Abundant
LIVING

E. STANLEY JONES

EDITED AND UPDATED BY DEAN MERRILL

Summerside Press™
Minneapolis, MN 55438
www.summersidepress.com

Abundant Living

ISBN 978-1-935416-58-6

Cover and Interior Design by Müllerhaus Publishing Group, www.mullerhaus.net

Photo used with grateful acknowledgment to Asbury College and Asbury Theological Seminary Archives.

Summerside Press™ is an inspirational publisher offering fresh, irresistible books to uplift the heart and engage the mind.

Printed in China.

Abundant LIVING

E. STANLEY JONES

EDITED AND UPDATED BY DEAN MERRILL

AN **ESJ** DEVOTIONAL

summerside

CONTENTS

A MAN AHEAD OF HIS TIME

E. Stanley Jones (1884-1973) was a Methodist missionary to India during the colonial period. His prolific writing and speaking brought God's truth in fresh ways to audiences both Eastern and Western, often challenging their assumptions and stretching their souls.

Born in Maryland, Jones first arrived in India in 1907 and was assigned to an English-speaking congregation in the city of Lucknow. But he soon showed a gift for connecting with the wider Indian culture, particularly the educated castes. He was a keen student of Hindu and Muslim mindsets, and he carried a deep passion that Christianity not present itself as a Western import. In a sense, he was "seeker-sensitive" at least seventy years before North Americans invented the label.

In 1930 he founded his first "ashram," a place for spiritual retreat that fit the Indian tradition but led many to consider the person of Christ. No doubt the richness of his devotional writing sprang in part from the times he spent there in reflection before God.

A good friend of Mahatma Gandhi (even when they disagreed), Jones spoke out for peace, justice, and racial harmony. He saw clearly that the British rule of this massive nation would have to cease—and said so with enough cogency that the British pulled his visa for six years.

A widely sought speaker in his day, E. Stanley Jones wrote twenty-eight books in all, the best known of which was *The Christ of the Indian Road* (1925). In 1938, *Time* magazine called him "the world's greatest Christian missionary." He was nominated for the Nobel Peace Prize in 1962, and received the Gandhi Peace Award the next year.

> *[Jesus] said to them, "Therefore every teacher of the law who has been instructed about the kingdom of heaven is like the owner of a house who brings out of his storeroom new treasures as well as old."*
>
> *Matthew 13:52*

Yet he never compromised his message. "The straightforward, open proclamation of Jesus is the best method," he wrote with all sincerity. "Jesus appeals to the soul as light appeals to the eye, as truth fits the conscience, as beauty speaks to the aesthetic nature. For Christ and the soul are made for one another.... But the Hindu insists, and rightly so, that it must not be 'an encrusted Christ.' It must not be a Christ bound with the grave clothes of long-buried doctrinal controversy, but a Christ as fresh and living and as untrammeled as the one that greeted Mary at the empty tomb."

In this book, re-edited for the twenty-first century, that Christ becomes real and vibrant again through the insights of a man who was, in more than one way, ahead of his time.

NOT YOUR ORDINARY DEVOTIONAL

This second full-year devotional by E. Stanley Jones is like the first in that it intends to give far more than just a little morning boost, a miscellaneous thought or story to spark up a person's day. His goals were substantial.

"As in *Victorious Living*," he wrote in the preface, "I try to supply a threefold need. First, there is the need for a daily devotional book to be used in the Quiet Hour, a page a day. Second, I have gathered up the discussion into units of a week, one subject having at least a seven-day treatment. This makes it possible for the book to be used in study groups on a weekly basis. Third, I have written it as an ordinary book which can be read straight through. In other words, I have carried one theme, abundant living, right through, beginning at the lowest rung of the ladder and going on to the application of the theme to the social relations of life."

What this means is that we don't end each day's reading with a pretty bow tying up the package. We are rather being drawn along a trail, day after day, that takes us deeper and further into spiritual understanding. If we don't sense a "hurrah" or an applause line at the bottom of every page, that is because Jones was not aiming for such a response. He meant instead to make more solid Christians out of us.

Brace yourself to be ruffled occasionally by his convictions on certain topics: war, for example, or alcohol, or sickness origins. He does not mean to be either controversial or trendy; he is instead working out a full-orbed faith as he sees it. Listen to the scriptural basis for his views and decide for yourself if they are valid or not.

The Bible selections printed at the start of each day's reading in this edition are almost always the ones Jones chose himself. When he noted a preference for a certain translation that was popular in his day (for example, "Moffatt"), that text is preserved here.

Curiously, this book was written "in exile," so to speak—that is, in America during the early days of World War II. Jones had been strongly impressed by the Holy Spirit not to return to his work in India for the moment (see his account in the September 7 entry)—and then had gotten stranded, away from his wife, when the British colonial masters would not renew his visa. No official explanation was ever given, but their logic was fairly easy to see: The British had enough headaches during the war without having to manage the prominent evangelist's sympathies for Indian independence.

On March 15, he writes about the loneliness he felt and how he was coping. It is but one example of the author's deep and instructive walk with God.

Abundant LIVING

WE BEGIN THE QUEST

In the beginning God created the heavens and the earth. Now the earth was formless and empty, darkness was over the surface of the deep, and the Spirit of God was hovering over the waters. And God said, "Let there be light," and there was light. (Gen. 1:1–3)

Let us start at the very foundation.

Life can never be abundant unless it has abundant resources. It is obvious that no organism can expend more energy than it takes in from the outside. Just what does "the outside" consist of—physical nature and human society only? Or is there another dimension—an "Above"?

Many people have decided there is none—at least, none they can contact; so they have short-circuited life to "the inside" and "the outside." But, to their dismay, they find that these put up resistances instead of offering resources to abundant living. "The inside" is clashing, and "the outside" is contradictory.

Someone has said, "If we don't have something inside of us that is above us, we will soon yield to that which is around us." We become circumstance-conditioned and circumstance-fed, growing weak and anemic on the fare. And if we turn inside for our resources, we find the well is dry. There ensues what an able and earnest man called his "sense of cosmic loneliness. I am not sure whether my doings have anything cosmic back of them, whether I am working with anything significant, or just working meaninglessly alone with no one to back my work or care." In that, he was like an atheist, who has been described as "a person with no invisible means of support."

That is a frigid thought. It lays its cold hand on our hopes and our endeavors. Can it be replaced with a warm, living, cosmic Presence who is with us and for us? If so, that would touch our central need.

O warm, living, cosmic Presence, help me as I begin this quest for You and Your resources. I need Your help even to inspire me to begin the quest, for I am not entirely sure that You are there. I am only sure of this—that Something beyond myself ought to be there. So I begin. Help me. Amen.

IS THERE A COSMIC PRESENCE?

Then Job replied: "Even today my complaint is bitter; his hand is heavy in spite of my groaning. If only I knew where to find him; if only I could go to his dwelling!" (Job 23:1–3)

If Christ has not been raised, then your faith is useless and you are still guilty of your sins. In that case, all who have died believing in Christ are lost! And if our hope in Christ is only for this life, we are more to be pitied than anyone in the world. (1 Cor. 15:17–19†)

If there isn't Anything there, then we have no framework of reference, no star by which to steer our little boat. We are tossed from wave to wave of inane and meaningless existence.

If we lose God, then we lose the meaning of life—the bottom drops out. If there is no God to give worth and meaning and goal to life, then we are only animated bubbles that rise to the cosmic surface, glisten briefly in the sunlight, and then burst, leaving a nasty wet spot. It is all over.

An artist said of his nature paintings, "I can get the picture right if I get my sky right." We know now that, if we lose our Sky, we shall soon lose our earth. If you can get hold of God, or God gets hold of you, then the Sky is right and everything falls into its place. The whole thing is meaningful.

A modern man of insight reported a dream. "I thought," said this friend, "that I saw you standing on a hilltop and we, a great host of us, were crowding around eagerly waiting for what you might say. We could see your lips framing the word, but no sound came…. We tried to help you by calling out the word your lips were shaping; but we also were mute! And that word was…"

Was it *God?*

O God, help me to get this matter clear, for my Sky is overcast. In the words of the Brittany sailors, "Our boats are so small and Your seas are so great." I need a star to steer by. Open the clouds and let me see—really see. Amen.

FADING OUT

The scripture was fulfilled that says, "Abraham believed God, and it was credited to him as righteousness," and he was called God's friend. (James 2:23)

So Jacob took an oath in the name of the Fear of his father Isaac. (Gen. 31:53)

When Esau heard his father's words, he burst out with a loud and bitter cry and said to his father, "Bless me—me too, my father!" But he said, "Your brother came deceitfully and took your blessing." (Gen. 27:34–35)

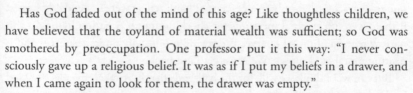

Has God faded out of the mind of this age? Like thoughtless children, we have believed that the toyland of material wealth was sufficient; so God was smothered by preoccupation. One professor put it this way: "I never consciously gave up a religious belief. It was as if I put my beliefs in a drawer, and when I came again to look for them, the drawer was empty."

The thing that has happened to this generation happened to the three generations of Genesis. God was real to Abraham; he had walked with Him as his "friend"; He was intimate and firsthand. But regarding the next generation, God was only referred to as "the Fear of Isaac." He had faded and become secondhand. In the third generation, this gradual fading began to show up in moral rottenness of Jacob, who stole his brother's birthright.

The same things have happened with us. Our ancestors had a firsthand experience of God through the past revivals. The next generation clung to the church for their parents' sake, but God was only the afterglow of a fading faith. The third generation is now showing clear signs of decaying morals, which is producing a decaying civilization. We are going to pieces morally.

But Jacob met God afresh at the stream bank during his midnight wrestle (see Gen. 32:24–30). He emerged a new person.

O God, I know that with the loss of You, some chord has dropped out of my symphony. But now I see I must find You again, as Jacob did. Amen.

WE CANNOT LIVE BY A "NO"

"I will hide my face from them," [the Lord] said, "and see what their end will be; for they are a perverse generation, children who are unfaithful." (Deut. 32:20)

But we are not of those who shrink back and are destroyed, but of those who believe and are saved. (Heb. 10:39)

If God goes, then the basis of our moral universe is gone. A recent survey discovered that only three percent of department store employees were honest due to character; that only five percent of bank tellers were dependably honest if there were no external measures for checking fraud. A nation living on this narrow margin of moral reserves is drawing too heavily on its resources and is nearing moral bankruptcy. We must get God back.

But can we? I think we will, for the half-gods that have taken the place of God are letting us down. People today are beginning to see that they cannot live, as they once thought, on the denial of other people's faith. The generation of people that lived on denials soon found themselves disillusioned even with their disillusionments. They had "three sneers for everything and three cheers for nothing." And they soon found they couldn't live by sneers. If we walked to the table each day and looked over the food, then turned away in high disdain, we could get away with this attitude for a while. But in the end, hunger would bite us.

Both physically and spiritually, we are positive beings. We cannot live by a "No"; we must live by a "Yes." And that "Yes" must be God, or it will let us down. The future of the world is in the hands of believers, for non-believers are suffering from "the paralysis of analysis." They only deny.

O God, I come to You for clearer light. I see that without You, my universe tumbles to pieces. With You it makes sense; my sums come out right. Help me to find You—the Key. Amen.

THE UNIVERSE BY CHANCE?

Can you direct the movement of the stars—binding the cluster of the Pleiades or loosening the cords of Orion? Can you direct the sequence of the seasons or guide the Bear with her cubs across the heavens? Do you know the laws of the universe? Can you use them to regulate the earth?... Who gives intuition to the heart and instinct to the mind? (Job 38:31–33, 36 †)

The situation is clearing as people see more and more that they must affirm some "Yes" about the universe, and that "Yes" may be God. For how could this universe come by chance into a cosmic orderliness that stretches from the molecule to the outermost star, and controls everything in between? And how could this orderliness just happen to preserve itself by chance through millions of years? That would be a stark materialistic miracle—universal chaos by chance gives birth to universal order! The one who believes that must spell *chance* with a capital *C,* and mean God by it.

How long do you think it would take to throw up a font of type into the air and have it come down into a poem by Robert Browning? I asked a printer that question, and he replied, "Both you and the type would wear out first."

Someone has figured the odds for the world to have happened by chance, and the numbers go round the world thirty-five times. "A preposterous figure," says Dr. Robert Millikan, the esteemed physicist and Nobel laureate.

When I pick up a book and sense intelligence in it (this sometimes does happen!), then I know that behind that intelligence is an intelligent mind expressing itself. When I look at the universe, I find that it responds to intelligence—it can be intelligently studied. Intelligence has gone into its very structure. The simple conclusion must be that behind that intelligence is an intelligent mind. And since that built-in intelligence seems to be universal, I will have to spell it in capitals—a Universal Mind.

O God (I say the word now with more confidence), I begin to see You. You are beginning to come into my intelligence. Help me this day to take You into the rest of my life. Amen.

INTELLIGENCE HAS A SOURCE

Only fools say in their hearts, "There is no God." (Psalm 14:1 †)

Someone may say to you, "Let's ask the mediums and those who consult the spirits of the dead. With their whisperings and mutterings, they will tell us what to do." But shouldn't people ask God for guidance? Should the living seek guidance from the dead? (Isa. 8:19 †)

"Out of nothing, nothing comes" is a universal law. But here is intelligence—you and I have it. Did that intelligence come out of the nonintelligent? If so, that is a materialistic miracle. Nature brought forth something she didn't have.

Again, you and I have purpose—we choose. Did that purpose come out of a nonpurposeful universe? That too would be a materialistic miracle. If people do not believe in God, they are forced to believe in miracles, the very thing they condemn in the believer.

Suppose in the end I find that there is no God, that belief in God was all a mistake. I would still not regret having held to a God, for life works better with this hypothesis. The universe is meaningful, and my life is happier. Furthermore, I would rise up in the end and confront the universe to say: "Well, I thought better of you; I thought there was Intelligence, I thought there was Purpose; now I see that you have let me down. I am superior to you, for I acted on a higher hypothesis than you could sustain. I cannot regret that I did."

A professor of electrical engineering, after passing through agnosticism to faith, put it this way: "If anyone could prove to me scientifically that this thing I have found is not true, I would still have to believe it, for the universe wouldn't make sense without it." He was profoundly right. The universe does not make sense without God.

O God, I am being hemmed in to a faith in You. Life is closing in on me; faith is becoming inescapable. And yet I do not wish to escape, for that would be to forfeit sanity. Help me to enter the Open Door. Amen.

GREATER THAN THE GAPS

Do you not know? Have you not heard? The LORD is the everlasting God, the Creator of the ends of the earth. He will not grow tired or weary, and his understanding no one can fathom. (Isa. 40:28)

But doubts still linger in the modern dialogue. Has not the doctrine of evolution made God unnecessary? Is not the whole thing being worked out by resident forces? Isn't science gradually filling up the unexplained gaps in nature—gaps into which we used to put God?

We Christians made a mistake in trying to put God into the unexplained gaps, for science has come along and has filled them up, leaving no room for God. Instead we should have put Him into the intelligence, the order, the dependability of the very process. That is where He belongs. The universe is orderly and dependable because God is an orderly, dependable God. He works by law and order instead of by whim and notion.

About evolution: When you say that "resident forces" are capable of producing the universe, the next question becomes: How could resident forces move toward intelligent ends without being intelligent? Toward moral ends without being moral? You cannot smuggle the attributes of God into the process and then say He is not necessary.

Which takes the more intelligence—to strike a billiard ball straight into the pocket with one stroke, or to strike a ball that in turn strikes another, and that another, and that another, until the last one goes into the pocket? Obviously, the latter stroke. If God seemingly creates something, which creates something, and the whole chain of events moves along to today's moral universe, a framework has been created in which the greatest thing in the world can emerge by choice, which is character.

O God, I begin to see the school, the framework in which I have to win or lose the battle of life. It is hard, unbending, exacting, but I am grateful; for while the rules of the school are strict, they are working for one end—my character. Help me to obey and help me to win. Amen.

OUR PEGS COME DOWN

And then—so the Lord of hosts declares—the peg driven in so firmly shall be wrenched out and give way, till everything that hung upon it shall come down. (Isa. 22:25 MOFFATT)

This prophecy, spoken centuries ago about Jerusalem's forthcoming collapse, echoes still in our time. When the peg of material civilization upon which we have hung everything is wrenched out of the wall by economic turmoil, then everything we have hung on it—our plans, our hopes, our futures—gives way and goes down in a crash. We have hung everything on the wrong peg, the insecure anchor of money. That peg should have been God; He holds steady amid the stress of things.

One of the richest men of a Midwestern city pondered what he could give his daughter as a heritage. He began with financial securities, went on down the list, but eventually rejected all material legacies as too precarious. He finally settled on faith as the only secure inheritance he could give his child—an interesting conclusion, since he himself was not religious! (Of course, there was another problem: For faith to become really hers, the daughter would have to choose it herself. Her father could not simply bequeath it to her.)

But it is not easy to choose a faith now, for the intellectual climate has changed from traditional to scientific. In the traditional climate you simply took what was passed on from generation to generation without question. But in a scientific climate, everything has to be verified. The knowledge in the schoolrooms is verified knowledge; can the knowledge in the churches go on as unverified hypothesis? This is an impossible dualism for modern minds.

So the pegs on which we have hung much of our civilization are coming down. Will we take up a new anchor point—God? Will He verify Himself to us as self-authenticating?

O God, I want to find You with my whole being, for I know that a faith which does not hold my intellect will soon not hold my heart. I want both to be held by You. Help me. Amen.

TESTING, TESTING...

Test everything. Hold on to the good. Avoid every kind of evil. (1 Thess. 5:21–22)

[Jesus]: *If anyone chooses to do God's will, he will find out whether my teaching comes from God or whether I speak on my own. (John 7:17)*

If possible, we must work our way through this scientific climate to God. Science refers to that which can be weighed and measured. Faith, on the other hand, is about that which can be evaluated. The one deals with the quantitative aspects of life, the other with the qualitative.

Science comes to a mother's tear and defines it in terms of so much water, so much mucus, so much salt. But is that an adequate definition? Hardly, for there are ideas, emotions, values, and meanings in the physical structure of the tear. Faith evaluates those imponderables.

Of course, you can verify and double-check that which can be weighed and measured. But can you verify values? I say yes. You can put them into the test of life to see what life will do with them. If they are real, life will back them up; if they are not real, they will wither. When you try to live by them, you will fight a losing battle. They will let you down.

I was about to leave a broadcasting station when an announcer followed me to the elevator, saying: "I am supposed to be hardened by hearing speeches all day long, but you got me. And the reason is that my life has broken down at the center. The central thing upon which I have leaned has fallen out from under me. My life hypothesis hasn't worked. Tell me about yours."

I could tell him that since I have committed myself completely to God, life has become one long verification of my central hypothesis. Everything corroborates it. My values hold up under the strain of life. This way works.

O God, I want to test Your way. Show Yourself to me, for all other ways let me down; all their joys give me a hangover. I want something that stays permanent amid change, has sweetness amid sorrow, and light amid darkness. Amen.

FREE TO CHOOSE?

Don't be misled—you cannot mock the justice of God. You will always harvest what you plant. Those who live only to satisfy their own sinful nature will harvest decay and death from that sinful nature. But those who live to please the Spirit will harvest everlasting life from the Spirit. (Gal. 6:7–8†)

In any scientific endeavor, the first step is to state the problem to be investigated. This is the starting point of the scientific method.

It is equally useful to apply this to the realm of value. The problem for us all is how to live in a universe of this kind, and to live well. It is, after all, a moral universe, and it seems to take sides on moral questions. In this moral universe we are free to choose, but not free to choose the results of our choosing—they are in hands other than ours. This moral universe is not something we create out of our taboos and rules—it is something we discover; it is a "given."

A father was explaining Newton's Law of Gravity and how it held things together. His son answered, "Well, Dad, what held things together before they passed this law?" Just as Newton did not pass the Law of Gravity, but simply discovered it, so we do not pass the moral laws written in the constitution of our world; we discover them. And we must come to terms with these moral laws, just as we must come to terms with the Law of Gravity. If not, we will be broken.

We do not break these moral laws; they break us. If we run afoul of them, they will throw us back—bleeding, broken, blighted creatures. These laws are color-blind. Whether you are white, black, yellow, or brown, if you break them, you will be broken. The laws are also religion-blind. Whether you break them as a Christian or an agnostic, in any case, you will be broken.

O God, I see that I am free only to obey. I must come to terms with Your laws written in me and in this world. Help me this day to find my freedom in obedience to You. Show me how to begin. Amen.

THE KINGDOM WITHIN

Once, having been asked by the Pharisees when the kingdom of God would come, Jesus replied, "The kingdom of God does not come with your careful observation, nor will people say, 'Here it is,' or 'There it is,' because the kingdom of God is within you." (Luke 17:20–21)

In this exchange Jesus was talking not to His disciples, but to the Pharisees—unchanged people. Is the kingdom of God then in us all, changed and unchanged? Yes.

Of course, it is true that those who have been spiritually changed go ahead to "see," "submit to," "enter," and "inherit" the kingdom of God in a way the unchanged do not. They have embraced the laws and the God of the kingdom, and therefore receive the resources of the kingdom, so that the sum total of the kingdom works with them and not against them. Those who are unchanged find the kingdom is within them, but they are at cross-purposes with it. In the changed person the kingdom works as self-realization, and in the other as self-frustration. But in both it is present.

The laws of our being are not a novelty; they are the laws of God. Just as the engineer builds into an engine the way it is to work, so God has stamped His kingdom within the structure of our being. The Old Testament calls this stamp "creating man in his own image" (see Gen. 1:27). If we live according to it, we live. If we don't, we don't.

A railway engine is made to run on tracks, and if it remains on the tracks, it finds its freedom, pulls its loads, and gets to its destination. But if, in order to gain its freedom, it jumps the tracks, the result is not freedom but ruin to itself and everybody concerned.

There is a track to freedom, to efficiency, to full living, built into your being and mine. It is the kingdom of God—it is within you.

O God, I have looked for You to split the heavens and come down, and here I find Your fingerprints within my own being. You have been so near that I have run afoul of You and thought I was only running afoul of law. Forgive me. Amen.

RUNNING FROM OURSELVES

As he neared Damascus on his journey, suddenly a light from heaven flashed around him. He fell to the ground and heard a voice say to him, "Saul, Saul, why do you persecute me?"

"Who are you, Lord?" Saul asked.

"I am Jesus, whom you are persecuting," he replied. (Acts 9:3–6)

If the laws of our being are in fact the laws of God, we then come to this breathtaking conclusion: *We cannot revolt against God without revolting against ourselves.* I say it reverently: God has us hooked!

The result of the modern revolt against God is this: We who decided we would not live with God find that we cannot live with ourselves. A sinner is one who is literally a problem to himself. The hell that modern people banished from the universe by politely putting it out the door has now come back through the window in the form of neuroses, fears, inhibitions, inner conflicts, and guilts. It has moved into the center of their being.

So the counterpart of "The kingdom of God is within you" is "The kingdom of hell is within you too." Obey the kingdom of God within you, and you have heaven; disobey it, and you have hell—you have it right now as a condition, a state of mind.

When you obey the kingdom of God, you find heaven here and now, for its other name is "the kingdom of heaven." If you take heaven with you at the end of this life, you will get heaven, for you will have brought it with you. On the other hand, if you take hell with you when you die, you will get it, for you will have brought it with you. I do not know where heaven and hell are as places, but I know that sin is hell begun—it is disruption, disintegration, disease. Goodness is heaven begun—it is fellowship, harmony, life.

The kingdom of God will work with you or against you according to whether you obey it or disobey it.

O my God, I cannot run away from You. Nor do I want to. In fact, I fly toward You. Take me. Amen.

SELF-ACTING LAWS

Evil people are trapped by sin, but the righteous escape, shouting for joy.
(Prov. 29:6 †)

The laws of the kingdom of God, which are written in us, are self-acting. The result is not something imposed by God from the outside. It is something inherent. Sin and its punishment are one and the same thing. Sin is literally "missing the mark," the thing for which we are inwardly made; to miss the mark is to sin against oneself.

That fact has fooled this age. We have been taught that God will punish us for our sins in some extraneous way. But since no thunderclap of punishment followed our sins, we began to think nothing had happened. A little girl put it this way: "We don't have grace at our table, or pray in any way—but nothing has happened yet." No, my child, nothing outwardly, but the inner deterioration, the decay that has set in, as God has been shut out, is the real punishment.

Said a puzzled minister: "I preach just as well now as I did before I committed adultery." Perhaps so, but the inner chaos and conflict, the lack of self-respect, the deterioration of character is the punishment.

"A grasping nature is its own undoing," says Proverbs 15:27 (MOFFATT). Even in ancient times this was seen: "As the old proverb runs, 'Evil men bring evil on themselves'" (1 Sam. 24:13 MOFFATT). The Old Testament speaks of Achan's forbidden wedge of gold, a symbol of his greed, as "the doomed thing" (Josh. 7:12 MOFFATT). Evil is doomed, not because God pronounces judgment on it, but because of its own nature.

When you do right, that act is written in the ledger of life. It has the seeds of permanence in it. When you do wrong, that act is written in the ledger of death. It has the seeds of its own ruin.

O my God, this moral universe closes in on me. I must come to terms with it. Or is it an It? Is it You? Are You in these very laws? I want You, for I am not a subject asking for a law, but a child asking for a Father. Help me. Amen.

WALKING WITH THE GREEN LIGHTS

Tainted wealth has no lasting value, but right living can save your life.... People with integrity walk safely, but those who follow crooked paths will slip and fall. (Prov. 10:2, 9 †)

The converse of what we are discussing is also true: If the nature of reality guarantees the instability of evil, it also guarantees the stability of good. Evil, by its very nature, is unstable; good, by its very nature, is stable.

In fact, evil could not long exist unless it had enough good in it to keep going. If it were pure evil, it would collapse. There is "honor among thieves"; if there were not, they could not hold together long enough to loot the rest of us. The honor is the cement that temporarily makes them a group.

Dr. Richard Cabot of Harvard says, "When you speak the truth, the whole universe is behind you; when you lie, the universe is against you." The universe is simply not built for the success of a lie. You may try to hold lies together with all the cleverness and scheming possible, but in the end they will break down. In the words of a historian: "There is one fact that history sounds—the moral law is written in everything." It is "the way" stamped into the nature of things, and if another way is tried, it works its own ruin.

A friend of mine was about to walk across a street against the traffic light. A plainly dressed stranger stepped up to him and said, "My friend, if you want to live long, walk with the lights; if you don't, then walk against them." That is the lesson of life: If you want to live well, walk with the green lights God has hung in the makeup of things. If you don't, then walk against God's red lights—and be hurt.

O God, my Light, help me to walk with Your green lights. Forgive me that I have walked against Your red lights. I thought I was only hurting You. I was hurting myself too. Amen.

KINGDOM RELATIONSHIPS

On being asked by the Pharisees when the Reign of God was coming, he answered them, "The Reign of God is not coming as you hope to catch sight of it; no one will say, 'Here it is' or 'There it is,' for the Reign of God is now in your midst." (Luke 17:20–21 MOFFATT)

The above translation is a little different from the one we quoted earlier: "The kingdom of God is within you." Others say, "The kingdom of God is among you." Which is correct?

All are profoundly true. If the kingdom of God is stamped into our own beings, it is also stamped into our relationships with one another. There is a way to get along with ourselves, and there is a way to get along with other people— and that way is God's way.

If you try to get along with others on some basis other than God's, you won't. Your relationships will break down. Try to get along with your family on the basis of dominating them. There will be seething revolt as well as your own frustration and unhappiness. In trying to dominate, you break the law written into the constitution of human relationships.

The central law of relationships was expounded by Jesus: "Love your neighbor as yourself" (Mark 12:31). Now, you don't have to obey that law, but if you don't, you can't get along with your neighbor. In this case you do not get rid of him; he comes back on your hands as a problem and a pain. The kingdom of God is "in your midst"—it is the way we get along with others when we get along with them well.

Psychologist Alfred Adler, who originated the phrase "inferiority complex," attributed all human failure to the inability to grasp that "it is more blessed to give than to receive" (Acts 20:35). Why does life break down if you do not love your neighbor as yourself? Because you are made that way.

My Father, I see that You are Father to Your family. You have made me so I cannot get along with myself without getting along with the rest of the family. I see I must live by love or live by loss. Help me this day to live by love. Amen.

FRUSTRATING OURSELVES

Where you have envy and selfish ambition, there you find disorder and every evil practice. But the wisdom that comes from heaven is first of all pure; then peace-loving, considerate, submissive, full of mercy and good fruit, impartial and sincere. (James 3:16–17)

Look at human relationships on a world scale. Why have they broken down? For the simple reason that we have tried to get along with other nations on the basis of pure selfishness. That broke the law of the kingdom which is among us. Hence, this war [World War II]. We cannot violate the law of love any more than we can the law of gravity and not get hurt.

Someone plaintively said, "I am wondering when God will come into this war and take a hand." Where is the kingdom of God? It is here in our very frustrations. Since we wouldn't take the kingdom of God for our collective fulfillment, we must now take it as our collective frustration. We cannot live the way we have been living without having the kind of a world we now have.

Suppose the opposite had taken place. Suppose our collective revolt against God had somehow produced prosperity, peace, progress, and mutual helpfulness. Then we could have asked, "Whatever happened to the kingdom of God?" The success of our revolt would have indeed struck a fatal blow to our faith. But this kind of messed-up world corroborates everything the Christian stands for. Revolt against God and the resulting chaos work out as prophecy and fulfillment, as seed and fruit. We cannot live on a collectively selfish basis without having a collective clash.

The Christian has the key to solving the situation—the kingdom of God is among us. Live collectively according to it, and we live; if not, we collectively perish—as is happening now.

O God, I begin to feel a sense of personal and collective guilt. We have been trying to live against the universe, and now we are up against it. I plead with You to help me, save me. Amen.

PICKING OUT A HYPOTHESIS

This day I call heaven and earth as witnesses against you that I have set before you life and death, blessings and curses. Now choose life, so that you and your children may live and that you may love the LORD your God, listen to his voice, and hold fast to him. For the LORD is your life. (Deut. 30:19–20)

We have now come to the end of discussing the first step in the scientific method, *stating the problem,* which is how to live well in a universe of moral law. We have in fact run afoul of it and wear great inner bruises—guilts, fears, inhibitions, frustrations, complexes. Or if not these, then just a sense of incompleteness, of something missing, of emptiness.

We now come to the second step, *picking out a hypothesis to meet that problem.* This inevitably involves choice. Some say: "Does the whole thing rest on my choice? Will God not choose for me and make me take His choice? I wish He would."

That would be the most fatal thing He could do. It would break down the citadel of personality, the will; and when will is gone, we are gone—we are things instead of persons. When God created another person, He had to limit Himself—to move back, as it were, to give room for that will to act. That was a terribly dangerous move, for free will might make a mess of things.

But God took the risk, just as a parent takes the risk when bringing a child into the world, for the child might break its own heart and the parent's. Still, God and human beings create, because, well, they each say, "I'll take the consequences. The sins of these created persons shall be mine, their failures mine; but also their joys and developments shall be mine. We'll work it out together." Nothing but love could make God and humans take that risk.

Had God not seen a glorious end, He would not have dared to create. It took nerve to do it.

O God, I see that I have to choose. I want to shrink from that responsibility and push it over onto You. But I can't. I must stand up and choose. Help me to make the right choice, for the future is in this hour. Amen.

FREEDOM'S COMPLICATIONS

Be on guard. Stand firm in the faith. Be courageous. Be strong. And do everything with love. (1 Cor. 16:13–14 †)

Our freedom is a problem to God. Someone has put it this way: "Here is a chessboard, and all the figures on the board, instead of being made of wood, are flesh-and-blood persons with wills of their own. The game for God would be simple if the figures would go where He desires them to go. But suppose, when God begins to make a move in the game against Evil, that the figures balk and refuse to move, going instead on their own to other positions. That would complicate the game and mess it up badly." That has happened. And that is God's problem.

But our freedom is also His possibility. Suppose those figures learn that failure and mix-up come through moves on their own and refusal to cooperate with the Player. Suppose that God and humans play the game in cooperation—and win! How much finer that would be than to win against Evil with only wooden pawns!

You and I can cooperate with God, aligning our wills with His, making His wisdom our own, and in the end the victory becomes a joint victory. What a possibility for God and us! I would rather be a discontented human being than a contented worm, for that discontent would drive me to His feet. "Blessed are the homesick, for they will come home," says a German proverb.

A little boy of five, after seeing a puppet show, expressed his reaction in this way: "I'm glad I'm not one of those pretending persons. They have to do what they are told." The boy was right—with all the hazards, possibilities for breakdown, and heartaches involved in freedom, we don't want to be "one of those pretending persons." We would rather be real persons, standing up and making our choices with all of their good and bad consequences.

O God, my Father, I want to cooperate with You. I have been making foolish and disastrous moves on my own, getting into a mess with myself and others, and spoiling the game. Help me to play Your game. Amen.

HOW GOD REVEALS HIMSELF

"In the beginning, O Lord, you laid the foundations of the earth, and the heavens are the work of your hands. They will perish, but you remain; they will all wear out like a garment."… But we see Jesus, who was made a little lower than the angels, now crowned with glory and honor because he suffered death, so that by the grace of God he might taste death for everyone. (Heb. 1:10–11; 2:9)

Since you are a free being and can do the most important thing in the world—you can choose—now you want to choose your highest hypothesis. What shall it be?

Let us come straight to the issue: Do you know of any better hypothesis than Christ? Let your mind sweep the horizon for possibilities. After eliminating this thing and the other thing, this person and that person, does it not settle upon Christ as your best bet?

The highest thing in our moral universe is moral character. If God can be found anywhere, He ought to be found here. Nature cannot tell me of my Father—not clearly. Nor could the perfect revelation come through a prophet or teacher, for in going through them, the revelation becomes limited, sometimes distorted. Nor could the revelation come perfectly through a book, for literature cannot rise higher than the life that surrounds it. The book would be pulled down to the level of our highest experience.

The only complete way of revelation is through a Life—a Character that shows us what God's character is like. That Character is Christ, the human life of God, that part of God we have been able to see. The revelation is seen in the face of Jesus Christ. I can be content with nothing less.

O God, I begin to see that You are coming to me in Christ. He seems to be that personal approach from the Unseen to me. Receive me, O Christ, for I receive You. Amen.

CAUGHT IN THE ORBIT OF CHRIST

In these last days [God] has spoken to us by his Son, whom he appointed heir of all things, and through whom he made the universe. The Son is the radiance of God's glory and the exact representation of his being, sustaining all things by his powerful word. (Heb. 1:2–3)

We now see that God could not show us Himself except through another self, a self who would be in human surroundings and would speak the language we speak. Jesus was God speaking the language of the person in the street, interpreting God in understandable terms. Just as when you listen to my words you get hold of my thought, so when you listen to the Word, Jesus, you get hold of the Thought, God. They do not rival nor push out each other. The Word is the Thought become available, near at hand, intimate, human.

If I were to try to think out the kind of God I'd like to see in the universe, I could think of nothing higher than that He should be Christlike. As one writer put it elegantly, "Jesus stands erect amid the fallen, clean amid the defiled, living among the dying." Surely here in Jesus is one spot in my universe that will not let me down, something that is utterly trustable. Here, if anywhere, I can commit my life and confess my sins; for this one spot is not only trustable, it is sympathetic—it loves, it cares.

Just as a planet rushing through space is only a comet on its way to destruction until it is caught by some central sun and begins to revolve around that sun, so my life is an aimless comet burning itself out in its own self-will—till it finds the pull and attraction of Christ's love, halts its deadly way, and forever revolves around Him.

O Christ, I am so grateful that You are God near at hand, God bending to my need. I cannot scale the heavens to find You, for I am mired in my own fears and sins. You come to me—and now I come to You! Amen.

DON'T STOP HALFWAY

When Judas, who had betrayed him, saw that Jesus was condemned, he was seized with remorse and returned the thirty silver coins to the chief priests and the elders. "I have sinned," he said, "for I have betrayed innocent blood."

"What is that to us?" they replied. "That's your responsibility."

So Judas threw the money into the temple and left. Then he went away and hanged himself. (Matt. 27:3–5)

You are on the verge of a great decision. But before you make it, I will utter one word of warning: *Go clear through; tolerate no halfway measures.* The temptation will be to start out to be wholly Christ's and end up feeling a little more relieved. As someone put it, "They want to feel a little less elderly, to experience a slight rejuvenation. They do not want to be born again."

On the prayer knoll at Sat Tal, our retreat in the Himalayas, I watched a vine stretching across space to attach itself to a pine tree. That vine was a form of aspiration, stretching to catch something higher. One morning I came out and found that the vine had arrived! It had securely fastened to a branch.

But the next morning brought catastrophe. A storm during the night had swept across the mountains. There the vine lay, a pathetic thing, with its face to the earth, still holding onto the broken branch. The tree had let it down. But not really, for what had happened was that the vine had grasped a dead branch rather than reaching for the central trunk.

Many people start out with high aspiration toward the Tree, God, and then they stop at some dead branch of religion. They fasten themselves to a good resolution; but no mere resolution can hold up amid the storms of life. Others attach themselves to an institution, a rite or ceremony; these will let us down in a crisis. Others fasten themselves to a favorite minister, or an idea about God instead of an acquaintance with God.

Go clear through to the central trunk—God Himself. Don't stop short.

O God, I know that anything less than You will ultimately let me down. I come to You. Amen.

THE FIRST STEP UPWARD

The path of life leads upward for the wise; they leave the grave behind.
(Prov. 15:24 †)

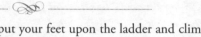

You are now ready, I trust, to put your feet upon the ladder and climb out to release and victory. I shall make that ladder very, very plain, for the greatest moment in life has come. This decision will decide all other decisions down the line—a master decision. In psychology there is what is called "a major choice," one that doesn't have to be made over again every day. Lesser choices fit into it, not it into them.

The ladder will have seven steps. It will be built around the concept of "turn," for that is a central word in Scripture.

(1) Turn over in your mind your present life—its direction and spirit. As you do this, you will be tempted to get defensive, for it is a hard thing not to defend your life patterns. But be relentlessly honest; look at yourself objectively and refuse to defend any wrong thing in your life.

That ugly self of yours, which you perhaps have dressed up in righteous clothing, will plead, excuse, and rationalize. It will try to keep the throne. You will be tempted to confess marginal sins and leave the central ones untouched. But nothing permanent has happened until the center of your difficulty, a wrong self, is replaced by another Self—God. He must be the center of reference, the center from which you get your life commands and orders.

You remember the blind beggar sitting by the roadside who was told that Jesus was calling him. "Throwing his cloak aside," he ran to Jesus (Mark 10:50). You must throw aside everything that would hinder you from getting to Christ—your inner dishonesties, and your outer ones too, your resentments, your wrong sexual relationships, your self-centered attitudes—yes, your very self—and run to Him.

O Christ, where else can I run? Help me to fling away everything and come to You. I cannot live any longer with myself until I find You, my true Self. So I come. Amen.

THE SECOND STEP

[Martha] saith unto him, Yea, Lord: I believe that thou art the Christ, the Son of God, which should come into the world. And when she had so said, she went her way, and called Mary her sister secretly, saying, The Master is come, and calleth for thee. (John 11:27–28 KJV)

Because of his great love for us, God, who is rich in mercy, made us alive with Christ even when we were dead in transgressions—it is by grace you have been saved. (Eph. 2:4–5)

After turning over in your mind your present self, you must now come to the next step:

(2) Turn to Christ. You need a Lord and Master. Perhaps you have been like the little dog that ran onto a football field. People called to it from every direction, but there was no dominant voice, so it stood confused. You have been listening to many voices, a perfect babel of them—the voice of money, of sexual passion, of self-interest, of pride. And you are confused, for there has been no dominant voice. Now above the din you are hearing one: "The Master is come, and calleth for thee." That Voice that grows authoritative. You feel there is Destiny in it. You have only one thing that is entirely yours—yourself. You can now decide what to do, who shall be your master.

A science student, making his way through the maze of possible choices, went out of my meeting, walked upstairs, and said as simply as a child, "I will say 'Yes' to Jesus." He kept repeating that to himself. It transformed him. Across that simple bridge of "Yes" he walked out of his personal swamp to abundant living.

Turn over all of yourself to one mastering will—the will of Christ.

O God, I need a Master. Chain me back into freedom, into light, into wholeness, into singing, into fullness. In Jesus' name, Amen.

THE THIRD STEP

We died to sin; how can we live in it any longer?... Therefore do not let sin reign in your mortal body so that you obey its evil desires.... For sin shall not be your master, because you are not under law, but under grace. (Rom. 6:2, 12, 14)

We come now to the third step:

(3) Having come to Christ, turn and look at your life through His eyes and break decisively with everything He cannot approve. Up to this moment, you may have been comparing yourself with yourself, or with others, and in the light of these you have not come out badly. But now, having come to Christ, you see things in a very different light. Things that, seen in the half-lights of our former standards, were not so bad, now turn out to be intolerable. They must go. Don't make excuses.

At our ashram (retreat) in Saugatuck, Michigan, one woman buried a little box, the symbol of the tyranny of a habit, in the sand at the foot of the cross. Another said she buried her fears and sins in the stars, so far out of her reach that she could not get at them again. Whether you dismiss them to the sand or the stars—dismiss them, and over their graves put the inscription, "No resurrection."

In the same ashram we were all assigned work to do with our hands; mine was picking up trash. I found that people's consciences became more sensitive as the days went on—but not far enough! I kept finding small pieces of paper in odd places; people would seem to hide their trash but not get rid of it!

Do not let this matter of getting rid of sin end in a stalemate, a compromise; don't be content with a conscience that hides sins but will not get rid of them. Go back into the hidden recesses where you have tucked sins away, to the margins of the subconscious, and bring them all out. They will plead, excuse, procrastinate—but be relentless. Not a thing must be left behind.

O God, I do not intend to look back. I am going all out for Christ. This will be no halfway business. Help me to cut loose. In Jesus' name, Amen.

THE FOURTH STEP

[Jesus] said to them all: "If anyone would come after me, he must deny himself and take up his cross daily and follow me. For whoever wants to save his life will lose it, but whoever loses his life for me will save it." (Luke 9:23–24)

We come now to the most important step of all:

(4) Turn over to Christ yourself and all you have. This is the crucial point, and if you bungle this, you block the process.

Between two persons there is no love without an inward self-surrender to each other. If either one withholds the essential self from the other, love is blocked; it will not spring up, no matter how hard you try.

A brilliant woman came to the end of her resources. Her self-centered life had exhausted its inner assets. She saw clearly that the self would have to resign to find itself. But the struggle was great. It always is. I told her that the initial battle was the hardest, that it takes twice as much power for an airplane to get off the earth as it does for it to fly. We then bowed in prayer.

At the close, she opened her eyes and said, "I'm off!" She had broken with the old life. There was wonderful release. She gave me her whisky bottle and her gold cigarette case, saying, "I have no more use for them." She gave up her sleeping tablets too.

For several days this woman was supremely happy. Then came a cloud. "I am like a child adopted into a new family; everything is beautiful," she reported. "But one thing is lacking—I cannot see my Father's face." And then the reason for it dawned. She had given her things in lieu of herself. She had tried to buy off God with those things!

When she saw what had happened, she hastened to add herself to the items. Then she saw her Father's face with nothing between.

O God, I see I cannot buy You off. You want the inmost shrine—myself. So I vacate the throne and give it to You, for I have no right to it. I am not God—You are. You command, I obey. Amen.

THE FIFTH STEP

Jesus said to the disciples, "Have faith in God.... I tell you, you can pray for anything, and if you believe that you've received it, it will be yours." (Mark 11:22, 24†)

If you have decided that God will have first place, then you are ready for the next step: *(5) Turn to Him in confidence and faith and believe that He receives you and that you receive Him.* Having given the one thing you have, you have the right to accept the one thing God has—Himself.

Many fail at this place. They are forever giving but fail to receive. Suppose you did that in a marriage relationship. If you always gave and did not allow your partner to reciprocate, would not the relationship be blocked? The alternate heartbeats of your relationship with each other and with God are *give, take; give, take.* If it's all giving and no taking, the heart will stop beating; it cannot beat in this lopsided fashion.

A great surgeon expressed it this way: "Christianity is pure receptivity. 'As many as *received* Him, to them *gave* He the right to be called the sons of God'" (John 1:12 paraphrased). If you are always breathing out and never breathing in, your breathing will stop.

A Roman Catholic girl, a student of sociology, entered this new experience and is alive with God. She puts her resolution this way: "More than ever before I am going to stop searching and let Christ permeate my life. He alone has the answer to life by giving us life itself—life abundant and real and not loaded with unanswerables." Stop mulling around on the inside of yourself, chewing on unanswerables. Go out in positive faith and accept the gift of God. He offers Himself. Take Him. You will find all you need—forgiveness, power, fellowship, motive, and energy to contribute to others.

O God, my Father, You have me. That sums up everything, for I now see the other truth: I have You. I am eternally grateful. Let my life spell out its gratitude day by day. Amen.

THE SIXTH STEP

Faith by itself, if it is not accompanied by action, is dead. But someone will say, "You have faith; I have deeds." Show me your faith without deeds, and I will show you my faith by what I do. (James 2:17–18)

You have taken the greatest of all steps. You wonder what will happen. A young man came to an editor friend of mine and said, "Stanley Jones ruined me in that meeting last night. All my plans I've had to surrender to God."

"Thank God," my friend replied. "Now God can do something with you. He can remake your 'ruined' life." That is the point: He shakes your life to the dust to rebuild it—but only with your cooperation. You and God now work it out together.

Take the sixth step: *(6) Turn and look at all your human relationships, then go into them with Christ.* Make Christ the basic fact. This fact must not be adjusted to your relationships—they must be adjusted to it.

You have six major relationships. (a) The church. Get into it. With all its faults, it is the greatest serving institution in the world, filling the earth with schools, hospitals, orphanages, leper asylums, and so on. (b) The home. Take Christ there as well. Set up grace at meals; begin family prayers. Start confessing your own sins, not those of your partner. (c) Your work. Make your business an outer expression of your chief business— serving God. You have no business to be in any business that cannot express your chief business. (d) Your class and race relationships. You now enter a new society—the Society of the Kingdom of God. This is a classless society, race- and color-blind. Recast all relationships that do not conform. (e) Your international relationships. You now have no more enemies because you have no more enmity! (f) Your relationship with the one next to you, in school, shop, office—they are all your neighbors. Share what has happened to you.

O God, I begin to see the greatness of my adventure. Nothing lies outside the domain of the kingdom—not as far as I am concerned. You demand a total obedience, and I give it—gladly. Amen.

THE SEVENTH STEP

Very early in the morning, while it was still dark, Jesus got up, left the house and went off to a solitary place, where he prayed. (Mark 1:35)

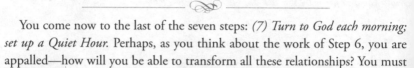

You come now to the last of the seven steps: *(7) Turn to God each morning; set up a Quiet Hour.* Perhaps, as you think about the work of Step 6, you are appalled—how will you be able to transform all these relationships? You must get resources, and you can get them from the Quiet Hour.

Many people say they can live in a state of prayer, without stated times for prayer. This is a mistake. Jesus felt the need of certain habits. He read the Scripture "as was his custom" (Luke 4:16). He went to the Mount of Olives to pray, "as usual" (Luke 22:39). He taught crowds of people "as was his custom" (Mark 10:1). These three simple habits: reading and meditating upon the Word of God, praying to God, and teaching others (passing on what we have found) are basic in the spiritual life. If He couldn't get along without them, how do we hope to do so?

Start the day right, and you will end it right. Someone asked me how I maintained my spiritual life. I replied with: first, by keeping up my prayer hours. I established the habit in college. A certain time does not belong to the day—it belongs to getting resources *for* the day. If I let down that time, the day lets down with it. I'm better or worse as I pray more or less.

The second is this: I am always up against a task I cannot do—deliberately so. This throws me onto the resources of God.

O God, I need a Quiet Hour with You just as I need physical food. I dedicate myself to them. I resolve to cut my physical food each time I cut my spiritual intake. That way, soul and body will go up and down together. For I am resolved to see this through, paying the price to do it. Amen.

REVIEW AND REVERSE

Repent, then, and turn to God, so that your sins may be wiped out, that times of refreshing may come from the Lord, and that he may send the Christ, who has been appointed for you—even Jesus. (Acts 3:19–20)

This matter of taking the initial step is so important that if you do not really take it, the rest of abundant living will be a sealed book to you. You won't have the combination to unlock the treasures of God.

At the risk of seeming tedious, we will go back over some of the same ground, this time using a different ladder. For I know that many may have gone through last week's study without actually taking the steps. I want to gather in that last hesitant soul before we go on!

This ladder will be even simpler than the other, using nine Rs upon which to step up and out. The first is this: *(1) Review.* Take an honest look at yourself. Perhaps you will find not so much positive sin as a lack of divine life. Or life may be at cross-purposes with itself, like bells jangling out of tune. Or you may feel you are not getting anywhere; you're sitting in a railway car that isn't hitched to an engine.

Then take the second step: *(2) Reverse.* Repentance is reversal. You have been going in a wrong direction; now you turn on your heel and reverse course. Don't confess other people's sins; confess your own. If you begin with yourself, they may confess theirs.

O God, I do begin with myself. I've been a coward. I've blamed others for my condition. But I myself am to blame for what I am. I now turn about-face. I honestly, even bitterly, repent. Forgive me. Amen.

RETURN TO GOD

When [the prodigal] came to his senses, he said, "How many of my father's hired men have food to spare, and here I am starving to death! I will set out and go back to my father."... So he got up and went.... (Luke 15:17–18, 20)

You have taken two of the nine steps to release. Now comes the third: *(3) Return to God.* But you say, "Will God receive someone like me? Don't I have to make myself better, so I'll be worthy?" Worthy? No one ever is.

A minister was riding a train, the only occupant in the coach except a young man who seemed very ill at ease. He would sit in one seat, then move to another, start reading a book, then quit again. The minister went over to him and asked what was wrong. The young man shut up like a clam.

But at last the dam broke, and he told his story: "I ran away from home, and I've been away a long time. I've wanted to go back, and I wrote my father asking if I could. But there has been no reply. So I have now written my mother and told her I'm not going to wait, that I'm coming home regardless—and if they will have me back, she must hang a white rag on the crabapple tree down by the railroad tracks so I can see when the train goes by. If I don't see a white rag, I will understand and just keep riding. Now we're getting close—and I'm afraid to look."

The minister said he would do the looking for him. The young man sat with his eyes shut tight. In a few minutes they came to the fateful tree. The minister reported, "Son, there's a white rag on every limb of that tree!"

If you are returning to God, something like that awaits you. A welcome so ungrudging, so overflowing that it will break down all your hesitancies, fears, and doubts. Take one step toward Him, and He will take two steps toward you.

O God, now I come to You, just as I am. If anything can be made of me, do it. I am at Your disposal. I've come with all I have. In Jesus' name, Amen.

RENOUNCE, RESTORE, RECEIVE

Zacchaeus stood up and said to the Lord, "Look, Lord! Here and now I give half of my possessions to the poor, and if I have cheated anybody out of anything, I will pay back four times the amount." Jesus said to him, "Today salvation has come to this house." (Luke 19:8–10)

The next steps are:

(4) Renounce. At the heart of this word there is a "no." It is the hardest word psychologically to say—"Yes" is much easier. But you will have to say "No" to some things in order to say "Yes" to the real things.

A man promised a pastor he would not drink again. Afterward, he showed up late in the evening and said he must be allowed to drink, or he would die. The pastor calmly told him to go home and die; he then returned to his work. The next day the man appeared with a new confidence in his face and said, "I died last night." He had, but a new man was alive.

(5) Restore. As you go over your life, you will find things that need to be made right. You may have to ask forgiveness for wrongs done to others, for resentments harbored; you may have to repair a quarrel; you may have to restore money. In one of our missions, the hotel management called to thank us for what we were doing—a woman had come and returned an armful of towels she had taken when she had been a guest at the hotel. Make a clean sweep, with no compromises or half-performances.

(6) Receive. Here is the simple act of faith. To receive is to affirm that God is as honorable as you are. You have given what you have; now you believe He will do as much—He will give what He has. And the best thing He has to give is Himself.

O God, I do affirm. I have lived on denials too long. Now I live on the positive affirmation that You are love; that I can bank on that love; that that love will not let me down; that I can draw on it for all I need. And now, O God, I am in Your hands forever. I am glad to be there. Amen.

RELATE AND REPLENISH

I rise before dawn and cry for help; I have put my hope in your word. My eyes stay open through the watches of the night, that I may meditate on your promises. (Psalm 119:147–148)

Now that you have taken the step of receptivity, you are ready for the last three. *(7) Relate.* Jesus was not a moralist connecting you to an external code. He wasn't saying, "Do this," "Don't do that." Instead, His method was to get people into right relationships, and then everything would follow. His first word was, "Follow me." Out of that relationship with Him would flow all other relationships.

Now that you have your central relationship with Christ nailed down, make all your other relationships fit into it. Nothing is more central in the Christian way than bringing all your relationships under the guidance of this central relationship.

Your central principle with people is: "Do to others what you would have them do to you" (Matt. 7:12). For example, give your employees the same treatment you would like if you were an employee. And thus go on down the line with every human relationship.

But for the Christian there is something beyond even the Golden Rule: "Treat one another with the same spirit as you experience in Christ Jesus" (Phil. 2:5 MOFFATT). That puts a plus, a beyond-ness, into the whole thing. Surrender yourself to that plus.

To do this, you will need resources. Get them in the next step. *(8) Replenish.* This will be done in the Quiet Hour. Here is where you hear God's standard. Then you can tune up your life to His. Keep that hour intact.

O God, I know there is nothing better than what I have found, except more of what I have found. Help me to open every pore of my being to the incoming life that heals, sustains, reinvigorates, empowers. I do so now—come in. Amen.

RELEASED AND RELEASING

There is now no condemnation for those who are in Christ Jesus, because through Christ Jesus the law of the Spirit of life set me free from the law of sin and death. (Rom. 8:1–2)

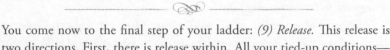

You come now to the final step of your ladder: *(9) Release*. This release is in two directions. First, there is release within. All your tied-up conditions—your inhibitions, your fears, your guilts—are now gone. You have entered abundant living.

But, second, there is release to serve. You are released *from* and released *to*—from fears to folks; from inhibitions to inspirations; from guilts to guidance. The doors now turn outward. You turn inward, no longer to mull around in useless regret over failure, but to get quiet in The Meeting Place, so that communion with Him will recoup the soul and make it adequate for the next outward step. That communion ends in commission. Life is now outgoing, positive, affirmative.

A woman who had gone through the ways of the world and had come out at zero put her experience this way in a letter: "I've been full of questions and doubts and wonderings. Then all of a sudden everything falls into its place like pieces of a jigsaw puzzle. And when this happens, I want to tell someone. I want to say, 'Why, there is no question about the reality of this. It's a fact.'"

Release is the last stage, and rightly so. The doors of the confined person all turn inward; the doors of the released person turn outward. His goodness now is good for something. Relief comes through releasing. You are released to follow the unfolding will of God.

O God, my Father, how can I express my soul's happy gratitude? Now help me to tell it not merely in ecstatic praise but also in quiet ways of human helpfulness. Help me to help the next person I meet, and so on through this day. Amen.

FOUR STAGES OF LIFE

Now that you have purified yourselves by obeying the truth so that you have sincere love for your brothers, love one another deeply, from the heart. For you have been born again, not of perishable seed, but of imperishable, through the living and enduring word of God....

Therefore, rid yourselves of all malice and all deceit, hypocrisy, envy, and slander of every kind. Like newborn babies, crave pure spiritual milk, so that by it you may grow up in your salvation, now that you have tasted that the Lord is good. (1 Peter 1:22–23; 2:1–3)

The spiritual life passes through the same four stages as the physical life: (1) gestation, (2) birth, (3) growth, (4) flowering.

Gestation is the period when this new life is forming spiritually. A brilliant doctor, after a period of awful struggle and darkness, said, "There is a little plant of faith growing in my heart. But I am almost afraid to look at it for fear it will wither."

After this period of incubation, when we alternate between doubt and faith, between hating God and surrendering to Him, between plunging deeper into sin and surrendering it entirely, there comes the birth. It may be as gradual as the opening of a flower to the sun, or it may be as sudden as a lightning flash. But even in the gradual birth there is a moment when the decision is made, as when the hand of the clock gradually turning round the dial comes to a moment when it strikes twelve o'clock.

An able woman said, "The terrible clouds of questioning and doubting have dispersed. I find I am no longer torturing myself about the 'rightness' and 'wrongness' of things. Victory is mine, and I find that praying has taken on a new vitality.... I scarcely know just what has taken place, but I do know that something within me has been released, something that had been throttled."

O God, I depend upon the certain faith that You and I have come together to be knit in a common purpose and a common life. This is the rock beneath my feet. Amen.

SWALLOWING SUNSHINE

Though you have not seen him, you love him; and even though you do not see him now, you believe in him and are filled with an inexpressible and glorious joy, for you are receiving the goal of your faith, the salvation of your souls. (1 Peter 1:8–9)

A college student put the wonder of the new birth in her own language: "I felt I had swallowed sunshine." Quite a contrast to some people who look as though they had swallowed a storm cloud!

A woman who had gone through the mazes of psychiatric analysis, and had been picked to pieces without getting a synthesis, experienced this change and described it this way: "I feel all clean within. All the old hymns about cleansing that I had laid aside as worn-out superstition have come back. I find myself singing them again."

Oliver Wendell Holmes, Jr., associate justice of the U.S. Supreme Court, expressed the same fact in stately words when he said, "You have a feeling of intimacy with the inside of the cosmos." You do. You are no longer orphaned, estranged, alone. You have a feeling of belonging—not only to "the inside of the cosmos," but to people.

The biggest grouch of a certain city called up a friend and said, "Everybody is changed here after that meeting last night in the high school with Stanley Jones. Everybody is different this morning. Of course, it may be that only I am different, but everybody seems different." His world was changed, for he was changed.

O God, I have come into a new world, for a new world has come into me. Help me to live so people will seem different to me and I seem different to them. For I am different, and I am so grateful. Thank You, Father. Amen.

NEXT COMES CULTIVATION

Just as you received Christ Jesus as Lord, continue to live in him, rooted and built up in him, strengthened in the faith as you were taught, and overflowing with thankfulness. (Col. 2:6–7)

You have now taken the preliminary steps in beginning the Christian way. Remember, it is a *way,* not merely a decision once made. A Christian may be defined as "one who is responding to all the meanings he finds in Christ." They will unfold as you respond to them, but only as you respond to them. Otherwise, those meanings will become meaning-less.

So many start well, but soon the glory fades, and they settle down to respectable mediocrity, without the spark of contagion. This often happens in the ministry. In one pulpit I know, there is a fire extinguisher fastened underneath. Probably the precaution is unnecessary—no fire would break out in that pulpit!

One man inadvertently prayed, "O God, grant that if any spark of divine grace has been kindled in this meeting, water that spark." Many of our sparks have been dampened out of existence, put out by mere neglect.

If conversion is the first law of the spiritual life, cultivation is the second. The way to fight germs is to raise the tone of health in the total organism. When disease does get a footing, nature sends up the temperature into a fever in order to get rid of the germs.

I went into a radio station and noticed the studio was marked off into portions: "Live End," "Semi-live End," "Dead End." You and I can live in the live end of the Christian faith, the semi-live end, or the dead end.

O God, I have started out on Your way, and I am all eagerness to continue. This new life has the feel of the real and the eternal. I would therefore cultivate my spiritual health so it will have plenty. Lead on; I follow with full consent. Amen.

SORTING OUT OUR ENEMIES

The sinful nature desires what is contrary to the Spirit, and the Spirit what is contrary to the sinful nature. They are in conflict with each other, so that you do not do what you want. But if you are led by the Spirit, you are not under law. (Gal. 5:17–18)

We come now to the stage where we must examine specifically some of the mental and spiritual germs that throw disruption and disease into human living. There is a par for life, but many of us are living below par—and when we do, germs rush in to gain a footing. We must now try to sort them out so we can deal with them intelligently and effectively.

In an earlier book I wrote about four enemies of the human personality. But subsequent weeks of study, discussion, and spiritual quest in our ashrams in America have expanded the list to fifteen. Here they are:

(1) A lack of faith in and loyalty to Something beyond oneself—a Something that gives ultimate meaning, coherence, and a goal in life. (2) Self-centeredness. (3) Anger, resentment, hate. (4) Fear, worry, anxiety. (5) A sense of unresolved guilt. (6) Negativism and inferiority attitudes. (7) Undisciplined desires. (8) Insincerity, whether conscious or unconscious. (9) Divided loyalties. (10) Unbalanced virtues. (11) Ignorance and a lack of judgment. (12) Physical disharmony. (13) An unchristian social order. (14) Lack of a total life discipline. (15) Lack of a creative, outgoing love.

Please do not think that these enemies are merely spiritual, throwing disruption only into the soul. They are enemies of the total life, causing physical disease, mental disruption, and spiritual disharmony. They attack the total person. They may begin in one portion, but in the end they extend their effects to all.

O God, I see my enemies. I have brought the hidden ones into the light. They are many, and they attack me in subtle, unseen ways. But if sin abounds, Your grace abounds much more. In that confidence I face them all, expecting You to give me nerve and courage to take them down one by one. Amen.

MADE FOR LOYALTY TO GOD

If the Spirit of him who raised Jesus from the dead is living in you, he who raised Christ from the dead will also give life to your mortal bodies through his Spirit, who lives in you. (Rom. 8:11)

The first of our fifteen enemies—*a lack of faith in and loyalty to Something beyond oneself*—points us in fact to Someone, namely, God. But whether you believe that "Something" is God or not, the basic necessity is the same. In order to be well, you must be loyal to something beyond yourself.

Why? You are structurally made that way. It is stamped into your being. Is that the statement of a minister and therefore supposed to be prejudiced? All right, then take the word of Dr. Carl Jung, who certainly was not prejudiced toward religion. To one patient he said, "You are suffering from loss of faith in God and in a future life."

The patient replied, "But Dr. Jung, do you believe the doctrines are true?"

"That is no business of mine," he answered. "I am a doctor, not a priest. I can only tell you that if you recover your faith, you will get well. If you don't, you won't." Why did this famous Swiss psychiatrist say that? He had found by experience that life works that way. Life needs something outside oneself to fasten its love and loyalty to, or it will break down.

I deal with hundreds of cases myself. The last one was an intelligent woman with a lovely family of four and a faithful husband. Because her husband would not go to church with her, she gave up going herself, gradually lost her faith in God, lost interest in her family, then suffered a nervous breakdown. There is nothing wrong with her, except that when God faded out, the meaning dropped out of life, and the whole of life sagged with it.

After she found God again, she slept that very night without medication for the first time in months. She has now regained the basis of health.

O God, can my lungs do without air, my eyes do without light, my aesthetic nature do without beauty? No more than I can do without You. I belong to You as a glove to a hand. Amen.

SUBSTITUTES FOR GOD

You were separate from Christ, excluded from citizenship in Israel and foreigners to the covenants of the promise, without hope and without God in the world. But now in Christ Jesus you who once were far away have been brought near through the blood of Christ. (Eph. 2:12–13)

If faith in and loyalty to Something beyond oneself is necessary to health, then could it not be that faith in *anything* beyond oneself is enough? Art, music, patriotism, causes of various kinds—will these not take the place of God? Why is God necessary?

There is no doubt that all these interests will help lift you out of yourself and are therefore helpful. But they do not ultimately hit the spot. For the last portion of the statement is important: "a Something that gives *ultimate* meaning, coherence, and a goal in life." Other things may offer local and temporary benefit to portions of life, but nothing can take us the whole way except God. Paul says of Christ, "In him all things hold together" (Col. 1:17).

The French psychologist and pharmacist Émile Coué suggested the method of autosuggestion, of saying to yourself, "Every day in every way, I am getting better and better." But Coué died of a broken heart because people made fun of his method, especially the world's newspapers. He could not stand the poking of fun, despite his own advice. He couldn't take it on the chin and get up smiling. His bootstrap method failed him, because it wasn't rooted in eternal reality.

As a friend of mine started out on a world speaking tour, a wise old lady advised him, "Give them nothing less than God." Anything less than God will let you down.

O God, I want to be able to "take it." Let all my being be rooted in You—my thoughts, my emotions, my will. Then I will live. Amen.

LETTING GOD FIND US

"Suppose a woman has ten silver coins and loses one. Does she not light a lamp, sweep the house and search carefully until she finds it? And when she finds it, she calls her friends and neighbors together and says, 'Rejoice with me; I have found my lost coin.' In the same way, I tell you, there is rejoicing in the presence of the angels of God over one sinner who repents." (Luke 15:8–10)

Many people wonder where they can find God. The answer is that you do not have to find Him; you have to allow Him to find you. If the New Testament teaches us anything, it teaches us not merely humanity's search for God, but God's search for us.

You must put yourself in the way of being found by God. That means, stop running away. Turn toward Him in an attitude of expectancy (another word for faith). Act as though God is, and is with you, and with you *now*.

Set up little habits to express that fact. Dr. Frank Laubach, missionary and literacy pioneer, suggests several, such as: Walk on the inside of the pavement with the suggestion that your divine companion is walking on the curb side to protect you from traffic. Leave a vacant chair at the table as a symbol of the Invisible Presence in it.

Take some time off during the day to quiet your heart in God's presence. Say to yourself, "As this physical breath I am taking into my lungs is cleansing the blood from impurities, so the breath of God purifies my life when I take it into my whole being."

O God, I now begin the practice of living in You; I am actually practicing the presence of God. Be in all things great and small. Make the small things great, and the great things possible. I thank You for the privilege of living on this cooperative plan. Amen.

GET THE CENTER RIGHT

See to it…that none of you has a sinful, unbelieving heart that turns away from the living God. But encourage one another daily, as long as it is called Today, so that none of you may be hardened by sin's deceitfulness. (Heb. 3:12–13)

You have to relate yourself to four worlds: (1) yourself, (2) things, (3) people around you, (4) God. Until you relate yourself to God in fellowship and obedience, none of the other three relationships will come out right. You will be out of sorts. But when you get the center right, the circumference takes care of itself.

The chapel steeple of a great university, where the minister is humanistic, has a weather vane on it instead of a cross. It symbolizes the fact that people point in every direction, turned by the winds of circumstance, until they come to faith in and a commitment to God. That gives life an unchanging steadiness.

Then why is it that we do not rest in Him? Because we try to rest in something else. We love God with the top of our minds but not with the bottom of our souls. Something else holds the seat of our affections. That deep affection then decides our thinking, for we think more with our emotions than with our minds. The affections draw reasons to themselves as a magnet draws iron filings.

People lose faith in God not so much by honest doubt as by dishonest sin. A brilliant headmaster, on an impressive salary, talked beautifully about faith in God. He had it—but then, his faith seemed to change. In giving a commencement address, he shocked everybody by saying, "Christianity is worn out; it has lost its hold on the world." At the bottom of that decay of faith was a decay of morals. He had begun to keep a mistress. The mind had tried to find reasons to justify the emotions. He was dismissed in disgrace.

O God, I cannot rest until I rest in You. I cannot find my peace except in Your will. For Your will is my peace. Help me settle down in You. Let the restless needle of my affections at last rest in You, northstar of my life. Amen.

IN HIM WE EXIST

[Paul speaking to the Athenians]: *"God...is not far from any one of us. For in him we live and move and exist. As some of your own poets have said, 'We are his offspring.'"* (Acts 17:27–28 †)

~~~~~~~~~~~~~~~~~~~~~~~~~~~~~~

Life is a restless, disrupted thing until we give ourselves to Something beyond ourselves, until we obey Something ultimate, and obey it supremely. Science corroborates that. A doctor said to me, "If three quarters of my patients found God, they would be well."

This being true, then why do not more of us find Him and live by Him? Here is one reason: The harboring of moral wrong makes God unreal. We will know as much of God as we are willing to put into practice, and no more.

Another reason is a lack of appropriating faith. As Paul said, we live and move in God, for He is the inescapable. We can only deny Him with the very powers He gives us. We have to live and move in Him even when we are throttling Him in our lives. In such a case, we are living on surface roots—the taproot has not gone down into God. We are failing to appropriate His amazing resources. And yet nothing is simpler.

Jesus says, "You believe—believe in God and also in me" (John 14:1 MOFFATT). Note, "You believe." Belief is the habit of your life; you have to believe in order to live. If you were to start a day without faith, you wouldn't eat your breakfast, for you wouldn't be quite sure it wasn't poisoned; the eating would be an act of faith in the cook. You wouldn't go to the university because you wouldn't be quite sure the professor would be there; the going would be an act of faith. All day long you are exercising faith. You live by it. Life would be paralyzed without it.

Since you do believe, then believe in the highest—God. Why expend your faith on lesser things?

O God, I see that faith is not some extraneous thing introduced from the outside. I must live by it, or not live at all. I choose to take this everyday fact of life and fasten it upon You. I will draw my very life from You. Amen.

CENTERED ON OURSELVES

We who are strong ought to bear with the failings of the weak and not to please ourselves. Each of us should please his neighbor for his good, to build him up. (Rom. 15:1–2)

We come now to the second major enemy of healthy, rhythmical human living: *self-centeredness.* This follows from the first, as fruit from root. When God is no longer the center, then *we* become the center—we become God. Deuteronomy 4:25 has the phrase, "…if you lose your freshness in the land and deprave yourselves by carving an idol" (MOFFATT). Note that when the freshness of God's presence is gone, we "deprave ourselves" by carving an idol. And that idol is usually just ourselves.

Aldous Huxley, the English humanist, says, "One strange result of scientific progress has been the reversion of monotheism to local idolatries." Those "local idolatries" can be state or race or class (which are simply enlarged versions of the self), or they can be just the personal self. When we lose God, we become a god.

On the face of it, it would seem that if we turn to ourselves and center on our own selves, we should grow under that cultivation. However, the very opposite takes place. Every self-centered person is a self-disrupted person. Whether you center upon yourself for artistic, religious, financial, or purely selfish reasons, the result is the same—the self goes to pieces.

Those who center upon themselves and have their way don't like their way; they do as they like, and then don't like what they do; they express themselves, and then find the self souring on their hands. This disruption and souring doesn't stop with the soul; it extends straight out into the nerves and tissues, poisoning them with disease. Apparently they are running against a fundamental law of life, deeply imbedded in the constitution of things. More people are being broken by that law than by any other single thing in life.

My Father God, I want to find adjustment in life. I want to live fully, abundantly, overflowingly. Teach me how. Amen.

SELF-CENTERED, SELF-DISRUPTED

Do not think of yourself more highly than you ought, but rather think of yourself with sober judgment, in accordance with the measure of faith God has given you.... Be devoted to one another in brotherly love. Honor one another above yourselves. (Rom. 12:3, 10)

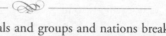

The law upon which individuals and groups and nations break themselves when they become egocentric is this: "If you cling to your life, you will lose it" (Luke 17:33 †). Concentrate yourself on yourself, and that self will go to pieces, not only spiritually, but mentally and physically as well.

The reason for this is obvious. There are just two driving instincts—the egoistic and the altruistic, the self-regarding and the other-regarding. Both of these must be fulfilled—and in the proper proportions—or life will be frustrated and unhappy.

Some people think Christianity teaches that they must love others, but not themselves. This is a mistake. Christianity teaches self-love: "Love your neighbor as yourself" (Lev. 19:18). If you did not love yourself, you would not develop yourself. So all attempts to eliminate the self end in hypocrisy and disaster.

On the other hand, if one organizes life around himself and becomes self-centered, then, as sure as fate, disaster overtakes that self. Does God pronounce judgment from heaven? No; by the very inherent laws within a person, judgment takes place. The person is at war with himself. His altruistic instinct is frustrated and undeveloped; hence, the person is dissatisfied and unhappy. He probably doesn't know what is the matter with him. But he is a house divided against itself. Every self-centered person is trying the impossible—to live against himself.

O God, my Father, I see that You have embedded Your laws into the texture of my being. How foolish for me to run against those laws and think I can get away with my folly! Forgive me for warring with myself and hence with You. Amen.

WHEN IT'S ALL ABOUT ME

[Paul speaking]: *Demas, because he loved this world, has deserted me and has gone to Thessalonica. (2 Tim. 4:10)*

When frustration sets in, self-centered persons often turn toward themselves in self-pity. They feel that life is hard on them. They blame everything except themselves. A case in point: A brilliant woman who had a nervous breakdown (for no other reason than that she lived in a state of constant self-reference) mulled over in her mind that people who tried to change her attitudes were persecuting her. Her life was all jammed up, and the one key log in the jam was self-centeredness. She could not say the words, "I'm sorry." The nearest she came was when she said, "Yes, I am sorry I did not take better care of my health." The repentance still had a self-reference to it.

She is clogged up still, and will be till that key log is pulled out. She has tied the hands of both God and people—they are powerless to help her.

Such a self-centered person usually attracts disease. While underprivileged people have my sympathy and also my efforts to gain equality of opportunity, it is overprivileged people who are in far greater danger. They are the disrupted souls—and bodies—of our civilization. I know a girl who has had thrown into her lap everything society can offer—money, opportunity, and all the rest. But since she is self-centered, she can enjoy none of them. Every sickness that comes into her neighborhood visits her. She draws melancholy to herself like a magnet, for that is the end of egocentric people. They start out to attract life to themselves—its joys, its thrills—and all they succeed in attracting is sadness, disillusionment and sickness—spiritual, mental, and physical.

O God, I see I cannot center on myself without that self going to ruin. I present this self of mine to You. Lift me out of myself into Yourself, so that I may find my freedom and myself. For Your will is my home. Amen.

WHERE EGOCENTRICITY LEADS

I pray that out of his glorious riches he may strengthen you with power through his Spirit in your inner being, so that Christ may dwell in your hearts through faith. (Eph. 3:16–17)

The egocentric person is his own punishment. Budd Schulberg, in his famous novel, *What Makes Sammy Run?* (which later became a Broadway play), tells the story of an aggressive copy boy at a newspaper who rises to the top of 1930s Hollywood by backstabbing others. The narrator says: "Unconsciously, I had been…hoping to be around when Sammy got what was coming to him. And now I realized that *what was coming to him* was not a sudden pay-off but a process, a disease…a cancer that was slowly eating him away, the symptoms intensifying: success, loneliness, fear….

"I thought…. You're alone, pal, all alone. That's the way you wanted it, that's the way you learned it…. All alone in sickness and in health, for better or for worse…till death parts you from your only friend, your worst enemy, yourself."

There is one way out of that hell of egocentricity. Dr. Fritz Künkel says: "It has been shown that all mistakes, weaknesses, and aberrations can be traced back to man's egocentricity. Accordingly, the fundamental problem of self-education may be described as the problem of overcoming one's own egocentricity" (*God Helps Those…: Psychology and the Development of Character*, p. 135).

How then do you overcome your egocentricity? By a deliberate act of self-surrender to Christ. It requires a willingness to die to this petty self, in order that a larger self might live.

Dear Lord and Father, You art leading me out of my petty self to Your ample self. I thank You that I have a door out of myself into You. I want to live this way, now and forever. Amen.

OUT OF SORTS WITH OURSELVES

What causes fights and quarrels among you? Don't they come from your desires that battle within you? You want something but don't get it. You kill and covet, but you cannot have what you want. You quarrel and fight. (James 4:1–2)

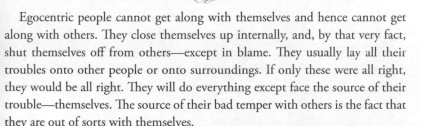

Egocentric people cannot get along with themselves and hence cannot get along with others. They close themselves up internally, and, by that very fact, shut themselves off from others—except in blame. They usually lay all their troubles onto other people or onto surroundings. If only these were all right, they would be all right. They will do everything except face the source of their trouble—themselves. The source of their bad temper with others is the fact that they are out of sorts with themselves.

Someone put it this way: "Do you want to find out a person's weak points? Note the failings they see most quickly in others." Usually they will point out what's wrong in others, or in the surroundings, as mental compensation for what is wrong in themselves.

That vicious circle must be broken. How? Either through a deliberate self-surrender into a larger center of life, or by an outside act of love that sweeps them off their center toward another. Dr. William Sadler, an outstanding psychiatrist, tells of a child of eight who was incorrigible; nothing was right. It turned out that she had once heard her mother say she was "an unwanted child." Now the child said bitterly, "Nobody loves me"—and in fact, nobody did!

Dr. Sadler heard her complaint and said: "Why, it isn't true. I love you. I really do like you." Soon the child came over and sat on his knee and kissed him, with tears streaming down her cheeks. In time she went back to her mother, made up, and was a different girl in school. Someone had broken the vicious circle of egocentricity by a love that swept her to a new center.

O God, You will have to do something like that to break the vicious circle of my egocentricity. Sweep me to a new center by Your invading Love. Amen.

DOWNWARD STEPS

One of his disciples, Judas Iscariot, who was later to betray him, objected, "Why wasn't this perfume sold and the money given to the poor? It was worth a year's wages." (John 12:4–5)

The most penetrating story of egocentricity's results is Judas. He began on a high level, a loyal disciple. But then came the slide:

First: He thought one could give too much to Jesus. He objected to the woman's lavish gift. His objection was a sign of an inward holding back.

Second: "What are you willing to give me?" he asked the chief priests (Matt. 26:15). Note, he was at the center. His request was the same as the prodigal son's: "Give me." This always starts the way down.

Third: "He watched for an opportunity to hand him over" (Matt. 26:16). He tried to arrange his world so it would not fall to pieces.

Fourth: But it didn't work. When Jesus at the Last Supper gave the fateful clue, Judas replied, "Surely not I, Rabbi?" The answer came back, "Yes, it is you" (Matt. 26:25). The heart of things began to be revealed.

Fifth: When Judas saw Jesus actually being condemned in court, he "was seized with remorse" (Matt. 27:3), but in the wrong direction. He turned to the chief priests and elders, trying to steady his tottering world with a halfway restitution. He brought back the money, but retained himself. "What is that to us?" they replied (v. 4). His companions let him down. Sin, you see, has no cohesion in it. Sin doesn't care. So he "threw the money into the temple" (v. 5), the thing that seemed to matter so much in the beginning. He then "went away" from opportunity, from life, from Christ. Sin is centrifugal. Finally, he "hanged himself." The self that was so central in the beginning had become impossible to live with. The egocentric self completely collapsed.

My Father, I see that this imperious, demanding self, like the camel's nose inside the tent, will soon push me out of this earthly habitation. I will soon not be able to live with it—unless I give it back to You for cleansing, for adjustment, for a new basis of living. I do. Amen.

SELF-FOCUSED RELIGION

There is no God apart from me, a righteous God and a Savior; there is none but me. Turn to me and be saved, all you ends of the earth. (Isa. 45:21–22)

Egocentricity may be very religious, seeking to save one's soul, or the souls of others. But it will still be egocentric, and as such destructive.

A very religious woman was suffering from arthritis. It was discovered that her anxiety to dominate her family, even for their own good, was the basis of her pain. She surrendered this anxiety to God, ceased trying to control the family—and both her spiritual life and her physical life cleared up. The arthritis disappeared.

A businessman was in the hands of a psychoanalyst. Over a period of five years he spent $60,000 having himself picked to pieces. He submitted over a thousand dreams for deciphering—often five or six a night. He kept a pad and pencil handy to note them down whenever he awakened. At the end of five years, he was thoroughly disrupted. The psychoanalyst didn't know how to put him together again. Self-knowledge was not healing. It straightened him out here and there, but could not heal the central hurt.

The man saw all this self-probing was ending in futility, so he gave up his last prop—the analyst. As he left the office, a sense of infinite sadness and loneliness came over him. He felt he had nowhere to turn.

Suddenly a Voice seemed to say, "Look this way." It was the Voice of Christ: "Look away from yourself, your misery, your fear, and your failures. Look to Me." These words came as a breath of health into the fetid atmosphere of self-concentration. He looked to Christ and found a lift that took him out of himself toward freedom. Today, with an entirely new lease on life, he is healthy, harmonious, useful.

O Living Christ, I do look to You. To whom else can I go? You have the words of eternal life, not only in the hereafter but in the here and now. I look to You for the power, the release, the victory I so deeply need. Amen.

THE THIRD ENEMY

They came to Capernaum. When he was in the house, he asked them, "What were you arguing about on the road?" But they kept quiet because on the way they had argued about who was the greatest.

Sitting down, Jesus called the Twelve and said, "If anyone wants to be first, he must be the very last, and the servant of all." (Mark 9:33–35)

We now come to the third of the fifteen enemies we face: *resentment, anger and hate.* Here we enter the realm of the emotions.

This age seems afraid of being emotional, and yet it is turning out to be a very emotional age; in fact, emotionalism is rampant. Most of this is self-disruptive. People who are afraid of emotion end up following the thing they fear, even as they try to suppress their feelings.

Emotions are a part of us. We cannot set them aside; we can only direct them, sometimes redirecting them, to great aims and purposes. The emotions are the driving forces of the personality. They can drive toward the rocks or toward the open seas of expanding accomplishment.

Take anger, for instance. It is an instinct of protection for ourselves and others. It causes us to stand up and fight against harmful enemies of the human personality. We are angry with evil, and therefore we stiffen ourselves against it. Nietzsche is right when he says, "Virtue is of no use unless it can be lashed into a rage." Otherwise we would be "moral cows in our plump comfortableness." Our capacity to love the good determines our capacity to hate the evil.

But note that it is our *virtue* that is to be lashed into a rage—not our pride, our hurt egoism, our fears. There is all the difference in the world between the two: one is harnessed to higher ends and hence constructive, the other is harnessed to the ends of a wounded self and hence destructive.

O God, I do not sail calm seas. I am driven by tempests of emotion. Help me to harness these to the purposes of Your kingdom. I surrender myself and my emotions to You. Amen.

A GOOD ANGER

Jesus asked them, "Which is lawful on the Sabbath: to do good or to do evil, to save life or to kill?" But they remained silent.

He looked around at them in anger and, deeply distressed at their stubborn hearts, said to the man, "Stretch out your hand." He stretched it out, and his hand was completely restored. (Mark 3:4–5)

If anger is to be constructive, it must be harnessed to great causes. It must be like the explosions in your automobile engine, which have a purpose, driving you to your destination. But if instead of harnessing the explosions, you lit all the gasoline in your tank at once, you would blow yourself and the car to pieces. That is what happens to the inside of you when you have a "blowup" of uncontrolled, nonconstructive anger.

Jesus was an example of controlled anger. When He was about to heal the man with the withered hand, He saw the hard faces of religious people who opposed the act because it was being done on the Sabbath. His anger was not personal offense or a wounded egotism—it was grief at the stubborn hearts that could block the healing of a poor unfortunate.

Anger is righteous if it carries grief on account of what is happening to others, not a grudge on account of what is happening to oneself. But we must be careful at this point, for the mind plays tricks on itself: it will dress up its personal resentments in garments of righteous and religious indignation so they will be justified before our religious self. Many a person fights "for principle" when they are fighting only for personal offense and pride.

But righteous indignation, even when it is purely righteous, should not be kept overnight. "In your anger do not sin: Do not let the sun go down while you are still angry" (Eph. 4:26). Here is an anger that is sinless—and yet it must not be kept overnight lest it corrode the soul into bitterness.

O God, give me clear insight to see myself truly, for I may be cloaking my resentment with garments of piety. I do not want to harbor any Trojan-horse enemies within me. Help me to be completely honest with myself. Amen.

ANGER AND THE STOMACH

Do not be quickly provoked in your spirit, for anger resides in the lap of fools. (Eccl. 7:9)

Now that we have seen the possibilities of righteous anger for good, we must look at the opposite.

There was a time when people thought getting angry and holding resentment made them difficult to get along with, but nothing much else happened. We know now, in the cold white light of science, that there are other effects.

First, upon the intestinal tract. Some doctors put a tube through the nostril of a man and down into his stomach. They tested the contents of his stomach according to his state of mind. When he was in good humor, digestion went on normally; but after they had purposely made him angry, digestion completely stopped. Only when they brought him back into good humor would digestion start again. This fact was the basis of a doctor's advice, "If you don't feel in a good frame of mind, you'd better lay off from eating."

Another doctor could not find any physical basis for the constant vomiting of one patient. One day she incidentally remarked that her mother-in-law was coming to visit at Thanksgiving. Taking this chance remark as a clue, he sent for the husband, persuaded him to ask his mother to postpone her visit, then told the wife that the mother-in-law was not coming—and the vomiting stopped.

Stomach ulcers are often caused by anger and resentment, we are told by those who know. The problem will even return after the ulcer is cut out by an operation, the edges of the wound becoming ulcerated again if the resentment is not eliminated. Such scientific revelation makes it quite clear that the stomach in its very constitution is made for good will and not for ill will.

O God, my Father, save me from any clinging resentment. Help me to pull it up by the roots. Amen.

ANGER IS POISON

Refrain from anger and turn from wrath; do not fret—it leads only to evil. (Psalm 37:8)

Better to be patient than powerful; better to have self-control than to conquer a city. (Prov. 16:32 †)

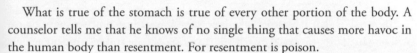

What is true of the stomach is true of every other portion of the body. A counselor tells me that he knows of no single thing that causes more havoc in the human body than resentment. For resentment is poison.

A doctor was baffled over the cause of a baby's sickness. One day he came into the home while the parents were quarreling, and saw the mother nursing the baby at the same time. The doctor threw up his hands and said, "Now I know what is the matter with your baby—you are poisoning it by this ill will." The poison was in the mother's milk, put there by anger. In two days the child was dead.

A pastor had his heart set on a certain appointment. When he did not get it, his wife became embittered and ill and died shortly afterward. He himself became spiritually so upset that he left the ministry. Resentment killed the body of one and the soul of the other. It was poison.

It is becoming more and more clear that qualities of character frequently determine a person's physical health. I do not mean to say that they determine all diseases, for there are contagions and they are real; there are structural diseases, and they too are real. But in all probability sixty percent of diseases have their root in the mental and spiritual realms.

O God, I want to be healthy in soul and mind. Therefore I welcome into my very being the health of Your mind. Let me be saturated with Your ways and Your thoughts, that I may live in radiant health. Amen.

SUBCONSCIOUS RESENTMENT

When the sun rose, God provided a scorching east wind, and the sun blazed on Jonah's head so that he grew faint. He wanted to die, and said, "It would be better for me to die than to live."

But God said to Jonah, "Do you have a right to be angry about the vine?"

"I do," he said. "I am angry enough to die." (Jonah 4:8–9)

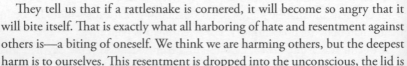

They tell us that if a rattlesnake is cornered, it will become so angry that it will bite itself. That is exactly what all harboring of hate and resentment against others is—a biting of oneself. We think we are harming others, but the deepest harm is to ourselves. This resentment is dropped into the unconscious, the lid is shut down on it, and there it works its havoc. Unconscious resentment is often just as potent for disruption as conscious resentment.

A man was constantly falling from his horse. He wondered why he couldn't stay on. It was discovered that he had a secret desire to commit suicide, and this falling was the outer sign. When he gave up the hidden resentment he held against life, he ceased falling from his horse.

A pastor and his wife disagreed over their pastoral appointment—he wanted to move, and she didn't. When the bishop decided to move them, she was very bitter and resentful—especially when the husband, wanting to avoid a crisis, stayed away and let her do most of the packing! After some weeks of harboring this resentment, she became ill—she could not get her breath. She went to the new city an invalid and resigned herself to a crippled life.

But when she saw that the harbored resentment had paralyzed the nerve fibers that control breathing, and that she literally was choking herself to death, she surrendered the whole thing to God. She became reconciled to the new place, arose, and is today a radiant, happy, and useful person.

O Christ, I now begin to see why You were always urging people to get rid of anger and ill will. Forgive us for not seeing, and forgive us for not surrendering. Amen.

ANGER DIMS THE VISION

Evil shall slay the wicked, and those who hate the righteous shall be condemned. (Psalm 34:21 NKJV)

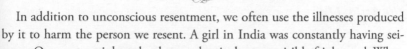

In addition to unconscious resentment, we often use the illnesses produced by it to harm the person we resent. A girl in India was constantly having seizures. One was so violent that her mother-in-law was visibly frightened. When the woman was out of the room, the girl whispered to the doctors, "I'll have these fits as long as I have to live with her."

Someone asked a husband why he got drunk. He replied, indicating his wife, "It's the only way I have of getting even with her."

Resentment and anger can dim our spiritual vision, so that the inner life becomes blurred. But did you know they can also literally dim the physical vision? Some doctors experimented with rats and found that after the rats had been kept angry for an extended period of time, opaque films came over their eyes. The report stated, "One realizes the picturesqueness and accuracy of the old expression 'blind with rage,' and the lesson to be learned is to avoid being angry. As the children say, 'One might freeze that way'" (*Southern Medical Journal,* Nov. 1940, p. 1237).

An optometrist tells me that he can never examine the eyes of an angry patient—such a person literally cannot see straight. As Dante puts it, "The wrathful travel in a cloud." Neither spiritually, mentally, or physically can we see straight if we hold resentment and anger. Our outlook on life is distorted because our inner condition is out of joint.

O God, we see that even in our physical constitution, You have made us for love. Forgive us for introducing the havoc of hate into the delicate fabric of our being. We are made for You, and Your way is love. Help us to live Your way. Amen.

SELF-PITY: A DEAD END

This is what the LORD says: "Restrain your voice from weeping and your eyes from tears, for your work will be rewarded," declares the LORD. "They will return from the land of the enemy. So there is hope for your future," declares the LORD. (Jer. 31:16–17)

A woman involved in an automobile accident suffered a broken neck and a severed nerve at the base of her spine, which left her lower limbs useless. After terrible initial suffering, she is now doomed to a wheelchair for the rest of her days. But she has met the whole tragedy in a spirit of faith, confidence, and good will. Hence she is radiant—in spite of everything!

At the table in the institution where she stays, she presides as a queen. Depressed patients are assigned to her table so her very presence may cheer them up. She is on top of her circumstances.

But her husband reacted differently. He was unhurt by the accident, except in his soul. He became embittered, resenting the man who was driving. This resentment has spoiled his lifework. One tragedy occurred to both wife and husband; they reacted oppositely. One emerged with a broken neck, but with her spirit intact; the other with his body intact, but with a broken soul.

It is obvious that to hold hate and resentment is to throw a wrench into the machinery of life. Structurally you are made for positive good will, in other words, for the Christian way of love. When you try the other way, the machinery of life breaks down, or at least works so badly that it leaves you exhausted and ineffective. Hate is sand in the gears of life; love is oil—and life works better with oil than with sand. Lovers love others—and themselves; haters hate others—and themselves.

O God, my Father, I have now come point-blank to the necessity of getting rid of all resentment, all hate. I ask for Your help to get rid of these things which have become rooted in me, which have become me. I offer them all to You. Amen.

HOW NOT TO DEAL WITH RESENTMENT
(PART 1)

Get rid of all bitterness, rage and anger, brawling and slander, along with every form of malice. Be kind and compassionate to one another, forgiving each other, just as in Christ God forgave you. (Eph. 4:31–32)

If we are to live abundantly, we must get rid of resentment and hate at all costs. But how?

Here are some ways *not* to proceed. *(1) We must not suppress them into forgetfulness and try to act as though we no longer have them.* This treatment drives them only into the subconscious mind, where they work to produce conflict and disturbance, the person scarcely knowing what is causing the upset. No one can play tricks on life and escape the consequences. We must bring the resentment to the surface and face it honestly, with no subterfuges, no evasions, no suppressions.

(2) Neither should we try the contrary—spilling out our hatred and resentment. Some psychiatrists prescribe this, and there is no doubt we can get temporary relief by giving the other person "a piece of our mind." A woman who had pains, first at the base of her spine, then in the middle of her back, and then between her shoulder blades, was asked by her doctor what was bothering her inwardly. She blurted out, "Well, I think I'd be well if I could tell my husband just once to go to _____." Perhaps she would have been relieved momentarily, but the resentment would only fill up again and be ready for another spillover.

No, expression is not the remedy; it merely deals with a symptom instead of the disease. While on the one hand *suppression* creates a sore boil at the center of our subconscious being, *expression* turns us into sore boils on the body of our social relationships.

O God, my heavenly Father, I am facing something too devastating to try to heal it lightly or to stall. Help me to go to the roots. But I will need more than Your help—I will need Your grace. Give me Your grace for this task. Amen.

HOW NOT TO DEAL WITH RESENTMENT (PART 2)

At one time we too were foolish, disobedient, deceived and enslaved by all kinds of passions and pleasures. We lived in malice and envy, being hated and hating one another. But when the kindness and love of God our Savior appeared, he saved us, not because of righteous things we had done, but because of his mercy. (Titus 3:3–5)

Other misguided ways of living are these:

(3) Trying to run away from circumstances that give rise to resentment. A doctor found a patient nervous, unable to sleep. He asked if his home relations were adjusted and happy, and was told that they were. Then as an afterthought, the patient replied that he and his mother-in-law didn't get along. That was the point of conflict. The doctor sent him and his wife off for a vacation. Good, but not good enough; for while there would be temporary respite and a letting down of tensions, yet they would tighten up again as soon as the prospect loomed for having to return home.

(4) Trying to divert one's attention. A woman said, "When filled with resentment, I go to the piano and bang out my resentment through Mozart's Sonatas—with apologies to Mozart." That would again give temporary relief and serve to drain the feelings, but it would not tackle the causes.

(5) Nursing resentment in the mind. This only makes it worse. It will carry over into the whole of life and spoil it. One woman said that when she entered the quiet time for prayer, the only thing she would end up doing was "chewing on my resentment." The quiet time simply brought to the surface what was a continuous fact—a nursed grievance.

All of these methods are attempts to heal over a boil—which is a dangerous act, because it may drive the poison inward.

O my Father, I am tempted to do everything about this resentment other than to get it up and out. The roots have now gone deep. I need to be relentless with myself. I ask Your help, for I cannot get it out alone. Amen.

FORGIVING, FOR CHRIST'S SAKE

When they came to the place called the Skull, there they crucified him, along with the criminals—one on his right, the other on his left. Jesus said, "Father, forgive them, for they do not know what they are doing." (Luke 23:33–34)

An Armenian said to me at the close of an address, "How can I forgive the Turks?" I could tell him only how one Armenian young woman had been enabled to forgive a Turk. She and her brother had been attacked in a lane, and while she had escaped by climbing over a wall, her brother had been brutally killed before her eyes.

She was a nurse, and later on while working in the hospital recognized one of her patients as the very Turkish soldier who had murdered her brother. Her first feeling was: *Revenge!* He was very ill, just hovering between life and death. The slightest neglect, and he would die—and no one would know.

But instead of revenge, she decided for Christ's sake to forgive him. She fought for his life and nursed him back to health. When he recovered, she told him who she was. The Turkish soldier looked at her in astonishment and said, "Then why didn't you let me die when you had me in your power?"

"I couldn't," answered the girl. "I just couldn't, for I am a Christian, and my own Master forgave His enemies who crucified Him. I must do the same for His sake."

"Well," said the hardened Turk in astonishment, "if that is what it means to be a Christian, I want to be one."

You can do what that Armenian young woman did: You can forgive for Christ's sake. No matter how you may have been bitterly wronged, nevertheless, for His sake, you can forgive the wrong and extend good will toward those who have wronged you. It isn't easy, but it can be done—by His help.

O God, the wrong has entered deep into my spirit. In my own strength I cannot forgive. But I am willing to be made willing. Through You I can do anything, yes, anything—even this. Amen.

UNDERNEATH OUR RESENTMENT

While they were stoning him, Stephen prayed, "Lord Jesus, receive my spirit." Then he fell on his knees and cried out, "Lord, do not hold this sin against them." When he had said this, he fell asleep. (Acts 7:59–60)

The central and fundamental motive for forgiving injuries is that God forgives us, and we therefore copy God as His children. But there are also minor motives and techniques we can use in dealing with resentment:

(1) Remember that the basis of most resentment is a touchy, unsurrendered self. The fact that we have been able to hold onto the resentment shows there is a self that is oversensitive. When surrendered to the will of God, we throw off resentment as a healthy skin throws off germs. Unless there is inner disease or an abrasion of the skin, germs can get no foothold. We should be suspicious of a self that can grow resentment—it is probably diseased with self-centeredness.

(2) Raise the question as to whether your resentment isn't rooted in imaginary slights, insults, and wrongs. A self-centered person can imagine a group is talking about him when in fact they are talking about everything else. An oversensitive person can by his very mental attitude throw other people into unnatural, closed-in attitudes, which he interprets as intentional hurts and slights. All the time he is oblivious to the fact that his own attitudes of self-centered sensitivity have created the very things in others against which he reacts.

Remember the old saying, "When you go around with a chip on your shoulder, it probably fell from the block above."

O God, my Father, help me to see myself clearly, for I seem to gather self-defensive arguments around myself. Now I lay myself at Your feet for cleansing and release. In Jesus' name, Amen.

PRAYER AND APPRECIATION

"You have heard the law that says, 'Love your neighbor' and hate your enemy. But I say, love your enemies! Pray for those who persecute you! In that way, you will be acting as true children of your Father in heaven.... If you love only those who love you, what reward is there for that? Even corrupt tax collectors do that much. If you are kind only to your friends, how are you different from anyone else? Even pagans do that. (Matt. 5:43–47†)

The next techniques for getting rid of resentment and hate are:

(3) Every time the name of the person arises in your mind, breathe a prayer. Meet every invading resentment with a barrage of prayer. Make the mind understand this practice and permit no exceptions. Soon you will have no enemies, for you will have no enmity.

(4) Say everything good you can about the person or persons with whom you are unfriendly. They probably have many fine points; focus your mind on those. In most cases, the good will outweigh the bad.

(5) Refuse to speak only of the negative. When you do have to speak of their faults, put them in terms of "I don't like certain things..." but then proceed to add, "But I do like these things..." and go on to name them. End on a positive note.

(6) Remember that focusing upon other people's faults is usually a defense mechanism. By doing so, you are probably attempting to lift yourself up by pushing them down. It won't work. By mentally picking flaws in others you create a worse flaw in yourself—you become a critical person.

God, my Father, I want to get rid of all that corrodes my soul. I know my attitudes of criticism eat like acid into my moral nature. I ask You to deliver me completely from the last tiny root of resentment. Amen.

LOVING PEOPLE FOR WHAT
THEY MAY BECOME

[Jesus to His disciple Peter]: *"Simon, Simon, Satan has asked to sift you as wheat. But I have prayed for you, Simon, that your faith may not fail. And when you have turned back, strengthen your brothers." (Luke 22:31–32)*

Dear brothers and sisters, if another believer is overcome by some sin, you who are godly should gently and humbly help that person back onto the right path. And be careful not to fall into the same temptation yourself. Share each other's burdens, and in this way obey the law of Christ. (Gal. 6:1–2†)

More ways to climb the ladder out of the resentment pit:

(7) If you find little to love or admire in a person, then love and admire what they may be. You do not have to be dishonest in your thinking. But you are now committed as a Christian, and you love people as Christ does. Your love then becomes real and redemptive.

(8) If there is a sudden flare-up in a relationship, get into the habit of settling disagreements at once. Don't let them get cold and rigid. Jesus said once, "Settle matters quickly with your adversary" (Matt. 5:25). This is sound, psychologically and morally. I know of one couple who have a beautiful wedded life. They decided, when they married, never to leave a room in which any disagreement was not resolved. Their difficulties, therefore, have always ended in laughs, because neither of them could go—they were prisoners of their own decision. There was no open door except into good will.

(9) See if there isn't a reason in the other person for the things you resent. If you notice a worker moving slowly, seeming to dawdle, is it truly a case of laziness? Or is the person sick, undernourished, perhaps depressed? Instead of criticizing, see if you can help rehabilitate—and in so doing, help yourself.

O God, I come to You to gain understanding. Give me clear insight, that I may read the lives of others. And when I understand, help me to forgive. Amen.

TOO GOOD TO BE AN ENEMY

"Do not judge, and you will not be judged. Do not condemn, and you will not be condemned. Forgive, and you will be forgiven. Give, and it will be given to you." (Luke 6:37–38)

Final steps for overcoming resentment:

(10) Go out each day to do some positive good to the person you resent. Wear down their hate and opposition with your own good will. A Japanese student intensely disliked a Chinese student in the same university. But when the Japanese was ill, the Chinese brought food to him every day. This kind attention broke down the enmity, and they became close friends.

(11) Be too glad and too great to be the enemy of anyone. Be so preoccupied with good will that you have no room for ill will. Dr. George Washington Carver, the great scientist and saint, rose to fame through his chemical discoveries and service to Southern farmers. Someone asked him for the name of the university that had accepted him as a student but then, upon discovering he was black, refused him admittance. Dr. Carver refused to say, passing off the incident as nothing. He possessed what somebody called "the peace that passes all understanding—and all misunderstanding."

A person said to me, "I don't think you know when you are insulted." I replied, "I am not looking for insults, and so I don't see them."

When Jesus announced His program at Nazareth, He read from Isaiah up through the words " '…to proclaim the year of the Lord's favor.' Then he rolled up the scroll, gave it back to the attendant and sat down" (Luke 4:19–20). Had he kept reading, the next phrase would have been "and the day of vengeance of our God" (Isa. 61:2). We should stop at the same place. Leave vengeance to God; use only redemptive good will.

O God, nothing anyone can do against me compares to what I have done against You. You have forgiven me—help me to forgive others. And help me to forgive graciously, not grudgingly. For Jesus' sake, Amen.

THE FOURTH ENEMY: FEAR

Fearing people is a dangerous trap, but trusting the Lord means safety.
(Prov. 29:25[†])

We have looked at three of the fifteen enemies of the human personality. We now come to the fourth: *Worry, anxiety, fear*.

Almost every evil is some perverted good—including worry. There is an instinct within us to look ahead, to plan, to think about how we will meet possible situations before they come. This capacity of foresight is one of the basic reasons for our rise beyond the animal. The animal stops at a dead end, while the human marches on to infinite goals.

Our capacity to foresee and foreplan and forestall is the power that lifts us out of the "is" into the "can be"—it is the secret of progress. As such, it must be cultivated. A lack of intelligent planning makes us prisoners of today, instead of pioneers of tomorrow.

Christians, above all others, are people of the long view, the long purpose, and the long plan. They plan how to live today, how to live tomorrow, how to live forever. And they plan this for all people, for they have not only the long view; they have also the wide view. They think in terms of the world as a whole. The idea that Christians are lackadaisical simpletons looking only at the moment because they are afraid to look further, like human ostriches with fearful heads in the sand, is false. We have been called to love God "with all your mind" (Mark 12:30), and a part of the mind is foresight.

Therefore, the Christian must cultivate this quality of intelligent planning, without succumbing to worry.

O God, You have taken the long view. The years of history tell us You are working out Your long-range purposes. Help me to catch the sweep of Your mind and the glory of Your purposes, and become a part of them. Amen.

ANXIETY: ASSET OR LIABILITY?

*Fear of the L*ORD *is a life-giving fountain; it offers escape from the snares of death. (Prov. 14:27†)*

There will be strange signs in the sun, moon, and stars. And here on earth the nations will be in turmoil…. People will be terrified at what they see coming upon the earth, for the powers in the heavens will be shaken. (Luke 21:25–26†)

If Christians are those who care about the past, the present, and the future, they are in the process of being sensitized on a world scale. This gives them drive, direction, and determination. It makes them progressive people. All other things being equal, Christians should be the most progressive people on earth. They are awakened in every fiber of their being.

But if this awareness is their greatest asset, it may also become their greatest liability. The fact that they are sensitive and aware may make them worry. If so, then their light has turned to darkness. Worry, anxiety, and fear can block the whole process of progress, paralyzing and disrupting the personality. Up to a certain point, fear may make surgeons more skillful and careful, lest they cut in the wrong places. But fear pushed beyond a certain point could paralyze them.

A healthy fear gives us skill and drive. An unhealthy fear inhibits us. Fear, like any other drive, has to be brought under control and used for constructive purposes. If out of control, it turns into worry and anxiety and becomes destructive to itself and others. "Do not fret—it leads only to evil" (Psalm 37:8). Jesus said this new life could often be "choked by life's worries" (Luke 8:14). It is probable that fear, worry, and anxiety form the greatest single trinity of evils a person can take into life.

O God, I fear the fear that gets rooted in my life. I am anxious about the anxiety that infects me. I am worried about the worry. Give me deliverance; help me to complete freedom from any cramping inhibition. Amen.

FEAR'S RELATION TO DISEASE

What I feared has come upon me; what I dreaded has happened to me. (Job 3:25)

So then, banish anxiety from your heart and cast off the troubles of your body. (Eccl. 11:10)

A doctor said to me, "Fears are the most disruptive thing we can have." All of life bears this out.

I know a lady who has a mortal dread of germs. She stays inside her house, the prisoner of her own fear. She doesn't realize that the fear itself is ten times more deadly than the germs. Besides, if she had a confident attitude toward life, germs would probably not get a foothold—her very confidence and faith would act as an antiseptic.

Doctors wanted to operate on a friend of mine for cancer or ulcer of the stomach. The facts were these: After he had failed in business, worry had stopped the gastric juices. But when he saw the cause and surrendered his worries to God, he gained thirty pounds in two months.

Indeed, San Francisco gastroenterologist Dr. Felix Cunha says, "The incidence of stomach ulcers goes up and down [in contrast to] the stock market." Investigation showed that when the Dow-Jones average skidded down, the number of business people with upset stomachs went up. Worry brings an over-acidity of the stomach, and that in turn upsets the digestive tract.

There is a definite connection between worry and disease. We ignore this at our peril.

O God, my Father, I see that in my inmost being I am made for confidence and trust, not for worry and anxiety. You have fashioned me for faith, not for fear. Help me this day to walk in confident faith, afraid of nothing. In Jesus' name, Amen.

FEAR IS COSTLY

You have not received a spirit that makes you fearful slaves. Instead, you received God's Spirit when he adopted you as his own children. Now we call him, "Abba, Father." (Rom. 8:15†)

On the evening of that first day of the week, when the disciples were together, with the doors locked for fear of the Jews, Jesus came and stood among them and said, "Peace be with you!" After he said this, he showed them his hands and side. The disciples were overjoyed when they saw the Lord. (John 20:19–20)

Sometimes fears are not basic, but marginal. Even so, they can upset the rest of the life. Marginal fear can push out basic courage. It can tie us up not merely physically, but mentally and spiritually as well.

A young minister began to complain of tightness of the chest and developed a hacking cough. The doctors found no physical reason. Then he began to complain of severe pain in the lower bowel, saying he had a cancer there. Examinations by several doctors found nothing physically wrong. He resigned the ministry, and now sits around moping and groaning most of the time. His mentality is giving way under the strain, and yet he is basically sound in body. It is the fear that is upsetting him.

Fear wrecks the machinery of life. And the repairs can be costly. Jesus, on the other hand, unlocks the doors shut by fear and leaves us, like the disciples, overjoyed.

My Father, I see that fear is indeed costly. But I cannot easily get rid of it, for it has put its roots within me. Help me tear it up, root and branch. Or do You have a better way? I will follow. In Jesus' name, Amen.

HOMEGROWN FEARS

Those who...do not call on God...were overwhelmed with dread, where there was nothing to dread. (Psalm 53:4–5)

I hear the slander of many; there is terror on every side; they conspire against me and plot to take my life. But I trust in you, O LORD; I say, "You are my God." My times are in your hands; deliver me from my enemies and from those who pursue me. (Psalm 31:13–15)

Fear attacks the body in a great number of subtle ways. Some friends brought a man into one of my meetings who was afraid of crowds, suffering from ochlophobia. When he got to the door, he tried to run away. But they insisted and took him in. During the whole service he sat with perspiration rolling down his pale and clammy face. The fear of crowds was an obsession. But there was nothing to fear except his fear.

In the last World War, doctors were amazed during the draft examinations to discover that so many perfectly healthy young men were convinced they had heart or kidney trouble, or some other malady. They had feared to undertake rigorous occupations for that reason. With very few exceptions, says the University of Wisconsin's Dr. Albert Wiggam, their fears had been started by hearing symptoms discussed at home. They were homegrown fears.

To implant fears in the minds of children is a crime. If parents try to rule the child by fear, then fear rules the child.

O God, our Father, we have filled Your world and our hearts with needless, devastating fears. Help us, we pray, to find release from these fears and power over them, for they are not our real selves—they are imported. In Jesus' name, Amen.

PHYSICAL EFFECTS OF FEAR

When [people] are afraid of heights and of dangers…then [people] go to their eternal home and mourners go about the streets. (Eccl. 12:5)

[Paul]: *When we came into Macedonia, this body of ours had no rest, but we were harassed at every turn—conflicts on the outside, fears within. But God, who comforts the downcast, comforted us. (2 Cor. 7:5–6)*

The physiological effects of fear and worry have been scientifically studied. One man was found worrying because a fellow worker had died unexpectedly, and he had an obsession that he would share the same fate. His stomach trouble had started after this worry began, and after he had tried to conceal it from everyone—even his wife.

Another sufferer had a flow of extra stomach acid even when sound asleep but dreaming of his troubles.

A man who had worked faithfully and long to get a promotion in his office was so upset when the turning point came that he could not take the new position when it was offered to him. Worry had so upset his heart that he had to go to the hospital instead of to the superintendency. Worry and anxiety snatched the prize from his hand and left him broken.

Such examples from the physical world reinforce that "Fear involves torment. But he who fears has not been made perfect in love" (1 John 4:18 NKJV).

O God, I see that I too have lost much of life's fullness and power on account of worry and fear. I cannot rise to my full powers until I have shed all fears and forebodings, marching out to meet life in triumphant faith. Help me to do this. In Jesus' name, Amen.

WHEN ANIMALS AND CHILDREN
ARE AFRAID

The wolf will live with the lamb, the leopard will lie down with the goat, the calf and the lion and the yearling together; and a little child will lead them. The cow will feed with the bear, their young will lie down together, and the lion will eat straw like the ox. The infant will play near the hole of the cobra, and the young child put his hand into the viper's nest. They will neither harm nor destroy on all my holy mountain, for the earth will be full of the knowledge of the LORD as the waters cover the sea. (Isa. 11:6–9)

Fears and anxieties upset the animal kingdom as well as the human kingdom. When aggressive dogs are around cows, the cows often refuse to give their milk; and even when they do, that milk causes colic in the calves.

A chicken farmer told me that after the Fourth of July with its explosion of firecrackers, many eggs had to be thrown out, for candling showed blood spots in them, which had been produced by fear. The same thing happened when an airplane flew very low over the chickens.

If worry and anxiety can stunt cows and chickens, they can stunt children as well. A schoolteacher said that when she is worried and upset, the students do not study well, and they quarrel with one another. Scholastic level is lower on those days, but it goes up when she is inwardly harmonious.

Now we have spent a week on the effects of worry, fear, and anxiety. Perhaps some of you have wondered if I would continue too long with this discussion, instead of going on to think about the remedy. I have no apology, for the first step in remedying fear is to see it as the fearsome thing it is.

O God, now I want to turn with an eager heart and mind from the devastation to the deliverance. Give me an expectant soul that believes freedom is at hand; I only have to take it. In Jesus' name, Amen.

FIRST STEPS IN DELIVERANCE

Then Peter said, "Ananias, how is it that Satan has so filled your heart that you have lied to the Holy Spirit and have kept for yourself some of the money you received for the land?… What made you think of doing such a thing? You have not lied to men but to God." When Ananias heard this, he fell down and died. And great fear seized all who heard what had happened. (Acts 5:3–5)

We now turn to the more joyous task of setting up a ladder so that defeated and harassed persons may climb to peace and poise.

(1) Let us clearly understand that any step must be honest and real. There must be no attempt to deceive the mind, no effort to entice it into a fool's paradise of make-believe. No one can play tricks on the universe, or on God. To try to wave a magic wand over fears and tell ourselves that they don't exist is the way of self-delusion. It leads to an inevitable breakdown.

The Christian way is the way of complete honesty. Jesus said once, "You will hear of wars and rumours of wars; *see and do not be alarmed"* (Matt. 24:6 MOF-FATT). He did not try to teach us to get release from alarms by refusing to see them. He told us to look fears straight in the face, and yet not to be frightened.

(2) Be sure you want to give up the thing you are afraid of. Very often fears produce bodily ills that in turn determine our life strategy. Some people use their illnesses to gain power over others. If they let go of their maladies, they would lose the attention that accompanies them. They, in fact, "enjoy" bad health. I know a family that lived by recounting to one another their various ailments, each bidding for sympathy from the others. They nearly all died before their time. The one member who survived found interests outside that circle of self-commiseration.

O God, I want to be completely delivered from fear and its results. I know how fears mark my soul and body. My subconscious mind plays tricks on me. Help me to be perfectly whole. Save me to complete honesty. Amen.

THE WILL TO BE WELL

There is in Jerusalem near the Sheep Gate a pool, which in Aramaic is called Bethesda…. One who was there had been an invalid for thirty-eight years. When Jesus saw him lying there and learned that he had been in this condition for a long time, he asked him, "Do you want to get well?" (John 5:2, 5–6)

If some people couldn't talk about their ills, just what would they talk about? You remember the old definition of a bore as "a man who talks about his rheumatism when you want to talk about yours." When people are self-centered, they will use any means to gain attention.

Jesus went straight to the heart of self-centeredness when He confronted the sick with this question: "Will you be made whole?" In other words, "Do you really want to be well? If not, I cannot do a thing for you!" Dr. Everett C. Drash of the University of Virginia told me he operated on a schoolteacher for tuberculosis, and she died. There was no apparent reason for her death until her relatives found among her papers a statement to a friend that she was convinced she would die. Her lack of faith had killed her will to live.

That brings us to the third step: *(3) Will to be well.* Throw your will on the side of deliverance. Just as there is a will to believe, so there is a will to be well. In contrast to the case mentioned above, there was a mother who died of tuberculosis and left six small children. Her sister stepped in to take care of them, and she too caught the infection. It seemed she too would die, for this happened in the days before modern science had begun to conquer this plague. Instead, the woman willed to live and raise that family. It was her life task, and she would perform it. Each day she had one of the children come and stand in the corner of her room while she said to herself, *I must live to raise this family!* She did live, she finished raising the family, and today is one of the most radiant and useful persons I know.

Whether you seek deliverance from illness or from fear, will to be well.

My Father, reinforce me at the center of my being, for I am inwardly flabby. Help me to take the strength of Your will into my own. In Jesus' name, Amen.

EVERY FOE IS A DEFEATED FOE

[Jesus]: *"In this world you will have trouble. But take heart! I have overcome the world." (John 16:33)*

So do not fear, for I am with you; do not be dismayed, for I am your God. I will strengthen you and help you; I will uphold you with my righteous right hand. (Isa. 41:10)

The words of Jesus quoted above display an open-eyed frankness that does not deny the fact of a world of tribulation in which we must live. And yet, after looking at it, with all its brutality and power to hurt, He says: "But take heart! I have overcome the world." In other words, every foe you face is a defeated foe.

That brings us to the fourth step: *(4) Remember that every fear, every trouble, every sickness, every sin you may face has been and is defeated and overcome by the One you follow—Christ.* When these forces come to overwhelm you and beat you into submission by their very overbearing presence, calmly look each one in the eye and say: "I am not afraid of you. You have been and are decisively beaten by my Lord. Let me see your neck. There, I knew it! The footprint of the Son of God is upon your neck!"

This confidence is your starting point: Nothing can touch you that hasn't touched Him and been defeated by Him. If you open your life to His power, every ill can be defeated again by you through His grace. You need not be defeated by anything unless you consent to be. Nothing can stop you except your refusal to cooperate.

Paul could say, "I do not frustrate the grace of God" (Gal. 2:21 KJV)—I do not block its redemption, nor frustrate its healing purposes. Therefore an Almighty Will worked within Paul's will, so that he arose a rhythmic, harmonious, adequate person. You can be the same.

O God, my Father, I have closed my heart to Your healing and deliverance. I have wrapped myself within myself—afraid of salvation! Forgive me. Amen.

WORRY IS ATHEISM

God has said, "I will never fail you. I will never abandon you." So we can say with confidence, "The LORD is my helper, so I will have no fear. What can mere people do to me?" (Heb. 13:5–6†)

When I say to you that you can live without fear and worry, I mean that. This is not an academic statement, but a fact. Here is my testimony:

By all outer signs, the week during which I was writing these pages should have been a week of worry and defeat, for everything had gone wrong. All my intensive efforts for months in Washington to find a basis for peace between Japan and America had come to naught.[1] Agreement had seemed so near and so possible—and then the crash. A long war stared us in the face. I was cut off from my work in India. My wife and family were there, cut off for the duration of the war—and worse, the war was slowly moving in upon them.

But—during this week, there had been peace. When a woman said to me one evening, "You have had a quiet day; you've had time to worry," I felt inwardly startled: *"Time to worry"*—as if a Christian ever has "time to worry"! The Christian has expunged worry from his vocabulary.

That leads us to the fifth step: *(5) Remember that worry or fear is a kind of atheism.* A person who worries says, "I cannot trust God; I'll take things in my own hands. God doesn't care, and so He won't do anything—I'll have to worry it through." But faith says, "God does care, and He and I will work it out together. I'll supply the willingness, and He will supply the power. With that combination we can do anything."

You remember the story of Martin Luther? One morning, when he was discouraged, his wife appeared in black. When Luther inquired what the mourning meant, she replied, "Haven't you heard? God is dead."

Luther saw the absurdity—and so should you. God lives—so will you!

O God, as long as You live, I too shall live. Nothing can shake the rock of Your existence on which I stand. Therefore, I shall not worry. Amen.

---

1. Throughout 1941, E. Stanley Jones worked tirelessly to prevent war in the Pacific—and nearly succeeded.

FEAR IS A TROJAN HORSE

"The eyes of the Lord are on the righteous and his ears are attentive to their prayer, but the face of the Lord is against those who do evil." Who is going to harm you if you are eager to do good? But even if you should suffer for what is right, you are blessed. "Do not fear what they fear; do not be frightened." (1 Peter 3:12–14)

Now we come to the sixth step: *(6) Hold in mind that nothing you fear is as bad as the fear itself.* I mean that seriously: Nothing can happen to you that is as disastrous and disruptive as the entrance of fear and worry into your life. If, however, you keep the center of life intact, you can come back from anything. Healed at the heart, you can say, "Let the world come on."

People who fight life's battles without fear fight only one enemy—the real thing confronting them. But those who fight with fears inside fight three enemies—the real thing, plus the imaginary things built up by fear, plus the fear itself. Actually, the greatest of these is fear. Fear is the Trojan horse that looses from within itself the enemies that capture us before the real fight begins.

> Then take your fear
> By the ear,
> And say, "See here,
> If the thing I fear
> Were already here,
> It could not cause a tear
> So scalding, nor could it sear
> My soul as much as you, the fear,
> So, now and forever, out of here!"

Even fear of the fear must go. How? By fastening our attention not on the thing to be feared, or on the fear of this fear, but on the Savior from fear.

O Christ, my Savior, You know everything that causes me to fear; You have gone through it all. And yet no fears or worries attached themselves to You. I want to know Your secret; unfold it to me. I obey completely and fully. Amen.

RELAX IN HIS PRESENCE

I have set the LORD always before me. Because he is at my right hand, I will not be shaken. Therefore my heart is glad and my tongue rejoices; my body also will rest secure. (Psalm 16:8–9)

It is a law of the mind that whatever gets your attention gets you. If your worries get your attention, they will get you. If Christ gets your attention, He will get you.

But how can you fasten your attention on Him? You find that you are pulled off from Him to worries. Then take the next step: *(7) Relax in His presence.* His power cannot get across to you unless you learn to relax. Fear and worry tighten you up. Faith relaxes you.

Often fear and worry keep the motor running even after you are parked. You are worn out even when sitting still. You are tense with anxieties and fears, using up energy. In that condition, nothing can get across, for it is a fact that you cannot engrave anything on a tense mind. Such a mind cannot take in energy; it can only expend it. The end of tension is bankruptcy.

But in quietness and confidence, you absorb; you are in a state of receptivity. A maid said to her employer: "I notice that when you sit, you sit tight. You are all screwed up and tight on the inside. Now look at me. When I work, I work hard; but when I sit, I sit loose." There was a real philosophy of life in that statement.

When you work, work hard; but when you stop working, then stop working—relax. The oft-repeated statement "Let go; let God" cannot be repeated too frequently, because it brings healing. Let go of your inward fears and worries, and let God absorb them in His grace and love.

My Father God, I've burned up the energy of my soul and body and mind through fear and worry. Such tenseness has taken me nowhere. Help me this day to receive the calm of Your purposes and the peace of Your power. Then I shall know harmony and accomplishment. Amen.

MEET TODAY, TODAY

I tell you, do not worry about your life, what you will eat or drink; or about your body, what you will wear. Is not life more important than food, and the body more important than clothes?... Do not worry about tomorrow, for tomorrow will worry about itself. Each day has enough trouble of its own. (Matt. 6:25, 34)

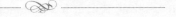

In India we have a bird we call the "Pity-to-do-it." It goes around all day saying what sounds like "Pity-to-do-it." And at night it sleeps with its feet in the air, to keep the sky from falling on it! It is a champion pessimist and worrier. Hence it is thin, scrawny, and fussy.

Some of us are like that bird. But we do not have to be. We can instead study the artist's picture of a bird on a nest overhanging a mighty waterfall. Amid the roar, that bird is the symbol of calm. We must learn that. How?

(8) Meet today, today. When Jesus talked about letting tomorrow do its own worrying, He was not saying there were no troubles to be met. There are. Life is bound to bring trouble. But don't telescope the troubles of tomorrow and of the next day into today. Meet today, today.

If you put the troubles of next week into today by anticipation, you spoil today. You are meeting two sets of troubles at once: one set that is actually here, and the set you bring in by worrying about tomorrow. You are therefore meeting your troubles twice—once before they come, and once when they are actually here. Such a telescoping of trouble is a double expenditure of energy.

Worry is the advance interest you pay on troubles that often never come. Some of them do come, and you can meet and conquer them separately. But tomorrow's troubles plus today's will break you. The theory of "divide and conquer" is applicable here. Divide your worries into one-day units; don't let them gang up on you and come piling all at once into one day.

O God, I see that I have been needlessly burdening myself. You give me a sufficient load for today, and You help me bear it. Forgive me for adding to my burden. I see that this is sin—a sin against myself and You. Amen.

IN QUIETNESS AND CONFIDENCE

Thus says the Lord GOD, the Holy One of Israel: "In returning and rest you shall be saved; in quietness and confidence shall be your strength." (Isa. 30:15 NKJV)

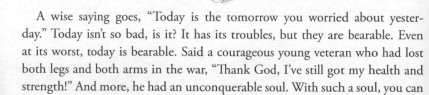

A wise saying goes, "Today is the tomorrow you worried about yesterday." Today isn't so bad, is it? It has its troubles, but they are bearable. Even at its worst, today is bearable. Said a courageous young veteran who had lost both legs and both arms in the war, "Thank God, I've still got my health and strength!" And more, he had an unconquerable soul. With such a soul, you can meet anything that belongs to today.

If the whole day seems too difficult, divide it up into hours. Meet each hour with your full resources, and pack it with God's resources too. Throw all your energies into meeting the enemies as they come one by one. Keep them segregated; fight them one at a time.

And fight them, not by strained endeavor, but by quiet faith. That leads to the next step: *(9) Say over and over, "In quietness and confidence shall be my strength."* Note two things there: quietness and confidence. You must quiet everything in the presence of God. Calm your being before Him and drink in His quiet strength. Let His healing quiet get into every pore, bathing the tired and restless nerve cells with His healing.

But quietness alone will not be enough—confidence is necessary. Quietness is passive, and we must be passive to God; but confidence is active, and we must be active to God. Confidence is *con* ("with") *fideo* ("faith"). In other words, it is not an alone faith; it is a "faith with"—a faith with God's faith. Your faith and God's faith flow together, and hence can do anything.

My Father, I begin to see that my poor faith alone is not all that is left to battle life's sorrows and troubles. I have a faith, plus Yours. And that plus is more than enough. I am no longer afraid—not with You. Amen.

FAITH IN HIS FAITH

The LORD is my shepherd, I shall not be in want. He makes me lie down in green pastures, he leads me beside quiet waters, he restores my soul. He guides me in paths of righteousness for his name's sake. (Psalm 23:1–3)

We did not quite finish the step of inwardly repeating the words, "In quietness and confidence shall be my strength." If confidence is having faith with God, then the Christian life is not lifting oneself by the bootstraps. It is linking our littleness with His greatness, our incompleteness with His completeness. It is doing what the little boy did when he offered his five loaves and two fish to Christ. That multitude could not be fed without his cooperation—and the feeding couldn't be done with his five loaves and two fish alone. He and Christ together did everything necessary.

Very often when I have no faith in my faith, I have to have faith in His faith. He makes me believe in myself and my possibilities, when I simply can't. I have to rise to His faith in me.

A woman who was inwardly collapsed said to me, "Well, I have no faith of my own, but I do have faith in your faith."

"Good," I replied. "Take faith in my faith as a first step, and then you will go on to something infinitely better—faith in His faith."

A passage in Deuteronomy touches your need: "For the Eternal…will not let you go" (4:31 MOFFATT). Faith is not merely your holding on to God—it is God holding on to you. He will not let you go! So keep believing that "Your strength is quiet faith" (Isa. 30:15 MOFFATT). Repeat to your soul these words: "To say what ought to be *cannot be*…is a brief and a complete statement of atheism." It is. Instead, say to yourself, "What ought to be *can be,* and I will make it so."

O living Christ, I see that life is communion—a union with You. Not merely in the quiet moments, but also in the moments of stress and toil. I now see I can be the happy warrior, for I am drawing heavily on Your power and going forward in Your confidence. I can actually do what I can't. I thank You. Amen.

SURRENDERING OUR FEARS

[Jesus] replied, "You of little faith, why are you so afraid?" Then he got up and rebuked the winds and the waves, and it was completely calm. (Matt. 8:26)

We come now to the next step: *(10) Surrender the thing you fear into the hands of God.* Ask Him to solve it with you. Fear is keeping things in your own hands; faith is turning them over to God's hands—and leaving them there.

A woman came to one of our gatherings from some distance away, suffering deeply. Sorrow and pain had left her with an upset heart. She had been in bed for a year and had various treatments. Now she said she had been afraid she would die on the way, as her heart began behaving very badly indeed. Her uppermost thought was, *How expensive it will be to ship my body back home.*

After a talk with her, I saw that anxiety and worry were causing the functional disturbance of the heart. The arrhythmia was not imaginary; it was real, but caused by worry and fear. I got her to surrender the whole matter to God. She did. The strained lines on her face relaxed, and she began to act like a normal person.

She tells the rest of the story: "Let me say that my body was not shipped home, but that I was very much alive, and scarcely tired, when I reached home after a 550-mile drive in one day! And there has been no relapse since. This recovery is so real; it is not neurotic, for my nerves are becoming steady, and my heart is beginning to act like a normal heart should. It is wonderful…. When the doctor saw me yesterday he said, 'Something has happened to you since you were here before. There is a transformation in you which is almost unbelievable. What is it?'"

My Father, forgive me that I hold my worries, troubles, and fears in my own incompetent hands. Now I do hand them over to You—not for an hour, but forever. I accept my own release. I am grateful—so grateful. Amen.

FILL THE VACUUM

Thank God! He gives us victory over sin and death through our Lord Jesus Christ. So, my dear brothers and sisters, be strong and immovable. Always work enthusiastically for the Lord, for you know that nothing you do for the Lord is ever useless. (1 Cor. 15:57–58†)

Now that you have turned over your fears and anxieties to God and have left them there, take the next step. *(11) Deliberately take up some task to help others.* You have relinquished your fears not to become a vacuum, but to have a heart with room and inward leisure for other people's troubles.

One woman was an invalid with high blood pressure and other ailments. She was always thinking about herself and rarely ever talked of any subject other than her disease; she lay in bed and performed no household duties. Then her husband suddenly grew very ill and seemed to be on the point of death. Aroused by this danger, she got out of bed and helped nurse her husband back to health. When she forgot her own ailments in her endeavor to help him, she herself got well.

A watchmaker told a friend, in reply to his question as to why he kept his various watches and clocks always wound up and running: "In order that they may be kept in better condition." You and I are made for constructive activity, and health will come to us as a by-product. Don't sit and talk about your ailments, or you'll have more and more of them to talk about.

Learn to be passive before God and active before people. Take in from God as you live in the passive voice; then give out to others as you live in the active voice. These are the two heartbeats of your life: passive, active, passive, active. You submit to God, but you don't submit to any fear or concern. You are creative and masterful.

O God, You are healing me in order to make me a center of healing. I hold this precious gift in my hand, not to gaze at it in reverence, but to pass it on. Freely I have received; help me freely to give. In Jesus' name, Amen.

FEARS DISSECTED (PART 1)

"My thoughts are not your thoughts, neither are your ways my ways," declares the LORD. *"As the heavens are higher than the earth, so are my ways higher than your ways and my thoughts than your thoughts." (Isa. 55:8–9)*

We are now in a position to look particular fears and worries in the face and take them apart. *(12) Look at your worst fears one by one.* They are already halfway defeated in Christ and are wholly defeated when you accept and act on the fact of their defeat.

Take, for example, *the fear of failure.* A great many people go through life in bondage to success. They are in mortal dread of failure. Why should this be? Jesus cared little about success or failure. The story of Jesus is a story of apparent failure: He ended on a cross. A faith that has a cross at its center cannot be a faith that worships success.

I do not have to succeed; I have only to be true to the highest I know. Success and failure are in the hands of God. On my way to India, I once said in England: "The romance of missions has gone for me. I know what I'm up against. If you should say to me that I would go back to India to see nothing but frustration and failure, with no more fruit whatever, I would reply: 'That is an incident. But I have the call of God to India, and to be true to that call is my one business.'"

I made that statement one day in a meeting, and a minister came up and said: "All my life I've been in bondage to success; I've looked at everything from the success standpoint. You have released within me the greatest tension of my life. I have only to be true—thank God."

Fear says, "There is a lion in the way." But when you walk straight up to the lion of fear, he turns out to be a mouse of fact. Suppose you should fail—is that so terrible? Not to have tried is a worse failure.

My Father, I've been afraid of failure. Forgive that I've looked at the verdict of others, instead of at the verdict of Your "Well done." Help me to be true—I care for nothing else. Amen.

FEARS DISSECTED (PART 2)

"Listen to me...you whom I have upheld since you were conceived, and have carried since your birth. Even to your old age and gray hairs I am he, I am he who will sustain you. I have made you and I will carry you; I will sustain you and I will rescue you." (Isa. 46:3–4)

Others are bound by *the fear of losing a friend's or loved one's affection.* To become anxious and worried about this is in fact the quickest way to lose, for it becomes difficult to love a person all inwardly tight. When you become strained about the love of a loved one, you defeat your very purpose.

Still others carry *a fear of being dependent in old age.* Why should you fear this? Your children were dependent on you; why would you fear being dependent on them? Life is so made that we grow by accepting responsibilities for which there is no return. Don't deny your children that privilege of growth. Be the kind of person they would love to take care of.

If it is fear of being taken care of by the state, then again, why should you be afraid? If you have been a good citizen and a useful member of society during your active life, contributing to the upbuilding of the state, then why shouldn't the state take care of you when you are no longer able to work?

What about *fear of the unknown future?* Many live in dread of what is coming. Why should we? The unknown puts adventure into life. It gives us something to sharpen our souls on. The unexpected around the corner gives a sense of anticipation and surprise. Thank God for the unknown future. If we saw all the good things that are coming to us, we would sit down and degenerate. If we saw all the evil things, we would be paralyzed. How merciful God is to lift the curtain on today, and as we get strength today to meet tomorrow, then to lift the curtain on the morrow. He is a considerate God.

O God, I am dependent on You. Help me not to be ashamed to be dependent on others. As for the future, I meet it with a salutation and a song. Amen.

FEARS DISSECTED (PART 3)

Since the children have flesh and blood, [Jesus] too shared in their humanity so that by his death he might destroy him who holds the power of death—that is, the devil—and free those who all their lives were held in slavery by their fear of death. (Heb. 2:14–15)

Many go through life spoiling life through *fear of death*. But why should we be afraid to die?

Some time ago I was being taken out to be hanged. On the way to the gallows my brother said to me, "It looks as though you're not going to get out of this, doesn't it?" To which I agreed.

But on the way we met the woman I was supposed to have murdered. "There," I said, "I told you so—here is the woman." We took her along. A large crowd had gathered, and I said, "I told you I was innocent; here is the woman."

But the crowd replied, "We've come here to see the minister hanged, and we're going to go through with it."

To which I replied, "You are doing an injustice, but I am not afraid to die." They were adamant; I was taken to the scaffold, the black cap put over my head, and the rope around my neck. I stood on the trapdoor.

But just as the trap was about to be sprung—I woke up! Of course, I was glad to find myself in bed rather than on a scaffold. But there was a sense of inner exultation, even joy. I said to myself, "Why, that wasn't so bad, even at its worst!" It couldn't be much worse than that.

Why should a Christian be afraid of death? To fear the larger life is a kind of atheism. Doubt of the future means doubt of the present. It means the Master is not dependable for the ultimate things, and therefore not for the immediate things. Real Christians live well and they die well.

O God, when I have You, I have more than everything. No death can touch that fact. You live amid earthly changes, and so shall I. I am invulnerable—with You. Amen.

MADE FOR FAITH, NOT FEAR

While the beggar held on to Peter and John, all the people were astonished and came running to them.... When Peter saw this, he said... "By faith in the name of Jesus, this man whom you see and know was made strong. It is Jesus' name and the faith that comes through him that has given this complete healing to him, as you can all see." (Acts 3:11–12, 16)

I had intended to finish the meditations on conquering fear last week, but the more we have faced this matter, the more fundamental it has become. As I wrote the above, a letter came from a highly gifted woman with this sentence in it: "Oh, Dr. Jones...everything is wrong, and I am so afraid I am going to crack up completely." She says "everything is wrong." She blames her circumstances; but nothing is wrong whatever except her fear, which is rooted in her self-centered attitudes. Her universe continually falls to pieces because of her attitudes giving birth to fears.

So this week we shall gather up our inward resolves and register them—not with a clenched jaw, but a calm relaxation committed to certain attitudes.

(1) I see that I am inwardly fashioned for faith, not for fear. Fear is not my native land; faith is. I am so made that worry and anxiety are sand in the machinery of life; faith is oil. I live better by faith and confidence than by fear and doubt. In anxiety and worry, my being is gasping for breath—these are not my native air. But in faith and confidence, I breathe freely—these are my native air.

A Johns Hopkins University doctor says, "We do not know why the worriers die sooner than the nonworriers, but that is a fact." But I, who am of a simple mind, think I know: We are inwardly constructed, in nerve and tissue and brain cell and soul, for faith. God made us that way. The need is not imposed on us dogmatically, but it is written into us intrinsically. We cannot live without it. To live by worry is to live against reality.

O God, I surrender myself to the healing and renewing of faith and confidence. With gratitude, I release it into every fiber of my being. Amen.

A FAITH FOR EMERGENCIES

"Why do you worry about clothes? See how the lilies of the field grow. They do not labor or spin.... If that is how God clothes the grass of the field, which is here today and tomorrow is thrown into the fire, will he not much more clothe you, O you of little faith?" (Matt. 6:28, 30)

The next declaration is this: *(2) I see that I cannot meet life's emergencies unless I have confidence and faith.*

A Mayo Clinic doctor told me about a patient being prepared for one of the wonderful new operations that reduce high blood pressure. She had passed every preliminary examination and thought no more were to follow. But she was mistaken. Before the surgeon would operate, he wanted to ensure that no spiritual or mental trouble was bringing on the chronic headaches and hypertension. He was firm and would not be sidetracked. So he questioned her closely: Was she happy? Worried over money? Was she satisfied with her home conditions? Her religion? Until she could pass that test, she was not ready to stand the operation, for if there were conflict and worry at the citadel of her life, she could collapse from within in spite of all scientific efforts.

A schoolteacher was suffering from heart trouble, her heart beating so loudly and rapidly that at the least exertion it seemed to jump out of her body. The doctors could find no physical reason, but they discovered she was worried over a lump in her breast. When she was assured that there was no cancer, she went home happy and relieved. The heart became normal, and she is now happy and efficient in her work. Fear and worry had caused functional disturbance. The disturbance was real, but it had been caused by an unnecessary fear.

O God, I see that I am the enemy of my possibilities if I harbor inward fear and anxiety. I throw disturbance into my organs, upset my brain cells, tire out my faithful heart, and paralyze my constructive energies. Forgive me. In Jesus' name, Amen.

THE BEST WE CAN BE

Let us draw near to God with a sincere heart in full assurance of faith, having our hearts sprinkled to cleanse us from a guilty conscience and having our bodies washed with pure water. (Heb. 10:22)

Fear and anxiety keep us from being at our best. They paralyze the center of life. A man saw a snake and, at the same moment, was nicked by a barbed wire. He thought he was bitten. He began foaming at the mouth and seemed about to die. The doctor arrived, however, saw there was no swelling at the abrasion, assured him he had not been bitten—and the man got well almost immediately. The fear had produced the symptoms.

Fear will often produce the very symptoms you fear. Why is it that people with a calm demeanor play a better game of tennis than those whose emotions go up and down with the score? The simple reason is their unperturbed confidence. Victory flows from that.

The worrier has a small set of lungs, made that way by the fact of worry. The person of faith takes in deep breaths of God's air, God's power, God's hope. The worrier is afraid to breathe deeply, afraid of the healing of fresh air, of the healing of God's hope, of God's power. He therefore smothers himself—sometimes to death. Said the man in Jesus' parable, "I was afraid, and went out and hid your talent" (Matt. 25:25). And that happens everywhere—those who fear bury their talents, and often bury themselves prematurely. Worry makes an eight-cylinder person into a four-cylinder person.

Worry is a species of myopia—nearsightedness.

My God and Father, I want to be at my best—at Your best. I now resolve to be a person without blockages anywhere in my life. For how dare I block You? Amen.

RESOLVE NOT TO ACT ON FEAR

[God's instruction to Moses regarding the Tabernacle items]: *"See that you make them according to the pattern shown you on the mountain." (Ex. 25:40)*

[Jesus]: *"Peace I leave with you; my peace I give you. I do not give to you as the world gives. Do not let your hearts be troubled and do not be afraid." (John 14:27)*

A third declaration: *(3) I resolve not to act on any fear, but to wait till I can act on faith.*

Never act on the basis of a fear, for fears are usually false. Note where Moses got his pattern for the Tabernacle: "on the mountain." Don't build your life according to any pattern shown to you in the valley of fear. Wait till you get to the mountain of faith, and then build your life plans.

I know of a strong healthy wife who was afraid to have a baby, and so allowed an abortion. There was no physical reason why she shouldn't have had that baby. But fear paralyzed her creative instinct. And now her arms are forever childless. Nothing that could have happened in childbirth would have been as hard as the lifelong pain of empty arms, the mother instinct frustrated. She loved herself—and hence had nothing to love except herself.

One of the greatest souls of this age says, "Whenever I get down, I shut off my mind from decisions—no decisions until I am on top of things."

All our decision moments must be faith moments, not fear moments. I will instruct my mind that no decisions are to be made except in faith. And there are to be no exceptions. I therefore use a mind purged of all acting on fear. It is marvelous what the mind will do when it is focused and decisive. Make a life choice that faith will be your permanent life attitude.

O living Christ, life has no retreats and no regrets with You. Give me the simple impulse of faith in every circumstance, and help me to act on nothing else. In Jesus' name, Amen.

CREATING FAITH IN OTHERS

We do not want you to become lazy, but to imitate those who through faith and patience inherit what has been promised. (Heb. 6:12)

Remember your leaders, who spoke the word of God to you. Consider the outcome of their way of life and imitate their faith. (Heb. 13:7)

Our fourth declaration: *(4) I resolve to create faith in other people. I will think faith, talk faith, live faith, impart faith.* That means I will turn over all my non-faith attitudes to God and help others to do the same.

A pastor told me he had been unable to eat, had stomach pains, and was getting thinner every day. He went on his knees and said, "O God, you delivered one man, Stanley Jones, from physical and nervous exhaustion; you can deliver another—you can deliver me." He turned the whole thing over to God, went to bed, relaxed, and received—breathed in the healing of God as the lungs breathe in the purifying air. Today he is the picture of health. In fact, he is contagious—he radiates health.

A father was about to be operated on, and the mother and son could not sleep. They sent word to a Christian layman: "Please come down and stay with us at night; we are afraid. Can't you come and talk to us? We have nothing to hold onto in the dark." The layman came. Mother and son both surrendered themselves to God and were changed. The son spoke to the father, who for a long time had lain there uncomprehending. But he finally recognized his son's voice, responded to his testimony, opened his heart to the love of God, and was himself converted. He died a happy man. The spark of faith in that son, a convert of just two days, kindled something in the father's heart.

You too belong to the great contagion—the contagion of faith.

O God, I want the doors of my spirit to turn out, not in, for You, the Creator, made me for creative activity. Help me to create hope and faith in others. In Jesus' name, Amen.

CULTIVATING YOUR FAITH

You know that the testing of your faith develops perseverance. (James 1:3)

Since we belong to the day, let us be self-controlled, putting on faith and love as a breastplate, and the hope of salvation as a helmet. (1 Thess. 5:8)

Our next declaration: *(5) In order to have faith and confidence to impart to others, I must deliberately cultivate faith.*

But this does not mean I will *try* to cultivate it. I will let go, relax, become a channel of a power not my own, and then God will do the rest. Does this sound like the pious statement of a minister? Then listen to Dr. Fritz Künkel, an outstanding psychiatrist who said in a lecture: "As long as I am confident, have faith, good humor, as long as I allow my body—my organs, my brain—to function as they want to function, I trust my nature, and all goes well. But when I distrust, become afraid, begin to control my nature, don't trust my nature, try to replace the unconscious function of my organs with willpower, then I find that willpower is powerless. I am trying to replace God with myself. My fear increases; therefore conscious strain increases; therefore the danger increases; therefore I strain the harder. The way out would be trust, faith, calmness, relaxation."

A businessman said to me: "I am physically and mentally well, but emotionally I am sick. I have hold of a 110-volt wire, and cannot let go." He was anxious. To let go means you have more faith in God and His processes than you have in yourself and your processes.

The essence of cultivation is relaxation. You will never be a good musician if you try too hard; you must let go and let the music get into your fingertips, so that you do not play the music—the music plays you. So with God: Don't use God; let Him use you.

O God, I have not been fighting the good fight of faith; I have been fighting the fight of fear. Now help me to go limp in Your presence, that You may impress on me Your ways, Your poise, Your power. In Jesus' name, Amen.

CHEERFUL ANTICIPATION

A happy heart makes the face cheerful, but heartache crushes the spirit. The discerning heart seeks knowledge, but the mouth of a fool feeds on folly. All the days of the oppressed are wretched, but the cheerful heart has a continual feast. (Prov. 15:13–15)

And finally, our sixth declaration: *(6) I shall face life cheerfully and with anticipation. I shall learn to laugh, even at myself.* This is what we can do once we follow the advice of 1 Peter 5:7—"Let all your anxieties fall on him, for his interest is in you" (MOFFATT).

The poet Elsie Robinson says: "Unpleasantness can be a disease. It provides an escape for our cowardice, an excuse for our laziness, an alibi for cussedness, and a spotlight for our conceit." I like the advice of the English humanitarian Muriel Lester: "Hunt for self-pity as you would hunt for lice"—and despise it with the same loathing. Whenever I get tense and take myself too seriously, I deliberately walk to a mirror and burst out laughing. Even if I do not feel like laughing as I walk, I do when I see the man's face there, laughing at me.

A doctor said to a friend of mine, "You will never suffer a breakdown, for you have a hair-trigger laugh."

Another physician, Emily T. Wilson, says, "Those [patients] who are cheerful and confident, who are free from anxieties and fear, make far more satisfactory progress than those who keep themselves in a turmoil of distress and worry.... The sincere Christian has no time for nerves. The religious man faces life confident and unafraid, and saves himself from countless ills."

"No time for nerves"—just too busy with faith and confidence to let them get a toehold, let alone a foothold.

O confident God, going steadily forward amid the deflections and betrayals of people, help me to have Your patience and confidence. From now on, I am eternally linked with You. If You ever fell, I would fall—but since that will never happen, I will stand! Amen.

WHAT ABOUT UNRESOLVED GUILT?

Have mercy on me, O God, according to your unfailing love; according to your great compassion blot out my transgressions. Wash away all my iniquity and cleanse me from my sin. For I know my transgressions, and my sin is always before me. (Psalm 51:1–3)

We have looked at four of the personality's fifteen enemies: (1) a lack of loyalty to Something that gives ultimate meaning in life; (2) self-centeredness; (3) anger, resentment, and hate; (4) fear, worry, and anxiety. Now we proceed to *(5) a sense of unresolved guilt.*

The older evangelism threw a great deal of emphasis on guilt, but it was in large measure connected with what would happen to you after death. How would you be able to stand before God's judgment, you guilty soul! That emphasis ceased to appeal to the modern mind and was discarded.

But it is now coming back through psychology. We are picking out of the wastebasket the need for the inner nature to be absolved from guilt. We cannot otherwise truly live.

Now, it must be acknowledged that a good many ideas about guilt *did* need to go into the wastebasket. They were false guilts that needlessly tormented many sincere people. For example, we now know that sexual feelings are not sinful; they are a part of our normal, healthy life. Everybody has them, saint and sinner. We also know that a normal self-love is right and natural; to act as if you had none is to end in hypocrisy.

The fear of having committed "the unpardonable sin" [speaking against the Holy Spirit (Mark 3:22-30)] is usually a false fear, for what Jesus meant was the act of a person saying He [Jesus] had "an unclean spirit," that the Holy Spirit within Him was of Satan. Seldom is that sin committed. We do not need to fear that form of guilt.

O God, I want to be inwardly absolved from all haunting guilts that rob me of confidence and power. Cleanse the depths, for I can only live with fellowship and reconciliation. Amen.

A GUIDE WORTH TRUSTING

Yes, we know that "we all have knowledge" about this issue. But while knowledge makes us feel important, it is love that strengthens the church. Anyone who claims to know all the answers doesn't really know very much. But the person who loves God is the one whom God recognizes. (1 Cor. 8:1–3†)

I said to a Hindu one day, "Suppose you broke caste [violated a social restriction], and no one knew it?"

"But I would know it," he replied, "for my conscience would trouble me if I broke caste." Conscience stands guard over the values you put into your moral nature. Thus, it is important what value you put there. The conscience should be trained at the feet of Christ; only then is it a safe guide.

This brings me to give a word of warning about some modern psychiatrists, who, finding persons at conflict with themselves—with ideals high and conduct low—try to dismiss the whole world of moral ideals. This usually results in greater disruption, for a new conflict is introduced at the level of conduct. The moral world cannot be dismissed by a wave of the hand or a slick phrase of a psychiatrist.

One such man, with outstanding credentials, urges his female patients who are nervous and upset to "find a boyfriend." Some of these women, after following his advice and practicing adultery, have come in great distress to a minister friend of mine. Through him they have found God and are today released and happy. Even this psychiatrist's wife, having divorced him (because he had acted on the advice he gave others), came to this same minister. She too found God and is radiant. The psychiatrist's false advice produced disunity in the personality and broke up homes—his own included.

The only possible level on which to be permanently unified is the level of your ideals. Everything else will let you down.

O God, my Father, I see that amid all the ways of humanity You have a way that is written into the nature of reality. Help me to find that way, for I cannot fumble this business of living. Time is too short, and living too serious. Amen.

THE KIND OF GOD WE NEED

We wait for the blessed hope—the glorious appearing of our great God and Savior, Jesus Christ, who gave himself for us to redeem us from all wickedness and to purify for himself a people that are his very own, eager to do what is good. (Titus 2:13–14)

The human heart will not be satisfied with subterfuges. It needs real reconciliation, forgiveness, assurance. A Korean girl came to a mission station asking, "Is this the place where they heal broken hearts?" Whether that broken heart comes from outer sorrow or inner guilt, the need is the same. We need a forgiving God.

Thomas Wolfe, the brilliant if erratic American novelist, wrote of the human condition as "a phantom flare of grieved desire, the ghostling and phosphoric flicker of immortal time, a brevity of days haunted by the eternity of the earth. We are an unspeakable utterance, an unsatiable hunger, an unquenchable thirst; a lust that bursts our sinews, explodes our brains, sickens and rots our guts, and rips our hearts asunder. We are a twist of passion, a moment's flame of love and ecstasy, a sinew of bright blood and agony, a lost cry, a music of pain and joy, a haunting of brief, sharp hours, an almost captured beauty, a demon's whisper of unbodied memory."

But Wolfe was not finished. He went on to a higher view: "We are the sons of our Father, whose face we have never seen…whose voice we have never heard…to whom we have cried for strength and comfort in our agony…to whom only we can speak out the strange, dark burden of our heart and spirit… and we shall follow the print of his feet forever" (*Of Time and the River,* pp. 869-870). Yes, we are children of the Father, and our spirits will never rest until they see His face. But when we see it, we must read in that face reconciliation and forgiveness.

O God, my Father, I did not know that Your footprints have been turned in my direction—You are seeking me. It is I who have been fleeing from You. I flee no more—I come, I come. Amen.

COMING TO TERMS

When you are on your beds, search your hearts and be silent.... Offer right sacrifices and trust in the LORD. (Psalm 4:4–5)

How precious is your unfailing love, O God! All humanity finds shelter in the shadow of your wings. (Psalm 36:7†)

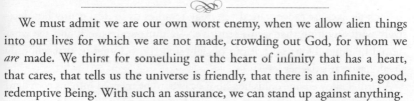

We must admit we are our own worst enemy, when we allow alien things into our lives for which we are not made, crowding out God, for whom we *are* made. We thirst for something at the heart of infinity that has a heart, that cares, that tells us the universe is friendly, that there is an infinite, good, redemptive Being. With such an assurance, we can stand up against anything.

But how can we satisfy this thirst? A girl who was used to being told just what to do and believe wrote to me, "Please tell me I am forgiven. If you say I am forgiven, I can be assured." I could tell her that, but the assurance of one person to another is slender. A stronger conviction is needed.

One route to that assurance is to relax in a room and let your mind roam freely across your life as it will. Do not debate with yourself, but bring to the surface anything to which the mind keeps returning. You may be startled by this alien thing buried within you—a sore point, a hidden guilt. At first you may not even want to acknowledge its presence, for you have argued with yourself that everything is all right; you have built up defenses against any questions about anything. But now, resolve to be perfectly honest and frank, even with yourself.

O God, I enter a life of complete openness. I am from now on "a child of light," with no secrets withheld, no sore points suppressed. I desire to be simple, unaffected—and Yours. Amen.

DEALING WITH SENSITIVE SPOTS

If we claim to be without sin, we deceive ourselves and the truth is not in us. If we confess our sins, he is faithful and just and will forgive us our sins and purify us from all unrighteousness. If we claim we have not sinned, we make him out to be a liar and his word has no place in our lives. (1 John 1:8–10)

Such an exercise as we started yesterday requires us to deal gently but decisively with anything that seems sensitive. We must segregate it and see what should be done. Don't push it out of sight and try to forget it; that will only wreak havoc at a deeper level.

A farmer allowed one of his neighbor's calves to be merged into his own herd and sold with the rest. But every time he looked to God, he could see nothing but that calf! Only when he restored and confessed did he find peace with himself and fellowship with God.

A young lady sensed a spiritual wall in her life, and she suspected the cause to be a hidden resentment against a minister for whom she had worked. She wrote a letter saying she was sorry for the resentment. She kept the letter several days, hoping the mere act of writing it would suffice. But the mind is a relentless thing—it won't say "Peace" when there is no peace. She finally dropped the letter into the mailbox. Only then did peace and release come.

Don't do as an intelligent, beautiful, fourteen-year-old girl did recently, when she came to me saying, "I'm all inwardly empty; worse, I'm in a mess. I've been kicked out of four high schools and am about to be kicked out of the present one. Isn't it too late to do anything now?" Too late at fourteen?! She had concocted new lies to cover up old ones, until now the law was closing in on her for check forgery. She started to be frank and have me help her—then suddenly decided to run away, literally. She ran from her surroundings, but not from herself.

Bring up everything that seems touchy.

O God, when I begin to untangle my life, help me to go clear through with it. I want to come clean. Amen.

BACK TO NORMAL

The people went out to see what had happened. When they came to Jesus, they saw the man who had been possessed by the legion of demons, sitting there, dressed and in his right mind. (Mark 5:14–15)

To find the way out, we perhaps are tempted to look to our surroundings, or to other people—to everything except to ourselves and God. But there is no other way out. Listen to a doctor's story of a once-desperate soul. A young woman only twenty-five years old was, oddly enough, suffering from arthritis. She had gone across the United States, consulting more than fifty doctors. She had sunk into a hopeless state of mind and was filled with fears: afraid of getting well; afraid of losing her home; afraid of losing her husband's love; afraid of never walking again. She was filled with a definite sense of guilt, convinced that life was a total loss. Many times nurses would come out of her room in tears because they could do nothing right—she was so hard to please.

Her first step toward God was to trust Him with some of her simple fears. She began to cooperate, so that nurses no longer dreaded taking care of her. Then she began to walk. When a malicious friend wrote that her husband had been unfaithful, she suddenly developed all the symptoms of a gastric ulcer. But she surrendered this sorrow to God, and the ulcer left. Then her husband came to visit, and the matter was straightened out.

This woman now confesses that two years prior to the arthritis, she had been running away from life because of a conflict, and that whenever her husband was studying, she had been living a double life, staying out late at night, drinking in order not to think, and smoking incessantly. What had broken down her health was not physical but spiritual. She concludes, "I'm back to normal, with the help of God." Sin is the abnormal; it is trying to live against life. And that cannot be done.

O my Father, I face, as this woman did, the tangled strands of my own sins and follies. Here and now I promise You that no stone will be left unturned, no pledge unfulfilled, until I am free in You. Amen.

A NEW FOCUS

Let us throw off everything that hinders and the sin that so easily entangles, and let us run with perseverance the race marked out for us. Let us fix our eyes on Jesus, the author and perfecter of our faith. (Heb. 12:1–2)

Bringing all conflicts and guilts to the surface leaves a vacuum that only Christ can fill. When He comes in and takes possession, we turn our attention not to ourselves but to the Christ who is within us. In this way, the most entrenched introvert becomes an extrovert! The focus is no longer inward but upward.

Our love, fastened supremely on Christ, will give all lesser, legitimate loves their meaning and place. They are hallowed by that supreme love. You can dare to love yourself if you love Christ supremely.

I was told of a brilliant woman, the mastermind of a drug ring, who listened to Christian radio programs to find arguments against God. She didn't merely disbelieve in God; she hated Him. At that time she was taking three times the legal dose of medication in order to sleep.

But something in the words she heard broke her antagonism. She was converted. And then the fight of disentanglement began. Again and again she would black out for want of the drug, but she refused to take it. She went among her gang and told what had happened to her. Her testimony broke up the ring. Five of them ended up going to England to help the war wounded in order to make atonement, they said, for what they had done to destroy others. She herself is now a radiant Christian, doing social work in a great city. A new loyalty and love broke the power of the old.

Love Christ, and then do what you like, for you will like the right. You will be free!

O my Lord and Master, I see that I can be free only when I am in love with You. I know now what the promise means when it says, "If the Son sets you free, you will be free indeed" (John 8:36). Thank You that I am free indeed. Amen.

WHEN GREATER IS SMALLER

Think of what you were when you were called. Not many of you were wise by human standards; not many were influential; not many were of noble birth. But God chose the foolish things of the world to shame the wise; God chose the weak things of the world to shame the strong. He chose the lowly things of this world and the despised things—and the things that are not—to nullify the things that are, so that no one may boast before him. (1 Cor. 1:26–29)

We come now to the sixth outstanding enemy of human living: *(6) Negativism and inferiority attitudes.* One is almost tempted to list these as Enemy Number One.

They are all the more dangerous because they are often displayed as their opposite—superiority attitudes. One who is not sure of himself talks loud, boasts, swaggers to impress others, trying to bolster himself with outward show. "I am coming to see you in a Cadillac," phoned a friend of long ago.

Jesus saw small people trying to be big and said, "Which of you by worrying can add one cubit to his stature?" (Matt. 6:27 NKJV). We try to add cubits to our stature by worrying about outer decorations to make up for inner inferiorities.

Those who try to appear great end up appearing ridiculous. Self-aggrandizing people defeat their own purpose. "Whoever wants to save his life," by concentrating on it, dressing it up to appear bigger than it is, "will lose it," Jesus said (Luke 9:24). Superiority attitudes and delusions of grandeur are the reverse side of an inferiority complex.

Shun superficial superiorities as you would shun the devil, for they are much the same.

O God, I want to be what I am without any sham. But I want to be more: I want to be the person You intend me to be. Then I shall stand with simplicity and dignity in Your will and purpose. In Jesus' name, Amen.

UNSURE PEOPLE

I say to every one of you: Do not think of yourself more highly than you ought, but rather think of yourself with sober judgment, in accordance with the measure of faith God has given you…. Live in harmony with one another. Do not be proud, but be willing to associate with people of low position. Do not be conceited. (Rom. 12:3, 16)

Sometimes aggressive attitudes alternate back and forth with periods of discouragement and self-deprecation. This cyclical behavior results in moodiness. Such a person ranges in temperament from very high mountains to very low valleys.

But often the attitudes of retreat and defeat show themselves differently. Professor David Eitzen, professor of pastoral counseling at the University of Southern California, says, "Slamming the door, walking rapidly, stamping the floor, arguing with one's associates…these are manifestations of a difficulty not faced and intelligently approached." Either way, the problem is the same sense of inward inferiority. The person is out of sorts with himself, so he vents his ill humor on his surroundings. He creates outer earthquakes in order to hide his own inner soul-quakes. Just as bodily shivers are an attempt of nature to bring up one's temperature when it has fallen below par, so these shakes of temper are a psychological attempt to bring up the temperature of the inner self! The person is inwardly slipping, and so takes to outward shouting.

This is the law of overcompensation at work. Touchy people are unsure people. They are looking for slights, for they have a subconscious feeling that they deserve them. You can tell the size of a person by the size of the things that upset him.

O God, I come to You to find power to be really strong. Save me from these make-believe strengths that leave me weak. I want to be the kind of person whom nothing can upset. But only as I am inwardly fortified by Your strength can this happen. In Jesus' name, Amen.

MADE FOR ACHIEVEMENT

"My righteous one will live by faith. And if he shrinks back, I will not be pleased with him." But we are not of those who shrink back and are destroyed, but of those who believe and are saved. (Heb. 10:38–39)

You and I are made in our inmost being for positive achievement—to be outgoing, to master our circumstances, to create. If we are not positively creating and producing, the machinery of life will get out of gear; for we are geared to creation. Negativism not only keeps us from achieving; it also keeps us from being.

I know a person whose first attitude toward everything new is "No!" She lives in the objective mood. Hence her life is frustrated when, with her powers, it might be fruitful.

A more dramatic illustration is that of a woman of intellectual ability who became afraid of life, pulled in, and made retreat her life strategy. When she refused to be outgoing, Nature began to take its toll. Her knees stiffened, and she became a confirmed invalid. Even her brain cells began to decay through worry and anxiety and fear. She became impossible—toward herself and others. The life forces were breaking down under this retreatism.

So the doctors decided to disconnect that part of the brain which presides over foresight, now corrupted through fear and worry, and let it atrophy, so that the rest of the brain would function normally. Fear and worry had to be expunged, either by operation or by the cleansing power of faith. She refused the faith: "I have run away too long. If you had got hold of me years ago, you might have headed this off—there is nothing now but the operation."

Retreatism and negativism are infections that corrupt the brain cells, make flabby the tissues, and poison the spirit. You must decide that they will have no part in you, since you want to live abundantly.

My Father, I belong to You, Creator God. I link myself with Your Creative Spirit. I do not belong to a wistful sighing over a dead past, nor to a fear of today—I belong to victory! Amen.

NEGATIVISM IS NOT YOUR FRIEND

It is for freedom that Christ has set us free. Stand firm, then, and do not let yourselves be burdened again by a yoke of slavery. (Gal. 5:1)

From this time many of his disciples turned back and no longer followed him.

"You do not want to leave too, do you?" Jesus asked the Twelve.

Simon Peter answered him, "Lord, to whom shall we go? You have the words of eternal life." (John 6:66–68)

If we are to get out of negativism and inferiority attitudes, we must take certain positive steps. Don't sit helplessly and expect either God or people to perform a startling miracle of deliverance *on* you. But they can perform a miracle *through* you if you cooperate.

Recognize negativism and inferiority attitudes as enemies; do not try to dress them up as friends. You will be tempted to look upon negativism as prudence, and inferiorities as humility. Strip off these false cloaks, and see these attitudes in their nakedness—as enemies of you and of your possibilities.

When a hard thing comes before you, you will take one of four methods in dealing with it, according to Dr. M. S. Congdon, a psychologist: "(1) Flee it! (2) Fight it! (3) Forget it! (4) Face it!" The first three ways will end in failure; only the fourth opens a door. Face the whole of the facts, and see your difficulty for what it is—not something to excuse, or defend, or explain away or rationalize, but something that must be ousted.

A minister took the first step when he arose and said in a meeting: "The twin evils of my life that are crippling me and my ministry are 'I can't' and 'tomorrow.' Whenever I say, 'I can't do things,' or 'I can't do them today,' paralyzing hands are laid on me." He was on his way to victory.

O frank and openhearted Christ, I want to be adequate and contributive. Take from my life all negative thinking, all refusal to accept responsibility, all fearful attitudes. Help me face life with a confidence and a song. Amen.

FRUSTRATING MYSELF

I am crucified with Christ: nevertheless I live; yet not I, but Christ liveth in me:
and the life which I now live in the flesh I live by the faith of the Son of God,
who loved me, and gave himself for me. I do not frustrate the grace of God. (Gal.
2:20–21 KJV)

Let this idea grip you: *I am made in the inner structure of my being for creative*
achievement; when I draw back from that, I frustrate myself.

One of the outstanding ministers of this country is in San Antonio, Texas, a
radiant and contagious soul. But he told me that as a boy he was the opposite,
due to an odd supersensitivity in his fingertips. To protect them, his mother
consented at last to let him grow long fingernails. But that made for problems
at school; one day his teacher called him up before the class and made him
cut his nails publicly. This humiliation turned him against school, so that he
invented sicknesses to keep away. One of these make-believe ills was a pain in
the hip. It became a real pain and grew so serious that a surgeon decided to put
him in a cast, for which measurements were taken.

When the boy saw what was happening, he broke down and told his mother
the cause. This man is a specimen of health today, even though he came near
being a cripple all his days. The negative retreatism was arrested in time by an
honest facing of the facts.

Another patient's life was running on half its cylinders. The doctor insight-
fully said, "I can see that all the 'don'ts' that you received before five years of
age are coming out in you now." It was true—the man had been brought up by
unreasonably cautious aunts. Those "don'ts" had gotten down in his subconscious mind and were controlling his conduct.

In the account of Pharaoh's refusal to let Israel go, one passage says, "The
land was ruined by the flies" (Ex. 8:24). Many a life is ruined by tiny things;
and the worst of all are fearful "don'ts."

O God, help me to link my littleness to Your greatness, my faintheartedness to
Your loving aggression—then nothing can stop me. Amen.

SHUT DOWN ALL NEGATIVE THOUGHTS

"Ah, Sovereign LORD," [Jeremiah] said, "I do not know how to speak; I am only a child."

But the LORD said to me, "Do not say, 'I am only a child.' You must go to everyone I send you to and say whatever I command you. Do not be afraid of them, for I am with you and will rescue you." (Jer. 1:6–8)

A country girl who had moved away fainted every time she saw a cow. That cow was connected with some trauma back on the farm, so that the girl's mind went into reverse at the mere sight of the animal. It was necessary for her to recognize that such a retreat was unnatural, something imported, something for which she was not made—a mind infection.

We can shut our minds against all negative thoughts the moment they come. Do not entertain those thoughts and give them a seat; for if they get your attention, they will get you. Meet them at the door and slam it in their faces; lock the door and throw the key away. Paul literally says: "Set your minds on things above, not on earthly things" (Col. 3:2).

Don't admit, even to yourself, let alone to anyone else, that you are inferior or afraid. Above all, don't talk about it as a virtue—it isn't; it's a sin. Said a racist white to a black person, "Why don't you admit your inferiority?" To which the reply came: "I am a child of God, and out of loyalty to my Father I cannot accept that I am inferior." As a child of God, the person was capable of infinite possibilities. So our faith is not lifting ourselves by our own bootstraps; it is a faith rooted in the fact of our relationship with God. The mystic Rufus Moseley puts it in these quaint and beautiful words: "The Holy Ghost makes me put back my shoulders."

My Father, I am Your child, made in Your image, enforced by Your mind, empowered by Your purposes, rekindled by Your love, and remade by Your redemption. I cannot be inferior since You are not, for I am in You. Amen.

NO ILLUSIONS OF GRANDEUR

Stop deceiving yourselves. If you think you are wise by this world's standards, you need to become a fool to be truly wise. For the wisdom of this world is foolishness to God. As the Scriptures say, "He traps the wise in the snare of their own cleverness." (1 Cor. 3:18–19†)

Alongside of shutting your mind to negative thinking, you must also *shut your mind to all illusions of grandeur.* The temptation will be for you to swing from one attitude to its opposite, indulging in extravagant notions about yourself. You are neither a worm nor a wonder—you are just a bundle of fine possibilities, if developed.

A father said to his daughter who had been slipping in her achievements, "You are not the least bit inferior." To which the girl replied, "No; the fact is, I'm superior in many things." That reply was revealing, for it showed the source of her ineffectiveness. She had rebounded from thoughts of inferiority to illusions of grandeur, nursing the idea that she was not like the common herd, and filling her mind with fantasies and daydreaming. From being in the dust, she had gone to living in fairy castles in the air.

You don't belong either in the dust or the clouds; you belong to the earth, with your feet on it, and walking straight into tasks you can do. So discipline your aspirations to what is possible. If you set up too high standards of achievement, beyond the reach of your powers even when they are used by God, then you may become discouraged and give up. I know a young man who, because he had such high aspirations of achievement that he couldn't reach those high goals, would lie on his bed and read most of the day. Since he couldn't do everything, he would do nothing. He should have disciplined his goals to the possible.

O God, stretch me to my utmost, but don't let me cry for the moon. Help me to evaluate what I can be in You, and then go out for that goal with all I have and all You can give to me. In Jesus' name, Amen.

YOUR POSSIBILITIES IN GOD

"Have faith in God," Jesus answered. "I tell you the truth, if anyone says to this mountain, 'Go, throw yourself into the sea,' and does not doubt in his heart but believes that what he says will happen, it will be done for him. Therefore I tell you, whatever you ask for in prayer, believe that you have received it, and it will be yours." (Mark 11:22–24)

Yesterday's word about setting aspirations that are possible is true—so long as we gauge our possibilities not in ourselves but according to what we can be in God. That leaves us with a disciplined but ever-expanding set of possibilities, for His are infinite. The situation is not about us alone, but us plus God.

Hannah sang this prayer: "My heart thrills to the Eternal, my powers are heightened by my God" (1 Sam. 2:1 MOFFATT). True, they are *our* powers, subject to limitations and not intended to do the work of someone else. But they are heightened—provided they are surrendered to God and His purposes. And then anything may happen—yes, anything.

Dr. Ray Allen translates into rigorous but true language the passage where the father of the epileptic boy pleads for Jesus' help (Mark 9:22-24). He says, "But if you can do anything, help us." To which Jesus replies, "'If you can'— everything is 'can' to those who believe." People of faith have thrown out "can't" and put in "can."

Across the hall from where I am writing once lay a hopeless cripple living in a darkened room. But faith worked through love there. "The Little Sister"—for so they affectionately called her—set up a home for cripples in China on the site of the pond into which people used to throw crippled children. Her faith inspired others, and money came in and was sent through her loving hands on its healing mission. A cripple has set up a home for cripples! Everything is "can" to those who believe.

O God, I have not much to offer, but what I have is Yours. Heighten these powers, so that I shall be a continuous surprise, even to myself. Amen.

DOING WHAT YOU CAN'T

What more shall I say? I do not have time to tell about [those] who through faith conquered kingdoms, administered justice, and gained what was promised; who shut the mouths of lions, quenched the fury of the flames, and escaped the edge of the sword; whose weakness was turned to strength. (Heb. 11:32–34)

At the funeral of the woman I mentioned yesterday, the eulogist spoke of "the miracle of her healthy mind." It was healthy because it was harnessed; it was disciplined to the possible, and yet how utterly impossible. Her faith had its feet upon the ground; but sometimes faith walked so fast that those feet seemed to leave the earth. A crippled body and a healthy mind resulted in a home for cripples—how? In and through it all, God worked as she worked. Someone has put it this way: "It is good to work; it is better still that our work should lead us to let God work."

That is what Jesus meant when, in answering the question, "What must we do to do the works God requires?" He said, "The work of God is this: to believe…" (John 6:28–29). When I am believing, then I am really working, for I become a channel of the Infinite.

One day in Washington as we waited on God in a small group to see what next step we could take to help bring peace between Japan and America, I told them I had a very difficult assignment that day: I was to see someone I didn't really want to see. A layman quoted this inscription on a tombstone (adapted from Mark 14:8): "She hath done what she couldn't." I went with those words ringing in my heart. I kept saying to myself, "I'll do what I can't." And I did!

When we are completely surrendered to God, we can do what we can't. We find ourselves becoming miracles to ourselves. We surprise ourselves.

O God, now I begin to see the way of open possibilities before me. I accept this adventure with You. Nothing is too small, beneath my dignity to do; and nothing too large, beyond my power to do. I am following—lead on! Amen.

WHAT JESUS SAW

As Jesus went on from there, he saw a man named Matthew sitting at the tax collector's booth. "Follow me," he told him, and Matthew got up and followed him. While Jesus was having dinner at Matthew's house, many tax collectors and "sinners" came and ate with him and his disciples. (Matt. 9:9–10)

See yourself not as what you are, but as what you are and can be in God. There were three persons in Matthew the tax collector: (1) the person his associates saw, (2) the Matthew whom Matthew saw, and (3) the Matthew whom Jesus saw. Each thought he saw the true Matthew. Who was right? The Matthew whom Jesus saw turned out to be the apostle and gospel writer, the Matthew of infinite possibilities.

Three people reside in you: the one your associates see (the outer you), the one you see (the present you), and the one Jesus sees (the future you). Everything depends on which "you" you center upon. If you center on the "you" your associates see, you will be in bondage to what others think about you; you will look around before you act to see what effect your action will have on others; you won't act, you will react. You will become an echo and not a voice, a thing and not a person.

If you center upon the "you" you know, then you will be discouraged. For who has not had some skeleton in the closet—something that made the cheeks burn with shame and humiliation? If you are centered on this "you," you will be caught in the bondage of inhibitions.

But there is this third "you" that Jesus sees. It is a "you" surrendered to God, cooperating with Him, taking His resources, working out life together. A "you" loosed from what you've been and done, reinforced with divine energy and insight. A "you" that does things beyond your capacity, amazing both yourself and others. That is the real "you." Center on Christ's "you," and you will become it.

God, I'm pushing back my small horizons as I see Yours. I'm leaving my outgrown self. I'm exchanging my "you" for what You see. Amen.

LOOK BEYOND SELF TO GOD

Those who belong to Christ Jesus have crucified the sinful nature with its passions and desires. Since we live by the Spirit, let us keep in step with the Spirit. (Gal. 5:24–25)

Clothe yourselves with the Lord Jesus Christ, and do not think about how to gratify the desires of the sinful nature. (Rom. 13:14)

What we said yesterday needs a further word, and that is: *Don't look too long at yourself in God—look at God.* A great many cults center upon self-cultivation and leave behind a multitude of wistful but frustrated people. They are lifted for a moment but limping for a lifetime.

As soon as Peter looked at himself or the waves around him, he started sinking. Only as he looked at Jesus did he walk firmly on the water. Look at yourself, or at others, and you will sink; look at Christ, and you can walk on anything. You must think not of yourself even to cultivate yourself; but think of Christ, and the self will be cultivated. Glance at yourself in God, but gaze at God.

This law of losing one's life to find it runs through everything. Jesus said, "See how the lilies of the field grow" (Matt. 6:28). How do they grow? By being self-conscious and fussily trying to look beautiful? No; they look at the sun, and in their sun-centeredness they themselves grow beautiful.

The beauty cults end in painted dolls, and charm classes lose their charm. The only beautiful people are people who lose themselves in a great cause. They grow beautiful as they continually gaze at beauty. We see heaven in their face.

O God, I gaze on You—and find myself. Now my eye is getting in focus. Thank You, Father. Amen.

WHAT GETS YOUR ATTENTION?

Whatever is true, whatever is noble, whatever is right, whatever is pure, whatever is lovely, whatever is admirable—if anything is excellent or praiseworthy— think about such things. Whatever you have learned or received or heard from me, or seen in me—put it into practice. And the God of peace will be with you. (Phil. 4:8–9)

Whatever gets your attention gets you—and you must not be the center of attention even when you are in God. Your faith is God-centered, not you-centered.

Look away from your sins and diseases. If your gaze is on sin and disease, you'll never get well. I asked some people in an American sanitarium to sew and knit for the needy in China. As they had countless hours upon their hands, I thought they would crowd the woman whom I designated to take their names. But not one person signed up. Then I saw what had happened: These people were more occupied with their own sickness than anything else. They needed to turn their attention from themselves to God and others.

I have noticed something curious while flying in Europe. French planes have a cup in front of each passenger with a sign that reads, "For airsickness." In British planes the notice reads politely, "In case you feel indisposed, the steward will help you." In the British planes scarcely anyone gets sick, but in the French planes it happens all the time! Passengers look at the word "airsickness," and that is enough. When they look at the British sign, they think of a steward; the attention is called off from self, and nausea is pushed to the margin.

A prominent minister preached ten consecutive Sundays on how to avoid a mental collapse—and ended up having one. His psychology was bad; he should have been centered instead on God's resources for health.

My Father, I see where I should be centered. In You I am safe and steady, for I am fashioned in my inmost being for You, the Homeland of my soul. I thank You. Amen.

WHOSE KINGDOM?

[Jesus]: *"Blessed are the poor in spirit, for theirs is the kingdom of heaven.... Blessed are those who are persecuted because of righteousness, for theirs is the kingdom of heaven." (Matt. 5:3, 10)*

Jesus called the children to him and said, "Let the little children come to me, and do not hinder them, for the kingdom of God belongs to such as these." (Luke 18:16)

Here is a fact you must grasp in regard to your resources: *You do not merely belong to the kingdom of God—the kingdom of God belongs to you.* This truth will turn the whole tide from defeat to victory.

Jesus said three classes possess the kingdom: "the poor in spirit," "the little children," and "those who are persecuted because of righteousness." The kingdom belongs to all of them; its powers are theirs. The first two classes are alike, in that they are simple, unaffected, teachable. Here we find the key that unlocks the storehouse.

This truth is applicable everywhere. The English writer Aldous Huxley once observed: "Science seems to me to teach in most unmistakable terms the Christian conception of entire surrender to the will of God. Science says, 'Sit down before the facts as a little child, be prepared to give up every preconceived notion, be willing to follow to whatever end nature will lead you, or you will know nothing.'"

How does the scientist gain mastery over nature? By surrendering to it! If scientists are proud and unteachable, they will learn nothing, master nothing. They advance, as it were, upon their knees; then they stand straight and are masterful. "The meek inherit the earth." So you too as you surrender to the kingdom of God; its powers are all yours.

O God, it seems too good to be true. I, who have been defeated and negative and afraid—can I dare take all these powers of victory and release and usefulness? Then I shall, in Jesus' name. Amen.

THE KINGDOM SPEAKS WHEN YOU SPEAK

[God] has committed to us the message of reconciliation. We are therefore Christ's ambassadors, as though God were making his appeal through us. We implore you on Christ's behalf: Be reconciled to God. (2 Cor. 5:19–20)

They called them in again and commanded them not to speak or teach at all in the name of Jesus. But Peter and John replied, "Judge for yourselves whether it is right in God's sight to obey you rather than God. For we cannot help speaking about what we have seen and heard." (Acts 4:18–20)

Ambassadors represent their country; all the powers and privileges of their country center in them. When they speak, the country speaks; when they decide, the country decides (provided they are not speaking on their own but are surrendered to the will of their country).

If you have merged your interests into the kingdom of God, if you are entirely surrendered to it, if you speak representing not yourself but the kingdom, then all the powers of the kingdom center in you. The resources of earthly kingdoms are so limited; the resources of the kingdom of God are so vast. God's government, which stretches from the lowest cell to the farthest star, comes to focus in you!

An earnest little boy of five, son of a minister, said to me, "We preach down in Troy." I loved that! As far as he was concerned, when the father preached, he preached. And when the little boy preached by his life, the father preached. The boy accepted the corporate responsibility and felt the corporate accomplishment.

You work with the Spirit of God and speak on His behalf.

O God, I merge my interests into the kingdom, accept its responsibilities, and—dare I say it?—I inherit its powers! Help me to be great in surrender, great in responsibility, great in resources, because of You. Amen.

FIRST, WE RECEIVE

To all who received him, to those who believed in his name, he gave the right to become children of God— children born not of natural descent, nor of human decision or a husband's will, but born of God. (John 1:12–13)

"I am the vine; you are the branches. Those who remain in me, and I in them, will produce much fruit. For apart from me you can do nothing." (John 15:5†)

To keep climbing our ladder out of negativism and inferiority, we must remember the two conditions for utilizing the resources of the kingdom: *receptivity* and *response.* These two words are not only the alternate heartbeats of the kingdom; they are also the alternate beats of the whole of life.

Take a plant—how does it get power to become? By being proud, self-sufficient, unrelated, and unresponsive? No; by surrendering, adjusting, and receiving. It gains power by surrendering to its environment. It takes in from air and soil and sun, thereby growing to fulfill its ultimate purpose.

Someone has defined life as "response to environment." You and I live physically when we respond to our physical environment; we take in food, light, and air. If response is shut off, we die physically.

Our spiritual environment is the kingdom of God. When we respond to it, surrender to it, adjust ourselves to it, receive our very life from it, then we live—and live abundantly. We are in a state of receptivity, which is a state of faith, confidence, appropriation. We absorb kingdom life as the body absorbs food; we breathe in its purifying breath as the lungs breathe in air; we take up its vitality as the skin takes in vitamins from the sunlight.

To believe is to receive, and to receive is to replenish.

O God, I choose to receive from You as my physical body receives from its environment. Then I shall live. Amen.

THEN, WE RESPOND

As servants of God we commend ourselves in every way: in great endurance; in troubles, hardships and distresses; in beatings, imprisonments and riots; in hard work, sleepless nights and hunger; in purity, understanding, patience and kindness; in the Holy Spirit and in sincere love. (2 Cor. 6:4–6)

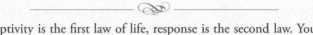

If receptivity is the first law of life, response is the second law. You receive from God, and you give back to God. In receiving from God you are completed and perfected, and in your responding to God—shall we say it?—God is completed and perfected. For, having created another personality, God is not complete till He gains the love and loyalty of that personality. Our response is as necessary to God as it is to us. A Love that loves, but is not responded to, is thwarted. God is all-important to us; we are important to God.

If receptivity and response are the two heartbeats of our relationship to God, they are also the two heartbeats of our human relationships. Love lets you receive from the other person; but, just as truly, it makes you respond in self-giving. Without this two-way traffic, the relation will break down. One who is always receiving and not giving will break down a relationship, and one who is always giving and not receiving will just as truly destroy the relationship.

Moreover, the receptivity and the response must be about equal. If one over-balances the other—if you are more of a receiver than a responder, or more of a responder than a receiver—you cripple the relationship. Impractical mysticism is strong on the receiving side, but weak on the responding side, and hence results in a lopsided religion, weak in positive contribution to human welfare. Activism is strong on the responding side, but weak on the receiving side, and hence ends in a religion lacking resources, depth, and permanence. A heart that tries to beat in one direction and not in the other ends in not beating at all.

O God, I never want to let You down. I want to humbly give back to You—a two-way traffic. I shall grow as I receive, and then give. Amen.

NEVER ALONE

Jesus made his disciples get into the boat and go on ahead of him to Bethsaida, while he dismissed the crowd.… When evening came, the boat was in the middle of the lake, and he was alone on land. He saw the disciples straining at the oars, because the wind was against them. About the fourth watch of the night he went out to them, walking on the lake. (Mark 6:45–48)

As you turn away from all negativism and inferiority attitudes to positive, abundant living, *remember that you are not alone—never alone.* At the time of seemingly greatest isolation, He is closest, watching your every move.

The American Indians trained their boys in courage by making them spend a night in the forest amid the wild animals. How dreadfully alone each boy would feel; but when the day began to dawn, he would see his father behind a nearby tree with drawn bow. Without the son's knowledge, the father had been watching all night to see that no harm should befall the son.

So is God with us. It is said of the English businessman and Quaker activist John Wilhelm Rowntree that, when he left a physician's office having been told that his advancing blindness could not be stopped, he stood by some railings for a few moments to collect himself. "Suddenly he felt the love of God wrap him about as though an invisible presence enfolded him, and a joy filled him such as he had never known before." That Presence will manifest Himself when most needed.

Say to yourself: "I live and move, in all inner thoughts and outer expression, in God's wealth every moment." Say this when you least feel the truth of it. When you lie down to sleep, say to yourself again: "Today I have lived and moved in God. He will guide and purify my dreams."

In the classic words of Brother Lawrence: "Those who have the gales of the Spirit are carried forward even in sleep."

O God, You and I will work this out together. I am yet weak and can take only a small part of the load—You'll have to take the heavy end. But You have my will, and when it develops, You'll have my strength too. Amen.

YOUR HANDICAPS, YOUR HANDLES!

He said to me, "My grace is sufficient for you, for my power is made perfect in weakness." Therefore I will boast all the more gladly about my weaknesses, so that Christ's power may rest on me. That is why, for Christ's sake, I delight in weaknesses, in insults, in hardships, in persecutions, in difficulties. For when I am weak, then I am strong.... The things that mark an apostle—signs, wonders and miracles—were done among you with great perseverance. (2 Cor. 12:9–10, 12)

In your going on to victory, remember this fact: *Your very handicaps may be new points of departure.* Perhaps you have had a bad start in life. Your heredity may be against you. But that can be a spur to you to pass on to others a better heredity. If you look back into the human heredity of Jesus, you will find some ugly spots: "David was the father of Solomon, whose mother had been Uriah's wife" (Matt. 1:6). What an embarrassment to have such a note stuck on one's life! But both David and Solomon survived that tragedy and contributed in spite of it. And think of the honest courage it took to put that statement into the genealogy of Jesus Christ. He who was going to begin a new humanity had the blood of the old humanity in His veins. But the divine inheritance so overcame the human inheritance that He passed on a new inheritance to us all.

Or suppose you are handicapped by a lack of attractiveness; you can make it up in accomplishment. Too many of the world's great beauties have nothing else; they get tangled up in their beauty and cannot move on to constructive achievement.

Look at your handicaps and make up your mind to use them as handles. Remember that a secondary failure may make you a primary success, whereas a secondary success (such as beauty) may make you a primary failure.

My Father, what I lack by nature I shall make up by grace. I cannot draw heavily on many things, but I can draw heavily on You. Make my very weaknesses into Your strength. In Jesus' name, Amen.

FLEE FORWARD

The apostles left the Sanhedrin, rejoicing because they had been counted worthy of suffering disgrace for the Name. Day after day, in the temple courts and from house to house, they never stopped teaching and proclaiming the good news that Jesus is the Christ. (Acts 5:41–42)

[Paul]: *I want you to know, my dear brothers and sisters, that everything that has happened to me here has helped to spread the Good News. For everyone here, including the whole palace guard, knows that I am in chains because of Christ. (Phil. 1:12–13†)*

Our handicaps may also serve as spurs that drive us forward. Jesus told His disciples that when the people turned them out of one village, they were to "flee to another" (Matt. 10:23). In other words, if you have to run, run forward—to the next opportunity on your list. All of us sometimes feel like running away. We differ only in that some of us flee forward, others flee backward.

Not having a college education made the poet Rabindranath Tagore the greatest literary figure of India. He fled from the lack of a college education— forward! He could have drawn back and bemoaned his inferior education; instead he turned it into a spur, became superior in himself, and founded a new type of educational institution.

Once I was sitting in the backseat of a car when the driver wanted to slide his seat closer to the wheel. He called to his wife in the backseat, "Please kick me forward, dear." Life is bound to kick you, for we all get knocked around, some more, some less. The important thing is the direction in which you are kicked. Make life kick you forward!

My Father and my God, help me not to run away from obstacles, but to run toward them, to tackle and overcome them. Help me to take the impulse to flee and compel it in a forward direction. In Christ's name, Amen.

NOBODIES BECOME SOMEBODIES

[Paul]: *I appeal to you for my son Onesimus, who became my son while I was in chains. Formerly he was useless to you, but now he has become useful both to you and to me.... Perhaps the reason he was separated from you for a little while was that you might have him back for good—no longer as a slave, but better than a slave, as a dear brother. He is very dear to me but even dearer to you, both as a man and as a brother in the Lord.* (Philem. 1:10–11, 15–16)

No matter what happens to you, or when it happens to you, it is never too late to become creative. I know a woman, wife of a professor, who did not touch a paintbrush until she was fifty. Then she awakened, began to paint, and now her paintings are being exhibited in this and other countries. She has also gathered around her a group of other women her age who had done nothing contributive but have now begun to be creative. One took up sculpting, and though she had never tried that branch of art, became a teacher of sculpture in a great college and exhibited her own products in America and Europe.

Some artists gathered on a farm to paint the landscape. The farmer, becoming interested, painted the landscape on his own. The teacher saw the painting and asked who had done it. Thus the farmer, sixty-eight, was "discovered" and became a famous landscape artist.

Jesus is the great Awakener. He stimulates the creative center in each of us, making it first aware of God, and then aware of the infinite possibilities in God. I was at the bottom of my class in school until I met Christ. Then I said to myself, "This is no place for a Christian"—and left it.

Jesus takes the nobodies and turns them into somebodies. He was the maker of humanity, and still is. No one can be in His company long without feeling an irresistible impulse to roll up the sleeves and say, "Where do I begin?" For creative impulse comes from contact with the creative God.

O Christ, enter into me to stimulate and quicken every fiber and nerve cell, so that I too may become creative. Amen.

PLAN TO ACHIEVE

God has given each of you a gift from his great variety of spiritual gifts. Use them well to serve one another. Do you have the gift of speaking? Then speak as though God himself were speaking through you. Do you have the gift of helping others? Do it with all the strength and energy that God supplies. Then everything you do will bring glory to God through Jesus Christ. (1 Peter 4:10–11†)

The top rung of the ladder to overcome negative attitudes is to *plan for creative achievement, and put your plan to work by however small a beginning.* Say with Jesus, "Do not weep for me" (Luke 23:28), and continue with, "I'm through asking for pity, for compassion—I don't want sympathy—I want a task, an open door. I'm through with living on a No; I'm going to live on a Yes. I'm not inferior since I have hold of a superior God, and He has hold of me. I no longer belong to those who look back, for 'no one who…looks back is fit for service in the kingdom of God' (Luke 9:62). The kingdom is forward-looking, and so am I."

Write down all your negative thoughts, and then tear them up as a symbol that they no longer exist. Next, write down your positive thoughts about what you can do, and begin at once to act on these thoughts. If you find you cannot do one thing, flee forward and do the next thing. Decide to do what you have decided to do, and do it now.

Ezekiel the prophet wrote, "The Spirit came into me and raised me to my feet" (2:2). The Spirit of God has entered you too—now stand up and do God's work in the world.

O Christ, at last I have risen out of the quicksand of self-pity. I have love in my heart, courage in my will, and faith in my inmost being. So let life come ahead. I thank You. Amen.

DESIRES UNLEASHED

[Paul]: *Even though I am a free man with no master, I have become a slave to all people to bring many to Christ.... I try to find common ground with everyone, doing everything I can to save some.... Don't you realize that in a race everyone runs, but only one person gets the prize? So run to win! (1 Cor. 9:19–20, 22, 24†)*

For two weeks we have been meditating on the negative side of the picture—people who are inwardly collapsed, afraid, negative. We now turn to the other side—to those whose desires are very positive, but uncontrolled, undisciplined. If there is danger from life being negative and afraid, there is just as much danger from life being desire-assertive. This is the next outstanding enemy of the personality: *(7) Undisciplined desires.*

One way of living may be likened to the horse that lies down in its harness and won't move; another way may be likened to the horse that runs away, breaking the harness and smashing everything. Abundant living has to find the poise between the two. It must find constructive but disciplined life.

Desires are the God-given forces of the personality, and as such are right. Without desire, life would vegetate. Buddha tried to make humans victorious over the desires of life by cutting the root of desire itself, so they would go out into desirelessness, into Nirvana. But you cannot cure the ills of life by reducing life; you cannot get rid of your headaches by getting rid of your head. You must have enough inward life to master outer environment and circumstance.

But if life is to be raised, it can only be raised through disciplined desire. The only way to manage a desire is to replace it with a higher desire, or to fasten it to higher ends and goals. Desires are the driving forces, and driving forces cannot be taken out of life—they must be redirected.

O God, we are now at grips with the raw material of human living, out of which we must fashion a person—Your person. Be the master of my desires. I give the reins into Your hands. Control them for me; I consent. Amen.

DESIRES REDEEMED

"Everything is permissible for me"—but not everything is beneficial. "Everything is permissible for me"—but I will not be mastered by anything.… Do you not know that your body is a temple of the Holy Spirit, who is in you, whom you have received from God? You are not your own; you were bought at a price. Therefore honor God with your body. (1 Cor. 6:12, 19–20)

The driving urges of the personality cannot be eradicated or replaced—they must be redirected through discipline. Take the self, for example. It is the primary urge and the first to be developed. When something crosses young children, they express their displeasure in various unpleasant ways. The same thing happens in grown-ups.

Now what does Christianity do with this primary urge of self? Does it try to wipe it out and make us selfless? Or try to crucify it and make it impotent? The answer to both questions is "No!" Christianity believes in the self, for the self is God-given: "Love your neighbor as yourself" (Luke 10:27). The self is to be loved, just as the neighbor is to be loved. It is your right and your duty to be the best possible self you can be.

Christianity therefore accepts the struggle for life that goes on in nature, expressed in the survival of the fittest. This is a hard and ruthless law, and some Christians have questioned whether such a merciless arrangement can have anything to do with God. It seems utterly at variance with redemption.

But I am coming more and more to feel that this process actually is redemption—it redeems those who fit into the physical environment and eliminates those who will not. The physically best survive and pass on their fine physical qualities to the next generation. If the law were otherwise, the survival of the *unfit* would end in physical degeneration. One generation would pass on its unfitness to the next, and so on to extinction.

My Father, I see that Your school is strict, but the end is redemption. Your laws are made for us, and they mean to make us. Help us then not to chafe at them as enemies, but to embrace them as friends. Amen.

OUR REAL ENVIRONMENT

"Who has ever given to God, that God should repay him?" For from him and through him and to him are all things. To him be the glory forever! Amen. (Rom. 11:35–36)

The struggle in nature to adapt to a physical environment, which we considered yesterday, is one thing. But we also have to fit into a moral and spiritual environment. The moral and spiritual world in which we live has its own laws of adaptation and survival. When we act in accordance with these laws, we survive and develop; when we don't, we decay.

In the spiritual universe, those who conform to the laws of the kingdom of God survive. This is the environment into which we must fit. If we do, we live eternally; if we don't, we are self-frustrated—the structure of our being breaks down. In the words of Jesus, we "perish" (Luke 13:3, 5 as well as the famous John 3:16). Here and now the process of perishing takes place, and the life forces break down through what we call evil.

A suicide note was found in England that read: "Many explanations will be given of this act, but I think it is this: It is the result of a private war going on inside myself, and which cannot be solved." This man was at war with the kingdom, the laws of which were written into the constitution of his being; when he fought with the kingdom, he fought with himself.

But when we embrace the laws of our real environment—the kingdom of God—we thrive. We grow in health and wholeness. We find ourselves in the state of abundant living.

My Father and my God, Your kingdom is written into my flesh and blood and bone and nerve cell. If I try to escape it, I escape from life itself. Help me therefore to come to terms with that kingdom, and hence with life. I want to live, and live fully. In Jesus' name, Amen.

MORALLY BLESSED

[At the end of the parable of the ten pounds, or minas]: *"Then he said to those standing by, 'Take his mina away from him and give it to the one who has ten minas.'*

"'Sir,' they said, 'he already has ten!'

"He replied, 'I tell you that to everyone who has, more will be given, but as for the one who has nothing, even what he has will be taken away.'" (Luke 19:24–26)

If we accept the law of the survival of the fittest in regard to the moral and spiritual life, we then redeem and make usable the two parables of the minas, or pounds (quoted above) and the talents (Matt. 25:14–30). Otherwise they are extraneous to the Christian system.

Those parables are disturbing in a way—the man who didn't develop the asset had it taken away. However, they are no worse than life itself, for that is what life does. If we do not develop any faculty or organ, it degenerates.

Accepting this law also validates the ideas of heaven and hell. Both of them are inherent results, natural corollaries. Good, by its very nature, is self-sustaining and self-perpetuating; evil, by its very nature, is self-disintegrating and self-destroying. A judge sentenced a man convicted of public intoxication to go look in the mirror. After the man took one look at his swollen, red-veined face, he immediately sat down and took the pledge to stop drinking. The signs of disintegration were obvious and compelling—the outer registration of an inner fact.

On the other hand, goodness within registers itself too. An unruly young artist, noting the change in his mother's face, asked her why. She said, "Your mother has prayed much for you." To which he replied, "Well, it makes fine lines." Response to the kingdom of God does make fine lines, for it makes fine lives. It is the way to live.

O my Father, I have taken guidance from too many things. I have obeyed this and that. But now the needle of my life, oscillating in many wrong directions, comes at last to rest in You and Your kingdom. It shall always be first. Amen.

DISCIPLINING THE SELF

[Christ] died for all, that those who live should no longer live for themselves but for him who died for them and was raised again. (2 Cor. 5:15)

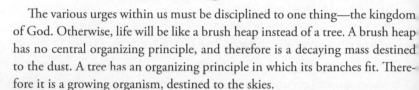

The various urges within us must be disciplined to one thing—the kingdom of God. Otherwise, life will be like a brush heap instead of a tree. A brush heap has no central organizing principle, and therefore is a decaying mass destined to the dust. A tree has an organizing principle in which its branches fit. Therefore it is a growing organism, destined to the skies.

The self must know its master. If the self is a servant of the kingdom of God, it will be rhythmical and harmonious; if it is a servant of itself, it will be halting and incompetent—its own slave. A woman who is entirely egocentric and has therefore had a breakdown said to me recently, "I spent all afternoon going from room to room before I found one to suit me, and now I don't like it." I gently replied, "The disorder is inside of you—you don't like anything because you don't like yourself." Her self was out of place on the throne, and the kingdom of her personality was in disorder.

Dr. Fritz Künkel says: "Every natural capacity for accomplishment, no matter how skillfully developed, is restricted sooner or later by egocentricity. Only the objectively oriented individual is unrestricted in accomplishment because he does not come into conflict with life's demands" (*Let's Be Normal!* pp. 97-98).

The self, then, must be disciplined to die. It must die to being first, in order to live being second. That is why at the center of the kingdom of God is a cross. You must go through spiritually what Jesus went through physically—you must die and be buried in order to experience a resurrection into freedom and fullness of life.

O Christ, I understand. I am to follow You to no trivial cross, but to one upon which I shall die—die to my own futile self-will in order to live to Your will; die to my own petty self in order to live to Your free and strong self. Help me from this moment to discipline my life to Your will. Amen.

WHAT GETS YOUR ATTENTION?

Work hard so you can present yourself to God and receive his approval. Be a good worker, one who does not need to be ashamed and who correctly explains the word of truth. (2 Tim. 2:15†)

One of the most radiant persons I know has overcome an invalidism stretching back forty-four years, making her room into the confessional booth of the city. She told me recently that the three words she is living by this year are *attention, meekness,* and *power.* She could not have chosen three more important words. They are so vital that we are going to use them as three steps to a disciplined self.

First, *attention.* If you give self your primary attention, self will be drawn to the center of your consciousness, and everything else will be arranged (or disarranged!) around self. To have self at the center is to have a cancer at the center, because cancer cells make other cells contribute to them, instead of making themselves contribute to other cells. A self-attentive person lives in a state of self-reference: "How will this affect me? What do I get out of this?" Such a person is disliked by others and even himself.

Decide, then, what shall have your primary attention. Decide, as you go into the shrine of your heart, to what you are going to bend the knee. If the kingdom of God has your allegiance, then make your loyalty absolute. Don't say "Yes" and "No." Don't say "Yes, but—." Put Christ once and for all at the center of your attention. Then you will live in a state of Christ-reference.

To shift the very basis of your life in this way will not be easy; the self will wriggle and twist and beg off and compromise. A pastor arose in our ashram and said, "I see what I need—and I see that I don't want what I need." He still loved himself first, even amid the wreckage caused by self-love. But this resolve to center Christ in your life is a seed decision; it decides all others.

O God, I have been out of focus, and all life's pictures have been blurred. But now life looks different, for I am looking upon it differently. My eye is now single, and my whole body is full of light. I am grateful. Amen.

THE MEEK INHERIT THE EARTH

The meek shall eat and be satisfied: they shall praise the LORD that seek him: your heart shall live for ever. (Psalm 22:26 KJV)

He guides the humble in what is right and teaches them his way. (Psalm 25:9)

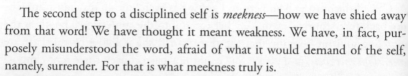

The second step to a disciplined self is *meekness*—how we have shied away from that word! We have thought it meant weakness. We have, in fact, purposely misunderstood the word, afraid of what it would demand of the self, namely, surrender. For that is what meekness truly is.

The scientist who is meek gains power over nature. The scholar who is meek gains power over knowledge. The Christian who is meek gains power over the universe, as Jesus stated: "Blessed are the meek, for they will inherit the earth" (Matt. 5:5). His words seem absurd. We could have understood if He had said, "…they will inherit heaven," but not earth, here and now.

However, who owns the mountains? The one who has enough money to buy them? Or the geologist who loves them, surrenders to them, gains their secrets, and is at home with them? Who inherits the world of the mind? Those who say they are free to think as they like? No, such people sometimes lose their minds! The mind belongs to the psychologist who meekly surrenders to its laws, who learns of the mind's ways.

Jesus was right (as always); the meek do inherit the earth. The English poet Robert Browning expressed the same thought when he wrote, "Who keeps one end in view makes all things serve." The one end is the kingdom of God; all things serve those who serve it.

O God, I now begin to feel the meaning of being disciplined. It is getting into my blood and brain cells. When I have become a disciplined soul, I shall be free. Help me to emerge in true meekness, true humility. Amen.

DISCIPLINED FOR POWER

If you fully obey the LORD your God and carefully follow all his commands I give you today, the LORD your God will set you high above all the nations on earth. (Deut. 28:1)

Brothers and sisters, I plead with you to give your bodies to God because of all he has done for you. Let them be a living and holy sacrifice—the kind he will find acceptable. (Rom. 12:1†)

Attention and meekness lead us to *power* over our desires, the third step to a disciplined self. We cannot gain power by tricks, by mental legerdemain. It comes by discipline alone.

A pilot in the air has to obey the laws of aviation. One moment's disobedience or carelessness, and there will be a terrible crash. There can be no "time off"; the obedience must be complete.

In the world of your desires, begin to be hard with yourself. Jesus said, "Anyone who puts a hand to the plow and then looks back is not fit for the Kingdom of God" (Luke 9:62†). Those who are undisciplined, soft, looking back toward things given up, cannot fit into the kingdom of God, which is a kingdom of the disciplined.

If this seems like a diminishing of life instead of an enrichment, let me say this: The control that discipline exerts on the self is the same kind of thwarting as when a dam is thrown across a river. Yes, the flow of the river is interrupted and restrained, but only so that a turbine might be installed to create power and light. The disciplined you is not free to do as others do, but free to do what others *cannot* do—to be a person who contributes. Some will say, "I am free to do as I like," but you will say, "I am free to do as I ought." You are dammed up on one level in order to raise the level of life, so you can function on a higher level.

My Lord and my God, I am putting my head into Your yoke—putting myself in bondage to You. But I am made for this yoke. Your laws are my life. I take Your weights upon my shoulders only to find they are wings. Amen.

A DISCIPLINED SEX LIFE

Flee the evil desires of youth, and pursue righteousness, faith, love and peace, along with those who call on the Lord out of a pure heart. (2 Tim. 2:22)

We have spent a week talking about how to discipline the first of the three driving urges—the self. We now come to the second, which is sex.

Life seems very heavily loaded on the side of sex, perhaps far too much for purposes of simple procreation. The human race, no doubt, could reproduce itself without the sex urge being so strong and imperious. It is quite probable that in normal human nature the sex urge is more occasional, as in animals and birds—active during mating seasons, dormant the rest of the time. This is true among primitive peoples.

But modern life has become strongly sexed. The sex appeal is everywhere. It seems to occupy the center of the stage, the center of literature, the center of dress, the center of advertising, the center of our thinking. Sigmund Freud ends up saying all life must be interpreted in terms of sex.

With all this emphasis, one would have expected this age to have found itself sexually. On the contrary, no age seems more sexually dissatisfied and thwarted than this one. The high rate of divorce tells the story of breakdown within marriage relationships. Evidently we are dealing with a problem that cannot be blamed simply on taboos and restraints. Can it be that the nature of reality is working against our modern sexual attitudes, causing them to break down?

O my Creator God, You will have to take me by the hand lest I be lost in the jungle of sexual desire. If I get off the track here, I will find myself more entangled every moment. Help me to see things clearly and to see the whole picture. Amen.

THE LAW OF DECREASING RETURNS

These people are…living only to satisfy their desires. They brag loudly about themselves, and they flatter others to get what they want…. They follow their natural instincts because they do not have God's Spirit in them. (Jude 1:16, 19†)

The London hospital for the mentally ill known popularly as "Bedlam" used to be called "Bethlehem," named after the place of the birth of Christ. Now the word stands for confusion, uproar, a madhouse. Is this not what has happened sexually in our day? The epitome of sexual purity (a divinely ordered virgin birth) has degenerated into a veritable bedlam of frustration.

The nature of reality is working against our sexual attitudes. We are experiencing the law of decreasing returns; we have to put in more and more to get a corresponding result. No age ever emphasized sex more than this age has done, or enjoyed it less. Restraints are gone; Puritanism has been banished. But now that the age is free to do as it likes, it finds it doesn't like what it does. We have gone in for thrills, only to find that "ills" are in thrills. We grow sick of our sexual liberties. Why? The nature of reality, which is Christian, is working against our unchristian desires.

Sex in itself is amoral; the way it is used is what makes it moral or immoral. Sex is like fire—you can use it wisely and be blessed, or you can use it unwisely and be burned. The way of moral use is embedded in the makeup of sex.

People thought that if they could only get rid of puritanical taboos and moral codes written in the Scriptures, they could be free to do as they liked. But they now find that the moral law is written into sex itself. Keep that moral law, and there is heaven; break it, and there is hell—here and now.

O God, I offer my sexuality to You for the best and highest purpose. I need wisdom and power, for sex clamors for attention and often drowns out Your still, small voice. Help me. Amen.

TEN STEPS TO SEXUAL VICTORY

Run from sexual sin! No other sin so clearly affects the body as this one does. For sexual immorality is a sin against your own body. Don't you realize that your body is the temple of the Holy Spirit, who lives in you and was given to you by God? You do not belong to yourself, for God bought you with a high price. So you must honor God with your body. (1 Cor. 6:18–20†)

If we are to use our sexuality correctly, we should take these steps: *(1) Recognize sex for what it is—a God-given power, neither moral nor immoral in itself, but moral or immoral according to its use.* This should take the shame out of the topic. There is no shame in sex; there is shame in the wrong use of sex. If people would be ashamed of what they do with sex instead of sex itself, there would be more normal, healthy attitudes toward it. Sex has brought more heaven and more hell into life than has any other thing. We make the heaven or the hell according to what we do with sex.

Every normal person has sexual desire—to act otherwise is to produce hypocrisy and probably complexes. So bring the fact of sex up into the open—look at it, but not too long, and then decide what you are going to do with it. Note: I said, "what you are going to do with it," not what it is going to do with you. Sex is a wonderful servant, but a terrible master. It can serve all the interests of life—or it can ruin all the interests of life. Lose the sexual battle and defeat will spread into every portion of your being; win the sexual battle and all of life will be uplifted.

(2) Recognize that sex does not belong in first place, nor is it an end in itself. If you put it first, it will corrupt your whole life. Those who most ardently give sex first place get the least out of it. The law of sex is this: He who saves his sex life (makes it first, an end in itself) loses it. Seek first the kingdom of God, making sex serve that kingdom, and every legitimate joy connected with sex will be added.

O God, I bring my sex life to the altar of Your love. May all lesser loves fit into my love for You. Amen.

TEN STEPS (CONTINUED)

God created human beings in his own image. In the image of God he created them; male and female he created them. Then God blessed them and said, "Be fruitful and multiply. Fill the earth and govern it." (Gen. 1:27–28†)

If sex is not meant for first place, nor to be an end in itself, then what is its purpose? *(3) Recognize that the foremost end of sex is the procreation of children and their nurture in an atmosphere of love.* In other words, sex is primarily intended for the creation of persons, not pleasures. Of course, there is a pleasure principle surrounding the procreation of children—but if this is detached and becomes an end in itself, it will cease to be pleasure and become the very opposite. Pleasure must be the by-product of the will to create.

A secondary purpose of the sexual urge is to produce an atmosphere of love surrounding the young life that has been created. If sex ministers to this love life, fosters it in the parents, lifts the whole tone of married life, then it is justified apart from procreative intention. But if it lowers the tone of married life, becomes a point of conflict in the individuals or between them; if it leaves life weakened mentally, morally, spiritually, or physically, then this use should be renounced entirely. As a sacrament of love—yes. As a sordid exploitation—no.

(4) Welcome the fact that sexual desire not only tones up the corporate life of the parents but the individual life too. It gives it sparkle, life, fire. It infuses every cell in the body with new energy and radiance—but only if it has found its proper place. When I say sex tones up the individual, I mean not only in its proper use, but in its proper restraints. A restrained sex life turns back and bathes the entire person with health. In the words of the French surgeon and Nobel Prize winner Alexis Carrel, to reach our "highest intelligence seems to require both the presence of well-developed sex glands and the temporary repression of the sex appetite."

O God, I thank You for this fire of sexuality within me. Let it be as a sacred fire upon Your altar, lighting up my entire being. I dedicate it to You. Amen.

TEN STEPS (CONTINUED)

Live by the Spirit, and you will not gratify the desires of the sinful nature.... Those who belong to Christ Jesus have crucified the sinful nature with its passions and desires. Since we live by the Spirit, let us keep in step with the Spirit. (Gal. 5:16, 24–25)

Continuing our discussion on using sexuality correctly: *(5) Recognize that both inside and outside the marriage relationship, the sexual urge can be redirected.* This leaves an open door to those who are denied the ordinary outlets of sexual expression. Sex is a creative urge—but physical creation is not its only outlet. It can become creative in the realm of the mind—creating new systems of thought, new attitudes both in ourselves and others. It can be creative in the social realm, giving birth to new movements for social betterment. It can be creative in the moral and spiritual realm, creating newborn lives, new hopes.

Some of the greatest work in the world is done by those who, when denied (voluntarily or otherwise) the normal outlets for sex, turn the tides of this strange power into creative activity in other ways. Their sex life is not suppressed, but expressed in other channels. If sex is dammed up with no outlet on any level, it may prove to be a source of conflict and frustration. But the way is always open in some direction.

(6) But beware of suggestions to short-circuit this power. There are only two ways of legitimately and helpfully using sex—inside the marriage relationship as physical creation, or outside the marriage relationship as redirection. All other roads are dead ends. Beware therefore of the advice from friends or various medical experts toward promiscuity or self-abuse as a way of release from passions. These are ways to deeper conflict in the moral nature. If anyone is fool enough to advise it, don't you be fool enough to take it. The right thing is always the healthy thing.

God, my Father, I offer You the turbulence of my urges. Quiet them with Your stillness, direct them by Your will, make them fruitful by Your creative love, and lift them by Your redemption. Apart from You, I can do nothing. Amen.

TEN STEPS (CONCLUDED)

Temptation comes from our own desires, which entice us and drag us away. These desires give birth to sinful actions. And when sin is allowed to grow, it gives birth to death. (James 1:14–15†)

In order not to follow the enticing sexual shortcuts, *(7) Make up your mind that none of them will work, except to work ruin.* When the suggestion comes, "Now is your opportunity," reply, as I often do, "Yes, I know it is my opportunity—to go to hell, and I don't intend to go." Then turn to the Tempter and say, "If I did this, I would be as big a fool as you are, and I won't be."

(8) Watch your thinking. As Ralph Waldo Emerson says, "The ancestor of every action is a thought." Don't dally with the alluring thought, saying, "I'll keep the thought but stop before the act." You won't, for as the psychologists teach us, in any battle between the imagination and the will, the imagination always wins. Mental adultery results in bodily adultery.

(9) Along with guarding the mind, guard the body. Bodily desires are aroused almost mechanically by the closeness of another attractive body. Don't put yourself close to the fire and then wonder why you get burnt.

(10) These suggested barriers are only fences alongside an open road—that open road is love for Christ. You can expel one desire only by a higher desire. Let the love for Christ be the fire that eats up these lesser loves. All the prohibitions against wrong use of the sexual urge will not save you unless love for Christ is at the center. Then the urge becomes marginal, and right. There are 32,000,000 statutes on the law books of America to make people good. The Christian has only one: "*Thou shalt love*" (Deut. 6:5 KJV). And "love is the fulfillment of the law" (Rom. 13:10). When you love Christ, you are free to do what you like, for you will like the right.

O Christ, I want to so fall in love with You and Your ways that all lesser loves become part of that central controlling love. You are the key to life—all life. I thank You. Amen.

OTHER DESIRES TO DISCIPLINE

As I have often told you before and now say again even with tears, many live as enemies of the cross of Christ. Their destiny is destruction, their god is their stomach, and their glory is in their shame. Their mind is on earthly things. (Phil. 3:18–19)

Sexuality is not the only desire in need of discipline. There are others—for example, the desire for food. If you are to live abundantly, you must be disciplined in your eating. Every meal should be a sacrament offered on the altar of fitter living and finer possibilities.

We must eat just enough to keep us fit, and a little less than will keep us fat. Why carry around excess baggage, overburdening the heart? Doctors tell us that excess of food destroys brainpower the same as too little food. What is in the stomach often affects what is in the head. Granted, "the kingdom of God is not a matter of eating and drinking" (Rom. 14:17)—and yet our eating and drinking often determine our fitness for the kingdom of God. The apostle advised that "whether you eat or drink or whatever you do, do it all for the glory of God" (1 Cor. 10:31).

The Israelites in the desert were told, "From heaven he made you hear his voice to discipline you" (Deut. 4:36). That divine, disciplining voice from heaven is turning out to be the same as that of modern medicine: Discipline yourself, or perish.

Everyone has a natural desire for security against want, whether hunger or some other kind. So we store up possessions. But this may make our inner selves insecure, by making outer securities the goal and aim of life. Trim your desire for security to your actual need. Beyond that is luxury and decay.

My Lord and my God, help me to harness all my desires and drive them according to Your purposes, lest they drive me. Let nothing master me except You. In You I find liberty, whereas in my desires I find tyranny. Take me entirely, desires and all. Amen.

DISCIPLINE OVER ALCOHOL

Wine produces mockers; alcohol leads to brawls. Those led astray by drink cannot be wise. (Prov. 20:1†)

What sorrow awaits you who make your neighbors drunk! You force your cup on them so you can gloat over their shameful nakedness. But soon it will be your turn to be disgraced. (Hab. 2:15–16†)

What we have said about the natural desire for food bears even more emphasis with regard to intoxicants. They are a personal and collective menace, increasingly so. In the last decade, insurance rejections for heavy alcohol indulgence have nearly tripled, to the point that one out of three otherwise insurable men and women had to be declined as unsafe risks. Cook County Hospital in Chicago made an eight-year study of 3,422 pneumonia sufferers between ages thirty and thirty-nine. The death rate among abstainers was 18.4 percent; among moderate users of alcohol, 29.1 percent; among heavy drinkers, 42.5 percent. Dr. C. C. Weeks, the English authority on alcohol, cites four medical writers who place it as one of the four great health scourges in modern civilization (alongside cancer, tuberculosis, and sexually transmitted diseases).

Should we teach "moderation"? I do not see the point in doing so, when the first effect of alcohol is to weaken the power to stop. Alcohol impacts the nervous system functions in inverse order to their development; it first impacts the traits that make us different from, and superior to, animals. It is not smart to drink—it is weak, an escape mentality, a failure of nerve.

O God, I need nothing but You—the exhilaration that comes from abiding in You, the sheer exuberance that results from being fully attuned to You, the rhythm and harmony that are mine in You. This is fullness enough. Thank You. Amen.

DISCIPLINE OVER TOBACCO

It is for freedom that Christ has set us free. Stand firm, then, and do not let yourselves be burdened again by a yoke of slavery. (Gal. 5:1)

What about another stimulant, the use of tobacco? Does it have any place in the life of a disciplined Christian?

It would be simpler for me to leave out this section, for many of my friends smoke, and they are Christians too. I do not doubt for a moment their sincerity and their piety. To skip over this would be easier—and more deadly. For the future of the world is in the hands of disciplined people.

Our society is about due for a reaction against tobacco. The time is ripe, for we have been propagandized into thinking it was the thing to do. Now we are finding that it is undermining the health of America. A heart specialist said to me: "Of all the poisons that people take into their system for supposed pleasure, the worst poison is tobacco. One puff of a cigarette, and you can register the effect upon the arteries; they tighten up and cause the heart to work faster."

Dr. W. J. Mayo, who with his father and brother established the world-famous Mayo Clinic, said at a dinner party: "Gentlemen, it is customary to pass around cigars after dinner, but I shall not do it. I do not smoke, and I do not approve of smoking. If you will notice, the practice is going out [fading] among the ablest surgeons."

Jesus refused any form of sedative even while hanging in torture on the cross. He wanted to face life matching His inner courage against outer circumstances. He refused to deaden Himself with drugs.

This area of desire, like the others, calls for clear-eyed discipline.

O God, I come to You for freedom. I do not want to be in bondage to a craving, a slave to a thing. I want to depend for comfort on a Savior. I want my joy to depend not on the most popular brand but on a quality—of life. Help me to shift my values. In Jesus' name, Amen.

DISCIPLINING OUR TIME

Be very careful, then, how you live—not as unwise but as wise, making the most of every opportunity, because the days are evil. (Eph. 5:15–16)

[Jesus]: *"As long as it is day, we must do the work of him who sent me. Night is coming, when no one can work." (John 9:4)*

We now turn to the discipline of our time. This is a process of making us burnished and fit—because we live in an undisciplined generation. Some people would retranslate the first line of Psalm 23 into "The Lord is my chauffeur; I shall not walk." We in the church are dealing with a society that, according to one writer, "is trying to drink its way to prosperity, war its way to peace, spend its way to wealth, and enjoy its way to heaven." It can't be done. We must discipline everything about our lives, especially our time.

In graphic design, the effectiveness of a photo depends not only upon what you put into it, but also on what you leave out. Your capacity to say "No" determines your capacity to say "Yes." You have to say "No" to lesser things in order to say "Yes" to greater things. Life depends upon elimination as well as upon assimilation. Someone asked a successful college president what was the first qualification for his post, and he replied, "A wastebasket." Throw away things in your schedule that do not contribute.

I believe in recreations when they re-create. But when they kill time and exhaust you, let them go. If you kill time, you kill yourself, for you are a part of time. Dr. William Osler, the great surgeon, used to tie knots in a string while riding in a streetcar, to prepare himself for quick tying in the crisis of an operation. He was "making the most of every opportunity."

My Father and my God, I want to be ready for the moment of my highest use, some great moment that calls for my best. Help me to be prepared. In Jesus' name, Amen.

DISCIPLINING OUR HANDS

After this, Paul left Athens and went to Corinth. There he met a Jew named Aquila, a native of Pontus, who had recently come from Italy with his wife Priscilla.... Paul went to see them, and because he was a tentmaker as they were, he stayed and worked with them. (Acts 18:1–3)

In our society we have set up the goal of reaching the place where we no longer have to work. We want to be "well-fixed"—others will work for us. It is a false goal. People who won't work deteriorate. They either get jittery and suffer from neuroses, or, after having eaten themselves all out of shape, they settle down to a bovine existence.

Nature seems to force us toward manual labor—and rightly so, for there is no health of mind and soul and body without it. Rehabilitation hospitals have been compelled to put in "occupational therapy" to help bring people back to balance and health. What irony: a civilization that strove to get rid of the necessity of work now has to pay doctors to put it back to work again!

Abundant living must include some form of creative activity with the hands. Our Christian ashrams include a daily period of manual labor as an integral part of our spiritual cultivation. This breaks down the barrier between those who normally work with their hands and those who do not. Big businessmen, doctors, professors, and bishops, when working alongside manual laborers, find a comradeship never known before. My job has been to go around with a bag and a sharp stick picking up litter.

Get in the habit of some manual work each day. Then organize your communities into volunteer squads, first to clean up the community and then to work on improvement projects. When people work together with their hands for the community's good, it lays the foundation for harmony in everything else.

O Son of a carpenter, take away our false pride in commanding the labor of others. We want to join You in making our communities places of health and beauty—veritable cities of God. Today I offer You my hands. Amen.

DISCIPLINING OUR FREE TIME

The apostles gathered around Jesus and reported to him all they had done and taught. Then, because so many people were coming and going that they did not even have a chance to eat, he said to them, "Come with me by yourselves to a quiet place and get some rest." (Mark 6:30–31)

Life must have its rhythms. There must be periods for creation and for recreation. All creation and no recreation makes "Jack" (and everyone else) a dull boy.

Since play is an inherent necessity, it should be carefully chosen, for recreation can wreck, or it can re-create. Here are ten things to remember:

(1) No recreation should be an end in itself—it should serve the ends for which you really live. To make recreation an end in itself is to defeat its purposes. *(2) Any recreation that takes from one part of your life to add to another is false.* For instance, if it takes from your necessary hours of sleep, it is not recreation, but a strain and hence a drain. More serious still, if it takes from your moral and spiritual life to add to your physical life, it is a snare and a delusion. *(3) Any recreation from which you have to recover is false.* Recreation should leave you with a sense of heightened vitality.

(4) Any recreation that leaves you with a sense of moral letdown will leave you physically let down. (5) Expensive recreation is usually expensive in more ways than one. Cultivate the simple, inexpensive pleasures. *(6) The Sabbath is psychologically sound as a means of quiet and recuperation.* To make it into a hectic day of running around is false.

(7) A movie, and anything else, must be judged according to the direction it MOVES you. (8) Any recreation that merely kills time kills you. (9) Gambling is not recreation—it is an attempt to get something for nothing, and that is not recreation, it is sin. (10) Any recreation into which Christ cannot be taken is not for a Christian. Make your recreations re-creations.

O Christ, I submit all my recreations to You. Select out of them what is real and vital, and let the rest be burned in the fire of my love for You. Amen.

A LADDER FOR DISCIPLINE

Do you not know that in a race all the runners run, but only one gets the prize? Run in such a way as to get the prize. Everyone who competes in the games goes into strict training. They do it to get a crown that will not last; but we do it to get a crown that will last forever. (1 Cor. 9:24–25)

Before we leave this topic, we must give a ladder on disciplined living:

(1) Decide what you are going to be disciplined to—your absolute. That absolute is Christ. You are going then to be a "Christ-ian." To be a Christlike person is the aim of your discipline. *(2) Discipline the center, the self, before taking on the circumference, the things around that self.* Bring the self into complete surrender to Christ. Otherwise, all disciplining of this, that, and the other is tinkering.

(3) Then, begin with the most difficult thing you have to discipline. I am afraid I cannot agree with those who advise picking out the easiest things first and then working out to harder things. For in so doing we seldom go on to the harder—we stay caught in the easier. I have made it a practice to pick out the worst looking letter in the pile and open it first. *(4) In tackling the most difficult thing first, don't try to taper off gradually.* Don't try to give up unnatural habits little by little—let them go all at once, bag and baggage. The tapering-off method seldom works.

(5) Since habits become power, make them work with you and not against you. Make good habits the friends and stabilizers of the new life. *(6) Remember that certain things are soils in which the new life grows.* Cultivate those soils that contribute. *(7) Don't allow any exception to your discipline.* The small victories count. Any exception you tolerate makes it easier to make the next exception, and so on down to undisciplined living.

O disciplined Christ, I want to be like You. May my disciplines become so naturalized within me that they become unconscious, and, therefore, effective. Amen.

SINCERELY INSINCERE

*Why worry about a speck in your friend's eye when you have a log in your own?
How can you think of saying to your friend, "Let me help you get rid of that speck
in your eye," when you can't see past the log in your own eye? Hypocrite! First get
rid of the log in your own eye; then you will see well enough to deal with the speck
in your friend's eye. (Matt. 7:3–5†)*

Now we come to the eighth of our fifteen major enemies: *Insincerity, whether
conscious or unconscious.* This can undermine the whole Christian structure we
build, and in a very hidden way. Insincerity is the termite of the personality.

Since we are all "only Christians in the making," we can find insincerities
and unconscious hypocrisies in the best of us. When we are not true and good,
we still attempt to simulate truth and goodness, thus acknowledging that we
ought to be true and good. From top to bottom, life is filled with these contradictions. The United States makes the bald eagle its national symbol—and yet
drives it almost extinct through pesticides and illegal shooting, among other
things. Our cities decorate for the birth of Christ—but underneath lies the
covetous commercial motive, which Jesus condemned. A big star hangs in the
sky at Bethlehem, Pennsylvania, ostensibly to lead our minds to Christ; but
underneath the star is a sign that says, "Hotel Bethlehem." The star is meant to
lead us to this hotel, instead of to the Inn of long ago.

A lady indignantly fired her housemaid, saying, "I had to dismiss her. I
found she was stealing those lovely Waldorf-Astoria towels I had." Her moral
indignation over someone else's dishonesty sought to make righteous her own!

*O Christ, we do not see ourselves, for we look at the sins of others with open eyes
and then turn a blind eye upon our own. Help us to be as honest with ourselves
as we are with others—and more. Amen.*

ARE YOUR EARS RED?

This is my prayer: that your love may abound more and more in knowledge and depth of insight, so that you may be able to discern what is best and may be pure and blameless until the day of Christ. (Phil. 1:9–10)

I have just been looking at a marvelous mosaic of the Last Supper, portraying the moment when Jesus says one of the disciples will betray Him. They are all asking, "Lord, is it I?" On the mosaic, all the ears of the disciples are red, but those of Judas are a little redder!

We often point accusingly at Judas, but our indignation covers up our own betrayals. If you want to find out a person's weak points, note the failings in others for which they have the quickest eye. We can defend our own inconsistencies because we compartmentalize life—our religion functions in one part, but doesn't go over into the other parts.

A YWCA manager urged an employer to give sufficient pay to his female employees so they could at least pay the low rates of the YWCA hostel. "No," said the proprietor, "but we will increase our gifts to the YWCA." He was willing to be charitable, but unwilling to be just. He would allow his religion to function as charity but not as justice.

A clever South Indian proverb says: "I will love you as my own child, provided you do not ask me for food and clothing." Another Indian proverb speaks of "*Hathi ke dant,*" the elephant's teeth—one set for show (the tusks); the other set for chewing (the hidden motives we keep in the rear).

The motto of Cortés, the Spanish conquistador, was "For God and gold." God was first in the motto, but gold was first in his heart. The important thing is not what is in our affectations, but what is in our affections.

O transparent Christ, probe deep within my heart and find the hidden infections of insincerity. Drain them to the last drop, lest they poison my whole system. Make me clean from every hidden contradiction, for I want to be harmonious and effective. Amen.

DUALISMS INSIDE OURSELVES

"I tell you the truth," Jesus answered, "this very night, before the rooster crows, you will disown me three times."

But Peter declared, "Even if I have to die with you, I will never disown you." And all the other disciples said the same. (Matt. 26:34–35)

We who preach the gospel—why do we do it? For self-display? To dominate others—their minds and souls, if not their bodies? Do we wait for the approving word at the close of the sermon, rather than the approval of God in the Quiet?

Do those who pay us really call our choices? Do we proclaim truth that is palatable to others, with an eye to our own stomachs? Are we afraid to offend a rich contributor, but not afraid to offend our own moral nature?

Our listeners wonder if we walk the talk. One pastor admitted to me, "I'm like a train depot announcer, calling out stations down the line to which I myself do not go."

Some recognize this dualism in themselves. "I am opinionated, and I call it conviction," said an honest soul. Another put his dualism this way: "I didn't sin, because I was so proud that I didn't want to have to apologize afterward." One sin, pride, kept him from other sins!

I was talking to a leading general of a certain country who was bitter and critical of other Christians. I suspected that underneath lay the motive of masking his own spiritual decay; so I stopped his outpouring by quoting Jesus' words to Peter when he inquired about John, "What is that to thee? Follow thou me" (John 21:22 KJV). The general went on worse than before. Again I stopped him with the same quotation. Then he pounded his knee and said, "Good; you've got me." That sentence was honest at last and opened the door to his eventual release from insincerity.

O Christ, relentless Lover and Redeemer, corner my soul. Don't let me wriggle and slip past Your redemptions. Help me to take my medicine, however bitter to the taste of self it may be. For I want to be whole. Amen.

BEHIND THE MASK

While he was still speaking, Judas, one of the Twelve, arrived. With him was a large crowd armed with swords and clubs, sent from the chief priests and the elders of the people. Now the betrayer had arranged a signal with them: "The one I kiss is the man; arrest him." Going at once to Jesus, Judas said, "Greetings, Rabbi!" and kissed him. (Matt. 26:47–49)

We fool ourselves if we think we can hide behind masks and remain a double person. Either the mask becomes us, or we become the mask. In the Greek drama, the actors wore masks. When the Romans took over the drama, they called both the mask and the actor by the same word: "persona." At first "persona" referred only to the mask; then it became the person behind the mask.

That is true—you become what your mask is. Listen to this *Saturday Review* poem by Helen Haiman Joseph:

Always a mask
Held in the slim hand,
whitely,
Always she had a mask
before her face—
Smiling and sprightly,
The mask.

Truly the wrist
Holding it lightly
Fitted the task;

Sometimes however
Was there a shiver,
Fingertip quiver,
Ever so slightly—
Holding the mask?

For years and years
and years I wondered
But dared not ask.

And then—
I blundered,
I looked behind,
Behind the mask,
To find
Nothing—
She had no face.

She had become
Merely a hand
Holding a mask
With grace.

Gracious Master, I want to be real—completely real. But there are many things to face. Help me to bring them up, until nothing is left for a mask to hide. Amen.

THE KICKBACK

Jesus began to speak first to his disciples, saying: "Be on your guard against the yeast of the Pharisees, which is hypocrisy. There is nothing concealed that will not be disclosed, or hidden that will not be made known. What you have said in the dark will be heard in the daylight, and what you have whispered in the ear in the inner rooms will be proclaimed from the roofs." (Luke 12:1–3)

All insincerities kick back. Secret motives write themselves into the lines of your face for the world to see. What you are behind the mask comes out into your eyes, creeps into your words, your looks, your attitudes, your very walk. "There is nothing concealed."

Rebekah persuaded Jacob to cheat Isaac and Esau. The result? Jacob had a feud on his hands and became a fugitive. His inner shiftiness got into his feet and made him run. The effect on Rebekah? She became unhappy: "These Hittite women tire me to death" (Gen. 27:46 MOFFATT). She was tired to death of her daughters-in-law because she was out of sorts with herself. The cheating she engineered only succeeded in cheating herself of inward peace.

A pastor I know allowed a love affair to develop. This illicit relationship kicked back—in fact, kicked him straight in the stomach. He developed stomach trouble as a result of this conflict in his life. It may be said in passing that such love affairs almost invariably result in frustration and unhappiness. No matter how they may be rationalized, excused, and dressed in cloaks of self-pity (for instance, due to unhappiness in each individual's own marriage), the results are the same. No matter how you may argue that the affair is of God since it seems "so sacred," you run against that law written not merely in sacred Scripture but in the constitution of things: "A man will…be united to his wife, and they will become one flesh" (Gen. 2:24). You must choose to follow that law, or suffer the kickback.

O God, I have tried to rationalize my insincerities. I am now through with explaining them away. I want a self I can live with; I cannot live while warring with myself. Help me now. Amen.

UP FROM INSINCERITY (PART 1)

Woe to you…hypocrites! You clean the outside of the cup and dish, but inside they are full of greed and self-indulgence…. First clean the inside of the cup and dish, and then the outside also will be clean. (Matt. 23:25–26)

Here are the steps to rise out of the pits of insincerities into the open light of frank and transparent living:

(1) Relax in the presence of God with all defenses down. In this condition, say to yourself, "Here, before God, I want every inconsistency to come to the surface, however disagreeable." Then let your mind wander at liberty across your life. Let it fasten on any place of insincerity it will.

(2) Recognize insincerities for what they are. Don't rationalize them. The mind is a part of the ego, whose pride is easily wounded, and it will immediately leap to the defense. It will gather flowers from everywhere, and sometimes from nowhere, to place them on the sore spot, trying to prove that it is a garden rather than what it is—a garbage heap.

(3) If you are not to rationalize insincerities, neither are you to religionize them. On the bottom of an art object given to an institution, I saw an inscription written so everyone could see: "Thine, O Lord, be the glory forever. Presented by ----." It was obvious that the first phrase was a pious religious frontage to justify the real intent of the donor—to get a good share of the "glory" for himself.

(4) Don't confess marginal insincerities and sins while leaving the central one untouched. This is a very definite tendency. I have seen people confess to impatience when they ought to confess to an egocentric life…to unkindness toward someone when they should confess to wholesale exploitation and greed…to an unkind deed when the whole life is filled with unkind attitudes. Someone defended Hitler because he did not drink or smoke.

O God, help me to be relentless. When I meet hard resistance, help me to go on through. For I want the clear living water of Your presence and power. In Jesus name, Amen.

UP FROM INSINCERITY (PART 2)

Confess your sins to each other and pray for each other so that you may be healed.
The earnest prayer of a righteous person has great power and produces wonderful
results. (James 5:16†)

The remaining steps:

(5) After throwing out these insincerities, don't smuggle them back. You will be
tempted to bring back those things that are artificial under different names and
guises. If you do, you will only add to your disharmony.

(6) Don't take up the cross and then cancel it. Perhaps you intended to pay any
price, do something worthy at any cost. If so, beware of trying it for a while,
then softening it, and finally canceling it. The Russian cross has, in addition to
the main crossbar, two additional crossbars, one of which is slanted. The legend
is said to be this: A priest said to his flock, "You will not obey the cross, you will
not live right—so I will take the cross out of the church." But there was such an
outcry that he brought it back with a line drawn through it, as if canceled. Look
for "canceled crosses" in your life—for toned-down resolutions, for softened
determinations, for slowed-up purposes.

(7) Deliberately go out and confess your insincerities to someone. The more you
do this, the more the self will become reluctant to harbor them, since they must
be exposed in the end.

(8) Be a part of a group that is disciplined to honesty and frankness. This will
keep you from holding secrets.

(9) Every day behold the glory of the Lord with "open face" as in a mirror, and
be changed into the same image "from clarity to clarity" (Luther's rendition of
2 Cor. 3:18).

O God, help me this day to stand before You with an open face, an open mind,
and an open being. I want to be changed into Your image. Day by day I want to
go from clarity to clarity, a transparent soul. Amen.

A HOUSE DIVIDED

Jesus knew their thoughts and said to them, "Every kingdom divided against itself will be ruined, and every city or household divided against itself will not stand. If Satan drives out Satan, he is divided against himself. How then can his kingdom stand?" (Matt. 12:25–26)

Next we come to the ninth major enemy of the fifteen, *divided loyalties.* It is similar to the one we have just been discussing (insincerities), and yet it is different. Persons may be truly sincere and at the same time find themselves split on the inside. They may not be covering up anything, and yet they may be trying to stay loyal to two or more mutually exclusive things. The result is the same: a canceling out of the person's abilities, effectiveness, and happiness. There can be no abundant living with inward division.

And yet how prevalent are divided souls. We believe in God with the top of our minds, but down deep at the bottom we obey something else as the way of life. We live by what the Quaker educator Dr. Thomas Kelly called "straddle arrangements and compromises.... We are trying to live several selves at once without all our selves being organized by a single mastering life within us."

A Supreme Court justice said to me as I was about to leave him: "We should discuss this subject [the war] for six hours. I am in a dilemma. For three days of the week I am a conscientious objector, and four days of the week I'm not." And since he believed in majority rule, he was an ardent militarist, smothering the conscientious objector, but not quite happy over the murder!

Many of us are living on a four-to-three majority, with little or no power left to implement the decisions of the majority. How much stronger we would be if we lived unanimously, with all our energies devoted to one great end.

O God, my Father, I am tired of being worn out by inward conflicts before I ever get to my problems. I must be unanimous for You. If You ever helped me, help me here. In Jesus' name, Amen.

A MAN OR A MENAGERIE?

[Jesus]: "Not everyone who says to me, 'Lord, Lord,' will enter the kingdom of heaven, but only he who does the will of my Father who is in heaven." (Matt. 7:21)

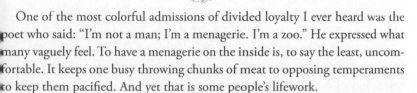

One of the most colorful admissions of divided loyalty I ever heard was the poet who said: "I'm not a man; I'm a menagerie. I'm a zoo." He expressed what many vaguely feel. To have a menagerie on the inside is, to say the least, uncomfortable. It keeps one busy throwing chunks of meat to opposing temperaments to keep them pacified. And yet that is some people's lifework.

We can see the outer fortunes of Israel go up and down with the inner divided loyalties. "Aaron…built an altar in front of the calf and announced, 'Tomorrow there will be a festival to the LORD'" (Ex. 32:5). They worshiped a calf today and the Lord tomorrow! Note which was the now, and which was "tomorrow"! The reason for this turning to the near-at-hand, immediate thing is that God has become vague. We make local idols because God is not fresh to us. God fades out, and idols barge in.

Then we try to put the two together and reconcile them. In the dark days of the judges, a woman said, "I solemnly consecrate my silver to the LORD for my son to make a carved image and a cast idol" (Judg. 17:3). Using God's silver to make an idol? That sentence is a transcript of a muddled soul expressing itself in a muddled purpose.

I saw a church notice board announcing the morning and evening sermon titles, which ran together:

THE CHURCH AT WORK

PLAYING SECOND FIDDLE

Not only is the church often playing second fiddle to something else that is leading the tune, but so are our own lives. Christianity has become subordinate, not supreme.

O Christ, help me to play second fiddle to You and You alone. Otherwise I will be out of harmony with the eternal realities. Amen.

MINDS AT WAR

I do not understand what I do. For what I want to do I do not do, but what I hate I do. And if I do what I do not want to do, I agree that the law is good.... I have the desire to do what is good, but I cannot carry it out. (Rom. 7:15–16, 18)

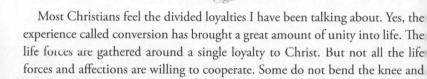

Most Christians feel the divided loyalties I have been talking about. Yes, the experience called conversion has brought a great amount of unity into life. The life forces are gathered around a single loyalty to Christ. But not all the life forces and affections are willing to cooperate. Some do not bend the knee and accept this new allegiance.

This residue of recalcitrance is variously named. Some call it "original sin," others "remains of depravity," "the old man," "another law working in my members." Psychology would probably explain it as "the driving urges in the subconscious mind." These three urges—self, sex, and the group—have a long history. They are strong and clamorous. They are used to having their way.

And now a new loyalty to Christ and His kingdom is introduced into the conscious mind through conversion. Intelligence, feeling, and will bend the knee to Him. But down in the subconscious mind are subjects that are subdued, but not surrendered. They obey, but moodily. They go on a rampage now and then to break free from this new Overlord.

As a result, there is a sense of inner strain. The soul is not relaxed and at ease with itself. Religion is not the natural expression of the whole person, but the forced will of a portion of it. *Duty*, rather than *spontaneity*, is the key word. The soul, instead of being composed, feels pursued; like the wild duck in the hunting season, it cannot rest to feed. The subconscious mind has not yet been converted.

O gracious Father, is this the best You can do? Can I not be released and spontaneous? I cannot bear this constant conflict. Make it cease; make me free. In Jesus' name, Amen.

CAN THE SUBCONSCIOUS BE REDEEMED?

I love God's law with all my heart. But there is another power within me that is at war with my mind. This power makes me a slave to the sin that is still within me. Oh, what a miserable person I am! Who will free me from this life that is dominated by sin and death? Thank God! The answer is in Jesus Christ our Lord. (Rom. 7:22–25†)

The new life is introduced in conversion, but is not fully reigning. A Presbyterian friend joked to me, "Being a Presbyterian may not save you from sinning, but it will take the joy out of it!" That is just the difficulty in many partly changed lives—the joy of sinning is gone, but the fact of sinning is not. We have just enough religion to make us miserable but not masterful.

Where is the snag? Is this the best that Christianity can bring? Some modern theologians frankly say, "Yes." In fact, this sense of guilt burden and consequent penitence is held up as the ideal. One theologian quoted the story of a one-hundred-year-old monk in a Palestine monastery who muttered with every breath, "Lord, have mercy upon us"—and the theologian added, "I hope I'll say that with my last breath."

As for me, I hope I won't! I hope I'll say, "My Lord and my God." I don't want the emphasis to be on my guilt, but on His goodness. Suppose a child should go around continually in the home muttering, "Father, Mother, have mercy upon me." That attitude would block the relationship as effectively as sin would. The attitude of penitence has to come, and come decisively; but it should lead us into pardon, which leads to fellowship, which leads to joy.

But even after the pardon and fellowship have come, the unchanged instincts remain in the subconscious. Can they be redeemed? Can salvation extend to the subconscious mind? Or is sitting on the lid the best we can do? This is one of the most important questions we can ask.

O God, have Your processes of redemption been stymied? Is there no cleansing for these depths? Must I go through life with this ghastly contradiction at the center of my being? I cannot. Help me. Amen.

INSIDE AGENT

[Jesus]: *"The Counselor, the Holy Spirit, whom the Father will send in my name, will teach you all things and will remind you of everything I have said to you."* (John 14:26)

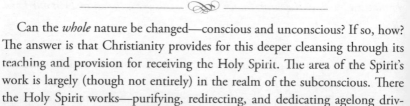

Can the *whole* nature be changed—conscious and unconscious? If so, how? The answer is that Christianity provides for this deeper cleansing through its teaching and provision for receiving the Holy Spirit. The area of the Spirit's work is largely (though not entirely) in the realm of the subconscious. There the Holy Spirit works—purifying, redirecting, and dedicating agelong driving instincts. The wild horses of nature roaming in all directions are tamed and harnessed for kingdom purposes. Only the Holy Spirit can work at those depths. "The Spirit fathoms everything, even the depths of God" (1 Cor. 2:10 MOFFATT)—and, I might add, the depths of our human nature. He refashions our depths and unifies us at the center, so that the conscious and subconscious speak the same language, understand each other, drive for the same goals, and own a common Lord.

But here is where the Christian church is weakest. It believes in and teaches the Holy Spirit—partly. The disciples were at this stage when Jesus said to them, "He lives with you and will be in you" (John 14:17). The same is true today. Most Christians know the Holy Spirit is with them—He disturbs them by momentary touches, by flashes of nearness, by illuminations and insights. But all this is "with," not "in." The capital and government are on the outside, rather than the inside.

This sense of "outsideness" will persist until we enter what the disciples entered at Pentecost. There they passed over from "with" to "in." Their faith was no longer a prodding but a penetration; no longer a restriction but a release.

O Spirit of God, I long for this "withinness." I want the seat of Your authority within me. Don't stop on the threshold—move inside. Come, Spirit, come, entirely within. Amen.

AFRAID OF WHAT?

Trembling and bewildered, the women went out and fled from the tomb. They said nothing to anyone, because they were afraid. (Mark 16:8)

On the evening of that first day of the week, when the disciples were together, with the doors locked for fear of the Jews, Jesus came and stood among them. (John 20:19)

Suppose Mark's gospel truly ended where several of the ancient manuscripts break off. The resurrection had taken place, the whole of the redemptive process was complete, the gladdest news that ever burst upon human ear was in the disciples' possession—but "they said nothing to anyone, because they were afraid." Suppose they had not gone on to Pentecost where those fears would be dissolved by a new invigoration of divine resource. How crippled, how unsatisfactory, how far short of human need our Christianity would have remained.

And yet that is where most of us have stopped. With glad good news entrusted to us, we have stopped in our tracks, "afraid." Of what? Our inadequate resources to grapple with challenges, afraid of our own selves as well as others.

Nothing less than the power of Pentecost must become our working capital. The new theologies of our time often seem to have no doctrine of, or emphasis upon, the Holy Spirit; hence they end in pessimism. The Christianity they produce is a sad, despairing type of the interim days between the crucifixion and the resurrection—of the first and second day but not the third. It is a broken-off gospel—a before-Pentecost message instead of an after-Pentecost—frustrated instead of fruitful.

Holy Spirit, I see what I need; I need You. Not as an occasional visitor, but as my constant Guest. This three-storied house of my body, mind, and soul is Yours. Take charge. Put heat in every room, and let light shine from every window. In Jesus' name, Amen.

DEEPER LEVELS

Peter replied, "Repent and be baptized, every one of you, in the name of Jesus Christ for the forgiveness of your sins. And you will receive the gift of the Holy Spirit. The promise is for you and your children and for all who are far off—for all whom the Lord our God will call." (Acts 2:38–39)

A young minister had a nervous condition, which the doctor diagnosed as follows: "You are trying to build a $200,000 house with $100,000 of resources. You are strained and worried over the inadequacy…. Cost of diagnosis: $50." That diagnosis could be given to the Christian church as a whole. We are trying to do things beyond our spiritual resources. We must tap into new ones.

For a long time in Texas, surface oil was used until the supply dwindled. Finally someone dared to drill down 5,000 feet and struck new levels of oil—in fact, gushers. Now almost all the oil is tapped at those low levels. When we as Christians go down to the deeper levels for resources the divine Providence has prepared for us, then we can be artesian and overflowing, ready for anything.

We need to be transformed from thermometers to thermostats. The thermometer merely registers the temperature of its surroundings; the thermostat *changes* the temperature. Our Christianity is often only registering its surroundings instead of remedying them. The early disciples did not go around registering the current pessimisms; they changed them. They didn't go around saying, "Look at the problems" but "Look at the Savior." Their emphasis was not on sin increasing, but on grace increasing much more.

And they spoke with transforming force. The book called "The Acts of the Apostles" records, in fact, the acts of the Holy Spirit working through the apostles. What they began, we can continue. The end of that book could well be appended with this line: "To be continued."

O Living Spirit, come within me and bring sparkle to life that has been dull, dead, and ineffective. Put Yourself into myself. In Jesus' name, Amen.

OIL FOR THE OIL PUMP

[Jesus]: *"If you, then, though you are evil, know how to give good gifts to your children, how much more will your Father in heaven give good gifts to those who ask him!" (Matt. 7:11)*

[Jesus in another account]: *"If you then, though you are evil, know how to give good gifts to your children, how much more will your Father in heaven give the Holy Spirit to those who ask him!" (Luke 11:13)*

Notice the slight difference (above) between Matthew's quotation of Jesus' statement compared to Luke's. The first promises us "good gifts," while the second is more specific: "the Holy Spirit." Indeed, the Spirit is the ultimate "good gift," the chief resource for abundant living. Seek, then, not just "good gifts," but go beyond them to their Source, the Holy Spirit.

A little boy, when asked what the Holy Spirit means, replied: "I suppose it is what puts the *oomph* in Christianity." He is, but very much more. He puts everything a Christian needs into Christianity. He makes the difference at every level.

An oil well was squeaking badly until a policeman went over and deliberately oiled it. Otherwise visitors would not believe it was an oil well when it itself was not oiled. Can the Holy Spirit put oil into the machinery of the Christian worker's own life while he is trying to pump oil for others? Unless our own machinery is well oiled and running smoothly, people will not believe we have oil for others. How can we lift others to an adequate life if we are living inadequately?

A young woman came home from college saying, "I just need the inspiration of the family life." She was rundown and needed recharging. That is what we need spiritually. We are not bad—just empty.

I come now, Spirit of God, to have my inmost being renewed and recharged. Teach me how to grasp Your resources. I want to be adequate for any hill, any load, any distance. Help me. Amen.

STEPS IN RECEIVING THE SPIRIT (PART 1)

[Jesus]: *"You will receive power when the Holy Spirit comes on you; and you will be my witnesses in Jerusalem, and in all Judea and Samaria, and to the ends of the earth." (Acts 1:8)*

We come now to the ladder for receiving the Holy Spirit. The steps are, in fact, simple.

(1) Believe it is the divine intention for you to receive the Holy Spirit. Fix it in your mind that the gift of the Spirit is not an exceptional gift for exceptional people in exceptional work, but the birthright of every Christian. Jesus spoke once to a large temple crowd about "the Spirit, whom those who believed in him *were later to receive"* (John 7:39). Note: It was in the divine intention and program for them. For whom? "Those who believed in him." Here is no exception. You, the ordinary Christian, are to receive the Holy Spirit, for you are among those who believe in Him. Peter said to another crowd, "You will receive the gift of the Holy Spirit. The promise is for you and your children and for all who are far off" (Acts 2:38–39). You belong to those "far off." You are in the stream of the divine intention.

(2) Make sure that YOU intend to receive the Holy Spirit. When I use the word *intend,* I mean *will.* This is more than wishes, passing emotions, or mental concepts. Do you *will* to receive the Holy Spirit, not as a passing influence that may get you out of spiritual difficulties, give you momentary satisfaction, lift and inspire you—not that, but as an abiding Power that will take over the citadel of yourself and reign there as a lifelong proposition?

(3) Bring the matter to a crisis. The soul grows by a series of crises. Conversion is usually a crisis; so is receiving the Holy Spirit. Wall yourself in on both sides, so there is no way around—you have to go forward or backward. The crisis moment has arrived.

O Spirit of God, I shall not sidestep into lame futilities and halfway compromises. I want nothing less than You. The marginal doesn't satisfy me anymore—the Center calls. I come. Amen.

STEPS IN RECEIVING THE SPIRIT (PART 2)

Brothers and sisters, I plead with you to give your bodies to God because of all he has done for you. Let them be a living and holy sacrifice—the kind he will find acceptable. This is truly the way to worship him. (Rom. 12:1†)

Continuing our quest: *(4) Remember the price you are to pay—yourself.* If you ask for the gift of the Spirit Himself, then it is obvious that you must offer yourself. You can ask for His gifts and, in return, give your gifts, but you cannot ask for the Gift of Himself without involving the gift of yourself. Let us repeat what we said before: There is no love between persons unless there is mutual self-surrender. If either withholds the inmost self, love is blocked. So it is here.

(5) Then pay the price of a complete surrender. I mean surrender, not just dedication. In dedication you still have your hands on the gift; in surrender you let go. The gift doesn't belong to you anymore—it totally and wholly belongs to Another. You now lead a Spirit-led life, instead of a self-led life.

Just as the canvas surrenders to the painter, the violin to the musician, the wire to the electricity, so you put yourself at the disposal of the divine. You surrender for better or for worse, for riches or for poverty, in sickness and in health, in life and in death—you will keep yourself only for Him. He has you.

Are you thereby lost, or thereby found? You lose your petty, isolated, defeated self in the universal Self of God and are harmonized with the heart of reality. As Rufus Moseley says: "I died and I died ungraciously, but I died to nothing but that which caused me to die." You die, just as a train engine dies to the thought of wandering free and surrenders itself to the bondage of the rails—only to find its freedom there.

Complete surrender means complete security, for God's will is our way—the way we are made to live.

O Spirit of God, bring this wandering, wavering will of mine to the bondage of Your freedom, to the narrowness of Thy universality, to the yoke that is easy, and to the burden that is light. I bend my neck. Amen.

STEPS IN RECEIVING THE SPIRIT (PART 3)

[Peter]: *"God, who knows the heart, showed that he accepted them by giving the Holy Spirit to them, just as he did to us. He made no distinction between us and them, for he purified their hearts by faith." (Acts 15:8–9)*

You are now ready for the next step, which is *(6) Accept the gift of the Spirit.* Remember: The gift is the Spirit Himself, not one of His blessings. Don't be put off with blessings—you want the Source of all blessing. Blessings come and go—He is the "Counselor to be with you forever" (John 14:16). Your choice is a permanent choice involving a permanent transaction with a permanent companion and master.

You cannot be worthy of His presence, nor earn the right to it. You can do only one thing—empty your hands and humbly accept the Gift. Having given yourself, you now have a right to receive Him. Repeat to yourself: "He comes—He comes. I let Him come. I welcome His coming with an open heart. I am grateful for His coming. We belong to each other forever."

His coming may be as gentle as the dew upon the newly mown hay—a subtle sense that you are not alone. Or it may be like the summer downpour. Welcome His coming, and do not dictate the manner. There is a reason for the particular manner.

(7) Be free to tell others about His coming; share it. You are not boasting; you are simply telling of the unspeakable Gift. The sharing of it fixes it. Nothing is really yours until you share it.

(8) Make the surrender and acceptance something once and for all, and yet continuous. Surrender in marriage is once and for all, and yet it is daily. Jesus told the Samaritan woman, "Those who drink the water I give will never be thirsty again. It becomes a fresh, bubbling spring within them, giving them eternal life" (John 4:14[†]). The water of the Spirit is here, and yet never finished—it is final, yet unfolding.

O Spirit of God, I have said a "Yes" that covers everything; now help me to live in a state of "Yes-ness" to Your unfolding will. In Jesus' name, Amen.

WHEN VIRTUES GET OUT OF BALANCE

Make every effort to add to your faith goodness; and to goodness, knowledge; and to knowledge, self-control; and to self-control, perseverance; and to perseverance, godliness; and to godliness, brotherly kindness; and to brotherly kindness, love. For if you possess these qualities in increasing measure, they will keep you from being ineffective and unproductive in your knowledge of our Lord Jesus Christ. (2 Peter 1:5–8)

It is not enough to be free from divided loyalties; we must have freedom from *unbalanced virtues*—the tenth of our fifteen enemies. A person may have only virtues in life, and yet those virtues may be out of proportion, unbalanced by opposite virtues. If so, they cease to be virtues and come dangerously near to being vices.

Some of the balanced virtues are: passive/militant…self-effort/God-dependence…world-renouncing/world-participating… introversive/extroversive… mystical/practical…being/doing…love/law…personal/social…freedom/law… artistic/artisan…self-renouncing/self-assertive…meekness/mastery…loving yourself/loving your neighbor.

Suppose you have only one side of those virtues; you are feeble. If you are only passive, or only militant, you are weak. The truly strong person is militantly passive and passively militant; not now and again passive, and now and again militant, but both in a living blend. You see both the passive and the militant in Jesus.

Each virtue must be held in tension by its opposite virtue. In that very tension there is strength. Otherwise, in the words of one wise writer, "It is easy for enthusiasm to become fanaticism, for zeal to become hysteria, for integrity to become hard and unforgiving, for thrift to pass over into stinginess."

O Jesus, so perfectly poised and harmonious, help my lopsided virtues to be corrected by Your amazing balance and sanity. Give me grace (and power) to correct them. For my virtues must be redeemed too. Amen.

VIRTUES MAY BECOME VICES

We are God's workmanship, created in Christ Jesus to do good works, which God prepared in advance for us to do. (Eph. 2:10)

This Scripture could actually be translated, "We are God's poem." If so, it reminds us that poems are rhythmical, each part balanced against the other. The same is true of virtues.

For instance, if your life-poem has nothing but self-effort, you are weak; if it contains nothing but God-dependence, you are also weak. But where the two are blended, so that you work as if the whole thing depended on yourself and you trust as if the whole thing depended on God, you have caught the rhythm of "receptivity and response," the alternate beats of a single heart.

One's firmness, a virtue, can become stubbornness, a vice. A minister said only half-jokingly, "I am opinionated, and I call it conviction." Many of us are like that—we get an idea and hang onto it as a dog hangs onto a bone. A Scottish theologian remarked, "God grant that I may always be right, for I never change." In fact, the person who is always right and never changes is always wrong.

Sensitivity rooted in selfishness is touchiness, but sensitivity rooted in thought for others is life. One may emphasize the material or the spiritual and make it into a vice—a materialist or a spiritualist is a part-person. But one who puts spirituality into material relationships is really strong. People can be so righteous that they are unapproachable, or so loving that they are sentimental. To be righteously loving or lovingly righteous is true strength.

When someone's right leg is longer than the left, they are lame. When one good quality is long in proportion to other good qualities, a person is morally deformed.

O Jesus, we see in You the perfect Man, all Your virtues so blended that we cannot tell where one ends and the other begins. You are everything we want to be and are not. So chip us here, mold us there; eliminate here, add to there, until one day we awaken in Your likeness. Amen.

CORRECTING THE IMBALANCE

If I speak in the tongues of men and of angels, but have not love, I am only a resounding gong or a clanging cymbal. If I have the gift of prophecy and can fathom all mysteries and all knowledge, and if I have a faith that can move mountains, but have not love, I am nothing. If I give all I possess to the poor and surrender my body to the flames, but have not love, I gain nothing. (1 Cor. 13:1–3)

If our virtues can topple over into vices, how can we correct them?

(1) Step off from your life and see it as a whole. Just what kind of total person is emerging? Am I unbalanced? Lopsided? What is the overall impression I make on people? When they think of me, what comes to mind?

(2) After looking at the large picture, now go over your life in detail. Consider each virtue one by one and see if it is a virtue still. Has your meekness become weakness? Has your strength become stubbornness? Has your outer "doing" gotten out of proportion to your inner "being"? Have the outer activities become more than your sustaining prayer life? Have you become more of a go-getter than a go-giver? Has your righteousness become rigid?

(3) Quiet yourself; let down the bars; let Christ point out what needs to be corrected. The tendency will be to defend yourself. Don't. Relax and let Him render the verdict. Accept that verdict. Don't try to amend it.

(4) Surrender your virtues into His hands for correction. He will make all your evils into goods, all your goods into betters, all your betters into bests.

(5) Sit down with an honest, sympathetic friend for review. They can see things you cannot, for each of us is prejudiced in our own favor.

(6) Having looked at yourself, now look away to Christ. Don't end up fussily trying to arrange your virtues. Fix your eyes on Christ; He has all your virtues perfectly blended. Be Christ-centered, not self-centered, even in this.

O Christ, I cannot be like You through my own futile efforts. But together, we can be and do anything. You have me—my lopsided virtues included. Remold me until I stand as Your workmanship. Amen.

THE PRICE OF IGNORANCE

[Paul]: *Since the day we heard about you, we have not stopped praying for you and asking God to fill you with the knowledge of his will through all spiritual wisdom and understanding. (Col. 1:9)*

Now we pass along to the eleventh of the fifteen major enemies: *ignorance and a lack of judgment.*

Goodness not guided by intelligence is almost as dangerous as intelligence not guided by goodness. Ignorance has produced as much confusion and suffering in the world as wrong intentions. Whether you learn right thinking through intellectual processes alone, or through moral teaching, it is necessary to learn right thinking. If the thinking goes wrong, life goes wrong with it.

In both nature and grace, ignorance is not ignored. It must be paid for in suffering. Sincerity amid the ignorance won't atone for the ignorance—the results are the same. I know Hindus who sincerely believe that smallpox is caused by the goddess of smallpox, Sitla. That sincere ignorance blocks scientific remedies, and people die, sincerity or no sincerity.

For a long time people believed malaria was caused by bad air—hence its name: *mal* = "bad," *aria* = "air." That ignorance let people die by the millions. Today, the same thing is happening spiritually. We are ignorant of the laws of mental and spiritual health, and as a consequence, humanity is tearing and lacerating itself like the demon-possessed man Jesus met (Mark 5:1–20). Neuroses and the jitters are the weapons with which we flog ourselves.

Since Jesus was the revealer of reality, He was always saying, "Don't you understand?" The stupidities of people astonished Him more than their wickedness. He saw they were trying to live against the nature of reality—attempting the impossible and getting hurt in the process.

O God, we hurt ourselves because we do not know Your laws, and when we know them, do not obey them. Give us minds that know and wills that obey. We want to know the truth and do it; then we shall be free. Amen.

A WELL-TRAINED CONSCIENCE

Anyone who lives on milk, being still an infant, is not acquainted with the teaching about righteousness. But solid food is for the mature, who by constant use have trained themselves to distinguish good from evil. (Heb. 5:13–14)

The Christian is a foe of ignorance, fighting it on every front. To get in touch with Christ is to have a mental awakening. It was no mere chance that so many great universities in America emerged from the Christian church.

Jesus said, "Love the Lord your God…with all your mind" (Luke 10:27). That last phrase was not in the original Old Testament command (Deut. 6:5); Jesus put it in. If scientists are correct in telling us we use only about half our brains, Jesus wants to awaken that other dormant half. Then we will love God with *all* our minds.

Jesus encourages people to think for themselves: "Why don't you judge for yourselves what is right?" (Luke 12:57). An ignorant conscience is a danger to the world. The conscience is not an infallible guide unless properly trained. It decides when a thing is right or wrong—but what it decides is determined by the training we give it. Paul killed innocent people in all good conscience until his conscience began to be trained under the tutelage of Christ. Then and then only was it a safe guide.

We make our consciences, and then our consciences make us. Many people have sensitized their consciences to very marginal sins and shortcomings, while hardly noticing central and fundamental sins. To give the safest and highest guidance, our minds must be Christianly informed. A truly Christian conscience is a great achievement, as well as a great gift of God.

O God, I begin to see that I must love You with an intellectual love as well as an emotional love. Awaken my brain cells so I may be the sharpest instrument I can be. Save me from intellectual laziness, and help me think Your thoughts after You. Amen.

TOWARD BETTER JUDGMENT

[Paul, writing from prison]: *When you come, bring the cloak that I left with Carpus at Troas, and my scrolls, especially the parchments. (2 Tim. 4:13)*

During the 1700s, one of John Wesley's preachers said, "I get my text and my sermons from God without studying." Wesley asked, "Does God ever give you a text you have not read?" "No," replied the preacher. Wesley added, "Then you would [be] better [to] read more."

An uninformed Christian is an uninspiring Christian. That which does not hold the mind will soon not hold the heart.

But Christians must not only be well-informed, they must also be well-balanced. A lack of judgment is as disastrous as a lack of information; you must know what to do with your knowledge after you acquire it. Said a judge to an oratorical young lawyer: "Young man, if you will pluck some feathers from the wings of your imagination and stick them in the tail of your judgment, you will fly better."

Here are steps to becoming better-informed, better-balanced Christians:

(1) Go over your life and see where you are illiterate. You will probably find vital areas that need information. *(2) See if your conscience is poorly trained, especially on the great social issues.* If your knowledge is neglected, your conscience will have little to work on. *(3) Determine to become educated in areas where now you are not.* Break up your mental assumptions by a mighty effort and a strict discipline. *(4) Set aside a certain amount of time each day to inform yourself in the areas where you need it.* Make a standing engagement with knowledge. *(5) Review your judgments and don't be afraid to reverse them.* Let the mind know that its judgments will be reviewed; this will make the mind more careful.

Be an informed and balanced Christian—the most beautiful handiwork of God.

O God, help me this day to begin a regimen of strict discipline, with no exceptions. I am serious about being my best for You. Amen.

PHYSICAL HARMONY

May God himself, the God of peace, sanctify you through and through. May your whole spirit, soul and body be kept blameless at the coming of our Lord Jesus Christ. The one who calls you is faithful and he will do it. (1 Thess. 5:23–24)

We pass on to the twelfth of the fifteen major enemies of the personality: *physical disharmony and disease.* We have been a long time getting to this topic. While some would have started out here, we have waited until now, because the physical is not all-important. Many people live abundantly in spite of physical conditions. One man I know was left crippled after the First World War. Yet he runs his business from his bedroom, which is a center of wholesome cheerfulness. He is one of the most magnetic persons in his town. He lives abundantly—in spite of.

Nevertheless, there is a very definite physical component to abundant living. Body and mind are so intertwined that one can scarcely say "body" and "mind," but rather "body-mind." If the soul and mind pass on their sicknesses to the body, then just as definitely does the body pass on its sicknesses to the mind and soul. The whole person becomes sick.

Many people are castigating their souls and loading them with guilt when they should attend to their nutrition, or have a tonsillectomy! If the nerves are starved for vitamins, they will kick back in spiritual depression, just as a starved soul will kick back in physical depression.

Christianity shows its absolute sanity by taking the body seriously. It is the only one of the great faiths that does so. It is founded, after all, on an incarnation.

O God, You have made me for health and rhythm; I present this body of mine to You. Make it into the very finest instrument, for Your purposes. Bring out of me harmony and effectiveness. Amen.

GOOD HEALTH—IS IT PHYSICAL OR SPIRITUAL?

We always carry around in our body the death of Jesus, so that the life of Jesus may also be revealed in our body. For we who are alive are always being given over to death for Jesus' sake, so that his life may be revealed in our mortal body. (2 Cor. 4:10–11)

There are those who say all disease has a physical origin—they are the materialists. There are others who say all disease has a spiritual or mental origin—they are the mentalists. To hold either position is to fly in the face of the facts. The first position alienates the whole mental and spiritual movement for health. The second position alienates the whole scientific movement for health. Both, as a result of their half-truths, have filled graveyards.

The time has now come to bring these two positions together. The truth in each has been established; now let the error in each be eliminated, and the two positions—the thesis and the antithesis—brought together in a higher synthesis.

The fact is that the balance will probably work out to about fifty-fifty—about half the diseases are mental and spiritual, and half are physical in origin. A young man once became ill after eating shrimp. Ten years later he became physically ill at the sight of the word *shrimp* on a menu card. The first time the illness was purely physical—he was allergic to shrimp; the second time it was purely mental.

O God of my mind and my body, I come to You to put both under the control of Your redemption and guidance. May I pass on to my body the health of my mind, and to my mind the health of my body. But in order to do this, will You pass on Your health to both my mind and body? Amen.

DOES CHARACTER AFFECT THE GLANDS?

If the Spirit of him who raised Jesus from the dead is living in you, he who raised Christ from the dead will also give life to your mortal bodies through his Spirit, who lives in you. (Rom. 8:11)

When the effects of glands were first discovered, many people felt they had found the basis of morality and character—the glands decided everything. One could change a person's moral character by simply adjusting the secretion of the thyroid or the adrenals. This seemed a terrific blow to Christianity, which says that morality originates in a spiritual being, God.

But now the further truth is emerging. If the secretions of glands affect character, character also affects the secretions of glands. A person's mental and spiritual state affects the proportion of glandular flow. Unchristian mental and spiritual attitudes upset the proper secretion of the glands. I asked an able practitioner of medicine this question: "If we live in a truly Christian way, will not the glands function perfectly, provided they are healthy?" The answer was an unqualified yes.

So apparently we have Christian glands! Unchristian fear, hate, selfishness, and guilt upset them, throwing them out of proportion. Christian confidence, love, unselfishness, and reconciliation make the glands function naturally and in the right proportion.

Perhaps the truth could be better stated this way: God made our glands, and into their structure He wrote the Christian law. When we obey that law, our glands are harmonious and rightly proportioned for health.

"You restored me to health and newness of life" said a radiant young woman. The two comments were connected—her newness of life brought health.

O God of harmony and peace, I bring to You my disharmonies and unrest. Take them all into Your hands. Where they are out of balance, balance them. I want to be harmonized like You. Amen.

THE MORAL BASE OF DISEASE

Ah, sinful nation, a people loaded with guilt, a brood of evildoers, children given to corruption! They have forsaken the LORD; they have spurned the Holy One of Israel and turned their backs on him.... Your whole head is injured, your whole heart afflicted. From the sole of your foot to the top of your head there is no soundness—only wounds and welts and open sores. (Isa. 1:4–6)

The physical basis of disease is so obvious that it emphasizes itself. Nor do we need to emphasize its effects upon the spiritual condition. The idea that you can be more spiritual if your body is chastened is false. The body kicks back and clouds the soul; mortified bodies produce morbid saints (and they are usually more morbid than saintly).

But the other truth—the effect of the mental and spiritual upon the physical—needs our attention. One lady put her case this way: "I had lost weight steadily in spite of medication. My mind had become so bad I was afraid to go out by myself, and I avoided meeting people. I was informed that there was very little organically wrong with me and that my mental state was causing my trouble. Then, a remarkable change took place in my life, and my health has steadily improved. My husband's love for me is growing stronger each day. The Lord is truly transforming our home from a morgue to a sanctuary."

From a morgue to a sanctuary! Not only are many homes morgues; many bodies are as well—they harbor death cells of anger, fear, self-centeredness, and guilt. Many a person, instead of having a vibrant body that is awake in every cell and harmonious in every relationship, lives in a body of death.

A Christian has no business with that kind of body. It can become a sanctuary.

O God, give me what the apostle Paul meant when he said our mortal bodies would be quickened by the Spirit. Let me be quickened. Amen.

DISEASE IS NOT THE WILL OF GOD

Be merciful to me, LORD, for I am faint; O LORD, heal me, for my bones are in agony. My soul is in anguish. How long, O LORD, how long? Turn, O LORD, and deliver me; save me because of your unfailing love. (Psalm 6:2–4)

If disease and physical disharmony are ours, it is probable that they come from one or more of four causes: (1) actual structural disease, brought about by heredity, accident, contagion, ignorance, or willful abuse; (2) functional disease (which may pass into structural disease), brought about by wrong mental, moral, and spiritual attitudes; (3) poor or unbalanced nutrition, brought about by poverty, ignorance, or willful neglect; (4) environmental factors that directly produce disease.

Note that in these four sources, I do not mention the will of God. He does not will disease; He wills health. Disease is an enemy Jesus fought against and healed whenever He could get cooperation. He never once told people to bear disease as the will of God. "I have come that they may have life, and that they may have it more abundantly" (John 10:10 NKJV)—that is the Christian note.

It is true that disease comes from breaking the laws of God, which He has written into the constitution of things. But God does not send it; we break His laws, and they break us. That makes us, not God, the author of that disease.

A friend once said to Dr. W. B. Cannon, the great Harvard physiologist: "When you know all the diseases it is possible to have…you wonder how anyone is ever well." To which Dr. Cannon replied: "When you know a great deal about the human body, you wonder why anyone is sick" (quoted by Dr. Russell L. Dicks, *Religion in Life*, 1941, Vol. X, No. 4, p. 515). The human frame is organized for health and, if the way is cleared by right cooperation with nature, will produce health.

Gracious Father, You have woven possibilities for health and rhythm into the structure of my being. Help me to cooperate with You, so that no crippling disease shall mar my efficiency for the kingdom. I want to keep fit for You. Amen.

SALVATION IS WHOLENESS

And, behold, a woman...came behind him, and touched the hem of his garment: For she said within herself, If I may but touch his garment, I shall be whole. But Jesus turned him about, and when he saw her, he said, Daughter, be of good comfort; thy faith hath made thee whole. And the woman was made whole from that hour. (Matt. 9:20–22 KJV)

The fact is that health is stronger than disease. A cancer expert tells me that cancer cells are more susceptible to radium than healthy cells. That makes it possible, by the proper use of radium, to kill the cancer cells with less damage to the healthy tissues.

Health is written into the constitution of things. God wills it. If we do not have health, then some law has been broken somewhere, either by our ancestors, or by ourselves, or by society, or by environmental factors. We can't be responsible for the body we begin life with, but we are responsible for the one we die with.

I have lived for thirty-five years in one of the worst climates of the world—India, a poverty-stricken and disease-ridden land, "the white man's grave," as some call it. And yet I have come out of it with a better body than when I went in. I have missed only about two engagements in twenty-five years: one from a flu germ (a gift from America!) and one due to a war regulation in Ceylon (Sri Lanka). Someone said recently, "You look ten years younger than you did five years ago—that is real religion." I found the linking of religion with health and vitality to be interesting.

Jesus defined salvation as health. Salvation is wholeness—health in total body, mind, and soul. If through ignorance or carelessness we are unhealthy, still the condition is not hopeless, for both nature and God are redemptive.

My gracious, healing Father, forgive me for the sins I have committed against this body of mine, and thus against You, its Creator. I want to work with You to make it the perfect expression of Your will. Give me insight into the laws of my body, and help me to obey them when I see them. Amen.

STEPS TOWARD HEALTH

God is able to make all grace abound to you, so that in all things at all times, having all that you need, you will abound in every good work. (2 Cor. 9:8)

If we are not at our best physically—if the physical basis of our abundant living is poor—we can improve it. The following steps may help.

(1) Get a thorough physical examination by a competent doctor, preferably one who is not a "materialist" but sees the interlocking of body and spirit. The doctor who sees disease as only physical in origin is as out-of-date as the medicine man puncturing patients to let the devils out. On the other hand, don't go to one who says disease is only of mental or spiritual origin. This one is equally dangerous and equally liable to write you a pass to a cemetery—or if not that far, to an infirmary.

(2) If there are physical weaknesses, take the next step and ask whether they are of physical or spiritual origin. Some may turn out to be physical, and an operation or medication may correct them. Don't hesitate to let God heal you in this way. Real surgeons or physicians recognize that they do not heal. As one doctor says: "I only clear the way; Nature or God does the healing." Jesus did not hesitate to use physical remedies; for instance, He made clay and anointed the blind man's eyes. Don't be more spiritual than God, who has planted in nature physical remedies for physical disease.

(3) Pay attention to the newest—and yet the oldest—branch of medical science: nutrition. Humanity has always been compelled to deal with it. But we are just now beginning to treat nutrition scientifically. It has much to teach us. More on this subject tomorrow.

God, my gracious Father, I want to live fully. Help me to face my physical situation with complete honesty and a willingness to know the truth, which alone can make me free. Save me from all self-deception and subterfuges. Amen.

WHAT WE NEED—AND DON'T NEED

Whether you eat or drink or whatever you do, do it all for the glory of God.
(1 Cor. 10:31)

--------------------------------- ∞ ---------------------------------

Seneca, the wise Roman philosopher, once said: "Man does not die; he kills himself." Now in our time, Dr. R. L. Greene, a professor of chemistry who specializes in nutrition, says: "The deadly weapons used by man in committing suicide are the knife, fork, and spoon." That suicide may indeed come from wrong food—or even the wrong eating of food. I was once in a restaurant absorbed in thought and paying no attention to my meal, when a bold waitress came up to me and said, "Sir, do you know that you are just gulping your food down?" I've since been grateful for that motherly soul. While I've not always obeyed her, I often feel her shadow over my shoulder in gentle rebuke.

Everyone needs a guardian angel to keep them from suicide by knife, fork, and spoon.

Continuing the steps toward physical health: *(4) See that you are getting the minimum requirement of vitamins.* Dr. Greene says: "Life's chemical reactions are disturbed more frequently by a deficiency of vitamins than by any other cause." For instance, "A deficiency of Vitamin A gives rise to kidney, skin, and gastrointestinal disorders, diarrhea, poor appetite, bad teeth, chronic colitis, bronchitis, malnutrition followed by a greatly lowered state of general health and a high death rate from infectious diseases, especially tuberculosis and pneumonia."

If there were space, we could show a table of other diseases caused by deficiencies in Vitamins B, C, and D. Just one example: Without enough Vitamin C, the teeth of guinea pigs or monkeys suffer a progressive mineral loss and soon become soft like rubber.

Nutrition is necessary to vitality. This is the way God created us.

Divine Chemist, thank You for hiding in the heart of food the seeds of vitality and health. Help us now to hunt them out and utilize them to the full, for they are Your gift. Amen.

THREE SECRETS FOR VITALITY

When Jesus landed and saw a large crowd, he had compassion on them and healed their sick. As evening approached, the disciples came to him and said, "This is a remote place, and it's already getting late. Send the crowds away, so they can go to the villages and buy themselves some food."

Jesus replied, "They do not need to go away. You give them something to eat." (Matt. 14:14–16)

The main facts about vitamins are becoming generally known. What is not so generally known is the relation of lack of vitamins to nervous diseases. Dr. I. S. Hughes, a vitamin authority, said to me at the beginning of the National Christian Mission, at which I was to speak three to five times daily for six solid months: "If you take some tablets I will give to you, I will guarantee that you will come out of this Mission without nervous exhaustion." (The tablets contained nothing more than wheatgrass, which contains all the vitamins in concentrated form.)

I replied that I would be his test case. I cannot prove that the tablets made the difference—but there is no doubt that I came out of that Mission after six months fresh and full of vitality, in fact far better than when I began. And this, despite the heavy demands of constant speaking and traveling.

Someone asked me how I was able to come through such a grind so well. I replied, "It was the combination of three things: grace, grass, and guts!" I sounded half-joking, but in fact I was in dead earnest. That combination will produce health and vitality in us all: (a) grace for the soul to avoid inner conflict; (b) nutrition for the body to provide the physical basis of abundant living; and (c) determination in the mind to use God's gifts intelligently.

Gracious Father, I come to You to be made into a vital person. I need Your grace to keep me from wearying conflicts. I need stored vitality from nature's storehouse. And I need a quickened intelligence to save me from foolish mistakes. Help me to use all three. Amen.

ATTITUDE CHECK

[David]: *"You, my son Solomon, acknowledge the God of your father, and serve him with wholehearted devotion and with a willing mind, for the LORD searches every heart and understands every motive behind the thoughts." (1 Chron. 28:9)*

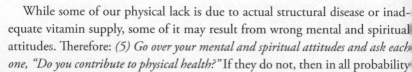

While some of our physical lack is due to actual structural disease or inadequate vitamin supply, some of it may result from wrong mental and spiritual attitudes. Therefore: *(5) Go over your mental and spiritual attitudes and ask each one, "Do you contribute to physical health?"* If they do not, then in all probability they contribute to disease and disruption. For, according to high British medical authority, "There is not a tissue or organ in the body not influenced by the attitude of mind and spirit."

One doctor told a patient he would refund her fee if she would come and listen to what I was saying on the relationship between mental and spiritual states and health. Her pains were real; she was not malingering. But their origin was in her mental and spiritual condition. She had passed on her mental and spiritual sickness to her body.

Another piece of evidence comes from a doctor's wife: "My husband says he would die if he harbored resentment." Many people do! Or they go on living at a half-dying rate. Heart disease has increased alarmingly in American life so that it now ranks first among the causes of death. The rise in worry and anxiety has been responsible for much of this increase. Stomach ulcers are now going up and down with the anxieties of the war [World War II]. In a dozen different ways, the mind does create disease—or destroy it.

O God, I see I must be healthy-minded if I am to be healthy-bodied. Purge my mind from all fears, worries, and resentment. I want to be strong for You. Make me the best I can be. Amen.

HEALING FOR THE WHOLE PERSON

Pleasant words are a honeycomb, sweet to the soul and healing to the bones. (Prov. 16:24)

Dear friend, I pray that you may enjoy good health and that all may go well with you, even as your soul is getting along well. (3 John 2)

The powerful influence of mind over body is illustrated by Dr. Adelaide Woodard, a medical missionary to India, who had a finger amputated after a painful infection. She still senses pain in her finger, though it is gone.

An elderly woman had vomiting spells, and the cause was found to be worry, brought on by financial insecurity. The worry threw functional disturbance into her digestive tract.

A doctor told me that his brother, a rather wealthy man, had refused to disburse a special portion of the family estate to a sister who had taken care of the parents during their old age. He grew selfish and resentful. A stomach ulcer resulted. The doctor then telephoned his brother, spending a good deal of money on the call, to say that the ulcer was the result of his brother's selfishness. The man was so impressed that he gave up his resentment, shared the money— and the stomach ulcer was healed.

The human being is a unit, and cannot be sick in one part without passing on the sickness to other parts. The entire person must be redeemed. The gospel provides for that total redemption. It provides healing for the body, cleansing for the mind from all conflicts and divisions, forgiveness and fellowship for the soul—the whole person is unified, coordinated, and made effective. This is full salvation!

O God, my God, I need You—body and soul. Give me radiant health in every part of my being. I yield every part to You for Your healing. Amen.

OUR SYSTEM PROBLEM

What sorrow awaits you who lie awake at night, thinking up evil plans. You rise at dawn and hurry to carry them out, simply because you have the power to do so. When you want a piece of land, you find a way to seize it. When you want someone's house, you take it by fraud and violence. (Micah 2:1–2†)

Blessed is the man who does not walk in the counsel of the wicked or stand in the way of sinners or sit in the seat of mockers. (Psalm 1:1)

--------------------------------- ✆ ---------------------------------

We come now to the thirteenth major enemy of abundant living: *an unchristian social order,* specifically the way it affects the individual.

We will not debate the question of whether heredity or environment is stronger in shaping such a life. The determinative influence, in fact, is the individual's own reaction to what is received from heredity or environment. Only what you respond to influences you.

But the fact must be faced that the individual usually responds to his or her social heredity—which then proceeds to bring about change. The social heredity has an amazing power to convert the individual for good or bad. Not mechanically, mind you, but in outcome nonetheless. A dean of girls in a public school told me straightforwardly that the three major factors in producing problem children are "poverty, broken homes, and a lack of attendance at Sunday school or church"—all social factors.

The psychoanalysts stress that the cause of maladjustment to life is inside the individual, while the Meyer school of psychologists stress environmental factors. Both assumptions are true, for the individual and the environment act and react upon each other. But if I had to choose between them, I think I would say that an unchristian social order produces more thwarted and disrupted lives than any other single cause.

O Christ, we are beginning to see more clearly why You present a new order on earth, the kingdom of God. We submit ourselves to that new order. We yield to it every impulse, thus responding to the highest. Amen.

HOW THE SOCIAL ORDER SHAPES US

*Hear this, you who trample the needy and do away with the poor of the land…
buying the poor with silver and the needy for a pair of sandals, selling even the
sweepings with the wheat. The LORD has sworn by the Pride of Jacob: "I will
never forget anything they have done." (Amos 8:4, 6–7)*

Many things that we think are born within the individual are, in fact,
imposed on the child through social heredity at a very early age. The social
heredity in China converts into its image hundreds of millions of people every
generation. On the other hand, a Chinese child transferred at birth to America
and put into a purely American home would grow up in the image of the
American social heredity, with the outlook, mentality, and spirit of America.

As a dyer's hands are colored by the dyes in which he works, so the souls
of individuals are colored by the social heredity in which they live and move.
A man makes a machine, and then the machine makes him. Someone has
expressed it this way: "Some machines lift us up, help us to make the most of
ourselves. Some tear us apart, grind us down…. One is human, giving you a
chance to be at your best self. The other is mechanical, working on you like a
gear cutter, whittling you down, chiseling at you, cutting grooves in you, making you like all the small gears on the line."

Social surroundings have a way of cutting into our being, chiseling us, and
making us after their own pattern. It is because I care deeply about individual
conversion that I am so committed to the need for social conversion. If anyone
shows no interest in changing an unchristian social order, then, by that very
act, the person has little interest in individual conversion. For apart from the
Holy Spirit, the greatest single power to change the individual is the social
order. Jesus sees this clearly. He wants to replace this unworkable, rotten order
with God's order, the kingdom of God.

*O God, forgive us for making You into a half god ruling over a half-realm. You
are God, and all life, individual and social, must bend the knee to Your will,
finding itself in that will. For Your will is life. Amen.*

THE NEED FOR TOTAL DISCIPLINE

Enter through the narrow gate. For wide is the gate and broad is the road that leads to destruction, and many enter through it. But small is the gate and narrow the road that leads to life, and only a few find it. (Matt. 7:13–14)

We now take up briefly (awaiting a fuller development) the fourteenth major enemy of abundant living: *lack of a total life discipline.*

The future of the world is in the hands of disciplined people. Actually, this statement must be modified to say that the future of the world is in the hands of people *who are disciplined to the highest level.* Very often our disciplines are too small; we are geared to modest concepts and purposes. Many, for example, are committed to their family, which is very good; but it is inadequate unless the family is geared to something beyond itself—an absolute. The discipline of a club, a union, a church, a country may be good, but these are not good enough. We must be disciplined to something that gives total meaning to the total life.

It is just this total discipline that is lacking in modern life. Things are so compartmentalized, specialized, and picked to pieces that they lack total meaning. Science, for example, extracts knowledge about specific things but fails to deal with the sum total of reality and its meaning. Psychoanalysis picks people to pieces but often cannot put them together again on a higher level. It uses psychoanalysis and not psychosynthesis.

Just as the spokes of a wheel hang loose without a hub, so the powers of life are at loose ends unless fastened into the central hub—God and His kingdom. There is simply nothing to which we can be totally disciplined except God's absolute order. That and that alone gives total meaning to life.

Gracious Father, I am hanging at loose ends; life lacks total meaning, and therefore lacks purpose and power. Help me to a complete discipline under Your kingdom. Amen.

DISCIPLINED TO THE KINGDOM

Do you not know that in a race all the runners run, but only one gets the prize? Run in such a way as to get the prize. Everyone who competes in the games goes into strict training. They do it to get a crown that will not last; but we do it to get a crown that will last forever. (1 Cor. 9:24–25)

We human beings are made for freedom, we say. But freedom can come only through obedience. I am free from police officers if I obey the laws they represent. Within that framework, I am free. The larger the unit I obey, the larger the freedom I enjoy. If I obey the laws of the United States, I am free within the boundaries of that country.

When I am disciplined to the kingdom of God and obey its laws, I am free within the limits of its area. That area is universal! Therefore I am universally free. The Christian who is disciplined to the kingdom of God is the only universal person, a cosmic person.

The thing works the other way. If you are disciplined only to yourself and your own desires, you are free within the area of yourself and your desires. You have chosen a small unit of allegiance; hence you become small. Moreover, you become disliked by others to whom you have no loyalty or love. In the end, you dislike yourself for being so small, and for being disliked by others. This is a vicious circle, a descending spiral.

But if you are disciplined to the kingdom, you will like yourself for the greatness and nobility of your loyalties and allegiances, and other people will respond to you. Best of all, the universe will take sides with you, backing you up, making you feel at home and free. This is an ascending spiral.

O God, I want every area of my life to hold but one allegiance. I cannot rest till I am under the sway of the Ultimate, nor until the Ultimate has the ultimate way. In Jesus' name, Amen.

A CREATIVE, OUTGOING LOVE

This is the message you have heard from the beginning: We should love one another.... If we love our Christian brothers and sisters, it proves that we have passed from death to life. But a person who has no love is still dead.... We know what real love is because Jesus gave up his life for us. So we also ought to give up our lives for our brothers and sisters. If someone has enough money to live well and sees a brother or sister in need but shows no compassion—how can God's love be in that person? (1 John 3:11, 14, 16–17†)

We come to the last of the fifteen major enemies: *lack of a creative, outgoing love*. I have saved this enemy for last, because to overcome it is the *sine qua non* of abundant living. If you were able to conquer all fourteen others, you would still lack the one needful thing. The person who loves not, lives not; and the person who loves most, lives most.

I have purposely put the word *creative* in the name, for there is another kind of love that goes out only to get for itself. It goes out to bring in. That kind of outgoing love is just as bad as a turned-in love, for it still says, "Give me." But *creative* love is the love that stimulates, helps, and awakens others. And as it stimulates, it is itself stimulated.

You can never get rid of your own troubles unless you take upon yourself the troubles of others. The saintly John Keble, for whom one of the Oxford colleges is named, said: "When you find yourself oppressed by melancholy, the best way is to go out and find something kind to do to somebody else." Or as someone else has put it: "When I dig a person out of trouble, the hole left behind is the grave where I bury my own sorrow."

Go out each day and do something that nobody but a Christian would do.

O God, I see You have fashioned me for creative love. You, Creator God, have made me to be a creator too. I share Your power to make and to remake. I am so glad not to be a negative being, but positive and outgoing. I thank You. Amen.

THE MIRACLE STARTS INSIDE

[Jesus]: *"A tree is identified by its fruit. If a tree is good, its fruit will be good. If a tree is bad, its fruit will be bad. You brood of snakes! How could evil men like you speak what is good and right? For whatever is in your heart determines what you say. A good person produces good things from the treasury of a good heart, and an evil person produces evil things from the treasury of an evil heart."* (Matt. 12:33–35†)

A creative, outgoing love is an imitation of what God Himself does and has always done. It is amazingly effective. Leslie B. Salter says: "Every normal man or woman longs more keenly for love, for warm friendship, admiration and human responsiveness…than for anything else in life…. Wouldst thou love life? Then start giving those about you the feeling they long for. Start passing out good cheer and brotherly love, and you will receive in return a personal friendliness and genuine happiness you never dreamed possible, and which will revolutionize your whole life."

Don't wait for some miracle to be performed on you from the outside, lifting you above your fears and self-centeredness. You help God from within by offering love to others, and miraculously your fears and self-centeredness vanish. The miracle starts from within, not from without. Throw your will on the side of outgoing love, and all the healing resources of the universe will be yours.

But neither God nor people can help you if you remain bottled up in yourself. You are not made to live that way. All the medicine, all the advice, all the praying will do you no good unless you throw your will on the side of outgoing love. Get out of yourself, or perish!

O You who are always reaching out after me in love and awakening me, help me this day to do the same. Help me to quicken some life by the touch of my friendliness and love. Amen.

A FINAL EXAM

Test me, O LORD, and try me, examine my heart and my mind; for your love is ever before me, and I walk continually in your truth. (Psalm 26:2–3)

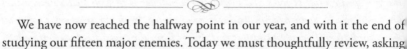

We have now reached the halfway point in our year, and with it the end of studying our fifteen major enemies. Today we must thoughtfully review, asking ourselves straight questions. As we do, let there be no blind spots.

Do I have a faith in, and loyalty to, Something beyond myself that gives ultimate meaning, coherence, and goal to life? And is that Something, God? Or are there still areas of self-centeredness? If so, do these uncleansed areas breed the offspring of self-centeredness—dishonesty? greed? prejudice? intolerance? pride? refusal of responsibility and cooperation? Have I really shifted the center of my life from myself to God?

What about anger, resentment, hate—any roots left? Am I still harboring worries, anxieties, and fears? Or are they turned over to Him?

Does any sense of unresolved guilt still lurk in me? Am I now forever turned away from negativism and inferiority attitudes? Are my desires disciplined? Do impure sexual thoughts have any part in my mind? Are my other appetites all under His control? Is there any insincerity left in me—conscious or unconscious? Are any divided loyalties still left within me?

Am I balancing my virtues with their opposite virtues? Do ignorance and lack of judgment still hamper me? Are there physical disharmonies rooted in wrong mental and spiritual attitudes? Is lack of proper nutrition weakening me? Am I doing my best to change the unchristian social order? Am I now under a total discipline in my total life? Am I released and outgoing in creative love to others?

If, on the whole, we can answer these questions in a way that honors God, we are on the way to abundant living.

O God, I have faced my enemies, and in Your name I have knocked them down. I thank You. Now help me to refuse any alliance with any enemy that pleads to stay. Help me make a clean sweep. In Jesus' name, Amen.

WE TURN TO OUR RESOURCES

Just as you received Christ Jesus as Lord, continue to live in him, rooted and built up in him, strengthened in the faith as you were taught, and overflowing with thankfulness.… For in Christ all the fullness of the Deity lives in bodily form, and you have been given fullness in Christ, who is the head over every power and authority. (Col. 2:6-7, 9–10)

Along the way as we looked at our fifteen major enemies, we glanced at our resources to meet and destroy them. This was necessary to keep up our confidence that they could be overcome. Now we must gaze full-faced until our resources take hold of us, down to every nerve cell and fiber of our being. We must gaze at them until we are possessed by them.

Someone has said, "The early Christians did not say in dismay, 'Look what the world has come to,' but in delight, 'Look what has come to the world.'" They saw not merely the ruin, but the Resources for reconstructing that ruin. They saw not merely that sin increased, but that grace increased much more. On that assurance the pivot of history swung from blank despair, loss of moral nerve, and fatalism, to faith and confidence that at last sin had met its match; that something new had come into the world. They saw that people could attain goodness, health of mind and body—not only here and there, but on a wide scale.

That same sense of confidence must possess you if you are to pass from being the anemic, noncreative, nay-saying type of person to being the master of self, circumstances, and destiny. This faith must not be based on a self-hypnosis, a fool's paradise; it must be based on the solid confidence that your life is connected to the sum total of reality, and that reality is working with you rather than against you.

The whole secret of abundant living can be summed up in this sentence: "Not your responsibility, but your response to God's ability."

O Gracious God and Father, my heart beats a little faster at the prospect of being the person I have felt I might be. I am ready to follow. Amen.

IS THE CHRISTIAN WAY REALISTIC?

[Jesus]: *"Do not let your hearts be troubled. Trust in God; trust also in me. In my Father's house are many rooms; if it were not so, I would have told you. I am going there to prepare a place for you. And if I go and prepare a place for you, I will come back and take you to be with me that you also may be where I am."* (John 14:1–3)

We have spoken more than once about aligning ourselves with reality, making sure we are working with the grain of the universe rather than against it. But how can we be sure the Christian way is the way of reality? What if the Christian way is just a beautiful but unrealistic dream that overlies a basis of hideous but solid reality?

Some critics say we Christians are endeavoring to be something for which we are not made, striving for goals we cannot, by the very fact of our human nature, attain. They say the Christian way of idealism breaks its delicate wings upon the hard facts of reality. It may work in some other world, but in this world we must not waste our time with the impossible, which only excites us with much ado about nothing; which only gives us an itch that cannot be scratched.

That is the haunting doubt of the modern mind, and we cannot make an inch of progress into the soul of this defeated age until that doubt is faced.

Clarity comes when we see that inherently we are made for the Christian way, and to try to live some other way will not only be wrong but also impossible. You cannot live against the nature of reality and get away with it. You will get hurt. Jesus was surprised not so much at people's wickedness as at their stupidity. "Don't you see?" he kept saying. "You are living in opposition to life, and that is impossible—you'll get hurt—in fact, you are hurt." Sin is an attempt to act against God without opposing ourselves—which is impossible.

My Father, You have fashioned my being for Yourself, and when I try to fashion it for something else, it gets all tangled. I want to take Your way. Amen.

TWO JUDGMENTS, ONE VERDICT

We make it our goal to please him, whether we are at home in the body or away from it. For we must all appear before the judgment seat of Christ, that each one may receive what is due him for the things done while in the body, whether good or bad. (2 Cor. 5:9–10)

The verdict of life and the verdict of Christ are the same. He is life ("I am… the life," John 14:6)—and to live against Him is to live against life. If that short statement is true, it is the most momentous truth ever presented to humanity.

Two lines of human experimentation, conducted for the most part independently, are now converging: the Christian way and the scientific way. Life is bringing them both out at the same place. Someday science is going to lay everything on the table and say, "This is the way to live, as opposed to this." And when we see it all, we will be astonished and exclaim, "But what you are recommending is the Christian way, and what you are disqualifying is an unchristian way." The scientist will reply: "Regarding that, we are not trying to take sides. But we can affirm that life comes out to this result."

The Christian way is written into the constitution of things. It is the natural way to live. I heard two thoughtful people render the same verdict. One was an outstanding specialist who had dealt with people's jagged and frayed nerves all his life, and this was his conclusion: "Christianity is just plain common sense." The other was a brilliant youth who, beginning to experiment with life, said, "The Christian way is just [common] sense." The youth by a swift intuition and the doctor by a lifetime of experimentation came out at the same place.

If you try to live against nature, you get all tangled up. Life goes from one snarl to another.

God of my inmost being, of my nerves and tissues and blood, I cannot sin against You without sinning against myself. I cannot escape Your swift and sure judgments, for they are inherent. I want to escape into You. Amen.

THE NATURAL WAY

All things were made through Him, and without Him nothing was made that was made. (John 1:3 NKJV)

"Therefore whoever hears these sayings of Mine, and does them, I will liken him to a wise man who built his house on the rock." (Matt. 7:24 NKJV)

The Christian way is embedded into the texture of life. The striking words of John 1:3 (see above) tell us there is a way stamped into everything. It is the way life is made to work, the Christian way—"without Him nothing was made that was made." It is the divine intention written into flesh.

Dr. H. F. Rall says that one does not say to a crocodile, "Now be a crocodile," for it will never be anything else. But one does say to a man, "Now be a man." Why? For men and women can and often do live against, or below, the way they are made to live. They can be unnatural—which is to be frustrated.

Sin is trying to live *unnaturally*—it is literally *missing the mark,* the mark woven into our blood cells, our tissues, our nerve cells—it is the will of God. The laws of our being are not different from the laws of God; they are the laws of God put into the constitution of our being. To be true to them is to be true to God, and to be true to God is to be true to them.

The early Christians sensed this when they spoke about those "who belonged to the Way" (Acts 9:2). Not merely "the Way of salvation," but "the Way"—the Way that life works. Sometimes in presenting the gospel we emphasize that blessed word "whoever" in John 3:16, and rightly so. It points to the unlimited offer of redemption. But there is another "whoever" in Matthew 7:24 (see above), which points to an unlimited fact: If you build on my words, said Jesus, your house will stand up under life; if you don't, it will go down in a crash. There are no exceptions.

O Christ, how can I thank You enough that amid my stumblings I happened onto this Way! It fills me with constant surprise. Now I go forward. Amen.

HOW TO SELF-DESTRUCT

Whoever of you loves life and desires to see many good days, keep your tongue from evil and your lips from speaking lies. Turn from evil and do good; seek peace and pursue it. The eyes of the LORD are on the righteous and his ears are attentive to their cry; the face of the LORD is against those who do evil, to cut off the memory of them from the earth. (Psalm 34:12–16)

Evil entangles every situation, for evil is against the nature of reality. To try to straighten out a situation by using an evil is only to entangle it more. Therefore, evil is not only evil; it is stupid.

Somebody mentioned that the English word *evil* is the word *live* spelled backward. Evil is putting the will to live in reverse; it is life turning against itself. Evil is the way our nature is *not* made to work. In evil, life desires to gain freedom, but gains only the freedom to destroy itself. It runs away—from salvation. It revolts—against life.

A group of students was allowed to take a slot machine apart to study its inner workings. They found that the machine had been so constructed as to yield up only one dollar in ten. The players might fuss and fume and call on Lady Luck, but in the end there would be just one result: a 10 percent return. Luck was not against the players—the machine was against them. So every morning the machine would be empty, and every night it would be full. The manufacturer had figured the law of averages scientifically and had built that knowledge into the machine.

Sinners turn out to be a problem to themselves and others. God has us hooked—we cannot revolt against Him without revolting against ourselves. The attempt to disprove this statement has filled the world with human wreckage.

My Father, I understand that the penalties attached to evil are not signs of Your wrath but of Your love—Your redeeming love. I desire to work with that love, not against it. Amen.

JESUS, THE STANDARD NOTE

[Jesus]: *"The Son of man has come eating and drinking, and men say, 'Here is a glutton and a drunkard, a friend of taxgatherers and sinners!' Nevertheless, Wisdom is vindicated by all that she does." (Matt. 11:19 MOFFATT)*

If sin is not only bad but also foolish, the opposite is true: Goodness is not only good but also wise. That is the reason Jesus identified Himself with wisdom. He had just been talking about Himself, specifically His habit of associating with imperfect people. Despite the criticism, He asserted that wisdom was on His side. In fact, He went so far as to generalize to "all" His actions. He was hitting right notes more than just here and there; He never *missed* the right note.

Paul takes up the same theme when he says: "We preach Christ crucified… Christ the power of God and the wisdom of God" (1 Cor. 1:23–24). Note that he connects the two—power and wisdom. The sum total of reality is behind wisdom; the whole moral universe backs it. Sooner or later, wisdom is bound to win. The stars in their courses work on behalf of good. Goodness is wisdom, and goodness is power.

At the beginning of every symphonic performance, the concertmaster stands and plays the standard note to which the rest of the orchestra is to tune their instruments. Anything that departs from that pitch is discord, and hence torture to the ear. This standard note is not arbitrary; it is inherent. In Jesus, the standard note of human living is struck. Everything that tunes to that note catches the music of the spheres; everything that departs from it is discord and torture. God does not inflict any torture. The variance itself produces the torture. It is inherent.

O Christ, the Standard Note of all human living, forgive me for trying to play by my own pitch. From this hour, I resolve to tune my life fully and wholly to You. Amen.

WHAT DOES IT MEAN TO BE "NORMAL"?

[Christ] is before all things, and in him all things hold together. (Col. 1:17)

One man cleverly said of himself, "The trouble with me is that I am in harmony with chaos." Such a comment actually befits *everything* not in harmony with Christ. The choice is literally this: Christ or chaos.

Christ is the Standard Note of life, the Norm—to depart from Him is to be *abnormal*, hence frustrated. To be "normal" is to be Christian. I will always remember a man who, at the close of an address, blurted out enthusiastically, "Well, we can't have too much of Christianity." Is there literally anything else in life of which we cannot have too much? Nothing!

New York psychologist and author David Seabury says: "Disease is a loss of balance in part or in all of the organism. It may begin in the spirit and end in bodily disintegration. [Or] it may start from physical causes and react upon the psyche. But always it is a loss of balance in one's basic being. Too little or too much emotion records itself at once on the endocrine system. Neither inhibition nor wild release of feeling tends to health…. Too much or too little food, exercise, sleep, indeed too much or too little of anything…destroys health. Only by achieving a psychical and physical equilibrium on and between each plane of life is a [person's] vigor maintained" (*How Jesus Heals Our Minds Today*, p. 310).

We can have too much of everything except one thing—Christ, for He is equilibrium; He is the Norm.

O Christ, now at long last I have something that needs no restraint. I cannot be too like You, have too much of Your Spirit. Let me drink deeply of Your mind and Your way. Amen.

AFRAID OF SANITY!

[Paul speaking at his trial]: *"I have had God's help to this very day, and so I stand here and testify to small and great alike...."*

At this point Festus interrupted Paul's defense. "You are out of your mind, Paul!" he shouted. "Your great learning is driving you insane."

"I am not insane, most excellent Festus," Paul replied. "What I am saying is true and reasonable." (Acts 26:22, 24–25)

The new birth comes through surrender and abandonment of this false world of evil in order to accept the true world of good. We become realigned to God's original purpose.

Humanity, unfortunately, has become so naturalized in evil that it thinks the Christian way is the unnatural way. When the people of Gadara came and saw the demoniac set free of evil spirits, they "asked Jesus to leave them, because they were overcome with fear" (Luke 8:37). Afraid of what? They were afraid of sanity! We have become so accustomed to our insane ways of life that we are afraid of the real sanity of the Christian way.

A man told me he had ridden a bicycle with crooked handlebars for so long that, when someone straightened them, he fell off. He had become naturalized in crookedness! To people who are naturalized in this world's crooked and impossible order, the realism of Jesus seems idealistic. In fact, His realism is simply too far ahead of us.

Evil is the great illusion—that you can live against the design of the universe and get away with it. In 2 Peter 2:19 we read about false teachers who "promise them freedom, when they themselves are slaves of depravity." They are given over to something that is under the doom of decay.

Meanwhile, the Christian way is life under the bloom of development. Hence, the Christian way is the natural way. It is the nature God stamped into us at creation.

O Christ, help me not to be afraid of Your splendid sanity. Help me become naturalized in the homeland of my soul—the kingdom of God. Amen.

THE HOMELAND OF THE SOUL

You, however, are controlled not by the sinful nature but by the Spirit, if the Spirit of God lives in you…. If Christ is in you, your body is dead because of sin, yet your spirit is alive because of righteousness. (Rom. 8:9–10)

In our prayer yesterday, we spoke of "the homeland of my soul—the kingdom of God." Is that true? Is the kingdom of God the soul's native air? When we find it, do we find ourselves? A recent letter from a brilliant but disrupted person said, "I am easy to please, but difficult to satisfy." Why would this be so? Is it because the soul knows its homeland and will not be put off with substitutes?

When Jesus said, "The kingdom of God is within you" (Luke 17:21), He voiced one of the most important things ever uttered. The seeds of a new humanity are in that statement. It has seldom been taken seriously by orthodox Christianity; only the cults have taken it up. It must now be reclaimed for the mainstream and become potent there.

I know the fear that has kept that verse from becoming current: If the kingdom of God is within us, in everybody—even the unchanged (for this verse was spoken to Pharisees who were unconverted)—then (so the argument goes) the necessity of a new birth is gone. A merely optimistic view of human nature replaces the tragic view that we are sinful and needing redemption. Therefore, salvation comes by insight, instead of by repentance and faith.

I appreciate that fear, but do not share it. If the kingdom of God is within us, written into the constitution of our beings, then sin is not less tragic, but more so. For then we sin not only against a God far off, but also against a God who is in our inner kingdom. This is intimate rejection, intimate slaying. We sin not only against God; we sin also against ourselves.

Sin, therefore, is not the nature of our being; it is against nature—*our* nature—as well as the God who made it.

O God, I see that if I sin against the kingdom within, I disrupt myself, my possibilities, my all. And I sin against You, the King. Forgive me. Amen.

ON THE DOORSTEP

[Jesus to his outbound disciples]: *"When you enter a town and are welcomed… heal the sick who are there and tell them, 'The kingdom of God is near you.'"* (Luke 10:8–9)

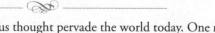

Two great streams of religious thought pervade the world today. One maintains: "Everything is within you; all you need is to awaken your latent powers; you have the spark of the divine within you—kindle it." Or in the extreme form, as in the Vedanta in India, "You not only have the divine within you; you *are* divine, you are God—realize it."

The other stream maintains: "You are a sinful creature; there is nothing good within you; you need the invading grace of God from outside to awaken you, to redeem you."

Do we have to vote with our lives on one side or the other? No. Each viewpoint has a truth, but it is only a half-truth—the truth is beyond each of them. That truth is in the kingdom of God. The kingdom fulfills the truth of *immanence*—"The kingdom of God is within you" (Luke 17:21). It fulfills the truth of *transcendence*—"The kingdom of God is near" (Mark 1:15). The kingdom is both pervasive and invasive; it is within us and beyond us.

We humans are sinful in that we sin not only against the God who made us but also against the kingdom written into the texture of our being. This view makes sin worse than if we viewed ourselves as naturally sinful. For if that were the case, then is sin so bad if it is natural? Why should I be punished for doing what is natural, for fulfilling my own nature? But if sin is not only sinful *but also unnatural,* then sin is doubly bad—it is revolt against God and myself.

Sin is not natural; it is an attempt to live against my real nature. Sin is anti-life.

O God, You have not formed us in our inmost being and then abandoned us, turning us over to forces too strong for us. You are protesting our self-ruin at every step. Help us not to consent to our own ruin. In Jesus' name, Amen.

MORAL TENSION

The one who is in you is greater than the one who is in the world. (1 John 4:4)

Count yourselves dead to sin but alive to God in Christ Jesus. (Rom. 6:11)

If the kingdom of God is within us, then one might ask why anyone needs tensions between the kingdom and ourselves that lead to crisis and repentance and the new birth? Doesn't this kingdom-within-you emphasis flatten out those tensions, doing away with the crisis?

On the contrary, this kingdom-within-you emphasis heightens those tensions and leads more definitely to crisis, for now we see that we are in revolt against God and ourselves. When I speak to an audience, I find I obtain twice the response for repentance and conversion from this kind of appeal, compared to saying that humans are naturally sinful and cannot do a thing about it unless God sovereignly rescues them. The emphasis that we are naturally sinful not only flattens out tensions—it flattens out the self. For if we are naturally sinful, why fight against nature? It will be a losing battle anyway. That paralyzes hope and, consequently, the will.

Often in India I have heard a man excuse his sin by saying, "I am a man." Well, if he is a man, then that is one of the most potent reasons for his *not* sinning. For when a man sins, he feels less than a man, out of harmony with himself, with God, with his fellow man—even Nature drapes herself in mourning. But when a man does right, he feels his personality heightened; he is at home in the universe; he is universalized; he walks the earth as a conqueror.

Goodness is native to us, and sin is unnatural, an aberration, a deflection, a defeat, a degradation. It may be customary, but it is not natural—no more than a cancer is natural, or sand in the eye.

O God, I revolt against my sin, repudiate it, break with it forever. I accept my native land—Yourself and Your kingdom. Here I am at home, free and at my best. I thank You. Amen.

WHAT ABOUT "ORIGINAL SIN"?

They have acted corruptly toward him; to their shame they are no longer his children, but a warped and crooked generation. Is this the way you repay the LORD, O foolish and unwise people? Is he not your Father, your Creator, who made you and formed you? (Deut. 32:5–6)

If the kingdom of God is within us, then what about "original sin"? Is it all a mistake? Should we be talking about "original goodness" instead? Yes, for our origin is in God, and therefore goodness is original, for God is good. He has stamped His ways within us.

But there is a truth in original sin, which we might call genetically acquired sin. The human race has sinned generation after generation and has passed on to posterity unnatural bents toward evil. The natural urges—self, sexuality, and the group—have been twisted by unnatural use. The self has become an end in itself instead of being a means to the ends of the kingdom of God. Sexuality has also become an end in itself instead of being dedicated to the ends for which it was intended. The social instinct has become focused on lesser entities such as class, race, or nation instead of on the kingdom of God. All of these have become perverted and therefore need to be *con*verted—to the ends for which they were originally intended.

If we are made in the image of God, then sin is not natural; it is acquired. It is an attempt to live against nature, against life—and to escape the consequences. We recognize this fact when we say someone is "crooked," implying that they have departed from goodness, from the straight. But if sin were natural, then it is goodness that would be the unnatural crookedness.

Impurity is unnatural; purity is natural. The sum total of reality is behind the pure person, because that person is aligned to the nature of things. Impurity is lined up against the nature of things; hence, the eyes are shifty, the face grows dull, and the personality sags.

O God, You are teaching me Your ways. I am beginning to be vocal with Your purposes and vibrant with Your vitality. Make me a vehicle of Your victory. Amen.

THE KINGDOM OF GOD IS THE NORM

[May you give] thanks to the Father, who has qualified you to share in the inheritance of the saints in the kingdom of light. For he has rescued us from the dominion of darkness and brought us into the kingdom of the Son he loves, in whom we have redemption, the forgiveness of sins. (Col. 1:12–14)

When we say the kingdom of God is within us, are we talking theological fiction or teleological fact? In other words, are we imposing our views on nature, or are those views written within the purposes of nature?

More than one psychologist, studying the human personality in the cold white light of science, has found there is a norm written within us, and that to depart from that norm is to end in disruption and self-frustration. While some of them spell that "norm" with a small "n," we who believe say the kingdom of God within us is that Norm. To depart from it is to lose ourselves, to frustrate ourselves.

Departure from the Norm is to be *abnormal*, hence unhealthy, frustrated, a little "off" (sometimes very much "off"). Such people are not merely bad, but foolish, trying to live against the Norm, which is impossible. They are bound to end in only one way—in self-defeat and self-frustration. These are inescapable, for the nature of things works that way. Sin and its punishment are one and the same thing, for sin is *amartia* in Greek—"missing the mark," departing from the Norm.

A cancer is abnormal tissue. One does not have to impose punishment on a cancer, because being a cancer is its own punishment—it is bound by its very nature to destroy itself as well as nearby tissue. The end is death.

The apostle Paul declared, "The wages of sin is death" (Rom. 6:23). The wages, the natural outcome, the payoff is bound to be so, for the sin itself is a departure from Normal.

O my Father God, I stand in awe of Your goodness. I see Your footprints everywhere. They are within me. I align myself with Your standard, Your definition of normality. Amen.

IS THE KINGDOM OF GOD "NATURAL"?

You were once darkness, but now you are light in the Lord. Live as children of light (for the fruit of the light consists in all goodness, righteousness and truth) and find out what pleases the Lord. (Eph. 5:8–10)

If the kingdom of God is our real nature, then what about Paul's statement that "The natural man does not receive the things of the Spirit of God"? (1 Cor. 2:14 NKJV). Moffatt recaptures the original in his translation: "The unspiritual man rejects these truths of the Spirit of God." The context shows that Paul's discussion is not between the natural and the unnatural, but between the "spiritual" (vv. 13, 15) and the unspiritual. Spiritual persons are controlled by the kingdom of God; hence, they are truly natural. Unspiritual persons are living against that internal kingdom; hence, they are unnatural.

Again, we ask, "What might psychology say?" Let Dr. Henry C. Link, an eminent psychologist, answer: "I define personality as the extent to which the individual has developed habits and skills which interest and serve other people…. [Personality's] essence is self-sacrifice, not self-gratification. Indeed, the pursuit of personality just to win friends and position is quite likely to result in self-consciousness" (*The Rediscovery of Man*, pp. 60-61).

Note the accent on self-losing service to others—and this with unmixed motives. Is that not the picture of a Christian? Dr. Link says this is "personality." When you discover the Christian way, you discover your own way as a person. To adopt the Christian way is to have your personality heightened, for it is unified, adjusted to the nature of reality, and therefore no longer under the law of self-frustration, but of self-fulfillment.

On the Day of Pentecost, "the Spirit enabled them to express themselves" (Acts 2:4 MOFFATT). True self-expression began when they were filled with the Spirit.

O God, I have been afraid to surrender to Your will, lest my own will be lost. How foolish I have been. I now see that to find Your purposes is to find my own person. I want to express myself in You! Amen.

THE KINGDOM IS OUR CAUSE

Then the King will say to those on his right, "Come, you who are blessed by my Father; take your inheritance, the kingdom prepared for you since the creation of the world." (Matt. 25:34)

We must pursue this thought of the kingdom of God within us until it becomes not an argument, but an axiom—something we no longer hold, but something that holds us.

Someone asked the renowned Prof. W. H. Kilpatrick of Teachers College (Columbia University) to name the greatest discovery of modern education. He replied: "He that saveth his life shall lose it, and he that loseth his life for some great cause shall find it again." No, Professor Kilpatrick, that was not a discovery of modern education—that was a rediscovery, for Jesus used that language five times, except He said "the kingdom" instead of "cause." The kingdom of God is our paramount cause.

Modern education, in its experiments with human nature, comes to the conclusion that if we center ourselves on ourselves, our self will go to pieces; only as we lose ourselves in some greater cause do we find our selves coming back integrated and heightened. That is a law of human living as deeply imbedded in the universe as the force of gravity.

A Roman Catholic businessman said to me at the close of a service club address: "You didn't preach to us; you just told us things." He saw that I was lifting up laws of the moral and spiritual world written into the constitution of things, and that they are self-authenticating. One doesn't have to argue them, just as in geometry you don't have to argue the axiom "Things equal to the same thing are equal to each other." You simply state it, and it argues itself.

The people who heard Jesus "were amazed at his teaching, because his message had authority" (Luke 4:32). It was the authority of the facts.

O God, we have been feverishly trying to support Your universe with our puny arguments. Forgive us and help us to trust implicitly in Your self-authenticating truth. In Jesus' name, Amen.

THE KINGDOM AND BUSINESS

An expert in the law tested him with this question: "Teacher, which is the greatest commandment in the Law?" Jesus replied: "'Love the Lord your God with all your heart and with all your soul and with all your mind.' This is the first and greatest commandment. And the second is like it: 'Love your neighbor as yourself.' All the Law and the Prophets hang on these two commandments."
(Matt. 22:35–40)

Even the world of business is stumbling upon the laws of the kingdom in its search for a workable way forward. I say "stumbling upon," because chance discoveries are being made. When someone asked Daniel Willard, the great head of the Baltimore and Ohio Railway, what was the outstanding qualification for a successful executive, he replied: "The ability and the willingness to put yourself in the other man's place."

But that is distinctly Christian—it is loving your neighbor as you love yourself, doing unto others as you would have others do, projecting yourself in understanding sympathy, and making the other person's difficulties and troubles your own. This great executive came to that conviction not through dogmatic assertion from a pulpit, but through trial and error. Life approved of this attitude and would approve of no other.

In a business journal I saw a statement in bold type: "More and more companies are finding it pays to treat [visitors] with friendly courtesy." Why? Because good will is written into the constitution of things; ill will is sand in the machinery. Life will work with good will, but not with ill will. You may try with infinite cleverness to make your universe hold together by ill will, but sooner or later it will topple.

"*Anima naturalis Christiana,*" said Tertullian at the end of the second century—"the soul is naturally Christian."

O God, You and my soul have been estranged, but they are not strangers; we have been separated, but are not separate. You are my life, my breath, my being, my all. I thank You. Amen.

"WITHIN" OR "AMONG"?

Being asked by the Pharisees when the kingdom of God will come, He answered them, "The kingdom of God is not coming with something observable; no one will say, 'Look here!' or 'There!' For you see, the kingdom of God is among you."
(Luke 17:21 HCSB)

What about translations such as the one above? Is the kingdom of God *within* us, as I have been emphasizing, or *among* us?

Both are so profoundly true that Jesus may have said either or both. We have seen that the kingdom of God is written into our physical, mental, and spiritual makeup, so that we have a Christian brain, a Christian nervous system, a Christian stomach, Christian glands, and so forth. St. Francis of Assisi said he sympathized with wicked people because they could not express the suppressed holiness within them.

But the kingdom of God is just as surely *among* us. There is a way to get along with other people, and it is God's way. Unless our relationships with one another proceed along the lines of certain inherent laws, they break down. You and I do not make or pass those laws —we only discover them; if we break them, we break ourselves and the relationship. You may try with infinite patience and skill to build on something other than God's way, but in the end you won't get along with yourself or others.

For instance, you need not love your neighbor as you love yourself—but if you don't, you transform him into a problem and a pain. Sociology does not construct the laws of human relationships—it discovers them. They are a given, written into our society by a pen other than our own.

Gracious Father, You have written the family spirit into us; when we break those laws, we turn the human family into a feud. Forgive us and help us to catch Your mind in our relationship to other minds, Your Spirit in relation to other spirits. In Jesus' name, Amen.

FIVE WAYS TO RELATE

Do not be deceived, God is not mocked; for whatever a man sows, that he will also reap. For he who sows to his flesh will of the flesh reap corruption, but he who sows to the Spirit will of the Spirit reap everlasting life. (Gal. 6:7–8 NKJV)

Note the ways people try to get along with one another: (1) Some try to dominate others; (2) some live aloof from others; (3) some are indifferent to others; (4) some work with others; (5) some work with and for others.

Which of these attitudes will life approve?

Suppose you choose the first and try to dominate others in one way or another. What happens? Relationships break down and get snarled up. A dictator tries to conquer the world and finds initial success; then he inevitably has to face the world turning against him, and goes down. Like produces like.

"Do not be deceived" by initial successes in domination, for "God is not mocked"—the nature of reality is against you, and in the end it will break you. Our text continues: "He who sows to his flesh," the flesh of domination, "will of the flesh reap corruption"—the situation (and you) will be corrupted, will deteriorate, go to pieces. The nature of reality foredooms the collapse.

But "he who sows to the Spirit," aligning with eternal realities, "will of the Spirit reap everlasting life." The sum total of reality will back you; you will have the power of survival, for you are living with and not against the grain of the universe. You reap an everlasting way to live.

Assistant Secretary of State A. A. Berle, Jr., says, "No group of human beings, however implemented, has been able to challenge the great Design." This Design is none other than the kingdom of God.

O Designer of the great kingdom, our hearts are set to fit into it, to mold our lives by it, to be fully surrendered to its purposes—and so to live abundantly. Amen.

MUTUAL ASSISTANCE IN THE KINGDOM

If someone says, "I love God," but hates a Christian brother or sister, that person is a liar; for if we don't love people we can see, how can we love God, whom we cannot see? (1 John 4:20†)

The eye cannot say to the hand, "I don't need you!" And the head cannot say to the feet, "I don't need you!".… God has combined the members…so that there should be no division in the body, but that its parts should have equal concern for each other. (1 Cor. 12:21, 24–25)

Most of us remember from early childhood what happens on the playground seesaw if one's playmate decides to jump off while at the low end. Suddenly the fun is ruined—if not the whole friendship.

We cannot violate the law of love any more than we can violate the law of gravity and not get hurt. This is part of what the kingdom of God has stamped into our relationships. Suppose our human bodies should violate the law of mutual assistance—the stomach disagreeing with the heart and refusing to give it nourishment; the heart retaliating and refusing to give the stomach any blood; the feet refusing to cooperate with each other, one going in one direction and the other in the opposite; the arteries withholding pure blood and the veins holding up the elimination of impurities. If the organs of the body became selfish and competitive, the whole system would collapse.

This law of mutual assistance is not something imposed on the body as an outside decree; it is written into the very constitution of its being. Since no one has imposed the law, no one imposes the penalties—they are inherent and self-acting. Break the law of mutual assistance, and the disastrous results come automatically.

Our Father God, we approach You as foolish children who sometimes try to live against Your ways and end only in hurting ourselves. Forgive us. And give us the plain sense to see that Your laws are Your love—and Your laws are our life. In Jesus' name, Amen.

RETREATING FROM PEOPLE

God sets the solitary in families; He brings out those who are bound into prosperity; But the rebellious dwell in a dry land. (Psalm 68:6 NKJV)

Having considered the first of five ways people relate—domination—we turn now to the second: *Some live aloof from others.* This is the opposite swing of the pendulum.

What happens to those who try this attitude? Can they cut human relationships, retreat into their own shell, without affecting their own being? Not at all. Such people deteriorate. If they cannot have a world of real human relationships, they build up a world of false relationships. They fill their mind with fantasies and daydreaming of superior personal grandeur. Or they look on themselves as inferior, unworthy to be connected to others. In either case, recessive individuals hurt their own mental and moral nature. Human beings are made inherently for relationships with others, and any attempt to live apart brings inherent penalties.

You break the law of love just as much by receding from people as you do by trying to dominate them. You can no more cut yourself off from people and live fully than a brain can cut off relationships with the heart and live. All life is bound up in a bundle, and one person cannot be separate without disruption. That is why a lonely recluse is off balance. They are trying to live against the kingdom of God, which is a kingdom of loving relationships.

Another false strategy is to recede from people in order to protect oneself from temptation. I find more temptations when I am alone than when I am with people. By their expectancy, people help us to be at our best.

If receding from people will not work, neither will the third attitude of *being indifferent to them.* Both methods end in self-frustration and a breakdown of relationships.

Gracious Father, You have set us within Your family. Teach us to enter into loving relationships with one another and to help and be helped in the interplay of life. You meet us in others; help us to see You in them. Amen.

THE BEST WAY FORWARD

Dear friend, you are being faithful to God when you care for the traveling teachers who pass through, even though they are strangers to you. They have told the church here of your loving friendship. Please continue providing for such teachers in a manner that pleases God. For they are traveling for the Lord, and they accept nothing from people who are not believers. So we ourselves should support them so that we can be their partners as they teach the truth. (3 John 5–8 †)

The fourth attitude we can take toward others is *to work with them.* This sounds like a great advance over the other positions, and yet, even this turns out to be inadequate. For we may work with others and yet reserve our inner life. So sensitive are these kingdom laws that an outer conformity to brotherhood will not do. If the inner self is withheld, relationships break down.

There is only one attitude toward others that will succeed: *Work with AND FOR others.* There must be positive, outgoing goodwill, a desire to help the other person as you would be helped. In the world of business, if labor and management work together only in a suspicious mood, fulfilling the letter of contracts, there will be minimal productivity—and open hostility at the first provocation. Only when the relationship is built on a generous and just basis will there be a new spirit—and a new increase in total output.

Just generosity is literally the best policy. It obeys the kingdom law to love one's neighbor as oneself. This law is written into the constitution of our relationships, and hence produces stability. Injustice and inequality produce instability, for they work against the kingdom. When John Hay, secretary to Abraham Lincoln and then later an ambassador as well as secretary of state, declared that the only way for nations to get along is to apply the Golden Rule, he was expressing a law that is inescapable.

God, our Father, forgive us that we have tried to live together on anti-kingdom principles. Open our eyes that we may see—and live. Amen.

CLOSE AT HAND

After John was put in prison, Jesus went into Galilee, proclaiming the good news of God. "The time has come," he said. "The kingdom of God is near. Repent and believe the good news!" (Mark 1:14–15)

We have seen that the kingdom of God is *within* us, also that the kingdom of God is *among* us; we now pass on to the further step that the kingdom of God is at our doors. It is prepared to invade us from without.

This kingdom is within history and beyond history; it is within time, it is beyond time—eternal; it is within us and yet stands at our doors awaiting our consent for a full invasion. The school of thought that emphasizes the kingdom is within us exclusively is based on a half-truth. On the other hand, the school of thought that insists the kingdom is found only in a divine invasion from the outside is also based on a half-truth. The kingdom is both. If you insist only on the-kingdom-within emphasis, you end in a vague mysticism that often flattens out into humanistic techniques for awakening your latent powers. But if you insist only on the-kingdom-from-without, you end up making sin natural, rendering ourselves helpless, becoming pessimistic about human nature, and making God more or less absentee.

So how do we see the nature of this kingdom—by looking at the kingdom within ourselves? Yes, but not supremely. Only as we look at the historical Christ do we see the full meaning of the kingdom. Only there do we really see the new order.

O Christ, we turn to You to see the meaning of the kingdom of God, for we must not get this wrong—if we do, all of life goes wrong with it. With our gaze on You we can never go astray. We thank You. Amen.

HOW GOD RULES

Philip said, "Lord, show us the Father and that will be enough for us."

Jesus answered: "Don't you know me, Philip, even after I have been among you such a long time? Anyone who has seen me has seen the Father. How can you say, 'Show us the Father'? Don't you believe that I am in the Father, and that the Father is in me? The words I say to you are not just my own. Rather, it is the Father, living in me, who is doing his work." (John 14:8–10)

The nature of the Divine Invasion is seen in Christ. He is the personal approach from the Unseen. In Him the nature of reality is uncovered. In Him we see into the nature of God and also into the nature of God's reign. God redeems in terms of Christ. He also rules in terms of Christ.

In Christ the kingdom is given content and character. If the kingdom were only in us and only among us, then we couldn't be sure of its character, for ours would blur the picture. But in Christ the character of the kingdom is determined. If God is Christ universalized, so the kingdom is the attitude of Christ reigning.

This is important, for it means we cannot bring in the kingdom by any methods other than Christlike methods. Otherwise, when we thought we had brought it in, it wouldn't be the kingdom; it would be something else. The ways we had used in our attempt to bring in the kingdom would spoil the very goal. The means would spoil the ends.

In Christ the kingdom is given not only a character content but also a personal content. In Him the kingdom is no longer merely an impersonal order. When I give myself to the kingdom, I give myself to the person who embodies that kingdom. In Him the kingdom looks out at me with tender eyes, loves me with warm love, and touches me with strong, redemptive hands. Christ is the kingdom personalized.

Christ, in You I see into the heart and meaning of God's kingdom. To such a kingdom I can surrender with complete abandon. I do. Amen.

A HOMECOMING FOR THE SOUL

Since we have been justified through faith, we have peace with God through our Lord Jesus Christ, through whom we have gained access by faith into this grace in which we now stand. And we rejoice in the hope of the glory of God. (Rom. 5:1–2)

The kingdom of God entails not just one awakening, but two.

(1) We must awaken to the kingdom within us, discovering the latent powers hidden in the recesses of our beings, becoming alive to our possibilities, realizing our divine origin and destiny.

(2) We must awaken to the kingdom outside of us—the invading kingdom. This kind of kingdom precipitates crisis. We sense a tension between this kingdom and what we are. For if it is true that the kingdom is written into the constitution of our beings, it is also true that we have tried to write something else there—incompatible ways, ways of sin. These ways set up a conflict between themselves and the kingdom. Inner conflict ensues. The external kingdom heightens that tension and brings it to crisis.

That crisis demands that we repent, that we submit, that we be changed, that we be converted, that we let this outside kingdom invade us with its healing, its reconciliation, its life. When we fling open the doors of our being, we are not letting in something strange or alien. We are letting in the very Fact for which we are made. The kingdom inside us rises to meet the outside kingdom, and together they cast out the unnatural kingdom of sin and evil.

The coming of this invading kingdom has the feel of a homecoming. We sense that estrangement is over, that reconciliation has taken place, that the homeland of the soul has been found. The inside kingdom and the outside kingdom are counterparts, are one. So we feel a deep sense of unity and universal being.

O Christ, when I welcome You, I welcome my long-estranged self; the prodigal comes home. Now I am at rest, at peace, at adjustment, at home. I thank You. Amen.

THE KINGDOM PERVADES—AND INVADES

God so loved the world that he gave his one and only Son, that whoever believes in him shall not perish but have eternal life. For God did not send his Son into the world to condemn the world, but to save the world through him. (John 3:16–17)

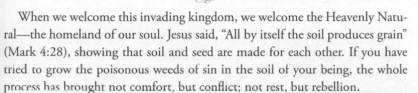

When we welcome this invading kingdom, we welcome the Heavenly Natural—the homeland of our soul. Jesus said, "All by itself the soil produces grain" (Mark 4:28), showing that soil and seed are made for each other. If you have tried to grow the poisonous weeds of sin in the soil of your being, the whole process has brought not comfort, but conflict; not rest, but rebellion.

When a child passes from the womb to the outer world, it finds a world for which it has been made—air for its lungs, light for its eyes, food for its stomach, love for its affectional nature, and a growth for its latent possibilities. The child and the world are made for each other. So you and I are made for the kingdom.

But Christianity is not merely awakening the internal kingdom; it is an invasion of the external kingdom as well. If it were only the first, we would grasp the nature of the kingdom by looking inside. But we have so overlaid that kingdom with unnatural ways of life that the interpretation is blurred. Only in the face of Christ do we see the true nature of the kingdom.

In fact, we see more than that; we see in Christ what it costs God to get to us in spite of our sin. The kingdom is at our doors only because Christ brought it down to us through an incarnation, a cross, a resurrection, down to the very threshold of our being, there to await our consent for entrance. Something crucial, something decisive had to happen in history before the kingdom could stand at our doors. The cross is therefore the pivot upon which history turns.

Gracious Christ, You have come to me at supreme cost. I want to respond to You with all I can pay. For Your kingdom knocks with nail-pierced hands. Help me to open the door with hands that are willing to be pierced. Amen.

CHOICE, CRISIS, CONVERSION

[Jesus]: *"He who is not with me is against me, and he who does not gather with me, scatters." (Luke 11:23)*

The wages of sin is death, but the gift of God is eternal life in Christ Jesus our Lord. (Rom. 6:23)

To realize, to grasp the kingdom of God is no afternoon tea affair. It cost God, and it will cost us. Sir Arnold Lunn satirizes current surface views of the gospel in these words: "God so loved the world that he inspired a certain Jew that there was a great deal to be said for loving your neighbor."

No. God gave up his only begotten Son to keep us from *perishing*. Those who do not receive this kingdom do perish literally, for their life forces break down through contradiction and strife. But when you let in this kingdom, you align yourself with the eternal realities of Being; hence you live, now and everlastingly.

The coming of that kingdom means crisis, choice, conversion. The schools of thought that tell you the-kingdom-within means you only have to evolve yourself are missing the deep tragic note of the faith. Paul did not say, "What a progressive creature I am! Who shall help me evolve myself?" But he did say, "What a wretched man I am! Who will rescue me from this body of death?" (Rom. 7:24) or, literally, "this dead body." The figure is that of a live man with a dead body chained to him, carrying around a decaying corpse as punishment. That figure is accurate: a sinner is a person with the kingdom of God written inside, carrying around a decaying corpse of sin. Sin is anti-kingdom, therefore anti-life and doomed to decay; the one who harbors it "perishes." That dead body of sin is a useless, infecting encumbrance.

O Christ, I gladly consent to let go of this sin, whose embrace is death. Forgive me if I hesitate, but I have lived with death so long that I think it is life. Still, I do consent, for I see, I see. Amen.

TWO CRISES

Then he said to the crowd, "If any of you wants to be my follower, you must turn from your selfish ways, take up your cross daily, and follow me. If you try to hang on to your life, you will lose it. But if you give up your life for my sake, you will save it." (Luke 9:23-24†)

The Divine Invasion precipitates crises within, making us either resist or surrender. Sometimes we resist. A brilliant doctor, whose inner life was a mass of conflicts, returned to me an inscribed New Testament with this written on the wrapper: "I hate Him, and I hate you." I had scarcely received this outburst when another letter came from the doctor, saying: "Where is God, and where are you?" Here was a soul resisting God, and yet reaching out for Him; telling Him to go, and yet entreating Him to stay! Rebelling, repelling—relenting, repenting: these are the alternate beats of the heart that feels the divine pressure.

When consent is given, the Divine Invasion usually takes place in two great crises: (1) the crisis of conversion; (2) the crisis of a deeper cleansing. The first brings release from festering sins and marks the introduction of a new life; it is a glorious release, but not a full release. The roots of the disease are still there.

I once had acute appendicitis and was operated on. When I came to consciousness, the doctor said, "I have drained the inflamed appendix, but I couldn't take it out, for there were too many adhesions. You'll have to have them all taken out later." After that I was better, but I wasn't well. Six months later I got rid of both the appendix and the adhesions.

Sin throws its adhesions around the organs of life. Salvation, in these two great crises, drains the poison, loosens the adhesions, and restores us to truly natural health.

Tender Invader of my soul, I yield my stricken life to Your healing. Drain every drop of poison from my being, and root out the adhering results of that poison. I want not only to be better; I want to be well. In Jesus' name, Amen.

THE KINGDOM OF GOD IS OUR OWN

To the Jews who had believed him, Jesus said, "If you hold to my teaching, you are really my disciples. Then you will know the truth, and the truth will set you free." (John 8:31–32)

If anyone harbors sin, they are caught between two fires: the kingdom of God within, and the kingdom of God at the door. They have to live out their life under a double protest: the protest of what they really are (in contrast to the false world they have built up), and the protest of what they might be. One protest is from the internal kingdom, the other from the external kingdom.

Sin is therefore caught in a pincer movement. This intrusion called *evil* must surrender and succumb if the person is to live. When it truly surrenders, then the internal kingdom and the external kingdom coalesce. The person is possessed by an inner unity. They are now truly natural, hence rhythmical and harmonious.

The kingdom is our own—it is written into the constitution of our very being; it is our real nature. But the kingdom is also given to us when we submit to it and let it possess us. The paradox is this: When we find this invading kingdom, we find ourselves. I do not argue; I only testify that when I most belong to the kingdom, I most belong to myself. When I try to live in un-kingdom ways, I lose both the kingdom and myself.

Here, then, in the kingdom I find my perfect freedom. Think of the paradox of that statement: A kingdom where you are ruled is a place where you are perfectly free! The freedom of the railroad engine is the confining rails; the freedom of electricity is the confining wires—for engine and rails are made for each other; electricity and wire are made for each other. So it is with the kingdom and me.

My God, I see everything clearly now; I take the yoke of the kingdom, and I find it easy. I take Your burden, and I find it light. I take You—and find myself. I thank You. Amen.

NATURALIZED IN THE UNNATURAL

[The prodigal son] went and hired himself out to a citizen of that country, who sent him to his fields to feed pigs. He longed to fill his stomach with the pods that the pigs were eating, but no one gave him anything. (Luke 15:15–16)

Though the kingdom of God is written into our true nature, we have been so accustomed to false ways of life that we think *they* are our true nature. We hold to our unnaturalness, suspicious of God's true nature.

A woman who had lived all her life in the foul, heavy air of the New York slums said she got physically sick when she went into the country and breathed pure, fresh air. Her lungs had become so accustomed to unnatural pollution that natural freshness was unnatural! In a South American city a new market was built, clean and sanitary, with tiled floors and walls. But the stall operators in the dirty old market would not move in. One woman explained: "That market is so clean it makes me sick. It is just like a hospital."

That is the tragedy of our humanity. We see that our ways won't work, and yet we hesitate to take God's way. The great-hearted mayor of a city in India, who had cleaned up vast portions of slums and built lovely, neat cottages and apartments in their place, said to me: "Sometimes I walk around the remaining wretched sections of the city at night and say to myself, 'If the people would only let me, I could do anything for them.' But they are naturalized in their filth, and cling to it, though it kills them off like flies."

Christ must be doing that today! He sees us with our unworkable ways, running into dead ends, ending in frustration and futility, losing our means of living, and our lives themselves, and He says again: "Seek first the kingdom of God…and all these things shall be added to you" (Matt. 6:33 NKJV). But we are seeking other things first, and all these things are being subtracted from us.

Gracious Father, our life strategy is wrong, and things won't come out right. Help us to have enough plain sense to abandon our ways of futility for Your ways of fruitfulness. Help us to seek first the kingdom. In Jesus' name, Amen.

WHAT SHALL WE SEEK FIRST?

Since, then, you have been raised with Christ, set your hearts on things above where Christ is seated at the right hand of God. Set your minds on things above not on earthly things. (Col. 3:1–2)

The struggle in the world is over one question only: What shall we seek above all else? What shall ultimately command us? I do not think you can understand the world situation, with its terrible clashes, unless you look on it primarily as a religious question. Sifted to its final issue, the question at bottom is this: What shall we finally obey? Where shall we bend the knee?

Someone has said that mistakes in war tactics may be forgiven, but a mistake in strategy, the general plan of large-scale action, is inexcusable. You may be forgiven if you make detailed mistakes within a right plan of life, but no such detailed actions can atone for a wrong life strategy.

What are the answers being given to this question here in our time [the early 1940s]? The Japanese have their answer: "Seek first the Emperor; be loyal to him in complete obedience, and all these things shall be added unto you." The Chinese have their answer: "Seek first the Family, and all these things shall be added unto you." Governments might come and go in China, but the Family has always been the unit of allegiance. Hindu India has its answer: "Seek first the Caste, and all these things shall be added unto you." If only you obey caste *dharma,* or duty, you will get a better birth when the Wheel of Rebirth turns next. The Muslim has a reply: "Seek first the fatalistic will of Allah, and all these things shall be added unto you." The word *Islam* literally means "submission"—surrender to your fate as decreed by Allah. Buddhism says: "Seek first *nothing;* cut the root of desire, even desire for life, and Nirvana will be added unto you."

Gracious Father, Your children are in obvious confusion. We live at cross purposes in our central aims, and hence we are at cross-purposes with each other. Take us by the hand and help us to see things from Your standpoint. In Jesus name, Amen.

CONTINUING THE ROLL CALL

[Jesus]: *"If…God clothes the grass of the field, which is here today and tomorrow is thrown into the fire, will he not much more clothe you, O you of little faith? So do not worry, saying, 'What shall we eat?' or 'What shall we drink?' or 'What shall we wear?' For the pagans run after all these things, and your heavenly Father knows that you need them." (Matt. 6:30–32)*

We shall continue our roll call of life strategies. The modern Communist says: "Seek first Society, as expressed in the will of its proletarian dictator, and all these things shall be added unto you." Society and its interests are supreme; the individual counts for little.

The Fascist has his answer: "Seek first the State, and all these things shall be added unto you." The State is supreme. The Nazi is ready with his reply: "Seek first the Race—the superior Aryan Race—and all these things shall be added unto you."

Modern Capitalistic Society has its answer: "Seek first Money, and when you have that, all these things shall be added unto you." Many who inwardly hold this view would hesitate to put it in such bold terms, but they believe in money and act upon their belief. It may be added that a corollary to the aims of Modern Capitalistic Society is: "Seek first to be able to live without working; get to the place where others will work for you, and all these things shall added unto you."

Meanwhile, Modern Hedonism, the search for pleasure, says: "Seek first the Thrill, and all these things shall be added unto you."

The Christian turns to Christ for His reply: "Seek first the kingdom of God…and all these things shall be added to you" (Matt. 6:33 NKJV).

Which life strategy is right?

God, we have come to life's supreme choice. Don't let us fumble here, for if we do, everything will tumble to pieces. We approach this question with a prayer on our lips, for our wisdom fails us—we need Yours. Amen.

ETERNALLY RIGHT

Even if everyone else is a liar, God is true. As the Scriptures say about him, "You will be proved right in what you say, and you will win your case in court." (Rom. 3:4†, citing Psalm 51:4)

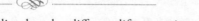

In the last two days we have listed twelve different life strategies—which is right?

Jesus had a reputation for being correct in everything; He was never misled by a subordinate issue, never once slipped to the marginal, the un-worthwhile. But was He wrong in telling us to seek first the kingdom of God? Did He miss the way here?

To ask the question is to answer it. His answer towers above all others. When we state it, it is self-verifying. When we really look at the ends of other life strategies, there is no choice—we must take this answer of Jesus, or brand ourselves as simple fools. If this answer of Jesus isn't the answer, then there is no answer.

I have often been puzzled about the words Jesus added: "Seek first the kingdom of God *and his righteousness.*" Why did he add this phrase? Is righteousness not included in the kingdom? Is it not a needless addition? Perhaps the answer is found if we put it, "and his rightness." This answer—the kingdom of God—is God's rightness. It is eternally right, and everything out of harmony with it is wrong, is crooked, is out of gear, is doomed to break itself. If that is not the correct interpretation of these words, it is a fact nevertheless. When you seek first the kingdom, you are right; the sum total of reality is behind you, working with you. But if you seek something else first, you are setting yourself against the sum total of reality; you are wrong.

The reason the world situation is going from snarl to snarl is that we are centrally and fundamentally wrong; we are seeking the wrong thing first.

O living Christ, Your answer is so right; everything within me says so. Now help me to give it the full consent of all my being. Amen.

FIRST THINGS FIRST

Let your gentleness be evident to all. The Lord is near. Do not be anxious about anything, but in everything, by prayer and petition, with thanksgiving, present your requests to God. And the peace of God, which transcends all understanding, will guard your hearts and your minds in Christ Jesus. (Phil. 4:5–7)

If we seek first the kingdom of God, what will be the product? Jesus said, "All these things will be added to you." Get the first thing straight, and everything down the line will come out right.

What did He mean by "all these things"? He had mentioned such simple things as food, drink, and clothing (Matt. 6:31). The kingdom of God is designed to supply us not merely with a heavenly world after this life, but also bodily sustenance in this life. In seeking first the kingdom of God, Jesus says, the material needs of human life will be guaranteed to you: "Your heavenly Father knows that you *need* them" (Matt. 6:32).

Note that you will get according to your *need*, not according to your *greed*. You have a right to as much of the material as will make you mentally, spiritually, and physically fit for the purposes of the kingdom of God.

You and I are constitutionally made in such a way that if we get less than we need, or more than we need, we harm ourselves. Therefore, anyone who is striving to get more than they need is working for their own harm. A friend of mine is in charge of the troubled children of a certain city, which has 25 percent below the poverty line (the underprivileged); 25 percent above the average level (the wealthy, the overprivileged); and 50 percent in the middle. She says nearly all of the children in her care come either from the underprivileged or the overprivileged. Apparently, if you have too little or too much, you tend more in the direction of problems.

God our Father, You have written Your laws into matter as well as into mind and spirit. Help us to discover those laws and live according to them. For if we do not, we hurt ourselves and others. Amen.

TOO LITTLE, TOO MUCH

Give me neither poverty nor riches, but give me only my daily bread. Otherwise, I may have too much and disown you and say, "Who is the LORD?" Or I may become poor and steal, and so dishonor the name of my God. (Prov. 30:8–9)

God has written into the constitution of things that too little and too much are alike, and equally dangerous. We all see the devastating effects of poverty—sickly bodies, stunted minds, and problem souls. Yes, it is true that, here and there, a person can struggle against grinding poverty, make it sharpen their wits, determination, ability—and rise to achievement regardless. But where one triumphs, a dozen are broken or stunted by poverty. Let not our boasting about the achievement of the one blind us to the devastation of the dozen. Poverty is wrong, for it produces wrongs to body, mind, and soul.

But if poverty is wrong, so are riches. The latter is not so easily seen, for it is covered up by refinements, culture, the glamour of prestige and power. The rich die beautifully. But they die; and I don't mean just physically. Decay of the total person sets in, unless the person arrests it by intentionally giving away their riches. Such people put back into life the adventure of dispensing to human need from what they have.

Those who hold on to what they have inevitably decay—their faces grow dull, bovine. The light of adventure goes out on the face because the light has gone out in the heart. Jesus described this leaden-eyed existence in these words: "They are choked by…riches" (Luke 8:14). Those who hold on to riches as an end strangle the life forces within, suffocating themselves.

I shed bitter tears for underprivileged children; I shed even more tears for overprivileged children. They are doomed to decay unless some miracle of grace or of personal effort rescues them from the dead hand of riches.

Gracious God, we have been blind. We have made our aim something that in the end turns out to be our poison. Forgive us this individual and collective suicide, slow though our dying may be. Help us to make the material our servant and not our master. In Jesus' name, Amen.

THE RESULTS OF TOO LITTLE, TOO MUCH

All the believers were one in heart and mind. No one claimed that any of his possessions was his own, but they shared everything they had…and much grace was upon them all. There were no needy persons among them. For from time to time those who owned lands or houses sold them, brought the money…and it was distributed to anyone as he had need. (Acts 4:32–35)

In order to have a proper physical basis for abundant living, we must surrender the will to be rich, determining to keep only enough wealth to supply our need—and no more. We must likewise surrender the will that reconciles itself to poverty, determining to make enough to supply our needs—and no less.

Two classes have to think too much about money—those who have too much, and those who have too little. I want just enough of material goods to forget about them and get on with the business of human living. Someone has said that "the poor have to think about their next meal, and the rich have to think about their last one." Both results are bad. Need should be supplied—no less, no more.

Now note: This law of "To each according to his need" is not something Karl Marx dreamed up recently. It is written into the above Scripture as the basis for the material life. The word *need* is used in the New Testament seven times in relation to the material. How did the early Christians arrive at this? They knew no economics, no sociology, no science, but out of an experience of God they arrived at that basis. They reached it by inspiration.

And now society, by trial and error, is slowly but surely coming to the same conclusion. Life will back nothing else. The frustrations in modern society, its instabilities, its wars, are in large measure due to breaking this law of the kingdom. God's way must be our way.

God, our gracious Father, You will not let us rest in wrong, for wrong is ruin. So You are letting us hurt ourselves against Your laws. May our bruises make us turn to You for healing and for sense. In Jesus' name, Amen.

GETTING REQUIRES GIVING

[Paul]: *We were not idle when we were with you, nor did we eat anyone's food without paying for it. On the contrary, we worked night and day, laboring and toiling so that we would not be a burden to any of you. We did this, not because we do not have the right to such help, but in order to make ourselves a model for you to follow. For even when we were with you, we gave you this rule: "If a man will not work, he shall not eat." (2 Thess. 3:7–10)*

Last week we stressed that God guaranteed our needs would be met. But all God's promises are conditional, for God does not merely give—He gives in such a way that the receiver is stimulated, not smothered. God does not merely make a gift; He makes a person.

Abundant living will not come through eternally receiving. Abundant living depends upon abundant giving. If we go no further than the thought "to each according to his need," we create a parasitic society that causes degeneration. The other side of the medal is, "from each according to his ability." If you do not give to the good of society according to your ability, then you will not get according to your need.

Someone will no doubt throw up their hands and say, "But that is socialism!" You cannot scare me with a label. The two principles I have mentioned are deeply imbedded in the New Testament, and were there long before the term *socialism* was thought of. The two principles are: "It was distributed to anyone as he had need" (Acts 4:35) and "If a man will not work, he shall not eat" (2 Thess. 3:10). You might just as easily say that this spirit of cooperation is democracy as to say it is socialism, for Andrew Jackson had the second principle on one of his coins: "No labor, no food."

Wherever the idea came from, it is sound: If you do not give, you cannot get. Life is receptivity and response—both.

Father, You have created us to be creators. Help us then to be channels of Your creative energy. Help us to take hold of our tasks and make them the demonstration of Your purposes. In Jesus' name, Amen.

SEEKING THE KINGDOM MEANS ACTION

Give, and it will be given to you. A good measure, pressed down, shaken together and running over, will be poured into your lap. For with the measure you use, it will be measured to you. (Luke 6:38)

I cannot insist too much that abundant living means abundant giving. You are made that way in the very structure of your being. If you only breathed in and refused to breathe out, you would smother yourself to death; so if you are not outgoing, the whole process of incoming will stop, and you will die spiritually, mentally, physically. God will see to it that "all these things" will *not* "be given to you" if you do not "seek first his kingdom."

What would it mean to fulfill the first portion of the command, to seek first the kingdom of God? Many would assume it means to "acknowledge as first the kingdom," mentally assenting to its primacy. But this goes deeper than that. I know a man who has engraved Colossians 1:18 on his letterhead: "That in all things he might have the preeminence" (KJV)—yet he lives in a constant state of self-reference. The motto is mere mental compensation.

Seeking first the kingdom means more than acknowledgment; it means action. It means committing the whole of life to the proposition that the kingdom is first, last, and always—and acting on the committal. Just as people "seek" food or clothing, you are to "seek" the kingdom. It must master your thinking, your emotions, your will, you. In every situation you ask, "In this situation, what does the kingdom demand I should do?"—and then you do it.

In two passages the kingdom and doing of the will of God are made identical. One is in the Lord's Prayer: "Your kingdom come, your will be done on earth" (Matt. 6:10). The other is in a warning: "Not everyone who says to me, 'Lord, Lord,' will enter into the kingdom of heaven; but only he who does the will of my Father" (Matt. 7:21). The kingdom and carrying out the will of God are one and inseparable.

O God, I commit my will to Your will. You have made me for strenuous endeavor; unless I work, I wither. Put Your zeal within me. Amen.

THE KINGDOM AND THE NATION

Day after day they seek me out; they seem eager to know my ways, as if they were a nation that does what is right and has not forsaken the commands of its God. They ask me for just decisions and seem eager for God to come near them. (Isa. 58:2)

The kingdom of God is to be first, both in our allegiance and our actions. It is the absolute, confronting all relativisms with the demand to surrender, submit, obey, lose your life to find it. The kingdom of God confronts the relativisms of nation, of race, of class, of church, of wealth, of family, of self, with a demand that all bend the knee and find the meaning of their relative life in the absolute life.

If the nation becomes an end in itself, saves its life by centering upon itself as supreme, it will lose its life. When a relative thing becomes an absolute thing, you have idolatry. I love my country and will give everything to it except one thing—my conscience. That belongs to the kingdom of God. If my country clashes with my conscience, then my conscience must cling to one authority and only one—the kingdom of God.

Our nation acknowledges this position when it gives the right of conscientious objection to war. In doing so, it acknowledges an authority beyond itself, to which the individual conscience is amenable. The nation will not ravage or coerce that conscience—it belongs to God. The standing of conscientious objectors is therefore legal, and their patriotism is not to be questioned. The danger to the nation is not from those who have consciences, but from those who have none. They are the fifth columnists (the enemy fighting from within) who undermine the morals and hence the morale of the country.

The nation finds its meaning and life in surrendering to the purposes of something beyond itself, namely, the kingdom of God.

O God, You have a plan for our nation. Help us as a people humbly to surrender to Your plan and work it out. For if we take our way, we shall lose our way. If we take Your way, we shall find ours. In Jesus' name, Amen.

THE KINGDOM AND RACE

You have taken off your old self with its practices and have put on the new self, which is being renewed in knowledge in the image of its Creator. Here there is no Greek or Jew, circumcised or uncircumcised, barbarian, Scythian, slave or free, but Christ is all, and is in all. (Col. 3:9–11)

We must continue to study the absolute order, the kingdom of God, as it makes an absolute demand on all relative orders to submit, to lose themselves in this higher order.

In Nazism the kingdom of race is supreme and absolute—but not just there. Many of us have the religion of being white. Where there is a clash between the kingdom of God and the kingdom of being white, we choose the second. It is our god.

We cannot live abundantly unless we offer our race on the altar of God. How can the white race be supreme? Only in one way: Let white people become the servant of all; then they will become the greatest of all (see Mark 9:35). No race can be great except as it greatly gives itself to service to others. Those who serve the world will rule it in the future. That is an inexorable law written into our universe.

But note: "servant of *all*." Some are willing to be the servant of some—their friends, their families, their class, their race. They pull back from being the servant of *all*. It is my observation that only two came out of the last war [World War I] with enhanced reputations—Christ and the Quakers. Why? The Quakers were willing to serve everyone. A Polish woman saw the Quakers feeding the starving on both sides of the conflict and said to one of them: "You are feeding everybody, aren't you? Poles, Russians, Germans, friend and foe. Well, I knew there ought to be people like that in the world, but I didn't know there actually were."

The future belongs to those who belong to others in loving service.

Gracious Master, help me to lose my racialism in Your passion for service—and thus I shall find myself again. Amen.

THE KINGDOMS OF CLASS AND MONEY

I appeal to you, dear brothers and sisters, by the authority of our Lord Jesus Christ, to live in harmony with each other.... Be of one mind, united in thought and purpose.... Remember, dear brothers and sisters, that few of you were wise in the world's eyes or powerful or wealthy when God called you. (1 Cor. 1:10, 26†)

The kingdom of class must bend the knee to the kingdom of God. We often think and act in class terms rather than in Christian terms. Before we act, we look around to see what our class approves. Thus we are not a voice; we are an echo. We don't think with our minds; we react with our emotions. This is bondage.

No Christian can allow himself to become prisoner of his class and hope to remain Christian. For the kingdom of God is a classless society. The Communists say they are striving for that. In the kingdom of God we have it already. How so? Simply by the fact that if anyone in that kingdom begins to obey the behests of class instead of the behests of the kingdom, he or she is automatically out of the kingdom! But as we lose our petty class-consciousness, we find a God-consciousness.

The kingdom of money must likewise bend the knee to the kingdom of God. In our acquisitive society, money is god. You succeed as you succeed in terms of accumulation. These values are false and must be surrendered. Following the god of money leads to a dead end. The wealthiest man in a certain city developed heart trouble. He said pathetically: "Now that I've made my money, the two things I most want to do I can't do, namely, smoke and play golf." The world he had laboriously built up fell to pieces.

When money is surrendered as an end and offered to be a means to the end of the kingdom, it is found again. Only those who surrender it enjoy it.

O Master of my heart, class has silently entered me and set up its shrine. I overthrow it today. And money wants to claim my allegiance. I tear out both altars, making You, O Christ, my sole Lord. Amen.

THE KINGDOM AND THE CHURCH

Christ loved the church and gave himself up for her to make her holy, cleansing her by the washing with water through the word, and to present her to himself as a radiant church, without stain or wrinkle or any other blemish, but holy and blameless. (Eph. 5:25–27)

Even the kingdom of the church must bend the knee to the kingdom of God. Just as we often want our nation, race, or class to be dominant, so we want our church to be dominant. The church can be our religious self on display—but it is still the self, covered up with religious trappings. If the kingdom of God comes in, we as a church would like to bring it in, since that would leave us dominant.

That any one denomination is the exclusive or particular channel of God's grace is a dead concept. God sometimes works through a denomination, sometimes in spite of it, but never exclusively in any one of them. If that statement hurts your denominational pride, it may help your Christian humility!

The saints are about equally distributed among all denominations. The degree to which God uses people is determined not by the denomination in which they are located, but by the depth of their surrender to God. (If God seems too broad or liberal nor not sufficiently mindful of denominational distinctions, then you must quarrel with Him, not with me!)

No one denomination has the truth. The truth is in Christ, who is "the truth" (John 14:6). What we hold are truths about the Truth. These truths more or less approximate the Truth, but are not the Truth. He is beyond us all, and more than us all. We need, then, to pool our truths, so that the sum total of our truths will more nearly approximate the Truth.

The kingdom of the church must surrender itself to the kingdom of God.

O God our Father, forgive us for making Your glorious church into an idol. We will do so no more. We offer the church to You as the instrument of Your redemption. In Jesus' name, Amen.

SURRENDERING FAMILY AND SELF

[Jesus]: *"If you love your father or mother more than you love me, you are not worthy of being mine; or if you love your son or daughter more than me, you are not worthy of being mine. If you refuse to take up your cross and follow me, you are not worthy of being mine. If you cling to your life, you will lose it; but if you give up your life for me, you will find it." (Matt. 10:37–39†)*

The kingdom of the family must be surrendered to the kingdom of God if it is to find itself. But the family often becomes an end in itself. Family interests decide the issues. Such a family is bound to deteriorate.

A family that lives in a state of self-reference will live in a state of self-frustration. The probabilities are that being self-centered it will be self-disruptive—the units, not being held together by lofty purposes, will fall apart. But to have something beyond the family, to which the family is devoted and loyal, will make that family hold together. The beyond-itself loyalty will be its cement. A family that loses its life will save it.

And now we come to the final unit that must be surrendered—the kingdom of the self. We have stressed this so much that we need only mention it here. Losing the individual in something beyond itself in order to find itself is no mere suppressing imposition; it is the law of life running from the lowest to the highest. You have to die on one level to live on the next. The mineral kingdom surrenders itself to the kingdom above—the vegetable kingdom—and is taken by that kingdom toward transformation from dead matter into living forms. The vegetable kingdom surrenders to the animal kingdom and is lifted into thinking, feeling forms. The animal kingdom surrenders to the human kingdom and becomes assimilated into a yet higher life. The human kingdom surrenders to the kingdom of God and shares the highest life. The law of life is: Lose your life to find it.

O God, we have found the Way! It is written in the ways of life from the kingdom of matter to the kingdom of God. Help us this day to accept Your way, surrender to it, and live according to it. In Jesus' name, Amen.

PRAYER IS SURRENDER

Teach me to do your will, for you are my God; may your good Spirit lead me on level ground. (Psalm 143:10)

[Jesus] went away a second time and prayed, "My Father, if it is not possible for this cup to be taken away unless I drink it, may your will be done." (Matt. 26:42)

To find ourselves, we must lose the "I-who-am" for the "I-who-ought-to-be." This is done by a once-and-for-all surrender—and it is also done as a continual process called prayer. Prayer is fundamentally and essentially self-surrender.

This idea cuts across the usual idea of prayer as a method of obtaining your wishes from God. That is called self-assertion. Am I saying that prayer should be passive submission? A denial of the will to live? Is it the will to die? Far from it. Prayer is a will to die on the level of a defeated, empty, ineffective, short-circuited life in order to live on the level of a victorious, full, effective, cosmic-connected life. It is self-renunciation in order to find self-realization. Your petty self is renounced in order that your potential self might be realized.

Prayer is the wire surrendering to the generator, the flower surrendering to the sun, the child surrendering to education, the patient surrendering to the surgeon, the part surrendering to the whole. A branch that is not surrendered to the vine but is cut off and on its own is not free; it is dead. People who don't pray aren't free; they are futile. They are the blind who won't surrender their blindness to the surgeon in order to see. They are free—to remain blind.

O God, my Father, forgive me that I fear to surrender my fractured will to Your saving will. Help me, as I begin this adventure of prayer, that it may be no sideline activity. For I must have Your life to live. In Jesus' name, Amen.

PRAYER IS ALERT PASSIVITY

Pray in the Spirit on all occasions with all kinds of prayers and requests. With this in mind, be alert and always keep on praying for all the saints. (Eph. 6:18)

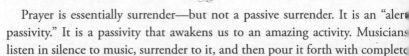

Prayer is essentially surrender—but not a passive surrender. It is an "alert passivity." It is a passivity that awakens us to an amazing activity. Musicians listen in silence to music, surrender to it, and then pour it forth with complete abandon. They are creative because they are receptive.

Scientists surrender to the facts of nature—they fling open the doors of their senses to be guided and directed by the facts. They are passive, but with an alert passivity. Their facts become factors as they are gathered up and put to work in factories, turning out finished products to serve the world. The surrender was really a mastery.

We must learn to live in the passive voice. Only those who do so know what it means to live in the active voice. The fussy activity of modern people is no life; it is the nervous twitching of their disordered and starved nerves. When animals lack certain vitamins, they become nervous, jumpy, and hysterical. The rush of modern life is not the calm, poised sureness of mastery. Rather, it is the jumpy hysteria of starved nerves crying out for vitamins of real life. Someone has said that no one commits suicide because they are tired of life—they are tired of a lack of life.

Jesus put the alternatives this way: "Men ought always to pray, and not to faint" (Luke 18:1 KJV). It is pray or faint—literally that. Those who pray do not faint, and those who faint do not pray. You can become alive to your fingertips—every cell in your body alert, active, creative—provided you pray. Otherwise you faint.

Pray or be prey—prey to fears, to futilities, to ineffectiveness.

Gracious Father, I thank You that power is open to me if I only take it. Help me to empty my hands of trifling toys, so that I may take the things You are offering me—release, power, victory. Amen.

IS PRAYER AUTOSUGGESTION?

Cast your cares on the LORD and he will sustain you; he will never let the righteous fall. (Psalm 55:22)

Ask and it will be given to you; seek and you will find; knock and the door will be opened to you. (Matt. 7:7)

Some say prayer is "autosuggestion," "wishful thinking," "an echo of your own voice." Suppose it were; even on that level it would be a healthy thing, for you would be suggesting the highest to yourself instead of the lowest.

But how is it that those who pray the most are convinced it is Other-suggestion rather than autosuggestion? Only those who use it least, or not at all, claim it is autosuggestion. Are they competent witnesses? Prayer would never have survived as a human practice had it been only autosuggestion, with no Voice answering our voice, no Heart answering ours. Can the flower believe that the sun is only the projection of itself?

The sense of Otherness is in true prayer. Something answers—and answers in terms that are worthy: release, power, vitality, insight, heightened accomplishment.

Prayer is the perfect instrument of development and of doing: It is outgoing, it is incoming; it is faith in God, and faith in oneself; it is active, it is passive; it is strenuous, it is calm; it works as if the whole thing depended on us, and trusts as if the whole thing depended on God. Is such a faith, so sound and health-giving, itself a delusion? Like produces like. How is it that bitter and disillusioned people deride prayer, while the calm, the poised, the hopeful, and the radiant delight in it?

My God and my Father, I want to live in You and have You live in me. Then my life will throb with energy and poise, with power and peace. Teach me to pray so I can live abundantly. Amen.

THE GREATEST SINGLE POWER

Are any of you suffering hardships? You should pray. Are any of you happy? You should sing praises. Are any of you sick? You should call for the elders of the church to come and pray over you, anointing you with oil in the name of the Lord.... The earnest prayer of a righteous person has great power and produces wonderful results. (James 5:13–14, 16†)

Dr. William Sadler, the psychiatrist, says that in neglecting prayer we neglect "the greatest single power to heal disease." He refuses to take a patient who does not believe in God; he says it is impossible to get patients straightened out unless they have something to tie to and love beyond themselves. We are literally coming down to this alternative: *meditation* or *medication*. And even the latter is not effective unless linked with the former.

Then prayer must be learned, for reservoirs of power are at our disposal if we can learn this art. "If we learn it"—that is the rub. People expect results without any practice of the art. We would consider a person to be foolish who stepped up to a musical instrument only occasionally but expected to be proficient. The little son of a British missionary bought a harmonica in India but came home upset: "That man cheated me. There is no 'God Save the King' in this thing." We just as foolishly believe we can get ready-made results without the *practice* of prayer.

We live in an open universe. Just as God has left certain things contingent upon the human will—and they will never be accomplished unless that will decides—so He has left certain things contingent upon prayer—things that will never be accomplished unless we pray.

Praying has three parts: (1) Listen; (2) Learn; (3) Obey. Without all three prayer will be a farce instead of a force. If we spent half the time learning to pray as we do learning any other art, we would get ten times the results.

Gracious Christ, teach me to pray. Give me the mind to pray, the love to pray, the will to pray. Let prayer be the aroma of every act, the atmosphere of every thought, my native air. Amen.

STEPS IN PRAYER (1-3)

If you need wisdom, ask our generous God, and he will give it to you. He will not rebuke you for asking. But when you ask him, be sure that your faith is in God alone. Do not waver, for a person with divided loyalty is as unsettled as a wave of the sea that is blown and tossed by the wind. Such people should not expect to receive anything from the Lord. Their loyalty is divided between God and the world, and they are unstable in everything they do. (James 1:5–8†)

We must now come to specific steps in the art of prayer. There are nine:

1. Decide what you really want. I want to stress the "you"—not a part of "you," a vagrant portion of "you" wandering into the prayer hour as a side adventure. It must be the whole "you." For prayer is not a luxury; it is a life. God cannot give things to you apart from Himself, and you cannot take things from God apart from yourself.

2. Decide whether the thing you want is a Christian thing. God is a Christlike God; His actions are Christlike actions; and He can answer prayer only if the thing desired is in accord with Christ. That is what Jesus meant when He said, "Whatever you ask in my name" (John 14:13)—in my character, according to my Spirit. Don't try to get God to do something that isn't Christlike. He can't, for He can't do something against His own nature. Within that limit, He gives you freedom to ask for "whatever."

3. Write it down. The expression will deepen the impression. I find that to write something down is almost destiny. I think I will change it, but once written it is almost impossible to change. If you are willing to commit your prayer to paper, you probably really mean it. In writing you do two things: You write it more deeply on your own heart, and you commit yourself more fully to a line of action. To write it down is one step in self-committal.

Patient Christ, my feet stumble on this pathway of prayer. I am learning to walk—help me over the hard places. I do want to learn this art. Amen.

STEPS IN PRAYER (4-6)

Find rest, O my soul, in God alone; my hope comes from him. (Psalm 62:5)

Continuing our specific steps in the art of prayer:

4. Still the mind. Just as the moon cannot be reflected well on a restless sea, so God cannot get to an unquiet mind. "Be still, and know that I am God" (Psalm 46:10)—be unstill, and you do not know, for God cannot get to you. In the stillness, the prayer itself may be corrected. For God does not only answer prayer, He also corrects prayer and makes it more answerable.

One night I bowed my head before a sermon and whispered, "O God, help me." Very quickly came back the reply: "I will do something better; I will use you." That amendment was decidedly better. I was asking God to help me—I was the center; I was calling God in for my purposes. But "I will use you" meant that something beyond me was the center, and I was only the instrument of that purpose beyond myself. God's answer shifted the prayer's whole center of gravity.

5. Talk with God about it. The order of these steps is important: Listen to God before you talk. As someone has noted, "Instead of saying, 'Speak, Lord, for Thy servant heareth' (1 Sam. 3:9 KJV), many say, 'Listen, Lord, for Thy servant speaketh.'" Let God have the first word and the last word—you take the middle word. Let your speaking with God be largely a turning over of the whole matter into His hands—you becoming the instrument of His purposes.

6. Promise God what you will do to make this prayer come true. The accomplishment needs to be a double affair as well, a cooperative endeavor. God answers the prayer, not for you, but with you. God's interest is not to give you things, but to build you through the getting of those things. The end of the whole process of prayer is not the request but the person.

O Father, I begin to see that my objective has been things I thought I needed; now I see that Your objective is to build me. I asked for the little; You are giving the great, the permanent, the everlasting. Help me to respond at the depth of Your purposes. In Jesus' name, Amen.

STEPS IN PRAYER (7-9)

I waited patiently for the LORD; he turned to me and heard my cry. He lifted me out of the slimy pit, out of the mud and mire; he set my feet on a rock and gave me a firm place to stand. (Psalm 40:1–2)

The last of our nine specific steps in the art of prayer are:

7. Do everything loving that comes to your mind about your request. That word *loving* is important. If the thought in your mind is unloving, it is from below, perhaps from the depths of your subconscious; but if it is loving, it is from above. The willingness to do the loving thing is important, for if you are unwilling, you have tied God's hands—He can't do, if you won't. Prayer is the working out of what God works in.

8. Thank God for answering in His own way. Remember that "No" is an answer, as well as "Yes." Sometimes He has to save us, as the great Bengali poet Tagore says, "by hard refusals." But if He refuses on one level, He does so only to make an offer on a higher level.

However, it is probable that if our prayer has run the gauntlet of the previous seven steps and has survived to this stage, it is answerable by "Yes." But that "Yes" may be delayed in order to put persistence and toughened fiber into us. God often holds us off to deepen our characters, so we won't be spiritual crybabies if we don't get everything at once.

9. Release the whole prayer from your conscious thinking. If the prayer is real, it will keep working in the subconscious mind—there will be an undertone of prayer in all you do. But release it from the conscious mind lest it become an anxiety center and make you tense. The very releasing is an act of faith in God. You relax and trust God to do the right thing in the matter.

These nine steps are the ladder by which you climb from your emptiness to God's fullness.

Gracious Spirit, I cannot pray as I should unless I become Spirit-taught. I want to pray according to Your will, and hence be answered according to Your power. In Jesus' name, Amen.

RELAXED RECEPTIVITY

Just as you received Christ Jesus as Lord, continue to live in him, rooted and built up in him, strengthened in the faith as you were taught, and overflowing with thankfulness. (Col. 2:6–7)

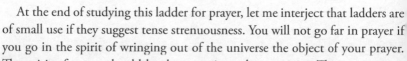

At the end of studying this ladder for prayer, let me interject that ladders are of small use if they suggest tense strenuousness. You will not go far in prayer if you go in the spirit of wringing out of the universe the object of your prayer. The spirit of prayer should be the opposite—alert passivity. This term means that while your spiritual, mental, and physical sensibilities are awake and alert to God, they are also relaxed and receptive.

Thus there are two sides to real praying. If we are only relaxed, we are weak. Prayer puts relaxation and tension together, and is therefore the perfect instrument of human well-being.

Since prayer has been presented so strongly by so many as strenuous alertness (the Luke 18 parable of the persistent widow being the special text for this), we must stress the relaxed attitude in prayer. A stenographer who is all tense and keyed-up and anxious to be a good stenographer will probably be a very poor one, for the anxiety literally ties up the energies.

Relaxation is receptivity, which in turn becomes resource. In the relaxed attitude you are allowing God to get to you; it is an invitation to come; you wait expectantly.

Gracious Father, I come to You to learn to receive. In Your presence I let down all the bars of my being. As the blood courses through my body to cleanse and heal and restore and empower, so You are going through me—body, mind, and soul—cleansing, healing, restoring, empowering. I thank You. Amen.

PHYSICAL RELAXATION

Great peace have they who love your law, and nothing can make them stumble.
I wait for your salvation, O LORD, and I follow your commands.
(Psalm 119:165–166)

In order to put ourselves into a mood of alert passivity, we will begin with the body, the outer framework of prayer. Jesus said, "When you pray, go into your room, close the door and pray" (Matt. 6:6). Close the door! All outer distractions should be reduced to a minimum. Every home should have a little corner, or room, or private chapel, and it should be understood that anyone who is there is not to be disturbed. They are in "the Trysting Tent" (Ex. 27:21 MOFFATT). Who would disturb a person having an audience, say, with the king or the president? To be in that Trysting Tent should make one inviolable.

As the surroundings are freed from disturbance, so attend to yourself and relax every muscle in your body. Say to your organs in succession something as follows: "My brain, you are now in the presence of God. Let go, and listen. He speaks, He penetrates, He heals. Receive, receive."

And to the eyes: "My eyes, weary with looking at a distracting world, close… and inwardly see nothing except Him into whose presence you have now come. He touches my eyes; they are rested and calm, single and healed."

And to the nerves: "O nerves, intelligence department of my being, strained and torn by living in a world of chaos, I now set you to work on the job of reporting better news—your God comes with calm, with poise, with resources and redemption. Receive, receive, receive."

And to the whole body: "He is now in every part, untying knotty nerves in His gentleness, bathing every brain cell with His presence, reinforcing every weak place with His strength, healing all your diseases, coordinating all parts and making them into a cooperating whole. Open every door; give Him all the keys."

O God my Lord, this body in every part is Your temple—hallowed by Your presence, cleansed by Your purity, and grasped by Your purposes. Amen.

RELAXED IN SPIRIT

May the Lord of peace himself give you peace at all times and in every way. The Lord be with all of you. (2 Thess. 3:16)

The Nobel Prize-winning surgeon Dr. Alexis Carrel bemoans the fact that "in the midst of the agitation of the new city," there are so few "islands of solitude, where meditation would be possible." Both the city and the home are impoverished without them; instead, a surface civilization and surface personalities are produced. As Kenneth Fearing whimsically writes:

"And wow he died as wow he lived,

Going whop to the office, and blooie home to sleep and

biff got married and bam had children and oof got fired.

Zowie did he live and zowie did he die."

The body must find places to be relaxed and restored, as we saw yesterday. But deeper than that, the spirit must be relaxed; otherwise, moral and spiritual tensions are passed on to the body. No amount of physical relaxation techniques will avail if the tension is in the soul.

In Romans 12:2 we read: "Instead of being moulded to this world, have your mind renewed, and so be transformed in nature, able to make out what the will of God is" (MOFFATT). Note: "have your mind renewed, and so be transformed in nature." Evidently the renewed mind can renew the nature. The mind is the key. The mind decides what shall or shall not be the nature of your nature. It decides to what molding influences the inmost and the outmost nature shall be exposed.

But the mind cannot be told to be calm and reassured unless it rests in some assurance beyond itself. Its final calm is found in being "able to make out what the will of God is." It must ultimately acquire its poise by linking itself to an eternal Purpose.

My Father, I see that I need all the techniques I can master; but in the ultimate analysis, my surest technique is to align with Your purposes. I want to be right with You in order to be right with myself. In Jesus' name, Amen.

SETTLING DOWN IN GOD

*Great is your faithfulness. I say to myself, "The L*ORD *is my portion; therefore I will wait for him." The L*ORD *is good to those whose hope is in him, to the one who seeks him; it is good to wait quietly for the salvation of the L*ORD. *(Lam. 3:23–26)*

You must not try to get merely a foothold in life by techniques of relaxation, but a roothold in the nature of divine reality. Only then can you be unshakably calm and poised. Otherwise, you have no secret of victory. "How did you like the airplane ride?" a nervous man was asked after going up for the first time. "Very well," he replied, "but I never did put my whole weight down." There can be no enjoyment of an airplane ride, or of this larger journey through life, unless you learn to put your whole weight down. Obviously there is nothing, absolutely nothing, upon which you can rest your whole weight except God.

Those who refuse to do as the Quakers suggest—to "settle down in God" or "center down in God"—are frustrated. The most disrupted woman I know believes that if she ever let go and turned over her frustrations to God, her universe would go to pieces. She has to hold it together, and is intensely and pathetically trying to do so.

One of the most nervous, frustrated men I know feels if he did not worry about his wife's business affairs, they would go to pieces. His wife is poised and able, more businesslike than he is; but it satisfies his self-respect to think he is holding their world together by his worrying. In fact his nervousness is self-defeating and is making him a problem, instead of solving anything.

All the attention these two people give to their nerves will be in vain unless at the center they let go and let God—unless they surrender in complete confidence to His will, living and working as joyous children in line with it.

O God, forgive my little antics of self-dependence—how invariably they let me down! I want to live on God-dependence, working out purposes not my own. Then shall I truly live—in You. In Jesus' name, Amen.

RELAXED, EVEN IF NOT RELEASED

Shadrach, Meshach and Abednego replied to the king, "O Nebuchadnezzar, we do not need to defend ourselves before you in this matter. If we are thrown into the blazing furnace, the God we serve is able to save us from it, and he will rescue us from your hand, O king. But even if he does not, we want you to know, O king, that we will not serve your gods or worship the image of gold you have set up."
(Dan. 3:16–18)

Relaxing in the ultimate love and goodness of God does not guarantee immediate release, however. Sometimes God may deny the thing asked for in order to give something better. The three Hebrews did not rest their confidence in a particular happening, but in the goodness of God, which would be the same whether that particular thing happened or not. Sometimes you have to live on "…but even if he does not."

A row of beautiful trees were laid low in a storm. Reason? The water was too near the surface, so the trees had not been forced to put their roots deep down. God may deny us a surface answer in order to get us to put our roots deeper into eternal reality, so that in some future storm we shall be unmoved.

When war was raging over Europe and engulfing everybody, some Christians reported: "On the surface there is storm, but twenty fathoms down it is quite calm." Someone asked a happy Christian in America how he remained poised and cheerful. He replied, "I have learned how to cooperate with the inevitable." That is the secret! You cooperate with the immediately inevitable because you know that in and through things God's will is being worked out and that Will wills your good.

My God and Father, I must not center down in the immediate; I have to center down in the ultimate. My faith looks not at a panorama, but at a person. As the hymn says, "Change and decay in all around I see; O Thou, who changest not, abide with me." Amen.

THE SECRET COMPANIONSHIP

King Nebuchadnezzar leaped to his feet in amazement and asked his advisers, "Weren't there three men that we tied up and threw into the fire?"

They replied, "Certainly, O king."

He said, "Look! I see four men walking around in the fire, unbound and unharmed, and the fourth looks like a son of the gods." (Dan. 3:24–25)

We must learn to live simultaneously in time and in eternity. If the time-side of life is all awry, the eternity-side holds us steady and lets us relax "in spite of."

A missionary in China said: "Christianity is a secret companionship. Hence when I am out for months where no one of my race is found, I am not lonely." You may have to walk through life arm in arm with disappointment; but on your other side, holding your arm, is the Secret Companion, and "the one who trusts will never be dismayed" (Isa. 28:16). You are disappointment-proof, for you always have the Secret Companion. Since that center holds steady, you need not grow tense at the unsteady happenings around you.

An intelligent woman told me she was so worked up over what she thought would be an inevitable marriage for her son that she began to have terrible pains in her head. She was soon in the hospital, unable to breathe. Pneumonia developed, until she lost consciousness. Only then did she relax. When she came out of the blackout, she surrendered the whole affair to God, and returned to poise and health. She had come near to choking herself to death by her resentment.

If your happiness is based on happenings, it will be a fleeting, evanescent thing. Your love for God must be so strong, so elemental, that if everything around you were stripped away—your work, family, prestige, power—this thing within would go on, regardless.

Gracious God, I rest not in the immediate; I rest in the ultimate, which is You. I am therefore impregnable. I view the panorama of life in quiet confidence that the last word will be spoken by You, for my good. I thank You. Amen.

SELF-REFERENCE OR GOD-REFERENCE?

They came to Capernaum. When [Jesus] was in the house, he asked them, "What were you arguing about on the road?" But they kept quiet because on the way they had argued about who was the greatest. (Mark 9:33–34)

When you are tense and unrelaxed, you are still centered in yourself. You are the center of reference—you are trying to hold your world together. When you relax, you shift the center of reference from yourself to God. You are no longer a self-centered person, but a God-centered person.

Relaxation means release—from yourself. When you live in a state of self-reference, you automatically shut yourself off from the guidance of God, and hence from His resources. The town of Lyons, Iowa, was situated at the narrow place in the Mississippi River where the railway bridge would certainly be built, so the citizens thought. They insisted on an exorbitant price from the railway company for the land. The railway company therefore decided to cross at Clinton instead, which offered them land free. Clinton has prospered; Lyons has withered. If you live in a state of self-reference, you will end in self-impoverishment.

Dr. Alexis Carrel says: "Thus psychoanalysis, in directing the mind of the patient upon himself, may aggravate the state of unbalance. Instead of indulging in self-analysis, it is better to escape from oneself through an effort that does not scatter the mind." The only way to escape from yourself is to make God and His will the center of your consciousness and your life plans.

It is virtually impossible to make an impression on a tense mind. Relaxation, on the other hand, is receptivity.

My Gracious and Redeeming God, I have been blocking Your power in my life by my tense fears and withholdings. Let me this day be as relaxed and as receptive as a little child. Then life shall become play and my hardest tasks simply joy. I thank You. Amen.

A TIME FOR QUIET

In the morning, O LORD, you hear my voice; in the morning I lay my requests before you and wait in expectation. (Psalm 5:3)

I cry to you for help, O LORD; in the morning my prayer comes before you. (Psalm 88:13)

I rise before dawn and cry for help; I have put my hope in your word. (Psalm 119:147)

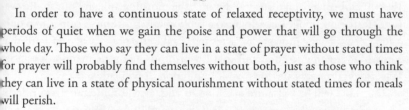

In order to have a continuous state of relaxed receptivity, we must have periods of quiet when we gain the poise and power that will go through the whole day. Those who say they can live in a state of prayer without stated times for prayer will probably find themselves without both, just as those who think they can live in a state of physical nourishment without stated times for meals will perish.

I asked a couple who were living defeated spiritual lives if they kept the Quiet Time. The naive reply came, "Yes, for a half hour after breakfast, my husband and I sit in the quiet and smoke." The modern equivalent of the Quiet Time! No wonder the husband had a nervous breakdown. Those sincere but defeated souls found release and victory only when they set up a real Quiet Time in which they took in the resources of the living God instead of nicotine. Breathing God deep into your inner recesses gives a genuine lift.

Set up the Quiet Time, preferably in the morning before you go out into the day. James Russell Lowell, the famous American poet and abolitionist, wrote that "the nurse of full-grown souls is solitude." It is best to have the Quiet Time in the pure, strong hours of the morning, when the soul of the day is at its best. Wash your thinking in the Thought of Christ before you face any other.

O God, without You we are empty and distracted and out of sorts. With You we are calm, poised, full, and adequate. We can go anywhere. Amen.

QUIET EXPECTANCY

When your words came, I ate them; they were my joy and my heart's delight, for I bear your name, O LORD God Almighty. (Jer. 15:16)

Very early in the morning, while it was still dark, Jesus got up, left the house and went off to a solitary place, where he prayed. (Mark 1:35)

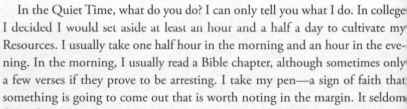

In the Quiet Time, what do you do? I can only tell you what I do. In college I decided I would set aside at least an hour and a half a day to cultivate my Resources. I usually take one half hour in the morning and an hour in the evening. In the morning, I usually read a Bible chapter, although sometimes only a few verses if they prove to be arresting. I take my pen—a sign of faith that something is going to come out that is worth noting in the margin. It seldom fails. If you do not write down your inspiration, it will fade out.

The Bible will be self-authenticating to you. It will find you at your deepest depths. You will know it is inspired, for you will find it inspiring. You will know God has gone into it, for God comes out of it. It is a revelation, for it reveals. It is an inexhaustible mine. You think you have exhausted it, and then you put down the shaft of meditation and strike new veins of rich ore. Your very brain cells will be eager and alert with expectancy. You will have what the Dutch philosopher Spinoza called "an intellectual love of God."

Perhaps you will have to be primed and prodded into thought by one of these "helps," such as this book or other devotional literature. But they are secondary, and not a substitute for firsthand contact with the Word of God. If the best Man who ever lived fed upon the Word of God, so must you.

O God, You have breathed into these words, and they have become the Word. Help me to saturate my inner thinking, my inner motives, with Your mind until I cannot tell where my mind ends and Yours begins. Then I will live fully and safely. In Jesus' name, Amen.

NOT A RESERVOIR, BUT A CHANNEL

He gives power to the weak, and to those who have no might He increases strength. Even the youths shall faint and be weary, and the young men shall utterly fall, but those who wait on the LORD shall renew their strength; they shall mount up with wings like eagles. (Isa. 40:29–31 NKJV)

Now that you have read the Word of God, let us turn to the negative side of prayer, which is getting rid of accumulated hindrances that have blocked the flow of power. I say "blocked the flow of power," for we are not reservoirs, but channels. David Seabury writes: "Many people have the idea that in each of us there is a reservoir containing a certain supply of energy. This is…supposed to be strictly limited in amount. If our expenditure is excessive, they say, our energy is depleted and we suffer from fatigue. So we take the attitude of economizing our little store of strength, conserving our resources, lest the tingy springs run dry.

"In contrast with this point of view is one akin to the teaching of Jesus. That is, our energies seem to be used up, not because the flow is checked, but because either the channel is blocked or we have not learned to use our capacities in the right way. In other words, we are tired not when we do too much but when we do too little…. Our hidden springs are not of body but of spirit; we are not receptacles but conductors….

"Jesus knew the human tendency to live far too frugally, to forget the source of our strength and fail to make God a perpetually sustaining power. Even more, he recognized our habit of hoarding both our material and our spiritual possessions" (*How Jesus Heals Our Minds Today*, pp. 170-72).

Jesus' method was this: "Give, and it will be given unto you. A good measure, pressed down…and running over" (Luke 6:38). Let the concept burn within us: "We are not resevoirs, but channels!"

O God, I've been meager and afraid my resources would run dry if I used them. But now I see that only as I give, will I get. Help me, then, to give with complete abandon. I shall draw heavily upon Your resources. Amen.

OPENING BLOCKED CHANNELS

It is for freedom that Christ has set us free. Stand firm, then, and do not let yourselves be burdened again by a yoke of slavery…. You were running a good race. Who cut in on you and kept you from obeying the truth? (Gal. 5:1, 7)

If we are not reservoirs, but channels, then one of the first things to do in prayer, after reading the Word, is to become silent before God and let Him put His finger on any blocked channel. The tendency will be to try to pray around that blocked place, to slide over it, to act as if it were not there. But don't defend yourself, overtly or covertly. Face the blocked place frankly; confess where you have been wrong; turn your problem over to God simply and honestly; tell Him you will do anything at any cost to correct it, with His help.

Or better still—He will do it with your help. For He is taking the initiative to make you the best you can be.

To be relaxed is to be released. Relax, then, toward God and be eagerly open to any suggestion for clearing up your life. But perhaps you are not relaxed toward people. You are holding resentments toward them. Surrender those resentments into the love of God. That love will dissolve them.

Perhaps you are tense toward others because you want to live out their lives for them. Surrender those loved ones to God. I wrote my daughter and her husband when they were married: "I would like my attitude to be, never in the way, and never out of the way." If you are fussily trying to manage other people's lives in their supposed interests, surrender that fussiness—it is pure selfishness. That attitude ties up yourself and others.

O Tender Silence, speak the word that will release me, heal me, and make me adequate. I consent without reservation to the draining of every swamp of self-centeredness and fear. Clean me to my depths. For the world is sick, and I want to be a part of the cure instead of the disease. In Jesus' name, Amen.

WHEN THE MIND WANDERS

We demolish arguments and every pretension that sets itself up against the knowledge of God, and we take captive every thought to make it obedient to Christ. (2 Cor. 10:5)

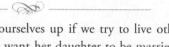

Yesterday we saw that we tie ourselves up if we try to live other people's lives for them. A mother did not want her daughter to be married—she was self-centered, wanting the attention of her daughter for herself. The daughter waited till she was thirty-one before she married. The mother fainted at the wedding. Through her self-pity she developed all sorts of diseases. But then, her husband developed cancer of the colon. In fighting for him and attending to him she forgot herself, becoming a well woman to this day. She shifted the basis of her relationships with others from self-interest to other-interest, which righted the relationships—and herself.

In prayer let God show you the places where you have tensions. If God in the silence brings up nothing, then assume there is nothing. Now you are ready for positive communion.

But another difficulty arises: As you begin, your mind wanders. This greatly distresses some people. It shouldn't. You can let the thing to which your mind wanders become the medium through which you commune with God. For instance, suppose you are distracted by a siren. Then say: "God, warn me by an even louder siren of the danger that besets a careless soul!" Make the distraction into a direction—toward God. Ride even on the wings of the storm—to God.

After a while you will be able to "take captive every thought to make it obedient to Christ," as the Scripture says. The more you obey Him, the more He becomes the center of your affection: and "where your treasure is, there your heart will be also" (Matt. 6:21).

Strong Son of God, You are becoming more and more my treasure. I am at rest, at poise, at power. Amen.

BUILDING FROM THE SUBCONSCIOUS

Out of the depths I cry to you, O LORD. (Psalm 130:1)

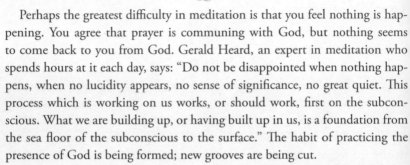

Perhaps the greatest difficulty in meditation is that you feel nothing is happening. You agree that prayer is communing with God, but nothing seems to come back to you from God. Gerald Heard, an expert in meditation who spends hours at it each day, says: "Do not be disappointed when nothing happens, when no lucidity appears, no sense of significance, no great quiet. This process which is working on us works, or should work, first on the subconscious. What we are building up, or having built up in us, is a foundation from the sea floor of the subconscious to the surface." The habit of practicing the presence of God is being formed; new grooves are being cut.

Prayer will then soon become an undertone, as well as an overtone of your life. Someone said of John Forman, a saintly missionary, "All his thoughts of people gradually turned to prayers." This means you need never waste time, no matter in what circumstances you are placed. If people are making you wait, thus wasting your time, you can immediately turn on your prayer-attention and begin to pray for the people who are making you wait, thus dissolving your resentment and making you use an otherwise wasted period constructively. You can pull the world's need into that blank moment.

The Christians of Europe undergoing persecution said: "Our people can stand solitary confinement better than others." Why? Because they could populate their cells with people in need, reaching out hands of prayer and gathering them in.

So prayer can become habit, easier to do than not to do. But habits are formed by regularity. Pray by the clock, if necessary, and soon you will pray by inward urge. Then you will know the meaning of "detained in presence of the Eternal" (1 Sam. 21:7 MOFFATT). You will not be able to tear yourself away.

Here in Your presence, O Eternal, I place myself, my affairs, my worries, my frustrations, my possibilities. I have narrowly held them; now I entrust them to You. Amen.

RELAXED STRENUOUSNESS

As long as it is day, we must do the work of him who sent me. Night is coming, when no one can work. (John 9:4)

Continue to work out your salvation with fear and trembling, for it is God who works in you to will and to act according to his good purpose. (Phil. 2:12–13)

Relaxation is release—not only from cramping inhibitions and fears, but also for otherwise impossible tasks. According to the writing of a well-known minister and a renowned psychiatrist: "Relaxation of the personality is really an evidence of faith and trust…. The man who believes absolutely in God, in the divine reliability and goodness, does not hold himself mentally and spiritually rigid, fearful that any moment something is going to happen to him, but, on the contrary, rests in complete confidence that all things work together for good to them who believe in God. As a result, he has peace in his mind and quietness at the center of his life…. This relaxed and peaceful state of mind gives him a clear brain, makes possible the free exercise of all his faculties, and thus he is able to attack his problems with every ounce of ability he possesses. The relaxed man is the powerful man. The rigid, tied-up personality is defeated before the battle starts" *(Faith Is the Answer,* Norman Vincent Peale and Smiley Blanton, pp. 84-85).

The goal of relaxation periods is relaxed strenuousness. The worship becomes work. Instead of "Now I lay me down to sleep" (which too many grown-ups are prone to pray), we can say:

> Now I get me up to work,
> I pray the Lord I will not shirk.
> If I should die before the night,
> I pray the Lord my work's all right.

Gracious Father, I place my life into Your hands, knowing that only things for my highest good will come to me. You and I will work them out together. We begin the Great Cooperation. Amen.

PHYSICAL AND MENTAL RELAXATION

I lift up my eyes to the hills—where does my help come from?
  My help comes from the LORD, the Maker of heaven and earth.
  He will not let your foot slip—he who watches over you will not slumber;
  indeed, he who watches over Israel will neither slumber nor sleep.
  The LORD watches over you—the LORD is your shade at your right hand;
  the sun will not harm you by day, nor the moon by night.
  The LORD will keep you from all harm—he will watch over your life;
  the LORD will watch over your coming and going both now and forevermore.
(Psalm 121)

A woman who spends most of her time in a city school system teaching children and parents to relax gave me her routine. It included the usual exercises of sitting in a chair, letting the arms go limp, then the legs, letting the head fall forward on the chest, then rotating it in a circular pattern, and so forth.

To these worthwhile movements I add the following:

I imagine I am seated before a calm lake, surrounded by strong silent hills that rise into the clouds. The trees lift their arms in silent prayer, absorbing the strength of God. The grass also lifts its blades and receives—in fact, everything receives.

And so do I. I breathe in God's peace and breathe out His calm: peace—calm, peace—calm, a gentle rhythm. In every portion of my being I am taking in the life of God, so that I am at rest in Him.

I am relaxed…receptive…released.

My Father, gently and quietly I breathe Your calm and peace into all parts of my life. My fever is gone in the great quiet of God. The healing of God goes through me. I am grateful. Amen.

MEETING TODAY, TODAY

Do not worry about tomorrow, for tomorrow will worry about itself. Each day has enough trouble of its own. (Matt. 6:34)

May I pause in this discussion to add a personal word?

Besides living physically relaxed, I live mentally and spiritually relaxed, because I believe the central hypothesis of my life is right. Life is one long verification of that central hypothesis. This fact gives an inner steadiness.

This attitude was tested in an airplane over St. Louis when we circled for two hours, trying to land. I had time to think. So I wrote down a life conclusion: "I am up in this plane, and we have been circling over these clouds for about two hours. If we do not land safely, I would like to leave my last will and testament to my friends and fellow followers of Christ: There is peace, perfect peace. Apart from my unfaithfulness to the highest, there are no regrets about the general course of my life. Life with Christ is the way to live. In this hour there is assurance—God is underneath all the uncertainties of human existence. So I rest in God. God's best to you all. Living or dying, I am His—His alone. Glory! Signed, E. Stanley Jones."

I try to take that central assurance into my work. That which is centrally right will not let me down in the details. I meet these details in confidence. I meet today, today. I do not telescope all next week into today. I clip off my engagements one by one as a person clips coupons. Dr. William Osler, the great surgeon, said: "The load of Tomorrow, added to that of Yesterday, carried Today, makes the strongest [person] falter. We must learn to shut off the future as tightly as the past." A voice greater than Osler's said: "Each day has enough trouble of its own."

Bishop Quayle told of lying awake, trying to hold the world together by his worrying, until God said, "Now, William, you go to sleep, and I'll sit up."

My Gracious Father, how can I worry and fret when You live and care? As Your happy child I play in Your house. You have taught me to laugh—I laugh incredulously that I have found this treasure. Amen.

DIRECTED BY CIRCUMSTANCE?

"Do not resist an evil person! If someone slaps you on the right cheek, offer the other cheek also.... You have heard the law that says, 'Love your neighbor' and hate your enemy. But I say, love your enemies! Pray for those who persecute you! In that way, you will be acting as true children of your Father in heaven." (Matt. 5:39, 43–45†)

We come now to the matter of guidance. If life is to be at its best, we must have the sense of instrumentation, of carrying out purposes not our own, of fulfilling a Will that is ultimate. We must be willing to be led; otherwise, life hangs at loose ends, lacks a goal, lacks the dynamic to move toward that goal.

If we lose the sense of being led, we become victims of our circumstances. The men of a church were having a dinner and, being unused to managing meals, kept giving contradictory orders to the hired caterer. He became upset and objected. At this, one man asked him, "Well, Henry, what do you do when the women are here?" He replied, "That's simple—I just throw my mind in neutral and go where I'm pushed."

A great many people simply throw their minds into neutral and go where circumstances push them. Or they allow other people's actions to determine their conduct. They are circumstance-directed instead of Christ-directed. In the above scripture, Jesus warned us against allowing the other person to set our course. The best revenge you can have on enemies is not to be like them.

A bishop told me that something I wrote cured him of "a mild species of swearing." When driving at night on a two-lane road, if the oncoming car would not dim its lights as it approached, this man would flash his lights into the other driver's face to express his irritation. "Now," he said, "I dim my lights no matter what the other fellow does, and keep them dimmed. It's safer, and I feel more like a bishop! I don't let him determine my conduct."

O Christ, help us to be impelled from the inside instead of being compelled from the outside. I want to submit to Your direction, lest I be the victim of my circumstances. I want to be a person, not a thing. Amen.

SECONDHAND GUIDANCE

Jesus replied, "Every plant not planted by my heavenly Father will be uprooted, so ignore them. They are blind guides leading the blind, and if one blind person guides another, they will both fall into a ditch." (Matt. 15:13–14)

We saw yesterday that if we are not God-led, we will probably be mob-led. We will not act; we will only react. In trying to find a way out between America and Japan, I recently said to some high officials: "Don't you see what's happening? You are allowing the Japanese to determine your conduct. You say, 'If they do this, we will do that.' Such an approach leads straight to war. Why don't you work from your own principles outward to the situation and find a settlement in that way?"

We Christians must work out from principles, not from pressures. No matter what the other person does, we should remain Christian.

Without a sense of guidance, life turns dull and insipid. Thomas Kelly, the Quaker mystic, observed: "The years have been [moving along] in average mediocrity. There is no special excellence, no special defeat in it. It's just it. And that is damnable. For the world is popping with novelty, with adventure in ideas. And we are not getting them here. We are safe and sane." Yes, safe and sane and secondhand!

When the Israelites disobeyed God, the punishment was this: "I will send an angel before you,…. But I will not go with you" (Ex. 33:2–3). Their religion was about to become a secondhand affair instead of a direct contact with God.

O God, we are afraid, and so become led by things and surroundings. Our faith becomes secondhand and vague, instead of firsthand and vivid. We want to regain the sense of being led by You, the sense that we are in direct contact, and that life has firsthand meaning. In Jesus' name, Amen.

LED BY GOD, OR BY THINGS?

Someone may say to you, "Let's ask the mediums and those who consult the spirits of the dead. With their whisperings and mutterings, they will tell us what to do.' But shouldn't people ask God for guidance? Should the living seek guidance from the dead? Look to God's instructions and teachings! People who contradict his word are completely in the dark. (Isa. 8:19–20†)

The growth of astrology in America is a sign of the lack of firsthand contact with God. If we are not led by God, we will try to be led by stars. Turning to stars for guidance is a sign of decay, mentally and spiritually. It is sheer materialism to believe your life is determined by lumps of matter floating in space.

Astrology laid its paralyzing hand on the mind of Greece and killed it. The Greek mind was a good mind, facing bravely the facts of life, until it lost its nerve and turned to the stars to find destiny. The mind of India was a creative mind, producing the amazing Sanskrit literature, until astrology made it sterile and noncreative.

About two years ago when ready to sail back to India, I announced that the Inner Voice had insisted that I stay in America, saying, "I want you here." This aroused widespread comment, some of it unfavorable, as if it were a strange and superstitious thing to be led of God directly. This reaction was most revealing. It showed how much of American Christianity was at least one step removed from firsthand reality. There seemed to be knowledge of God but not acquaintance with Him.

If there is a God, He must have some plan, some purpose for every life. When He made each of us, He apparently broke the pattern—we are all different. Each life has particular significance. If we find that plan of God and work within it, we cannot fail. Outside of that plan, we cannot succeed.

Gracious Father, You have paid attention to the smallest, lowliest cell; have You no plan for me and my life? You do! Help me to pay the price of working out that plan, making it my adventure. In Jesus' name, Amen.

A SENSE OF MISSION—AND SUBMISSION

[Jesus]: *You did not choose me, but I chose you and appointed you to go and bear fruit—fruit that will last. Then the Father will give you whatever you ask in my name. (John 15:16)*

Whenever I stand up to preach, I ask the audience to bow their heads in prayer, and I invariably remind God of the above verse, which was given to me years ago at the very beginning of my ministry. Repeating this verse gives me the sense of being sent, of having the backing of the Eternal, of speaking in a Name not my own. But it does another thing: It lays on me the obligation to surrender and obey the outworking of this plan. It gives life a sense of mission—and submission.

National ambassadors weigh their words, for they are speaking in the name of their government. We, too, must feel that same representative capacity, that we are speaking, thinking, and acting in a Name not our own. The significance of a life is determined by the significance of what it is identified with and what it represents.

But that sense of mission brings a sense of submission. Instead of making you proud and cocky, it has the opposite effect. You are awed and humbled. You feel you must walk softly before God.

Guidance strikes at the citadel of personality and demands surrender of self-sufficiency. God is taken into the center of the life choices. Guidance is the shifting of life from self-will to God's will. That will, not your own, becomes supreme. God's will becomes your constant frame of reference.

Instead of guidance being a spiritual luxury for rare souls, it is a minimum necessity for every Christian soul: "As many as are led by the Spirit of God, they are the sons of God" (Rom. 8:14 KJV). No leadership, no sonship. Guidance is of the very essence of Christianity.

O God, I begin to see that I must live in You or not at all. When I find Your plan, I find my person. Your will is my peace. My will is my war. I am eager for Your mind. Amen.

LISTEN, LEARN, OBEY

Moses commanded them: "…Assemble the people—men, women and children, and the aliens living in your towns—so they can listen and learn to fear the LORD your God and follow carefully all the words of this law." (Deut. 31:10, 12)

Since God has a plan for every life, we must become skilled in the art of knowing and working out that plan. I suggested earlier that when we come to prayer we should have three attitudes: listen, learn, obey. Some of us listen but won't learn, and some of us learn but won't obey. If we do not approach God in all three attitudes, then soon there will be nothing to listen to, or to learn, or to obey. The Voice will grow silent.

If we do not have guidance, then it is probably withheld for one of two reasons: we are untrained, or we are unwilling. Guidance doesn't just happen. It is a result of placing oneself in the way of being guided. A radio doesn't just happen to pick up messages; it is deliberately tuned, and then it receives. Receptivity is necessary to perceptivity—you perceive only as you receive. When the king of France complained to Joan of Arc that he never heard the voice of God, she replied, "You must listen, and then you will hear."

But many of us don't want to listen to God, for we are afraid that if God reveals His will to us, it will be disagreeable. We have changed "Thy will be done" into "Thy will be endured." We consider it something that mortals must accept with a sigh, like the death of a loved one.

That view must be completely reversed, or we shall get nowhere with guidance. Jesus said, "My food is to do the will of him who sent me" (John 4:34). The will of God is food to every tissue, every brain cell, to everything that is good for us. My will is poison when it conflicts with God's will. As far as real living is concerned, the will of God is reinforcement, not restriction.

Forgive me, O God, for hesitating to throw down every barrier to Your guidance. Why should my eye be afraid of light? I will not be. Every part of me is sensitive and open to Your suggestions. Amen.

BE SILENT TO GOD

Although the Lord gives you the bread of adversity and the water of affliction, your teachers will be hidden no more; with your own eyes you will see them. Whether you turn to the right or to the left, your ears will hear a voice behind you, saying, "This is the way; walk in it." (Isa. 30:20–21)

We must be trained to listen, to learn, to obey. Many of us talk fast in the presence of God, afraid that if we keep quiet, God will say something unpleasant to us. We must learn to listen, to live in the passive voice. A pastor arose in one of our ashrams and said, "God is showing me that I must shift the emphasis of my life from talking to taking." He was learning receptivity.

One Bible translator interprets the command, "Be still, and know that I am God" (Psalm 46:10) this way: "Be silent to God and He will mold you." He will shape you to become the instrument of His purposes. An almighty Will will reinforce your weak will, but only when that weak will is aligned to His purposes. An all-wise Mind will brood over your mind, awakening it, stimulating it, and making it creative. An all-embracing Love will quicken your love into world-sensitivity.

God has three things in mind for us: purpose, plan, person. His purpose is to make you the best you can be. He has a plan that embodies that purpose. The next step is for you to be the person who carries out that purpose and plan. In the silence you listen for it all to unfold. You literally become the plan and purpose of God—an embodied thought of God, His word made flesh.

A piece of disconnected wire is one thing, but a piece of wire attached to the electrical grid is quite another. Alone, you are one thing; attached to God's purposes, you are quite another thing.

O God, alone I am a dead wire; but attached to You, I am throbbing with energy and glowing with light. Make my connection sure with You, so I will not be periodically going dead and dark. In Jesus' name, Amen.

FOLLOWING THE PATTERN

[God to Moses]: *"See that you make them according to the pattern shown you on the mountain.... Set up the tabernacle according to the plan shown you on the mountain." (Ex. 25:40; 26:30)*

We must be willing to be guided by God, not merely now and then, but as a life proposition. You cannot get light in a crisis unless you are willing to get light in the continuous. God must not be called in to get you out of scrapes in which you have entangled yourself by continuous self-will.

A Swedish literary woman wanted God to tell her what her next career step was to be. At length, she seemed to hear God saying, "How could you expect Me to speak when you have gagged Me so long?" Don't gag God in the continuous and expect Him to speak in the crisis.

In the beginning, then, make a decision that decides all decisions down the line—the decision that the will of God is first, last, and always in your life. Nail that down. Let there be no loophole. Make it absolute.

The plan of your life may be unfolded in a moment of sudden insight, or it may be gradual, as in Psalm 37:23 (NKJV): "The steps of a good man are ordered by the LORD"—every two and a half feet. "Your word is a lamp to my feet" (Psalm 119:105). Note "to my feet"—just enough light by which the next step can be taken, and then the next. That puts adventure into life, and a moment-by-moment trust. There is a surprise around every corner.

But the life guidance may also be a sudden insight. One day, as a young man, I placed a letter on a chair and knelt before it. The answer to that letter would determine my lifework. The Inner Voice said, "It's India." I arose and said, "Then, it's India." That clear moment was real and has held me steady amid low moments of discouragement about the details in India.

The Inner Voice brings inner unity.

O God, help me to build according to the pattern I see when Your voice is clear and I am receptive. I cannot live on a surmise, but on a summons; not on a guess but on a goal. I await Your bidding and Your blessing. Amen.

THE SEVEN WAYS OF GOD'S GUIDANCE

He guides the humble in what is right and teaches them his way. All the ways of the LORD are loving and faithful for those who keep the demands of his covenant. (Psalm 25:9–10)

If guidance gives life a sense of mission and accountability every moment, then how does God guide us?

I suppose the great problem to God is how to guide us and not override us. He must guide us and develop us as persons at the same time. To lead us and simultaneously produce initiative in us is a task worthy of divine wisdom.

To do this, God will guide in many ways, awakening the personality to aliveness, making the mind and spirit alert to His hidden leadings. God's leadings should be obvious enough to be found, but not so obvious as to do away with the necessity of thought and discriminating insight. They must be "an open secret"—open, yet sufficiently secret to make us dig.

God will guide us in one or more or all of these ways: (1) He gives general guidance through the character and person of Christ. Jesus lets us know what God is like, and, therefore, what we must be like. (2) He guides us through the collective experience of the church—the corporate wisdom gathered through the ages. (3) He guides us through the counsel of good people. (4) He guides through natural openings, matching us against some opportunity or need. (5) He guides through natural law and its discoveries through science. (6) He guides through a heightened moral intelligence and insight—we become personalities who are capable of exercising sound moral judgments. (7) He guides us through the direct voice of the Spirit within us—He speaks to us in unmistakable terms in the depths of our being.

It is probable that God will guide us in more than one of these ways. If He were to use only one method, it would narrow us.

Gracious Father, I am excited to find out Your way and be led into it. I seek it with my whole being and without reservation. For I know that Your hand is my health. In Jesus' name, Amen.

GUIDANCE THROUGH CHRIST'S EXAMPLE

To this you were called, because Christ suffered for you, leaving you an example, that you should follow in his steps. "He committed no sin, and no deceit was found in his mouth." (1 Peter 2:21–22)

We now look at those seven ways of guidance in a little more detail.

(1) God gives general guidance through the character and person of Christ. Christ has revealed to us the nature of God—has shown us what He is like. He has lifted up into bold contrast the laws that underlie our moral universe as well as those that underlie our own spiritual, intellectual, and physical beings. In short, He has revealed to us the nature of reality. If we want to live according to the nature of reality, then we must live according to Christ.

The Muslim says you cannot get guidance from Christ, for He was not married; He can give no guidance to the married. There are two ways to be an example: One is to live in every possible situation—as a husband, as a mechanic, as every other station in life. This is obviously impossible. The other way to be an example is to live by universal principles that can be applied anywhere. Jesus took the latter method. There is no situation conceivable where His spirit is not the norm. He is the universal conscience of humanity.

When you have this general guidance in Christ, there is no use to ask for specific guidance. Often we ask for specifics because we are unwilling to take the general guidance in Christ. Ask the question in any situation, "What is the Christlike thing to do?" And if you do it, you will not go wrong. There is no use trying to prevail upon God to approve of any act or attitude that is other than Christlike.

O God, I see I am predestined to be conformed to the image of Your Son. What a destiny awaits me! I want to be willing to fulfill it. Amen.

GUIDANCE THROUGH THE CHURCH AND ITS LEADERS

In the church at Antioch there were prophets and teachers.... While they were worshiping the Lord and fasting, the Holy Spirit said, "Set apart for me Barnabas and Saul for the work to which I have called them." So after they had fasted and prayed, they placed their hands on them and sent them off. (Acts 13:1–3)

The next methods of guidance are these:

(2) God guides us through the collective experience of the church—the corporate wisdom gathered through the ages. The Roman Catholic Church makes this the sole instrument of guidance to the individual. We cannot accept it as the sole method, but certainly as one of the chief methods. The accumulated experiences of the ages are at the disposal of the individual.

The church has been the mother of my spirit; and just as a child turns to its mother in a crisis, so I can turn to the church for direction. Pastors are the mouthpieces of that collective wisdom. They should therefore not seek to be novel, but to interpret the wisdom of the ages to the people before them.

(3) God guides through the counsel of good people. As we look back across the years, we find that a word here, a phrase there, a conversation yonder with a friend, has lifted horizons, untangled snarled situations, and sent us on our way rejoicing, with clarified minds and purposes. Counseling is no hit-and-miss affair; it is becoming an art and a science.

The minister who cannot combine public utterance with private counsel is disqualified as a safe guide. The people of the East have a saying that you don't drop eye medicine into a person's eye from a third-story window. Guidance must be personal and confidential. It is a heavy responsibility.

Gracious Father, thank You for those who have come into my life with kind words and deep insights. Help me this day to be the agent of Your mind to some other person. Help me to speak the word that will lift the darkness for some fumbling soul. In Jesus' name, Amen.

GUIDANCE THROUGH PROVIDENCE AND NATURAL LAW

These are the words of him who is holy and true…. What he opens no one can shut, and what he shuts no one can open. I know your deeds. See, I have placed before you an open door that no one can shut. (Rev. 3:7–8)

Continuing with God's methods of guidance:

(4) God guides through opening providences, matching us against some opportunity or need. A little waif boy on the streets of London sidled up to a doctor and said, "Do youse want to see where wese live?" He took the doctor by the hand and led him into alleyways where boys slept in boxes and under steps, huddled together to keep one another warm. Before morning that doctor knew his life belonged to those boys. He went out and set up Dr. Barnardo's Homes, through which thousands of boys have been blessed. God's guidance was the opening of the doctor's eyes to see a need.

If God lets you see a need, it well may be His invitation for you to meet that need.

(5) God guides through natural law and its discoveries through science. We have a primary faith in revelation and a secondary faith in science. But in a sense, science is revelation—God speaking to us through the natural order. That natural order is God's order. It is dependable because God is dependable.

There was a time when we tried to put God into the unexplained gaps in nature—we said God must be there, for these gaps are mysterious and unexplainable. But when science began to fill up these gaps, God was pushed out. To relegate God to those gaps was a mistake, for God reveals Himself in the very order and explainable facts of nature. They express God far more than the unexplainable and mysterious. He is in it, is the author of it, works through it—but is not straitjacketed by it. For this order is still full of surprises and of freedoms. A closed system of nature is now considered unscientific.

O God, whose will is worked into the natural order, help us to accept and rejoice in that discipline. Your disciplines are our freedoms. Help us to hear your guidance in these ways. In Jesus' name, Amen.

GUIDANCE THROUGH MORAL INSIGHT AND THE INNER VOICE

All who are led by the Spirit of God are children of God. (Rom. 8:14†)

Here are the last two methods that God uses to guide us:

(6) God guides through a heightened moral intelligence and insight—we become persons who are capable of exercising sound moral judgments. This is the usual and perhaps the most dependable form of guidance. I would think it would be the form God most delights in. It is certainly the form that delights discerning parents, when they see their children now no longer leaning parasitically on them, but exercising sound moral judgments of their own. That is the sign of a free personality. Fellowship with Christ stimulates and heightens our moral insights and judgments.

(7) God guides through the direct voice of the Spirit within us. I am surprised that this method of guidance is looked on by so many church leaders as something strange and occult. Yes, it is capable of being abused. Thoughts may arise from our subconscious that we mistake for the voice of the Spirit. Any suggestion that speaks to us must be tested, particularly as to whether or not it fits in with the guidance we receive through the person and teaching of Christ. If the guidance is not in thorough accord with that, then suspect it and reject it.

And don't depend on the Inner Voice as the usual method of guidance, for if you do you may be tempted to manufacture guidance through your own desires when no Inner Voice comes. The guidance of the Inner Voice comes, at least to me, when none of the other ways can meet my particular need. I need a special word for a special crisis. Then the Inner Voice speaks.

And it is authoritative. When a voice rises from my subconscious, it argues with me. The Voice doesn't argue; it is self-authenticating.

O God who guides us when the choosing is not a question of right and wrong but perhaps of good and best, help me to be sensitive to the voice of Your Spirit. And help me to obey at any cost. In Jesus' name, Amen.

COOPERATE, OR DIE

All the believers were one in heart and mind. No one claimed that any of his possessions was his own, but they shared everything they had. With great power the apostles continued to testify to the resurrection of the Lord Jesus, and much grace was upon them all. (Acts 4:32–33)

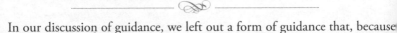

In our discussion of guidance, we left out a form of guidance that, because of its importance, needs separate treatment—group guidance. This was hinted at in "guidance through the church," but that sounds too official and stilted to express what group guidance truly is.

I am afraid of individual guidance that isn't checked up on by a group. The individual needs the correction or the corroboration of a larger body. People who say, "God told me such and such," should be willing to submit that to a disciplined group for their reaction. In the end, the individual may have to act on his or her own guidance, but it is not safe to do so unless one has been open to group judgment on it.

Christianity began as a group movement. Jesus gathered a dozen men and implanted His outlook and Spirit into that group. But in Christian collectivism the individual found perfect freedom. You cannot find your freedom in isolation and detachment. You find it only through a group. You are social by your very nature. Two cells came together to produce you.

A civic example: Galveston, Texas, had all the advantages of being situated on the gulf with a wonderful harbor. But three Galveston families began to compete with each other for domination of the city. They canceled out each other. Galveston was stunted. Houston had almost none of Galveston's advantages, for it was situated fifty miles up the winding river. Yet Houston has pulled away from Galveston to become the largest city of Texas. The secret? The leaders of Houston learned to cooperate.

The inexorable law of life is: Cooperate, or disintegrate and die.

O God, You are our Father, and we are Your family. Help us to learn to live with mutual aid at the very center of our beings and purposes. Amen.

THE REDEMPTIONISTS

A prophetess, Anna…was very old…. She never left the temple but worshiped night and day, fasting and praying. Coming up to [Joseph and Mary] at that very moment, she gave thanks to God and spoke about the child to all who were looking forward to the redemption of Jerusalem. (Luke 2:36–38)

Before Jesus gathered a group movement around Him, there was an earlier group movement, which has been called "The Redemptionists"—those "who were looking forward to the redemption" of Israel. The land was decaying; the voice of prophecy had ceased; religion was formal and dead. After all, Isaiah had prophesied that the Root, Jesus, would emerge "out of dry ground" (53:2).

But the Redemptionists held aloft the torch of reality amid the encircling gloom. They were the seed plot of a new order, the germ of a new world. The group was made up, in all probability, of Zechariah and Elizabeth, Mary and Joseph, Simeon, Anna, the shepherds. They were intensely nationalistic, and yet they were agents of a new order based on equal opportunity to everybody. In Moffatt's translation the word *just* runs like a refrain through their accounts. Zechariah and Elizabeth were "both just" (Luke 1:6). The angel spoke to him about "the wisdom of the just" (Luke 1:17)—a phrase that should burn itself into modern civilization: To be *just* is to be wise; to be *unjust* is to be unwise. Joseph was "a just man," but with a new kind of justice: He was "unwilling to disgrace her" (Matt. 1:19). Here was a justice that was merciful; it was redemptive, not punitive.

O God, we see the workings of Your purposes through those who are given to each other and to You. May I be a part of a nucleus in whom the future lies as an embryo in the womb. May I carry within me the germ of Your new order. In Jesus' name, Amen.

A COMPLETE PERSON

There was a man in Jerusalem called Simeon, who was righteous and devout. He was waiting for the consolation of Israel, and the Holy Spirit was upon him. It had been revealed to him by the Holy Spirit that he would not die before he had seen the Lord's Christ. Moved by the Spirit, he went into the temple courts. (Luke 2:25–27)

One member of the Redemptionists who epitomized the new order was Simeon. He was unadorned by any title, office, or rank; the Bible says only that "there was a man." This plain layman, however, was a vehicle of God's thought for the new age.

Though only "a man," we read four remarkable things about Simeon that show his complete stature: He "was righteous." He was "devout." He was "waiting for the consolation of Israel." Finally, "the Holy Spirit was upon him." His faith made him sound in every relationship, a well-rounded personality. Some people are righteous toward others but not devout toward God. Some are devout toward God but not righteous toward people. Some are patriotic lovers of their country but are inwardly empty—the Holy Spirit is not upon them. And some are devoutly mystical and spiritual, but not interested in the affairs of their nation—they are narrowly personal. In Simeon, God's kingdom was working as total wholeness and health.

Simeon was on right footing in general, and as a result found particular guidance in a particular situation: "Moved by the Spirit, he went into the temple courts." You must not expect particular guidance if you refuse to allow God to give you general guidance in the whole of your life. God cannot be called in as a Cosmic Bellhop to run your errands in particular situations of difficulty if you shut Him out of the total management of your life. He is not the Bellhop; He is the Owner and Manager of this hotel called the world. We must come under His general and particular guidance.

O God, help me to be fit every moment, so that I, too, may be ready to be used in the crisis. Help me to be disciplined. In Jesus' name, Amen.

SEEING HUMAN POSSIBILITIES

Simeon took [the child Jesus] in his arms and praised God, saying: "Sovereign Lord, as you have promised, you now dismiss your servant in peace. For my eyes have seen your salvation, which you have prepared in the sight of all people, a light for revelation to the Gentiles and for glory to your people Israel." (Luke 2:28–32)

The whole nature of Simeon was fit and attuned, so that when the great moment of his life came, he was not caught off guard. He was ready with insight to see its meaning.

Simeon was a patriot, "waiting for the consolation of Israel" (v. 25), and yet he was not narrowed by his patriotism. He saw that God's salvation was to be for "all people." How prophetic his vision was.

Even further, he saw that Christ would be "a light for revelation to the Gentiles"—or, if we accept the alternate translation of this text, "a light for the unveiling *of* the Gentiles." Christ was to unveil the worth of the Gentiles, uncovering their possibilities. Jesus uncovers our Father; He also uncovers our brother and sister—lifts the veil from our prejudiced eyes and lets us see the infinite value in every person, of every race, of every color, of every class. The Gentiles were no longer to be a "problem"—they were to be possibilities.

Some people in our time speak of "the black problem"—they should speak of "the black possibility." The problem is not in people of a certain skin color; it is rather in those who make that color into a problem. White Christianity needs a baptism of the spirit of Simeon to make our faith into a revelation of people's possibilities instead of a bolster for our prejudices. Christianity is a double revelation—of God and humanity. We need a faith that brings faith in people as well as in God.

O God, You are our Father—and the Father of all people. Help me this day to catch Your vision of the infinite possibilities in everyone, however overlaid by various wrappings they may be. And help me to begin the great adventure of bringing out those possibilities. In Jesus' name, Amen.

A SWORD IN THE SOUL

Then Simeon blessed them and said to Mary, his mother: "This child is destined to cause the falling and rising of many in Israel, and to be a sign that will be spoken against, so that the thoughts of many hearts will be revealed. And a sword will pierce your own soul too." (Luke 2:33–35)

But Simeon was no sentimentalist—he saw the deep issues involved in Christ. His patriotism did not blind him to the fact that Jesus was destined for the downfall of many Israelites as well as the rise of others. The nation would stumble to its doom over Him. Patriotism is mere babbling if it doesn't see the role of Jesus. Said one Russian author, "Europe has lost Christ, and Europe will perish." The same can be said of any nation that loses Christ.

Jesus is the world's conscience. Just as we struggle with and sometimes fight against conscience, so we struggle with and fight against this Man. Some people shrink from the One who came to unveil all people, so that they attack the Light. Jesus is the Man we ought to be, struggling with the man or woman who is. He brings out the secret aims of many a heart.

Simeon went on to prophesy that this would drive a sword into Mary's soul. She suffered vicariously. The nation would suffer because of its rejection, and Mary would suffer as well. Christ causes a twofold suffering—to those who reject, and to those who love those who reject.

But Mary knew full well the essence of His revolution. She had declared in her own Magnificat (Luke 1:46–55): "He has scattered those who are proud in their inmost thoughts" (frustration for the unbending)…"He has brought down rulers from their thrones" (political revolution)…"but has lifted up the humble" (social revolution)…"He has filled the hungry with good things but has sent the rich away empty" (economic revolution). With that message, no wonder she suffered.

O God, I see that bringing in Your new order is no child's play. It will cost blood and struggle—not of others, but of us who are dedicated to bringing it in. Help us to be strong, as Jesus was. Amen.

KEYNOTE FOR THE KINGDOM

As is written in the book of the words of Isaiah the prophet: "A voice of one calling in the desert, 'Prepare the way for the Lord, make straight paths for him. Every valley shall be filled in, every mountain and hill made low. The crooked roads shall become straight, the rough ways smooth. And all mankind will see God's salvation.'" (Luke 3:4–6)

Out of this Redemptionist group at Jerusalem came two mighty movements—one led by John the Baptist, the other by Jesus. John's movement emphasized the equalitarian attitude. "Every valley shall be filled in"—the depressed and underprivileged will be leveled up; "every mountain and hill made low"—the overprivileged will be brought down; "the crooked roads shall become straight"—people will be judged by merit rather than by cleverness and cunning; "and all mankind will see God's salvation"—not just one racial or national group, but "all mankind."

John continued this equalitarian emphasis in very practical application when he said to the crowd: "If you have two shirts, give one to the poor. If you have food, share it with those who are hungry" (Luke 3:11 †).

Jesus took up the same note when he said to the rich young man: "Go, sell your possessions and give to the poor…. Then come, follow me" (Matt. 19:21). In His parable of the vineyard workers, the landowner said to the complainers, "I want to give the man who was hired last the same as I gave you" (Matt. 20:14). Equality of opportunity before God was the keynote of the Redemptionists, and their message was caught up and fulfilled in the kingdom Jesus proclaimed. This small group, then, was the seed plot of a new order.

Today, while the old order is going to pieces, we must have groups that contain in themselves the germ of a new order. These small disciplined groups are the hope of the future.

O God, our Father, help me to become a part of those who belong not to yesterday and today only, but to tomorrow. Help us to be ready with our answer when the half-answers break down. In Jesus' name, Amen.

DOING THE IMPOSSIBLE

"How can this be?" said Mary to the angel, "I have no husband." The angel answered her, "...With God nothing is ever impossible." Mary said, "I am here to serve the Lord. Let it be as you have said." (Luke 1:34–38 MOFFATT)

The key to the Redemptionists is to be found in these words. They put themselves at God's disposal.

The most absolutely potent thing on this planet is a small group disciplined to great ends. A group of raindrops gathering on a mountainside is the beginnings of a mighty river. A seed is a group of forces dedicated to growth. Jesus speaks of the seed as "the message about the kingdom" (Matt. 13:19), but He goes on and says, "The good seed represents the people of the kingdom" (v. 38[†]). Here, the message becomes real flesh. The people of the kingdom are the seeds of the new order. They do not give the message—they are the message. They do not seek an answer—they are the answer, the kingdom in miniature. There is nothing so absolutely potent as a group unbreakably bonded to each other and unreservedly given to God.

It doesn't take many people to accomplish things. A determined, disciplined minority can do anything. A handful of people made Germany Nazi, and Italy Fascist. In 1914 someone said that to find two Communists in Paris (the home of Communism) would be a wonder, and to find four would be a miracle. And yet in five years the Communists had captured Russia and challenged the world.

Less than a hundred people produced both the Renaissance and the Reformation in Europe. Dr. W. H. Welch of Johns Hopkins University School of Medicine, with a small disciplined group of young doctors around him, changed the medical life of America for decades to come.

Gracious Father, I see that if I am in a minority with You, then anything can happen. I am determined to stay in this minority at any cost. I am at Your disposal; like Mary, "I am here to serve the Lord." Amen.

A TRACK FOR FELLOWSHIP (1-3)

You are no longer foreigners and aliens, but fellow citizens with God's people and members of God's household, built on the foundation of the apostles and prophets, with Christ Jesus himself as the chief cornerstone. (Eph. 2:19–20)

If we are to be a small disciplined group, we must look at the laws that underlie corporate living. There is a way to get along with people, and that way is God's way. Let it be burned into our consciousness that life is social and that there are definite laws of association. Corporate living requires intelligence as well as good will.

(1) You must not try to dominate the group. That is fatal, for it begets the same thing in others, setting the stage for strife. At the threshold of corporate living is self-surrender. A bewildered man who was dealing with a strong-minded woman in his company said to me, "I cannot control her mind." I told him he had to give up the desire to dominate and begin to cultivate the will to cooperate. That changes your attitude and allows you to see the truth in the other person's position rather than always trying to get your position across.

(2) You must not try to use the group. People can sense at once if you are pursuing any ulterior purpose—self-aggrandizement, self-display, business, social climbing.

(3) Cultivate the power to put yourself in the other person's place. Such imaginative sympathy is the key to life, in fact, is life itself, for life is sensitivity. One secret of Jesus' power over us is just this quality. But it is not just sympathy in imagination—it is sympathy in fact, or, literally, "suffering with." Our hunger becomes His; our bondages are His very own. To the degree that we acquire and cultivate this spirit of imaginative sympathy we are Christian and can get along with other people.

O God, in this delicate, difficult, but delightful business of getting along with people, give me skill, insight, and patience. You are patient with me in spite of my blunderings; help me to be the same with others, for they have to put up with me. Amen.

A TRACK FOR FELLOWSHIP (4-8)

Settle matters quickly with your adversary who is taking you to court. Do it while you are still with him on the way, or he may hand you over to the judge, and the judge may hand you over to the officer, and you may be thrown into prison. (Matt. 5:25)

We continue with laws that underlie corporate living:

(4) Determine to conduct no secret criticism of one another. A motto in our ashram says: "Fellowship is based on confidence; secret criticism breaks that confidence; therefore we will renounce all secret criticism." If there is no outer criticism, then we know there is no inner criticism; so the fellowship is relaxed and unrestrained.

Of course we welcome the mutual helpfulness of constructive criticism, for the best of us are only Christians in the making. If we are afraid of criticism, we are on the defensive, living by fear rather than by faith. Let us lower the barriers and welcome the worst. We will probably find the best!

(5) Don't look for perfection in people. You have to get along with yourself in spite of yourself, so make up your mind to get along with others in spite of themselves.

(6) Look on others not as they are, but as they can be. That was the secret of Jesus' influence on people. He believed in them when they couldn't believe in themselves. This attitude will give you not a querulous mood of dissatisfaction with others, but a constructive mood of expecting possibilities.

(7) Determine to settle differences as they arise—don't let them get cold. Most misunderstandings can be dissolved by quick action.

(8) Refuse to look for slights. Those who look for them usually find them. Have a great purpose that absorbs your attention, so you will actually not know when you are slighted.

God, my Father, Your way is the way not merely of theology, but of life. Help me to bring Your unfailing patience and good will to my relationships, that I may be the dissolver of misunderstandings and the healer of hurts. In Jesus' name, Amen.

A TRACK FOR FELLOWSHIP (9-14)

Don't get involved in foolish, ignorant arguments that only start fights. A servant of the Lord must not quarrel but must be kind to everyone, be able to teach, and be patient with difficult people. (2 Tim. 2:23–24†)

We continue our steps for corporate living:

(9) Don't allow yourself to become petty. When some elements in Israel would not acknowledge Saul as king, he "kept silent" (1 Sam. 10:27). A smaller man would have gone into a fit of temper. Saul was never more kingly than in that silence under provocation.

(10) Look for privileges of service rather than for your rights. The person who goes around insisting on rights never gets them. Rights are not something that can be given—they have to be earned. And they are earned as you give service to others.

(11) Don't try to do people good—instead, love them. If anybody wants to do me good, I feel like dodging around the corner; but if anyone loves me, I'm conquered at once. A loving attitude opens all doors, anywhere in the world.

(12) Often decide with the group against yourself. The group can see more objectively than you can. Maintain the power to say, "I'm sorry." Those who are always right are always wrong.

(13) If there is any basic injustice in the group's relationships, deal with it; don't just advise patience. It is impossible to have real fellowship over and around a basic injustice. That will plague your fellowship and spoil it. Correct the injustice, and fellowship will come naturally.

(14) Don't try to have fellowship—work together for great ends, and fellowship will follow. If you try simply to have fellowship, you will achieve only stilted niceties. But if you work for great kingdom ends, the fellowship will come as a by-product.

O Christ, we thank You that in discovering the ends of Your kingdom, we are discovering one another. The cause makes us coalesce. Fuse us together in bonds of great endeavors. Amen.

A TRACK FOR FELLOWSHIP (15-19)

Just as we have in the one body many organs, and these organs have not all the same function; so collectively we form one body in Christ, while individually we serve as organs for one another. (Rom. 12:4–5 WEYMOUTH)

Today's list will complete our steps for corporate living:

(*15*) *Remember, we are "organs for one another."* This concept from Paul will keep us from jealousies. If we are one another's "organs," then the other person fills out and complements me where I am weak. If a person can sing better than I can, that person is my set of vocal cords—I am complemented by his or her strength. If another can manage things better than I can, I must not be jealous but recognize this person as my organ of executive ability. Perhaps there is something I can do better than the other person—I am his or her organ in that particular thing.

(*16*) *Expect the best from others.* If you do, you will probably get it; if you expect the worst, you will probably get that. As Jesus said once in a different context, "According to your faith will it be done to you" (Matt. 9:29).

(*17*) *Help others to help themselves—don't smother them.* Instead, shape them for great things. On the day a great YMCA secretary saw an Indian protégé elected to take his place, he commented, "Now I've really succeeded." Don't be a benevolent tyrant. Let people around you grow.

(*18*) *Keep your power of laughter.* When things become tense, burst out laughing, if only on general principles. If you lose your laugh, you are sunk. Make your voice smile when you talk.

(*19*) *Never let your group forget that it is disciplined by something beyond itself—the kingdom of God.* The group must never become an end in itself; if it does, it will become self-righteous and holier-than-thou. It must have a constant sense of accountability to the kingdom.

O God, help me in this group to be the kind of person I want others to be. Help me to remember that people are lonesome and need love. Help me to provide that love without reserve. Help me take the initiative, not waiting for others to do so. Amen.

GEARED FOR CONCRETE GOALS

How good and pleasant it is when brothers live together in unity!... It is as if the dew of Hermon were falling on Mount Zion. For there the LORD bestows his blessing, even life forevermore. (Psalm 133:1, 3)

We all [must] reach unity in the faith and in the knowledge of the Son of God and become mature, attaining to the whole measure of the fullness of Christ.

Then we will no longer be infants, tossed back and forth by the waves, and blown here and there by every wind of teaching and by the cunning and craftiness of men in their deceitful scheming. Instead, speaking the truth in love, we will in all things grow up into him who is the Head, that is, Christ. From him the whole body, joined and held together by every supporting ligament, grows and builds itself up in love, as each part does its work. (Eph. 4:13–16)

God abides in and uses group life especially. It is safer for God to use a group than an individual, which may result in individualism. The use of a group results in corporate emphasis. Individuals find themselves in that corporate living.

But group life must be organized around embodied objectives, not hazy ideas. The Redemptionists at Jerusalem lived on in the movement of Jesus because they were organized around the idea of equality for all. That idea is fermenting in the world, and may yet save it.

If any group's driving ideas are hazy, disembodied, and out of gear with concrete reality, then the group will be pushed aside by other movements in which the members have a definite task to accomplish. Let the church take this to heart. The future belongs to movements that are geared into concrete, accomplishable tasks.

God, I seek to find my will and affection purified, clarified, and enlarged by the group life. Help me to lose my life that I might find it again. Amen.

FOR MARRIED COUPLES (PART 1)

Wives, submit to your husbands, as is fitting in the Lord. Husbands, love your wives and do not be harsh with them. (Col. 3:18–19)

·············· ✺ ··············

While we are discussing disciplined corporate living, let me pass along some suggestions for making the marriage relationship the best it can be. Most of these come from the eminent marriage counselor Dr. Paul Popenoe.

General guidance for both spouses: (1) Don't nag. (2) Don't try to remake your partner. (3) Don't criticize. (4) Give honest appreciation. (5) Give attention to your partner in the small things. (6) Read a good book on the sexual side of marriage, which has a physical basis that should be satisfactory to both.

For husbands: Here is a questionnaire. Give ten points for each "yes."

1. Do you still "court" your wife with an occasional gift of flowers, with remembrance of her birthday and wedding anniversary, or with some unexpected attention and tenderness?

2. Are you careful never to criticize her before others?

3. Does she have money to spend entirely as she chooses?

4. Do you make an effort to understand her moods and help her through periods of fatigue or irritability?

5. Do you share at least half of your recreation hours with your wife?

6. Do you take a definite interest in her intellectual life—the books she reads, the groups she belongs to, her views on civic problems?

7. Do you keep alert for opportunities to praise her and express your admiration for her?

8. Do you thank her for the little jobs she does for you?

9. Do you ever pray together? Go to church together?

10. Do you keep the shrine of your heart intact for her?

Our Father, train us in the art of living together, so that we might make a Family of God out of the world's chaos. Help us to begin where we are. Help us to make the kingdom operative in the little things of the home. Amen.

FOR MARRIED COUPLES (PART 2)

I urge you to live a life worthy of the calling you have received. Be completely humble and gentle; be patient, bearing with one another in love. Make every effort to keep the unity of the Spirit through the bond of peace. (Eph. 4:1–3)

Continuing our study of how to live together in the family unit, here is a list of questions *for wives*:

1. Do you have an intelligent grasp of your husband's business so you can discuss it with him helpfully?

2. Can you meet financial downturns bravely, even cheerfully, without criticizing your husband for his mistakes, or comparing him with others who are more successful?

3. Do you make a special effort to get along amiably with his side of the family?

4. Do you compromise little differences of opinion in the interests of harmony?

5. Do you keep track of the day's news, the new books, and new ideas in order to share an intellectual life with your husband?

6. Do you keep up your own prayer life so you can meet every situation in the home with poise, divine direction, and insight?

7. Have you made a quiet place in the home where your husband, you, or your children can get away for undisturbed meditation and prayer?

8. Have you learned to say, "I am sorry"? Or are you always right?

9. Are you tending your church relationships and making them real, or do you just send your children to Sunday school?

10. Are you the kind of person you want your children and your husband to be?

God, keep me from all divided loyalties, from all querulous attitudes, and from all anxiety. Let me approach each day with confidence. Amen.

NOT FOR SALE

"Everything is permissible for me"—but not everything is beneficial. "Everything is permissible for me"—but I will not be mastered by anything. (1 Cor. 6:12)

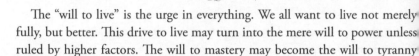

The "will to live" is the urge in everything. We all want to live not merely fully, but better. This drive to live may turn into the mere will to power unless ruled by higher factors. The will to mastery may become the will to tyranny unless controlled by the will of God.

Paul's phrase "I will not be mastered by anything" is one of the greatest phrases ever uttered. The man who was completely mastered by the will of God said he would not be mastered by anything else. The opposite of that is also true: If you are not mastered by God you will be mastered by things, by yourself, by other persons, by circumstances, by the world, or by sorrows and disappointments.

Some people are indeed mastered by the world. It is usually a very slow, silent process. We scarcely know what is happening, but a materialistic outlook slowly overtakes us. The legend goes that a robin was offered a worm for a feather. The bird thought this would be a good bargain—it would save a lot of hunting for worms, and he would not miss a feather. But after accepting many such offers, the dreadful day came when the robin awoke to the fact that his feathers were gone and he could not fly. He had sold his power to fly for worms. He was earthbound.

The counterpart of that is happening all around us—the powers of soul, the ability to soar, are bartered for physical attractions. Soon the person's soul is dead though surrounded by many things.

Other people are mastered by some bereavement or disappointment. They retreat into the kennel of life like a whipped dog. There they give themselves to self-pity. The "will to live" has become the "will to complain" about life.

O God, apart from You I will be mastered by this, that, or the other. With You, however, I am free. Help me to rise, like an airplane, against resistances. In Jesus name, Amen.

LIVING ABUNDANTLY "IN SPITE OF"

Who shall separate us from the love of Christ? Shall trouble or hardship or persecution or famine or nakedness or danger or sword?... No, in all these things we are more than conquerors through him who loved us. (Rom. 8:35, 37)

Abundant living happens sometimes on account of situations, but more often in spite of. When circumstances are against us, we must be able to set the sails of our souls and use even adverse winds. The Christian faith does not offer exemption from sorrow, pain, or frustration—it offers the power to use these adversities. This is in many ways life's greatest secret. When you have learned that, you are unbeatable and unbreakable.

A young doctor said to me: "Your way of life is different from psychoanalysis or psychology. You go beyond them; you give people a knowledge of themselves, trying to change their environment where possible, but then getting the patient to lay hold of the resources of God, so that if they can't change the environment, they can use adverse surroundings to serve God's purposes. Yours is a more complete and adequate way of life." He was right, except that it isn't my way! It is Christ's way.

A teacher of slum children asked the class to name the qualities in Jesus that appealed to them. When the list was apparently completed, a boy put up his grimy hand and said, "They hung him on a cross, and he could take it." The boy was right—but the reason He could take it was not because of a stoic attitude. Jesus could take it because He could use it. You cannot bear a cross for long—it will break your spirit—unless you take that cross and make it serve higher purposes. The stoic bears the cross; the Christian makes the cross bear fruit.

Any movement that has learned the secret of making the most bitter tree—the cross—bear sweet fruit has learned the secret of abundant living.

O Christ, we begin to see Your secret. You seized life when it spoke its cruelest word and turned it into God's most redemptive word. Give me power to do just that. Then, in You, I will be invincible. Amen.

PEACE GIVEN, PEACE RECEIVED

[Jesus instructing the Twelve]: *"Whatever town or village you enter, search for some worthy person there and stay at his house until you leave. As you enter the home, give it your greeting. If the home is deserving, let your peace rest on it; if it is not, let your peace return to you. (Matt. 10:11–13)*

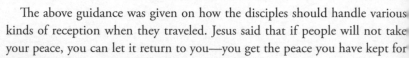

The above guidance was given on how the disciples should handle various kinds of reception when they traveled. Jesus said that if people will not take your peace, you can let it return to you—you get the peace you have kept for yourself, plus the peace you gave away! You win either way.

Christians thrive on difficulties, for they turn their very difficulties into doors, their Calvaries into Easter mornings. Are you criticized? Then, if the criticisms are true, correct whatever needs correcting. Make your critics "the unpaid guardians of your soul." If the criticisms are false, then do not let them affect your attitude toward the critics. Let your thoughts of them turn to prayer.

Out of the injustice you will extract a moral victory. You will have no enemies, for you will have no enmity. It is an easy and bloodless way to get rid of your enemies! You turn them into friends.

The only way to overcome your enemies is to not be like them. Don't let them put their weapons into your hands. If they give enmity, you give love. Two hates never made a love affair. You be the master of the situation.

Breathe peace upon everybody. If they don't take it, then it comes back to you.

Gracious Master, I want to walk amid adversity with my head up. But I cannot do this unless I lay my head in the dust at Your feet to learn Your ways—the ways of mastery. Nothing daunted You; nothing stopped You. Help me to be so overflowing that I may swamp everything—including enmity. Amen.

PAIN IS GOD'S PREVENTIVE GRACE

The Spirit himself testifies with our spirit that we are God's children. Now if we are children, then we are heirs—heirs of God and co-heirs with Christ, if indeed we share in his sufferings in order that we may also share in his glory. (Rom. 8:16–17)

Christianity survived the worst thing that could happen to it, namely, the death of its Founder. It turned this into the very best thing; it redeemed the world through a catastrophe. A faith that can do that has survival value.

We can see why God allows pain—it is His preventive grace. Had there been no pain in the world, the human race would not have survived. For instance, if there were no pain attached to disease, we would probably allow disease to eat on and on—it doesn't hurt, so why bother? But pain stabs us awake and says: "Look out! Something is wrong here; pay attention to it." Pain is God's red flag run up the pole to warn of underlying danger.

Unless pain is working toward some end, it breaks us by its meaninglessness. That is why the prophet saw that "pagans waste their pains" (Jer. 51:58 MOF-FATT). Those who live without the God-reference don't know what to do with pain; they waste it. Their pains end in mere dull, fruitless, meaningless suffering. It gets them nowhere.

So much of the world's suffering is wasted. During 1914-18 we suffered dreadfully, and yet we wasted that world pain. The best we could do with it was to forge it into the Versailles Treaty—and now we are back at war again, compelled to go through the whole miserable business once more. We may do the same thing with this present world pain unless we can transmute it into a determined purpose to make a new world, so that war may never happen again. Only where we see redemption in pain can we find any release while in the midst of it. Purposeless pain is paralyzing.

Christ, help us to master both the central and the marginal pains. Help me to take hold of life when life is hard and impossible. The struggle is on—I am to master, or be mastered. Help me, O Master. Amen.

DEFLECTED GRACE

[Paul]: *Everything that has happened to me here has helped to spread the Good News. For everyone here, including the whole palace guard, knows that I am in chains because of Christ. And because of my imprisonment, most of the believers here have gained confidence and boldly speak God's message without fear. (Phil. 1:12–14†)*

We Christians must learn to make our pains productive. Second Corinthians 7:10 speaks about "the pain God is allowed to guide" (MOFFATT). There can indeed be a God-guided pain. It can be swept up into the purposes of God and transformed into finer character, greater tenderness, and more general usefulness. It can be made into the pains of childbirth, bringing forth new life.

Take one of the most difficult pains to bear—the frustration of one's life plans. This often throws confusion into everything, for everything had been geared to those plans. How did Jesus meet such a situation?

A small incident reveals His secret. When Jesus healed the demoniac, the people came and saw the man, then quickly "pleaded with him to leave their region" (Matt. 8:34). It is disconcerting to find one's best endeavors blocked by ignorance and self-centered greed. But was Jesus blocked? No, He was simply diverted. His grace was deflected toward other people and situations.

In the next chapter of that gospel, he did some of the greatest things of His life. He healed a paralytic, called Matthew, taught regarding conservatism, healed a woman with a hemorrhage, raised the dead, and so on. The frustration turned to fruitfulness. If He couldn't do this, He would do that. He gained not only victory, but victory plus!

O Christ, I will not be deterred by petty blocking of my plans. If I cannot get through, I will find a way around. Give me a resilient spirit that bends but is never broken. Help me to be equal to anything, through Your power. Amen.

FROM FRUSTRATIONS TO FRUITFULNESS

"I John…found myself in the island called Patmos, for adhering to God's word and the testimony of Jesus. On the Lord's day I found myself rapt in the Spirit, and I heard a loud voice behind me like a trumpet calling, 'Write your vision.'"
(Rev. 1:9–11 Moffatt)

Opposition and frustration can in fact be a spur for us. Glenn Cunningham, who in our time runs the fastest mile, was so badly burned as a lad that the doctors thought he would always be in a wheelchair. The boy who was destined to be an invalid turned that destiny into becoming the world's fastest human. James Whistler, the painter, wanted to be a soldier, but he failed at West Point and turned to the brush as a second choice. Walter Scott wanted to be a poet and gave up because he could not equal Lord Byron. Ashamed of being a novelist, he wrote anonymously—but gave the world *Ivanhoe*.

A young university man had both his hands blown off in an explosion. Since he could no longer use his hands, he decided to concentrate on using his head and became a teacher in a great university. Phillips Brooks wanted to be a teacher, failed miserably, and turned reluctantly to being a preacher, becoming one of the world's greatest.

Perhaps you find yourself in difficulties and frustrations because of your Christian stand as the apostle John did in the text above. Isolated from people, he saw heaven opened and received the vision of the coming victory. Isolation became revelation.

Are your life plans broken up? Then you can, by God's grace, make new and better ones.

Victorious Christ, impart to me Your secret. I am powerless to change my surroundings, so let me change my soul. I shall make my surroundings into the whetstone upon which my soul shall be sharpened for Your purposes. With You, I cannot be beaten. Amen.

ON USING ILLNESSES AND HINDRANCES

[Paul]: *As you know, it was because of an illness that I first preached the gospel to you. (Gal. 4:13)*

[Paul]: *There was given me a thorn in my flesh, a messenger of Satan, to torment me. Three times I pleaded with the Lord to take it away from me. But he said to me, "My grace is sufficient for you, for my power is made perfect in weakness." Therefore I will boast all the more gladly about my weaknesses...for when I am weak, then I am strong. (2 Cor. 12:7–10)*

The apostle Paul, though undercut by an illness in Galatia, used that frustration and preached the gospel, raising up a Christian church to which he later wrote a letter that has enriched the world. That is victory.

In response to Paul's "thorn in the flesh" God promised not deliverance, but power to use the infirmity. If the "messenger of Satan" were to buffet him, Paul would determine the direction in which the blows would send him. They sent him forward!

This great preacher said, "I am no speaker, perhaps" (2 Cor. 11:6 Moffatt)—but did that lack of oratorical ability stop Paul? It only spurred him on to primary successes. Had he been a good speaker, he probably would have depended on that, and a secondary success would have blocked a primary one. Many people are ruined by secondary successes—they become entangled in their techniques and never get to the goal.

One of the most spiritually useful men in America admits to being his "state's worst speaker." He is, but he has made that kick send him forward. He functions where his usefulness really matters.

Jesus, You were master of every situation—even on a cross, where You dispensed forgiveness to crucifiers and gave absolution to a dying thief. Give me this mastery over circumstances. Abide with me; then I can abide with anything. Amen.

WORKING WITH A WOUND IN YOUR SIDE

The king…ordered that her request be granted and had John beheaded in the prison…. John's disciples came and took his body and buried it. Then they went and told Jesus. When Jesus heard what had happened, he withdrew by boat privately to a solitary place. Hearing of this, the crowds followed him on foot from the towns. When Jesus landed and saw a large crowd, he had compassion on them and healed their sick. (Matt. 14:9–14)

So important is this power to turn the worst into the best that we must spend another week on it.

It is simply impossible always to explain why suffering occurs. You cannot unravel the mystery and give a logical answer. But while you cannot explain the Why, you can learn the How—the How of victory over it and through it and around it. Cease worrying over the Why, and get to the How!

When Jesus heard that John the Baptist, His cousin and forerunner, had been beheaded, He wanted to be alone to let the wound in His heart heal a bit. But a large crowd broke up His plans. He readily began healing the sick who had come to find Him. And then He fed the entire group. He worked for others with a wound in His own heart. Instead of being bitter against the injustice of John's beheading, He became more tender with others: He "had compassion on them."

If you have to work with a wound in your side, remember that your very hunger for consolation can feed others. Just before a missionary was to speak in a chapel service in India, he received a cable that his father had died. He said nothing to us, but went on and preached a tenderly beautiful message—the transcript of his own beautiful soul. Only after the service did he tell us about the cable. He worked with a wound—and that wound was healing to others.

Master of the inward wound, may I not wince or glance back, even in thought, when wounded by life. Help me to go steadily onward. This is a hurt world. Make my hurts into healing. Amen.

USING LIFE'S LEFTOVERS

"I will repay you for the years the locusts have eaten—the great locust and the young locust, the other locusts and the locust swarm—my great army that I sent among you. You will have plenty to eat, until you are full, and you will praise the name of the LORD your God, who has worked wonders for you; never again will my people be shamed." (Joel 2:25–26)

The Christian has the power to transform every calamity into opportunity. Someone has spoken of "getting music out of life's leftovers." Sometimes life leaves you very little—but you can gather up those leftovers and make music out of them. I saw such a person yesterday—a face chiseled into strength and beauty. She had been stricken with polio at age twenty-eight; her husband died when she was forty-five. But she decided she would walk, even after the doctors told her the muscles were gone. She created new muscles out of her own will and the grace of God. At forty-seven she took a course in secretarial work and is now doing what everybody else is doing—and more; she is doing it in a radiant, triumphant way.

Christians are people who, when they get to the end of their rope, tie a knot and hang on. They know that each extremity is God's opportunity. Someone has suggested that the "silence in heaven for about half an hour," spoken of in Revelation 8:1, was God shifting scenes for the next act. The silent, suffering spaces in your life may be God getting you ready for the next great act. Hold steady; the next act will come. In the meantime, take hold of your dull, drab moments and make them musical.

The Russians say: "A hammer shatters glass but forges steel." The calamities that shatter some will forge character and achievement in you.

O God, my Father, I see I don't need to whine or complain. I can make music out of misery, a song out of sorrow, and achievement out of accident. I will turn everything—good, bad, and indifferent—into something else. Amen.

LIGHT IN THE DARKNESS

I will lead the blind by ways they have not known, along unfamiliar paths I will guide them; I will turn the darkness into light before them and make the rough places smooth. These are the things I will do; I will not forsake them. (Isa. 42:16)

A spirit of courage and faith is essential for every one of us. A brilliant young man, my first Sunday school student, was surveying a swamp near an ammunition factory. He struck a piece of board on which there was a blister of nitroglycerin, and it exploded, rendering him totally blind and deaf. At age twenty-six he was doomed to an existence without light, without sound.

"For twenty-four hours," he said, "I was beaten. None of my family ever seemed to die before eighty, and here I was—only twenty-six." But then he snapped out of it and determined to meet life as a Christian—he would find grace in the darkness. In fact, he has. He has brought a family into the world and supported them through a business he set up. There is no way of communicating with him except by printing out the letters of words on the back of his hand.

When I asked him how it felt to be cut off from the world, he laughed and said, "I'm not cut off from the world." Every portion of his being is vibrant with receptivity. He is informed on everything. To my question on what was his greatest disability, he replied, "I have a bad temper and get angry with those I love." Here was a blind and deaf man saying his greatest disability was a moral one!

This man illustrates the fact that what matters is not what happens to you, but what you do with it after it does happen. Christians are afraid of nothing, for they can use everything.

Brave Christ, make me brave. Even if the worst should happen to me, we can turn it into the best. I say "we," for I cannot do it alone. With You I can do anything, bear anything, go through anything. Otherwise, I will wither. But I am with You, so I face the future with calm joy. Amen.

MAKING ALL THINGS RESULT IN GOOD

We know that in all things God works for the good of those who love him, who have been called according to his purpose. (Rom. 8:28)

When the storm strikes the eagle whose wings are set in a downward tilt, it will be dashed to pieces on the earth. But if its wings are tilted upward, it will rise, making the storm bear it up beyond its fury. The set of the wings decides defeat or victory.

Christianity gives a set to the soul, so that when frustration and disaster strike, the soul goes up—its wings are set in that direction. The same disaster can strike other souls, and because of attitudes they writhe in anguish in the dust. Death strikes one home leaving bitterness and frustration; in another, the result is calmness, quiet victory, and greater usefulness.

Some students discussing the Scripture above said to a professor in Union Theological College, Richmond, Virginia, "But you don't believe that all the pain and suffering and misery can work for good—do you?" The professor replied, "The things in themselves may not be good, but you can make them work together for good."

That afternoon, his wife was killed in an automobile accident, and he was left a cripple. He sent for the seminary president and said, "Tell my students that Romans 8:28 still holds good." He died in a year. They inscribed this passage from Romans on his tombstone, for it was inscribed in his convictions. One of the greatest preachers of the South went again and again to that tomb with bowed head, praying that he might have that kind of grace.

The professor, through his triumphant spirit in that sudden tragedy, has gone further in his influence than he might have gone through long years of teaching.

O Christ, You lived and labored only three short years. But eternity was packed into those hours. Whether I live a short or long life, let my hours embody eternity. Then nothing can make me afraid. I thank You. Amen.

VICTORIOUS VITALITY

Thanks be to God, who always leads us in triumphal procession in Christ and through us spreads everywhere the fragrance of the knowledge of him. (2 Cor. 2:14)

Victorious vitality is able to master everything because it can use everything. It can take the raw materials of human living—justice and injustice, pleasure and pain, compliment and criticism—and weave them into the purposes of our lives, transmuting them into character and usefulness.

Just across the hall from where I was staying, a poor fellow, beaten by life, went into a closet and hung himself on a clothes bar only five feet from the floor, so that he had to hold up his feet until life was extinct. In deep contrast to this man is a woman in another town whom I went that day to see. She has been in bed forty-four years but is unbeaten by life. On the contrary, she has mastered it. She had three diseases, any one of which would have killed a normal person; but she is the "unkillable" kind. She reported, "These different disease germs fell into fighting each other down on the inside of me; and as they fought, they forgot about me—so I lived on."

Lying there on her back, she began to make exquisite butterfly pendants and set up a gift shop. She was soon making enough money to pay an income tax. She laughingly said, "I sent off my check to the government with my love." When you can pay your income tax with your love—well, that's a miracle! A magazine gave her $100 for the story of her gift shop and then gave her $1,000 for the best true story of the year. Her room is the confessional of the city. The bedpost upon which I leaned was literally worn down from people leaning on it and telling this invalid their troubles. Young and old go away renewed after opening their hearts to her gentle wisdom.

O Christ of the exuberant joy, give me this joy—in spite of. Save me from all self-pity, all feeling sorry for myself, and let me be outgoing and positive, taking on myself the problems of others. Help me to keep my sorrows in use as servants of the sorrows of others. In Jesus' name, Amen.

GOD WATCHES OVER OUR SPIRIT

May God himself, the God of peace, sanctify you through and through. May your whole spirit, soul and body be kept blameless at the coming of our Lord Jesus Christ. The one who calls you is faithful and he will do it. (1 Thess. 5:23–24)

When I asked the gift shop lady (introduced yesterday) what was the central thought of her year, she replied, "God's watch-care." Think of an invalid choosing God's watch-care as her central thanksgiving! If God cared about her, then why did He not heal her?

God heals in eight great ways: (1) through the surgeon, (2) the physician, (3) climate, (4) mental suggestion, (5) scientific nutrition, (6) deliverance from underlying fears, resentments, self-centeredness, and guilt, (7) the direct operation of the Holy Spirit, and (8) through the coming resurrection. Whatever He does not cure through the first seven ways He will cure through the eighth.

The "watch-care" of which God's noblewoman spoke was watch-care over her spirit, that her spirit should remain unspoiled and sound. Healed at the heart, she could say, "Let the world come on!"

A woman arose in one of our meetings and said the doctors had given her six months to live—cancer of the lungs. "At first," she said, "I was bitter and rebellious—how could I leave my children and my husband? Then I said to myself, 'If I have only six months to live, am I going to leave my children a heritage of defeat and frustration? Is that the last thing they will remember about me?' I decided I would surrender my rebellion and bitterness. Since then, there has been calm poise and even joy. The fact is, I've gained ten pounds." God's watch-care was over her spirit. Nothing else really mattered!

O God, watch over my spirit and keep me sound there. For if my spirit holds up, everything holds up with it. Then help me to live with abundance on the inside, so it will not matter much what happens on the outside. Into Your hands I commend my spirit this day—keep it positive and sweet. Amen.

MAKING LIFE COUNT REGARDLESS

*In all these things we are more than conquerors through him who loved us.
(Rom. 8:37)*

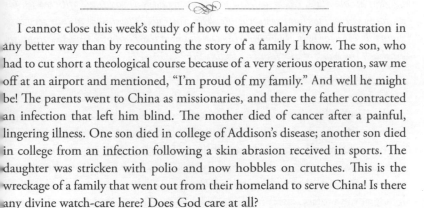

I cannot close this week's study of how to meet calamity and frustration in any better way than by recounting the story of a family I know. The son, who had to cut short a theological course because of a very serious operation, saw me off at an airport and mentioned, "I'm proud of my family." And well he might be! The parents went to China as missionaries, and there the father contracted an infection that left him blind. The mother died of cancer after a painful, lingering illness. One son died in college of Addison's disease; another son died in college from an infection following a skin abrasion received in sports. The daughter was stricken with polio and now hobbles on crutches. This is the wreckage of a family that went out from their homeland to serve China! Is there any divine watch-care here? Does God care at all?

The one surviving son was proud of his family because his father and sister, left at home, have only a seeing-eye dog and a pair of crutches between them—and yet they are meeting life gloriously. The father is pastor of a church, and the daughter keeps house for him—on crutches. She also organizes church activities, drives a specially equipped car, and is her father's right hand. Together they go on, amazingly useful. The father lectures all over the country. And, better than all, he keeps a radiant soul.

"This is the victory that has overcome the world [of sorrow and frustration], even our faith" (1 John 5:4). If faith is intact, nothing else really matters—you can rise unscathed from anything.

O Jesus, while hanging on the cross You said, "My God," even when the light had gone out and everything had collapsed. With those words You rose from gloom to glory. Let no sorrow or disappointment pluck those words, "My God," from my lips or my heart; and I, too, shall prevail over everything. Amen.

AGES AND STAGES

Teach us to number our days aright, that we may gain a heart of wisdom.…
Satisfy us in the morning with your unfailing love, that we may sing for joy and
be glad all our days. Make us glad for as many days as you have afflicted us, for
as many years as we have seen trouble. May your deeds be shown to your servants,
your splendor to their children. May the favor of the Lord our God rest upon us;
establish the work of our hands. (Psalm 90:12, 14–17)

As the years go by, they leave deposits of suffering in our minds, our memories, our bodies. We have been studying how to meet these deposits. But many people find that the greatest deposit of difficulty is just the fact of the aging process. To adjust ourselves and achieve abundant living at each stage is important.

Some people rebel and never really pass into maturity. They bring over infantilisms with them. They are misfits. Some who are growing old refuse to adjust to that fact, always sighing to be young again—fruitlessly, of course.

To be victorious at each stage of life, one must accept the fact of change and make the present period into something beautiful and effective. Each stage has something unique in possibility and achievement. Youth is not the only age of possibility. John saw in Revelation the tree of life "bearing twelve crops of fruit, yielding its fruit every month" (22:2). On the tree of life here and now, each month has its own fruit; each period has something distinctive in beauty and possibility.

God, as we live the adventure of each stage of life, give us insight and imagination
to make each stage distinctive and beautiful. Help us not to waste time in useless
regrets, or in reaching for the moon; instead, help us to beautify the hours as they
come and go, pressing the imprint of eternity upon each passing moment. Amen.

A LADDER FOR THE YOUNG (STEPS 1-5)

Don't let anyone look down on you because you are young, but set an example for the believers in speech, in life, in love, in faith and in purity. (1 Tim. 4:12)

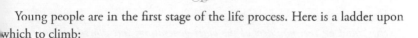

Young people are in the first stage of the life process. Here is a ladder upon which to climb:

(1) You are an awakening personality; let your whole being—body, mind, and spirit—come alive simultaneously. In the stage of physical awakening, some young people become acutely aware of their bodies, and especially of the fact of sex. This is normal and right. But it is possible to become so tangled up in sexual thought that you become body-minded. You must awaken in your total person—your mind and soul as well as your body—or you will be stunted in important dimensions.

(2) Find a cause to which you can devote your energies, giving life its meaning, coherence, and goal. That cause is the kingdom of God. Jesus said, "Seek first his kingdom...and all these things will be given to you as well" (Matt. 6:33). If you get the first thing first, then your life will come out right. If you get the wrong thing first, then nothing will come out right.

(3) Find a person who embodies that cause—a person to whom you can be loyal. That person is Christ. When you are loyal to Him, you are loyal to God's order that was embodied in Him—the kingdom. You are not giving yourself to an impersonal order but to Someone warm, tender, and personal.

(4) Make your life decisions yourself—don't drift. Some allow their circumstances or friends to decide for them. They don't act—they only react.

(5) Don't revolt against the older group and merely echo your own generation. That is substituting one bondage for another. When your group is wrong, dare to be different. Don't act in response to pressures, but to principles.

O God, I don't want to drift from wave to wave of meaningless emotion—I want a Way. You are the Way, and I will follow You through popularity or disfavor. I choose You. Amen.

A LADDER FOR THE YOUNG (STEPS 6-10)

Listen, my sons, to a father's instruction; pay attention and gain understanding.
I give you sound learning, so do not forsake my teaching. (Prov. 4:1–2)

Here are more steps on the ladder of life:

(6) Stand on the shoulders of the older generation, but don't kick their heads,
they're not made of wood—at least not all of them. Wisdom didn't begin with you,
and it won't end with you. You will soon belong to the older group; make sure
the next generation has a higher vantage point when it stands on *your* shoulders.

(7) Challenge everything, and then challenge yourself to make things better. That
is the kind of demonstration people will listen to. Protest must not be merely
verbal; it must be vital.

(8) Don't be impatient if the world doesn't change overnight at your command.
Some young people, because they cannot do everything, do nothing. Don't be
absolutist—do the next thing, and so prepare for the greater thing.

(9) Don't try to be a leader—be the servant of all, and out of that service you
will gain leadership as a by-product. Jesus said, "Nor must you be called 'leaders,'
for One is your leader, even the Christ" (Matt. 23:10 MOFFATT). The attitude
of many leaders is: "I lead; you follow"—it is self-assertive and thus cannot be
Christianized. It produces fussy managers of other people. Jesus said there was
one title He could trust us with—"servant" (Mark 9:35). In fact, "servant of
all." As you lose yourself in the service of *all* (not just some, such as your class,
your race, your color), you will become truly great.

(10) Be thorough in the small tasks and opportunities—out of these will grow
bigger ones. "You have been faithful with a few things; I will put you in charge
of many things" (Matt. 25:21).

God, my Father, I cannot do this alone. I need You. I am leaning heavily upon
Your strength, depending on Your resources, drawing on Your power. Walk with
me through the years. If You do, I cannot fail. Amen.

A LADDER FOR THE YOUNG (STEPS 11-13)

[Joshua]: *"Now fear the LORD and serve him with all faithfulness.... If serving the LORD seems undesirable to you, then choose for yourselves this day whom you will serve, whether the gods your forefathers served beyond the River, or the gods of the Amorites, in whose land you are living. But as for me and my household, we will serve the LORD." (Josh. 24:14–15)*

We're continuing to move up the ladder of life with the following steps:

(11) Take God into your choice of a life partner. Base your choice on something more than physical attraction. Find someone, if possible, in whom you will be interested and with whom you will be in love when the physical side of life has been dimmed and only the mental and spiritual remain. In other words, find somebody in whose conversation you will have a lifelong interest. But don't expect perfection, since you yourself will not bring it to the marriage.

(12) Youth is the age of struggling for freedom—gain freedom through discipline. There are two ways to seek freedom: one is to throw off all restraint, and the other is to find freedom through disciplined obedience to high, chosen ends. You don't gain freedom from the police by disobeying the law; in fact, they will haunt you every moment. You gain freedom by obeying the laws for which the police stand. When you are disciplined from within, then you are truly free.

(13) Start the day right, and you will probably end it right. Set aside some part of the morning for a quiet time with God. Fix the habit so that it is not a decision to be made daily. It is something automatic, with no exceptions. Pray whether you feel like it or not—pray by the clock, if necessary. Then there will be a Hand on your shoulder as you go out into the day to begin your adventure with God.

O God, as I begin this day and this new way of life, I put my hand in Yours. May I not miss a step with You today. May my strong urges be taken over by Your love and turned toward kingdom ends. I offer You my strengths as well as my weaknesses. In Jesus' name, Amen.

A LADDER FOR MIDDLE AGE

[Paul]: *When perfection comes, the imperfect disappears. When I was a child, I talked like a child, I thought like a child, I reasoned like a child. When I became a man, I put childish ways behind me. (1 Cor. 13:10–11)*

A similar set of steps is needed for those in the middle of adulthood:

(1) Watch out for decaying enthusiasm and ideals. Beware of the desire for softness and comfort. You are very liable to settle down, become safe—and start decaying. A middle-aged woman in one of our ashrams admitted: "I'm about to jell into the kind of a woman I don't want to be."

(2) Watch the growing power of money over you. Persons may gradually become purses—stuffed and stuffy.

(3) Watch the growing power of the crowd upon you. In middle age we cease being different, take on protective resemblance to our environment, fit into the group—and die of suffocation.

(4) Watch for a flare-up of sex. "The dangerous forties and fifties" must be guarded. Don't be afraid of this period, for it has its compensations. But watch and control any temptation.

(5) Watch your middle. There are four signs of approaching age: baldness, bifocals, bridges, and bulges! You may not be able to prevent the first three, but you can do something about the last one.

(6) Be reconverted to Christ at age forty, simply on general principles. It will take you through the days ahead with a growing spiritual vitality.

(7) Remain a hero to your children. Be the kind of parent they actually choose to quote as well as emulate.

(8) Keep a growing mind and soul after the body stops growing. "Education is change," the saying goes—so be continually educated.

(9) Amid all the changes, keep a living center—God.

My Father God, I am now getting to the time of life when the fires of life tend to burn low. Don't let them go out within me. As I go along, I am gathering experience—help me to grow in usefulness, power, and love. Amen.

A LADDER FOR SENIOR YEARS
(STEPS 1-4)

[Paul]: *The time has come for my departure. I have fought the good fight, I have finished the race, I have kept the faith. Now there is in store for me the crown of righteousness, which the Lord, the righteous Judge, will award to me on that day—and not only to me, but also to all who have longed for his appearing. (2 Tim. 4:6–8)*

There is only one way to remain young and that is to grow old gracefully. Here are some keys:

(1) Accept your age. Don't fight the fact that you are getting old—use it. You can't be twenty-eight again; then make fifty-eight or sixty-eight beautiful and useful. Each age has its own peculiar beauty and makes its own contribution. I am fifty-eight, and I love it! I wouldn't be twenty-eight again for anything; fifty-eight is too interesting, too full, too adventurous.

(2) Accept the liberties that come through advancing age. A wonderfully useful nurse said this to a group: "Beyond fifty, I found a freedom and a calm, and an interest in people as people, not merely as sexual beings." Her liberty to love and help others was very real. Accept the liberty to love more fully and widely when it comes.

(3) Accept the responsibilities that come along with that freedom. Your children have grown up and gone; now see what you can do for other children. I know one woman who, after her own children grew up, was responsible for putting through school not less than a dozen children; and she was not wealthy either, except in spirit and in good works. But what other wealth is there?

(4) Never retire—simply change your work. The human personality is made for creation, and when it ceases to create, it creaks…and cracks…and crashes. You may not create as strenuously as before, but keep creating. Otherwise you will grow tired of all the resting.

Creative God, may my mind and my soul be ever creative. This vehicle of body may not respond as well as before, but help me to keep it alert and fit for purposes of the kingdom of God. I am at Your service—forever! Amen.

E. STANLEY JONES | 293

A LADDER FOR SENIOR YEARS
(STEPS 5-7)

The righteous will flourish like a palm tree.... They will still bear fruit in old age, they will stay fresh and green, proclaiming, "The LORD is upright; he is my Rock, and there is no wickedness in him." (Psalm 92:12, 14–15)

We are completing the ladder for senior years:

(5) Don't try to tie your children to you too closely—give them rope. They must have sufficient room to grow on their own. The Bible says: "A man will leave his father and mother and be united to his wife, and they will become one flesh" (Gen. 2:24). This recognizes the necessity of young people leaving home in order to grow. Don't interfere. Remember, you wanted liberty to make mistakes when you started out too.

(6) Surrender to God your loved ones who have died. Do not mourn over them in useless regret. A mother monkey will often carry around the decaying corpse of a dead baby. Such grief is pitiful, dangerous, and useless, but not more so than that of a human parent who refuses to surrender the loved ones who have passed on. Many older people spoil their lives by useless mourning over departed loved ones. I know an intelligent woman who is making her life, and the lives of those around her, miserable by her useless mourning. She thinks it is showing loyalty to her husband, but really it is a species of self-pity.

(7) Develop the mind up to the end, keeping fit for tasks here and hereafter. They tell us that the *mind* never ages. Yes, the brain (the instrument of the mind) does grow old; but the mind can keep the brain fresh and alert if the mind doesn't let down and sag. Compel yourself to read some portion of a good book each day. Above all, fill your mind with *the* Book. Then you will never be empty or alone.

Gracious Father, help me to grow old gracefully and beautifully, to come to maturity majestically. Fill my mind and soul with Yourself, so that when physical beauty fades, spiritual beauty may take its place. Amen.

DO OUR WORDS FIT THE FACTS?

These men began to argue with Stephen, but they could not stand up against his wisdom or the Spirit by whom he spoke. (Acts 6:9–10)

We have been studying how to adjust to the passing of time. We turn now to another modification—adjusting our vocabulary to fact. Words often lose their relation to what is real. They are like institutions in this respect, which are formed at first to express life but often end up throttling that very life.

This is particularly true of religious words. They become sacrosanct, but all out of touch with reality. We must go over our vocabulary relentlessly to see if we are using words out of which the content has dropped. This is important, for the younger generation has a strong sense of what is real—it can sniff unreality from afar. The young people of our high schools and colleges usually give speakers the first five minutes to prove they have reality. If they hear only words, they will instead take out a book to read!

We must reclothe the eternal truths of the gospel in the language each age can understand. But even that will not do, if the reclothing is just adopting the words of a new age—terms that are contemporary. The words must have content in them, or they will say nothing.

Language is a symbol, and has to be changed constantly to fit the facts. The symbols are not the facts. A map is not the territory it represents—in fact, maps often have to be changed to bring them nearer to the facts on the ground, or they will mislead the users. Vocabularies that are not being constantly changed to fit the facts of life become dangerous.

But we dislike change, especially in words. An elder in a certain denomination felt the statement of its 1911 Conference was sacrosanct—and when the church changed it, he committed suicide. But the church would have committed suicide if it hadn't made the words fit the facts.

O God, perhaps I, too, am a prisoner of my vocabulary. Then break up my speech; tear down unreal and hollow words. I surrender my words and phrases to You. Make them over; I will try to cooperate. Amen.

LABELS CAN BECOME LIBELS

LORD, who may dwell in your sanctuary? Who may live on your holy hill? He whose walk is blameless and who does what is righteous, who speaks the truth from his heart and has no slander on his tongue, who does his neighbor no wrong and casts no slur on his fellowman. (Psalm 15:1–3)

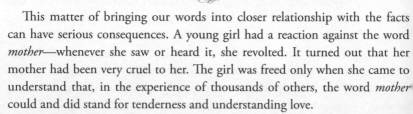

This matter of bringing our words into closer relationship with the facts can have serious consequences. A young girl had a reaction against the word *mother*—whenever she saw or heard it, she revolted. It turned out that her mother had been very cruel to her. The girl was freed only when she came to understand that, in the experience of thousands of others, the word *mother* could and did stand for tenderness and understanding love.

We stick labels on whole groups of people during this war [World War II] by saying, "Japs are tricky," or "Americans are materialistic." These labels are false and unjust. Some Japanese are tricky, as some Americans are; but many Japanese are not. Some Americans are materialistic, and some are not. Such labels are libels.

After a man was introduced in a flamboyant manner, he arose and said, "The adjective is often the enemy of the noun." We must cleanse our adjectives and see that they fit the nouns. Gandhi is an example of this. He has said he would use ornate language no more than he would use ornate clothing. He has reduced life and language to simplicity. When he speaks, his words are a revelation of fact.

In Jesus this simplicity of speech came to its perfection. His words were so stripped of embellishment that they were pure fact. His statement was: "By your words you will be acquitted, and by your words you will be condemned" (Matt. 12:37). We must surrender our vocabulary, then, for cleansing.

O Christ, I do surrender my vocabulary to You, for I want my words to come out of a heart of truth. Cleanse from my speech all unreality, all pretension, all veneer, and let me speak only that which has been cleansed by the Word. Amen.

BRIDGING THE SPEECH GAPS (PART 1)

A good person produces good things from the treasury of a good heart, and an evil person produces evil things from the treasury of an evil heart. And I tell you this, you must give an account on judgment day for every idle word you speak. (Matt. 12:35–36†)

When I speak about bringing words into closer relationship with facts, I must admit that the two can never be one—except on that single occasion when "the Word became flesh" (John 1:14). Just once in human history the symbol and the reality coincided, fusing together in Christ. In all other cases, the symbol of language must constantly be adjusted to the facts.

Here are steps for doing so, from Dr. Gordon Campbell, a medical psychologist and advocate for word-fact coherence:

(1) Date your statement. Why? Because people change; you change. Your statement about a person may become outdated; you may be talking about some other person than the one who lives today.

(2) Index the differences. When you make a statement about a person, proceed to add the ways in which your statement may not be the full picture. It may be true in general, but there are other factors that modify the generalization—state those other factors. As the quip puts it, "All generalizations are false—including this one."

(3) Put "et cetera, et cetera" after your statements. You have said certain things, but you have not said everything. For example, in describing a person, if you don't provide for the fact that the person is changing characteristics, your statement may be false. As Professor William James says: "If you start out to describe the universe in a sentence, put in a comma instead of a period."

(4) Be especially careful with labels. I find these days, for example, that the words "socialist" or "communist" are commonly used very loosely. Only when you are sure about someone should you apply any label.

O God, as You are cleansing my soul from all falsities, so cleanse my speech too. I want to be pure in both arenas. I want to be a clarified person. Amen.

BRIDGING THE SPEECH GAPS (PART 2)

Do not judge others, and you will not be judged. For you will be treated as you treat others. The standard you use in judging is the standard by which you will be judged. And why worry about a speck in your friend's eye when you have a log in your own? How can you think of saying to your friend, "Let me help you get rid of that speck in your eye," when you can't see past the log in your own eye? Hypocrite! First get rid of the log in your own eye; then you will see well enough to deal with the speck in your friend's eye. (Matt. 7:1–5†)

Here are the final two steps for word-fact coherence:

(5) Hyphenate your terms when appropriate. In speaking of body and mind, it is often inaccurate to separate them—they should be considered as "body-mind." For the two are closely intertwined.

(6) Stay with specifics. Seneca said: "A man who does not wash his hands is not a pig. He is a man who does not wash his hands." The difference in implication is profound. If you make one or the other of those statements, your whole attitude has to change accordingly.

Again, don't make the sweeping generalization of "I don't like that person." Instead, say, "I don't like such-and-such a thing about that person—but I rather like the person." That will make all the difference in the world. Sometimes we take a particular trait and keep chewing on it so we cannot see the rest of the person at all. We need to turn our attitude and say, "The person in general is right, but this thing isn't right." That would make us accurate, and the other person lovable.

Having segregated the thing you do not like in the person, do not end on what you do not like, but on what you do like. Let the last impression be positive.

Gracious Father, straighten me out from mental quirks that distort and disrupt. Help me to have a mind clarified of all prejudice and half-truths. May I be wholesome in mind and speech, for only in this way can I be the person You intend me to be. In Jesus' name, Amen.

OUR MONEY RELATIONSHIPS

[Jesus]: *"No one can serve two masters. For you will hate one and love the other; you will be devoted to one and despise the other. You cannot serve both God and money." The Pharisees, who dearly loved their money, heard all this and scoffed at him. Then he said to them, "You like to appear righteous in public, but God knows your hearts. What this world honors is detestable in the sight of God." (Luke 16:13–15†)*

We turn now to our relationship with money. None of us can live abundantly until we have found a Christian relationship here. Mark 12:41 says, "Now Jesus sat opposite the treasury and saw…" (NKJV). It is a solemn moment when we turn to our money, with Him sitting nearby and watching.

We know the life of the human body depends on balance—too much or too little produces imbalance, and hence disease. Too much food is just as harmful as too little. Too much or too little secretion of a gland threatens us.

Yet how we have neglected that word *balance* in relation to possessions. We have had no brakes on accumulation—the more we possess, the more successful we are supposed to be. One way we express the height of well-being is: "I feel like a million." This imbalance in possessions is producing disease in the body of society as well as its individuals. Decay invades the very poor and the very rich. Where is the place of balance?

Christianity has the answer. It teaches neither asceticism nor avarice—it teaches that you have the right and duty to have your needs met. In the early church, "it was distributed to anyone as he had need" (Acts 4:35). *Need* is the place of balance. Less than need produces disease, and more than need produces another kind of disease. Our civilization is unbalanced at this point because it is unchristian. Hence it topples over periodically into war.

O God, we are now in a real battle. Unnatural cravings have been created within us. We are victims of false values, of false goals. We have hurt ourselves and others in our madness. Help us to return to sanity, to equilibrium, to balance. In Jesus' name, Amen.

MASTERING OUR MONEY (STEPS 1-5)

Do not wear yourself out to get rich; have the wisdom to show restraint. Cast but a glance at riches, and they are gone, for they will surely sprout wings and fly off to the sky like an eagle. (Prov. 23:4–5)

In order to get mastery over money, here are the steps:

(1) Hold in your mind that money is a good servant, but a terrible master. If it gets on top of you, then your life is decided by a thing; consequently you are no longer a person, but a thing. If money is your god, then your enfeebled personality is the price you pay to worship that god.

(2) Reject the philosophy that you may hold vast accumulations as a trustee for the poor. Andrew Carnegie, who was the best illustration of this philosophy, said: "The millionaire will be but the trustee of the poor, entrusted for a season with a great part of the wealth of the community, but administering it for the community far better than it would have done for itself." If that is true, then democracy means little.

The poor do not need our charity, but our justice. When you give charity, they are mere recipients. When you give justice, you and they become equals. It is easy to be charitable; it is difficult to be just.

(3) Nothing you could do for your children would be more harmful than to leave them so much that they would not have to struggle and work. The surest way to flabby, irresponsible character is too much money.

(4) There are two ways to be wealthy—one is by having abundant possessions, the other is by having few wants. In choosing the latter way, you collect real wealth that cannot be taken away by depression or death.

(5) Where your needs end, set up a stop. After that, everything you make belongs to other people's needs. If you can create that stop, you are a person of character. You have mastered things; they do not master you.

O God, I live in an acquiring society where worth is judged by wealth. At the same time I am a Christian, and my judgments must be different. Help me to decide the Christian way, no matter how odd I may seem to be. Amen.

MASTERING OUR MONEY (STEPS 6-8)

[Paul]: *"I have not coveted anyone's silver or gold or clothing. You yourselves know that these hands of mine have supplied my own needs and the needs of my companions. In everything I did, I showed you that by this kind of hard work we must help the weak, remembering the words the Lord Jesus himself said: 'It is more blessed to give than to receive.'"* (Acts 20:33–35)

(6) *Keep your needs down to needs, not luxuries disguised as needs.* Needs contribute; luxuries choke. If you eat food beyond your needs, you simply clog the system and add useless fat—surplus baggage, which you then have to carry around. The same is true with money and things. If you find you have too much, invest it in people. This is the only bank that will not fail. It will pay dividends through eternity. Invest all surpluses in that bank.

(7) *Decide your level of need in the full light of the needs of others, of your enlightened conscience, and of the judgment of a disciplined group.* All three things are necessary. I speak of an "enlightened conscience," for a conscience trained in the half-lights of contemporary society is not an enlightened conscience. Train it at the feet of Christ. But when you come there, be sure you have adequate information about the needs of others. Conscience requires wide information to be a safe guide. A group is also necessary to help you make sound judgments, for it is more objective. An unchecked conscience is not safe.

(8) *As long as you are working to raise your income to the level of your need, give a tithe of what you earn. After you have reached that level, give everything you earn.* The tithe is but a token, a sign that you are not owner, but the one who owes. Just as you pay rent to acknowledge the ownership of another, so you pay a tithe to acknowledge the ownership of God over the nine-tenths. But when the level of your needs has been reached, then *all* you earn belongs to the needs of others—not as charity, but as right and justice.

O God our Father, I am digging deep around the roots of my life. I am trying to tie off this "root of all evil"—I cannot cut it entirely, but I can make sure it does not take too much nourishment from the soil of my life. Help me. Amen.

MASTERING OUR MONEY (STEP 9)

[Paul]: *Of course, I don't mean your giving should make life easy for others and hard for yourselves. I only mean that there should be some equality. Right now you have plenty and can help those who are in need. Later, they will have plenty and can share with you when you need it. In this way, things will be equal. As the Scriptures say, "Those who gathered a lot had nothing left over, and those who gathered only a little had enough." (2 Cor. 8:13–15†)*

Before we leave the subject of material possessions, we must spend one more day in gathering up our steps: (*9*) *Work for a cooperative system in which each will think and work for all, and all will think and work for each.* We would not produce less wealth in such a cooperative society—we would produce more, but it would be more widely distributed. The general level of life would rise for everybody. Wherever there are vast inequalities, there are bound to be instability, unrest, and clashes.

We had an interesting demonstration in American history of two attitudes toward money. In 1852 two sets of caravans with covered wagons started out from Omaha across the wide expanses toward the Far West. For days they went in parallel lines, and then they diverged—in more ways than one. The first group had written on their covered wagons: "God-seekers." The other group, part of the gold rush, put on their wagons: "Gold-seekers." The latter group was individualistic and competitive; the former group was a society of mutual aid, seeking the good of all and of each.

The "gold-seekers" found their gold, but it went through their fingers like water. Their gold is now, for the most part, in the hands of corporations. The "God-seekers" settled on unpromising land, developed it anyway, and now have a corporation for the good of the whole with significant assets.

The nature of life apparently approved of one and doomed the other.

O God, You are teaching us, through many a pain and frustration, that we must be a cooperative society. We have been slow to learn the lesson. Forgive us. Give us another chance, and we will learn Your ways. Amen.

WHAT CHRISTIANITY SAYS ABOUT RACE

Here there is no Greek or Jew, circumcised or uncircumcised, barbarian, Scythian, slave or free, but Christ is all, and is in all. (Col. 3:11)

A cooperative order must function not by class, color, or creed, but among persons as persons, apart from these extraneous things. Cooperation by class is snobbery; by color it is prejudice; by creed it is bigotry; by persons as persons it is Christian. But the moment we try to start a cooperative plan of living, we run into racial prejudice—one of the deepest we have to encounter. How can we master it? We cannot otherwise live abundantly.

If we are to make headway in this area, we will not do so by sentimental platitudes, but by facing irresistible facts. Are there such facts? Yes.

We have the backing of Christianity that humanity is one. "[God]…made every nation of men, that they should inhabit the whole earth" (Acts 17:26). "You have only one teacher, and all of you are equal as brothers and sisters" (Matt. 23:8 †). Paul spoke about a slave as: "no longer a mere slave but something more than a slave—a beloved brother; especially dear to me but how much more to you as a man and as a Christian!" (Philem. 1:16 MOFFATT).

The early church not only put people on a theoretical level but actually gave them equal authority. Paul was ordained at Antioch by a ministerium that included "Simeon called Niger" (Acts 13:1–3), literally, "the Black." There is no doubt whatever that our modern color prejudices were not present in early Christianity. In those times a person was looked on simply as a person— "someone for whom Christ died" (Rom. 14:15 †).

Christianity was to be a revelation of both God and humanity—and more: It was to be a faith in both. The Christian faith therefore brings out the best in all persons. Christ is the great believer in us—not some of us, but all of us. Hence, He is the hope of the world.

Our Father, give us a faith in You and in one another. Help us to look on people with the eyes of kindling faith, not with chilling doubt. You believe in us when we cannot believe in ourselves. Help us to pass on Your faith. Amen.

WHAT THE SCIENCES SAY ABOUT RACE

Dear friends, since God so loved us, we also ought to love one another. No one has ever seen God; but if we love one another, God lives in us and his love is made complete in us. (1 John 4:11–12)

Furthermore, another fact we must face is that *we have the backing of biology.* The idea of inherently superior races and inherently inferior races is being fast exploded by scientific investigation. There are undeveloped groups, but no permanently inferior or superior ones. The four types of blood found in one race are found in every race. A study showed that the IQs of black children in New York are as high as those of white children. The cultural background of their homes may help or retard their progress, but the raw material is the same.

An English judge in Burma, who had also been a judge in England, told me he had discovered that the brain of humanity is one, for the lawyers in England and in Burma argue from the same fallacies to the same conclusions!

Finally, *we have the backing of democracy.* If democracy means anything, it means equal opportunity for all—and "all" means all, of whatever race, color, or class. If it doesn't mean that, it is not democracy, but hypocrisy—the rule of the mask, instead of the rule of the mass. When I traveled to Soviet Russia, they said to me: "You are outdated. We are the real inheritors of democracy. You grew afraid of your principle, tried to confine it to the political scene; we went on and applied it to the economic and social as well. We are therefore the true practitioners of democracy." There is only one answer to that, and it cannot be simply verbal—it must be vital, a demonstration.

Remember the words of Peter: "The Holy Spirit told me to go with them and not to worry that they were Gentiles" (Acts 11:12 †). When we make racial distinctions, we break with the Spirit of God and accept the spirit of arrogance.

O God, I know that without justice there can be no community. Cleanse my heart of all divisiveness, all prejudice, all smallness. I want to love in spite of differences of color and race. Amen.

PRACTICAL STEPS AGAINST PREJUDICE

You are free, yet you are God's slaves, so don't use your freedom as an excuse to do evil. Respect everyone, and love your Christian brothers and sisters. Fear God, and respect the king. (1 Peter 2:16–17†)

Since we have the backing of Christianity, biology, and democracy that humanity is one, we can deliberately take steps to build up new attitudes toward other races. Here are five to consider:

(1) I will cease sticking labels on whole peoples. It is not true that certain groups are tricky, or materialistic, or shiftless—some individuals are, and some are not.

(2) I will deliberately cultivate friendships with people of another race. I will find that down underneath surface differences, we are fundamentally one. A German woman, after the last war, was applying for a job. Seeking to forestall prejudice, she said to the hiring agent, "Madam, we both shed the same tears." We do.

(3) I will deliberately set out to find what I can learn from people of another race. Each has something to teach the rest of us. It takes many differing notes to make a symphony. One year I realized that the three people who had influenced me most were Gandhi, Booker T. Washington, and Kagawa—not one of them of my color or race.

(4) I will deliberately try to bring people of other races into my church fellowship. The Christian church must be different from surrounding society.

(5) I will deliberately identify myself with the dispossessed and discriminated against. I will make their disadvantages my own, until all of life is thrown open to everybody on the basis of equal opportunity. Their cross shall be my cross; and their resurrection, my resurrection.

Gracious Father, here I will find my cross in modern life. I will become a part of the disabilities that fall on others. Help me to identify with the forgotten and despised in real ways, not as a mere gesture. In Jesus' name, Amen.

WHAT ABOUT WAR?

"The eyes of the Lord are on the righteous and his ears are attentive to their prayer, but the face of the Lord is against those who do evil." (1 Peter 3:12)

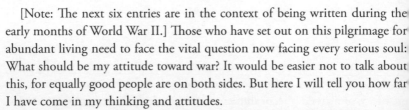

[Note: The next six entries are in the context of being written during the early months of World War II.] Those who have set out on this pilgrimage for abundant living need to face the vital question now facing every serious soul: What should be my attitude toward war? It would be easier not to talk about this, for equally good people are on both sides. But here I will tell you how far I have come in my thinking and attitudes.

First, *I have determined that I will not break my fellowship with those who differ from me.* I believe in liberty of conscience so much that I must give other people liberty to disagree without de-Christianizing them, even in thought. The fellowship must not be broken.

But second, *I have become completely disillusioned about the war method.* During the First World War I preached on two texts: "Herod with his men of war set [Jesus] at nought" (Luke 23:11 KJV), which I used to show that militarism cuts the impact of Jesus to zero. However, I offset that text with this one: "When the rioters saw the commander and his soldiers, they stopped beating Paul" (Acts 21:32). Military power, I contended, can be used to protect the innocent.

Since then, however, I have been completely disillusioned about war's ability to accomplish what its advocates believe it can. It cannot and does not protect the innocent. It protects the guilty, who are behind the battle lines, and involves the innocent, both civilians and soldiers alike, in insensate, useless slaughter. To compare the military method to that of protecting your wife or daughter from a would-be rapist is a false analogy; for war exposes wife and daughter—in fact, all innocents—to spiritual, mental, and physical ravishment. To compare war to killing a mad dog is a false analogy. In war the mad dog (Hitler *et al*) is not killed, but millions of innocent youth are.

O God, my Father, I come to You for light and guidance in this matter. I am involved in it whether I choose it or not. Help me. In Jesus' name, Amen.

WAR—A SURGICAL OPERATION?

Joab son of Zeruiah and David's men went out and met [the king's forces] at the pool of Gibeon.... Then Abner said to Joab, "Let's have some of the young men get up and fight hand to hand in front of us."

"All right, let them do it," Joab said. (2 Sam. 2:13–14)

It is the young men, who have little or nothing to do with precipitating wars, who have to bear the brunt of the fighting. Furthermore, in modern war some of the worst suffering falls on the civil populations. War seems to have lost any power to protect the innocent—it now exposes them. If it is said that there are some things worse than war, I am reminded of the reply one person gave: "Yes, and war produces every one of those things."

War is a means, a method that is out of harmony with the ends it hopes to accomplish. Nations everywhere hope to use it for good. But you cannot dismiss the means before they have shaped the ends. Evil means produce evil ends. If good has ever come out of war, it is only because other constructive influences were introduced into the process and produced constructive ends in spite of the war method.

To liken war to a surgical operation is a false analogy. Surgery must take place through the hands of an immaculately sterilized surgeon with immaculately sterilized instruments, or else it will do more harm than good—as I know from experience, for I was infected with tetanus when operated on for appendicitis. What nation going to war can claim immaculate sterility for itself and its instruments? If it did, then the first germ to infect the body of humanity would be hypocrisy. War is far from sterile—its weapons are lies, deceits, hypocrisies. It has been said that "the first casualty in war is truth."

The second casualty is love, for it is absurd to say you can go to war loving your enemies. If you loved them, you would be a very poor soldier.

Gracious Father, I ask You to wash my eyes and my heart. I want to see straight. Amid the hysterias of this hour, keep my soul and my mind clean. Instead of thinking with my emotions; help me to think with Your mind. Amen.

DID CHRIST APPROVE OF WAR?

[Jesus] said to them, "Then give to Caesar what is Caesar's, and to God what is God's." (Luke 20:25)

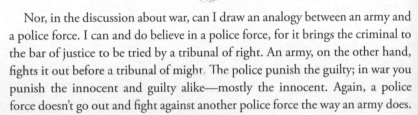

Nor, in the discussion about war, can I draw an analogy between an army and a police force. I can and do believe in a police force, for it brings the criminal to the bar of justice to be tried by a tribunal of right. An army, on the other hand, fights it out before a tribunal of might. The police punish the guilty; in war you punish the innocent and guilty alike—mostly the innocent. Again, a police force doesn't go out and fight against another police force the way an army does.

Nor can I, by any twisting of meanings, find the approval of Christ for war. It just doesn't fit. Several years ago, missionaries in Nanking, China, gave New Testaments to the occupying Japanese soldiers. At first the officers were glad, but later they came to the missionaries and said, "Please don't give our men any more. When they read this book, it takes the fight out of them."

To say that Christ used force in cleansing the Temple (John 2:12–17) is to twist the account. He used force as follows: (1) He "overturned their tables"—inanimate objects. (2) He "made a whip out of cords, and drove all from the temple area, both sheep and cattle"—animate creatures that could not understand moral force. (3) But on persons He used moral force: "Get these out of here! How dare you turn my Father's house into a market!" There is no scriptural warrant whatever that Jesus used physical violence on any person.

When He said, "give to Caesar what is Caesar's," He immediately added, "…and to God what is God's." The first phrase is qualified by the second. In His interpretation of the kingdom He taught that all life belongs to God. If Caesar fits into the kingdom of God, well and good; if not, then, "Seek first his kingdom" (Matt. 6:33). The idea that loyalty to Caesar is on a par with loyalty to God is foreign to the Christian faith.

Father, help me get my values and allegiances straight. I will give my loyalty to Caesar as long as it does not interfere with or contradict my loyalty to You. For You, not Caesar, are God and King—first, last, and always. Amen.

OVERCOMING EVIL WITH GOOD

Jesus said [to Pilate], "My kingdom is not of this world. If it were, my servants would fight to prevent my arrest by the Jews. But now my kingdom is from another place." (John 18:36)

Do not be overcome by evil, but overcome evil with good. (Rom. 12:21)

If we take seriously what Jesus said in the above passage, then Christ and war are indeed incompatible. Here He says definitely that His servants will not fight, for they belong to a different kingdom that uses different weapons.

The God I find in Christ overcomes evil with good, hate with love, and the world with a cross. Christ and the kingdom are one. He is the kingdom personalized. Jesus is both the revelation of God's character and the character of God's reign. The cross and the throne are one.

Now in our time, Gandhi has shown the possibilities of putting the cross into corporate life. Pacifism is not passivism—it is an activism from a higher level. Gandhi has shown us that a nation such as India need not slump down under its disabilities, nor does it need to engage in the barbarities of war—it can match its own capacity to suffer against the capacity of the other to give suffering—soul force against physical force. Gandhi has trained a nation to say: "We won't hate you, but we won't obey you. Do what you like." He, though not a Christian, has put the cross into public life.

If our nation took the Christian way of active good will toward all, we would probably do away with nine-tenths of the possibilities of invasion. If on the other tenth the Christian way should break down, we would not be lost, for we millions of people could sit down and say to a dictator: "We won't hate you, but we also won't obey you. Do what you like." We could overcome by our capacity to suffer. Is this nonsense? Christ tried it, and He rules the world.

O Christ, I am Your follower. And yet, I am afraid to follow You "all out." But I see Your way is right. I will take Your way, though the heavens fall—which they will not, for they stand with You. Help me to do the same. Amen.

ANY GOOD THINGS IN WAR?

God is pleased with you when you do what you know is right and patiently endure unfair treatment.... For God called you to do good, even if it means suffering, just as Christ suffered for you. He is your example, and you must follow in his steps. (1 Peter 2:19–21†)

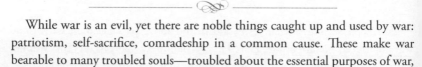

While war is an evil, yet there are noble things caught up and used by war: patriotism, self-sacrifice, comradeship in a common cause. These make war bearable to many troubled souls—troubled about the essential purposes of war, which are to kill and destroy.

The willingness of youth to sacrifice their lives touches me deeply. We can rescue these fine qualities and use them in a higher purpose. Gandhi's approach of nonviolent noncooperation links patriotism, self-sacrifice, and comradeship to advance constructive purposes. If we Americans would sit down, refuse to obey, and practice nonviolent noncooperation with a dictator, what would happen? The jails would fill up until jails would become ridiculous—an honor. They would line us up against a wall and shoot us until they would shoot themselves and their regime full of holes.

If it is said [here in the 1940s] that this might work against the British in India, but not against the Germans and the Japanese, the reply is that the early Christians used this method against the most brutal empire of the day—the Roman Empire, whose ordinary method of punishment was crucifixion. They broke that empire by their capacity to take suffering, not to give it. For the first three centuries, no Christian ever went to war or stayed in the army after becoming a Christian—it was incompatible. *After* the first three centuries, with the conversion of the emperor Constantine, no one but a Christian could get into the army. Christianity and the war method became entangled.

O God, strengthen my inner spirit to adopt Your way of nonviolence whether others take it or not. May I embrace the cross even if it means the added cross of being alone. For we must find a new way—this old way is ruinous to everybody. In Jesus' name, Amen.

CONSCIENCE IN A BODY

Let no debt remain outstanding, except the continuing debt to love one another, for he who loves his fellowman has fulfilled the law.... Love does no harm to its neighbor. Therefore love is the fulfillment of the law. (Rom. 13:8, 10)

Many will no doubt say, "Well, this idea of nonviolent noncooperation might work if we could convince enough people to try it. But we have schooled our population in the other method, not in this one." True. And how do we begin? With ourselves! We cannot wait until everyone is ready; we can embody this method of the cross in ourselves and in small groups we gather around us.

A college president sent word to an incoming guest speaker that he should go all out for war, since Rufus Jones, the eminent Quaker theologian, had recently been on the campus and had greatly influenced the students in the other direction. The speaker tried his best to do as requested, but didn't get far. The president asked him afterward why he hadn't made a better showing. The speaker replied, "Who can go all out for war with Rufus Jones on the platform?" Even in his absence, Rufus Jones had been the evening's Christian conscience. The speaker had to justify himself before that conscience, and the going was hard.

Will this method fail? All right, I would rather fail while using it than succeed in using the other. After all, the opposite of this method is failing to do anything for us except get us into universal ruin. Just sheer common sense should keep us out of war. Immanuel Kant, the eighteenth-century philosopher, once said, "Even a race of devils, provided only that they were intelligent, would be forced to find a solution other than war."

O Christ, my Lord, make me a Christian whether others become Christians or not. I need courage to take Your way, for so many are afraid the universe won't support it. Help me. Amen.

A SOCIETY WITHIN A SOCIETY

Since we are receiving a kingdom that cannot be shaken, let us be thankful, and so worship God acceptably with reverence and awe. (Heb. 12:28)

The discussion of our attitudes toward war has led to the necessity of getting small disciplined groups to be the seed plots of a new order. That way, if the old order goes to pieces, the group will raise up of a new one. The Christian church was just such a seed plot when the Roman Empire, founded on military might, fell apart. The Epistle to Diognetus, written at this time of decay, says: "What the soul is to the body, so the Christians are to the world—they hold the world together."

We are in a similar period of decay. Pitirim Sorokin, founder of Harvard University's department of sociology, says our culture, being oriented to the physical senses, has exhausted itself and is dissolving, so that the future must reform itself around other ideas and purposes.

The future must form around the kingdom of God or, in its turn, perish. For the kingdom is the final order, and whatever does not fit into it will perish. The church is the seed plot of that kingdom. In a large meeting, a singer was announced; her name was obviously Japanese. I held my breath to see the reaction. We were at war with Japan. Would the audience hiss her? She sang simply and beautifully: "How beautiful upon the mountains are the feet of him that bringeth good tidings, that publisheth peace."

At the end, the audience broke out in spontaneous applause. The Christian fellowship was unbroken. The church was not at war. It was a supranational fellowship that held together in spite of national bonds that had snapped.

The Christian church is different. It is a society within a society, a nation within a nation. It is, or ought to be, an expression of that "kingdom that cannot be shaken."

O God, I am so grateful for one island of sanity amid a raging sea of confusion and hate. Help me to be a worthy part of this glorious fellowship of those whose hearts have been illuminated and changed. In Jesus' name, Amen.

WHY BE LOYAL TO THE CHURCH?

I kneel before the Father, from whom his whole family in heaven and on earth derives its name. (Eph. 3:14–15)

After all, no one ever hated his own body, but he feeds and cares for it, just as Christ does the church—for we are members of his body. (Eph. 5:29-30)

In order to give full allegiance to the church, we should recognize these truths:

(1) There is no such thing as solitary faith. Jesus called us to love God *and our neighbor.* To be is to be in relationship. The Christian's life can be lived only in the give-and-take of corporate relationships.

(2) The Christian church is founded on a necessity in human nature. The social instinct is frustrated if I do not work out my spiritual life in a corporate fellowship. If the church were wiped out today, it would have to be replaced tomorrow by something similar, for human nature demands it. Those who try to cultivate their spiritual lives alone, apart from the church, are attempting to live vertically without the horizontal—which is impossible.

(3) The church, in a sense, is an extension of the Incarnation. The church attempts, in varying degrees, to reincarnate the Living Word (Christ) in corporate relationships. It is the only group in human society that lives not for its own purposes, but for eternal ones.

(4) With all its faults, the church is the best serving institution on earth. It has many critics, but no rivals in the work of human redemption. It has filled the world with schools, hospitals, and shelters for orphans, lepers, and the blind. There isn't a spot an earth where, if it is free to do so, it hasn't done so. Christians are people who care. And they care on a world scale—apart from race, birth, and color.

O God, I thank You that I can belong to a Family. Make me a good member of that Family. I want others to love this Family. Help me to bring to the Family the constructive spirit of love and mutual aid. In Jesus' name, Amen.

ONE UNBROKEN FELLOWSHIP

The churches here in the province of Asia send greetings in the Lord, as do Aquila and Priscilla and all the others who gather in their home for church meetings. All the brothers and sisters here send greetings to you. Greet each other with Christian love. (1 Cor. 16:19–20†)

Here are more truths about the church:

(5) The church, with all its faults, contains the best human life in the world. Its character is higher, finer, and more dependable. When a churchman goes wrong morally, it makes news. Something else was expected of him.

(6) The church is the one unbroken fellowship around the world. Various missionaries are now carrying on the work of the German missions until this war is over, but will return the work to them at the close. The church, as we said before, is not at war. It is holding an unbroken fellowship. The Christians are therefore the bridge across all chasms.

(7) The church lifts you from the present century and gives you solidarity with all the centuries. When you are in the church, you are not a prisoner of your era—you have a sense of belonging to the ages.

(8) The church, at its truest, breaks down all class and race barriers. A black minister arose on a train in Nazi Germany, gave a German woman his seat, and stood for the next four hours. When the woman was about to leave, she tried to thank him, but he couldn't understand her German, nor could she understand his English. Finally she wrote out a Scripture reference from Isaiah and handed it to him: "The LORD will guide you always…. You will be like a well-watered garden…" (58:11). Isaiah, a Jew, had brought together a black man and a German woman in Nazi Germany!

Celsus, the ancient Greek critic, said in derision: "These Christians love each other even before they are acquainted." Yes, they do.

O God, may no class, no caste, no color lines mar the open fellowship of the Family. Help us to have a relaxed fellowship in which everyone will be at home. Amen.

THE MOTHER OF MOVEMENTS

We want you to know about the grace that God has given the Macedonian churches. Out of the most severe trial, their overflowing joy and their extreme poverty welled up in rich generosity…. Entirely on their own, they urgently pleaded with us for the privilege of sharing in this service to the saints. (2 Cor. 8:1–4)

Finally, we can say about the church that:

(9) It has been and is the mother of movements. It gave birth to the arts, to education, to reform, to missionary advancement, to democracy. Democracy is a child of the Christian faith. The Baptists and the Quakers thought about God as Father, then proceeded to human beings as brothers and sisters, and then to democracy as expressing that equalitarian attitude in government. "Democracy," says Nobel Prize laureate Thomas Mann, "is the political expression of Christianity." If the root of democracy decays, the fruit will die.

(10) The denomination is not the church. The church is bigger than the denomination. I stood on top of a hill overlooking a valley. Here and there I could see isolated ponds of water. But they were not isolated ponds; they were portions of one winding river, only parts of which I could see at one time. The denominations are parts of a continuous river—the church. To think that we have roped off the grace of God within our denomination is as absurd as to say that the areas roped off for swimmers are the entire ocean.

(11) Similarly, the church is not the kingdom. The church contains the best life of the kingdom, but is not synonymous with the kingdom. It is a means to a greater end. It must lose its life for kingdom ends, and then it will find itself.

(12) The primary function of the church is the worship of God. Here we get in living contact with God, the Eternal, in order to face Time, the fleeting. Out of that worship, impulses and movements spring to serve humanity.

Gracious Father, in Your house I learn to live simultaneously in time and in eternity. I am the child of an eternal purpose. I can no longer be given to cheap ends. Help me to work toward Your eternal destiny for me. Amen.

THE OWNER'S STAMP

[Paul]: *Let no one interfere with me after this, for I bear branded on my body the owner's stamp of the Lord Jesus (Gal. 6:17 MOFFATT)*

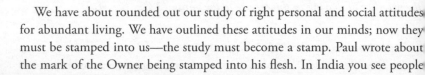

We have about rounded out our study of right personal and social attitudes for abundant living. We have outlined these attitudes in our minds; now they must be stamped into us—the study must become a stamp. Paul wrote about the mark of the Owner being stamped into his flesh. In India you see people who have the stamp of their god branded on their foreheads, put there by a hot iron. The bulls of the Hindu god Shiva are branded with the Shiva trident and are his wherever they roam.

Paul was thinking of this branding when he asserted that he was free from the obstructions of man because he was bound to the Man. He asserted his freedom through a deeper bondage. Strange way to find freedom! And yet he saw that Christ was the fulfillment of his being, the way he was made to live.

In another passage Paul says we are "predestined to be conformed to the likeness of his Son" (Rom. 8:29). People have argued for centuries over predestination. And yet it seems simple: If you carry out the destiny written into the constitution of your being, you will conform to the likeness of Christ. By the very nature of the universe, you are predestined to be a Christlike person. This is your destiny, and you can escape from it only by sinning against that destiny, against the God who wrote it into you.

"The Owner's stamp" is simply the outer sign of something stamped within you constitutionally. You give your consent to the constitution, and your way becomes the Way. Every single organ, tissue, and nerve cell is made to work in a Christian way. That is their destiny.

O Christ, I see that if I fulfill the thing I am made for, I will be like You. This is not an arbitrary decree written in a book and imposed upon me; it is written within me, inescapable. I consent with all my being to be branded as Your own. Amen.

MADE TO BE CHRISTIAN

You created my inmost being.... I praise you because I am fearfully and wonderfully made; your works are wonderful, I know that full well. (Psalm 139:13–14)

A wise man once said, "If the principles of Jesus were torn out of the heavens, they would spring up out of the earth"—and out of the nature of our very beings as well. It is not too farfetched to say that you and I have Christian lungs, Christian glands, a Christian stomach, a Christian heart, a Christian liver, a Christian nervous system—the total organization is Christian; and to put these organs to unchristian uses is to throw them out of gear. In fact, it grinds the gears of life against each other as you live in inner conflict.

Dr. Henry C. Link, a New York psychologist, gave up Christianity as an outmoded superstition. When, however, he began to try to untangle snarled-up lives, he found he had to give his patients something outside themselves to love. The only permanent thing he could offer was God; and soon he found he was talking himself back into being a Christian. Their lives wouldn't come out right in any other way. The Christian way, torn from the heavens, had sprung up out of the earth.

The study of psychology and the study of physiology will lead to the conclusion of the cartoon character Aunt Het, who says quaintly: "Nature tries to make us good. I used to get awful mad years ago, but I had to quit because it gave me bad digestion." The Presbyterian minister and newspaper columnist Dr. Frank Crane says: "Depression, gloom, despair, pessimism—these slay ten persons to every one murdered by typhoid, influenza, diabetes, or pneumonia." Nature is unfolding her book, and her finger points to its central passage, which reads, "Be Christian." It is, in fact, your destiny.

O loving, relentless, redeeming Owner, I find Your marks all throughout me. Brand Your stamp of ownership in me. Your will is my native air, Your mind the climate of my being. I thank You. Amen.

NOT FICKLE, BUT FIXED

You have taken off your old self with its practices and have put on the new self, which is being renewed in knowledge in the image of its Creator. (Col. 3:9–10)

Christ is our Owner, whether we acknowledge that fact or not. The declaration of that ownership is being more and more wrung from reluctant lips. Dr. Harvey Cushing, the great surgeon, said: "Don't operate on a person's stomach for a stomach ulcer—operate on their head." He was pointing to the true cause, which he viewed as worry or harboring resentment.

Faith, good will, and love are not imposed upon us as human beings; they are the things we are made for. The Owner's stamp is there within us. We must simply consent to them. Where shall we be branded? Paul says, "On my body" (Gal. 6:17). Perhaps you have had the Christian way painted onto you, not branded in. Therefore it has not endured. You have given yourself not to the Way but to the wayward; you are not fixed, but fickle. Now this whole Way must be burned in, beginning at the body.

Western civilization is body-minded, sensate, keyed to that which can be touched and tasted and smelled. If you say to someone today, "This will hurt your soul," the reply will be, "So what?" But if you say, "This will give you cancer," they will immediately sit up and take notice. All right—since our society is body-minded, let us begin at the body, asking Christ to stamp His mark into every brain cell, every nerve, every tissue—into the total physical life.

Every portion of our beings will cry out to be Christian, for that is our destiny.

Gracious Master, I know that this wandering, wobbling life must end. I want something that will brand me forever, so that no one will mistake my identity any longer. Let the fire of Your Spirit brand me as forever Yours. Amen.

ONE MARK OF JESUS: FORGIVENESS

Bear with each other and forgive whatever grievances you may have against one another. Forgive as the Lord forgave you. (Col. 3:13)

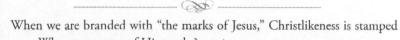

When we are branded with "the marks of Jesus," Christlikeness is stamped into us. What were some of His marks?

(1) Forgiveness of injuries. The most sublime prayer ever prayed was "Father, forgive them, for they do not know what they are doing" (Luke 23:34). The English essayist Sir John Robert Seeley said the distinguishing mark of a Christian is willingness to forgive injuries.

A bandit held up a man, who gave him his wallet. "Do you need money as badly as that?" the man asked. "I will give you some more," he added, handing over his other wallet. "If you will take a job, I'll help you to get one," he continued. The robber dropped his gun and said, "I can't take your money; you're a Christian."

Ralph was a converted prisoner serving a sentence. A fellow prisoner said of him: "No one can hold a grudge anymore when Ralph comes into the room." He evidenced the authentic sign of being a Christian.

A missionary in Japan was walking along the safety zone when her coat, blown by the wind, caught the door handle of a passing taxi; she was dragged and injured. In the hospital she begged that the driver should not be prosecuted, or his insurance taken away, as it was an accident. The driver was so moved by her attitude that when she died he attended her funeral and became a Christian.

You and I are to be branded with the spirit of forgiveness. It will go deep, very deep. Never again will we retaliate or harbor resentment. That all belongs to a dead past.

O Christ, brand me deep. I surrender all hurts, all resentment, all retaliation. I shall love everyone—friend and foe. Only by Your grace can I do this. From this point forward, let no hate trouble me: I bear Your brand. Amen.

TWO MORE MARKS OF JESUS

Sing and make music in your heart to the Lord, always giving thanks to God the Father for everything, in the name of our Lord Jesus Christ. (Eph. 5:19–20)

Continuing with the Christian's marks of Jesus:

(2) No self-pity. While on His way to the cross, Jesus said to a group of women: "Daughters of Jerusalem, do not weep for me" (Luke 23:28). This is a positive negative. Surrender all impulses to be sorry for yourself, all feelings of inferiority, all bidding for pity from yourself and others.

A pastor's father, himself a minister, lost his reputation through immorality. The disgrace left a stigma on the son—or so the son felt. He found himself shrinking back, feeling that others were holding this against him. I called his attention to the fact that in the genealogy of Jesus was this item about His chief ancestor: "David was the father of Solomon, whose mother had been Uriah's wife" (Matt. 1:6). And yet Jesus never pitied Himself because of His poor ancestry, nor did He surrender to inferiorities. He took the raw materials of life (some of them can be very raw) and turned them into a new posterity. The young pastor surrendered the self-pity, held up his head once more, and was released.

Now you are to do the same. This mark of "no self-pity" is being branded into you forever. It has no part in you from this point on. You are free. You can say after the manner of Paul: "Let no self-pity interfere with me after this, for I bear the brand of freedom from it."

(3) Joy, in spite of. Anyone can have joy on account of; but Jesus had joy in spite of. A Christian said in one of my Round Table conferences: "I have found that if you follow Christ, three things will happen: (1) You will be delivered from all fears. (2) You will be absurdly happy. (3) You will have trouble." The absurd happiness is in spite of the trouble!

O Christ, Your stamp is within me. Gloom, despair, and the blues shall no longer have a place in my life. They are burned out in the fires of Your joy. Amen.

TWO FURTHER MARKS OF JESUS

Trust in the LORD and do good; dwell in the land and enjoy safe pasture. Delight yourself in the LORD and he will give you the desires of your heart. Commit your way to the LORD; trust in him. (Psalm 37:3–5)

More brandings from the marks of Jesus:

(4) Calm receptivity. Jesus was constantly giving out, but only because He was constantly taking in. Jesus knew how to give because He knew how to receive. His relaxed spirit kept the channels free. There were no tight knots in His life blocking the power of God. He lived in a state of alert passivity.

You are to be branded with that spirit—branded—which means that alert passivity is to be a continuous state of mind, instead of an imported occasional thing in periods of relaxation. You are to live relaxed and receptive.

Mozart, when asked how he found his musical inspirations, said: "I do not know myself and can never find out. When I am in particularly good condition—perhaps riding in a carriage, or on a walk after a good meal…the thoughts come to me in a rush, and these are the best of all." He was receptive and attuned to Music. So Music played him all over.

You are now being branded by this mark of Jesus: You are not to live a nervous, overwrought, fussy type of life; you are going to be relaxed, receptive, and released. You are not a reservoir with a limited amount of resources; you are a channel, attached to unlimited divine resources.

(5) Courage. Jesus did not show the excited desperation of a battlefield, but the quiet courage that went on in the face of growing opposition and certain crucifixion. Yours will be the same kind of quiet courage: the courage to say "No" to enemies, also to friends; the courage to be in an unpopular minority with truth and right; the courage to go on undismayed when a loved companion drops beside the road and the future is all unknown; the courage of cosmic confidence. Never again shall you be afraid of anything. You are free!

O Christ of the undaunted faith, give me Your quiet confidence and courage. May that faith hold me when everything else is gone. I shall never again be afraid of anything, because I want only You. Amen.

THREE FINAL MARKS OF JESUS

The Lord Jesus Christ…gave himself for our sins to rescue us from the present evil age, according to the will of our God and Father, to whom be glory for ever and ever. Amen. (Gal. 1:3–5)

Three more ways a Christian can demonstrate the marks of Jesus:

(6) The power to take it. When things happened to Jesus, good or bad, He could take it. A judge made this comment to me: "There is an increase of the use of drugs, narcotics, and opiates because people can't stand frustration. The people who come before me have no religion, so they turn to the props of aspirin, drugs, liquor. They can't take it."

Jesus could—yes, when popularity tried to make a king of Him, and when those blinded by hate put Him on a cross. In either extremity He could take it. That power to take whatever comes is to be branded into you, so that never again will you whine, complain, or retreat. You will take everything that comes and you will use it—an unbeatable way to live.

(7) He cared. He cared little about what happened to Him, but He cared deeply what happened to others. He was so deeply sensitized that every person's hunger was His own; He was bound in every person's imprisonment and lonely in every person's loneliness. To be in touch with Christ is to be sensitized on a world scale. Christians are people who care beyond race, class, and color—they care indiscriminately. When this spirit is branded into you, it will deliver you from all smug, self-centered satisfaction and indifference to others. You will be hurt in the hurts of others and happy in their happiness.

(8) He gave Himself. His crowning mark was not just that He cared enough to give, but that He gave *Himself.* The ultimate test is there; we give money, interest, words, attendance—but do we give ourselves? If this last quality of life is being branded into you, you will give yourself to everyone who needs you.

O Christ, I want to be branded with Your total spirit. I thirst for You. One touch of You sets me aflame for more. I can be satisfied only when I awaken in Your likeness. Amen.

THE LAST FEW TWITCHES

Put to death, therefore, whatever belongs to your earthly nature: sexual immorality, impurity, lust, evil desires and greed, which is idolatry…. You used to walk in these ways, in the life you once lived. But now you must rid yourselves of all such things. (Col. 3:5, 7–8)

Perhaps you are questioning how absolute is the deliverance we studied last week. "Branded" is a decisive word. Don't be discouraged if the deliverance isn't all at once. It usually is. But it is sometimes gradual.

After Pentecost, which had burned many weaknesses out of Peter, there still lingered racial prejudice. A special aftertouch was needed to root that out: "The Spirit told me to have no hesitation about going with them" (Acts 11:12). There is a lot of mopping up to be done after the citadel has been taken by Christ—little pockets of recalcitrant, fighting rebels.

When I was in college, I caught poison ivy infection between my fingers and on my eyelids. It was so bad that even granulated tissue formed between my fingers. And then I got well. After I went to India, where there is no poison ivy, the infected places would still begin to itch every spring at the time when I had gotten the infection. The signs grew fainter and fainter each year; finally, after about twenty years, they faded out. Evil in your life will act in the same way. The roots are pulled out, and yet the dying twitches of dying habits will remind you of what was once there.

A woman who has helped many thousands into mental and spiritual health tells people that gradual deliverance is something like guests who have departed; good-byes are said and parting is all over…but soon the guests, having circled the block, come back to wave another good-bye. So it will be with evil habits; the good-byes are said, and yet there is often a last waving of farewell. But this one is final.

God, I want to find my fears dropping away, even if their specters may haunt me after they are buried. I belong to the victorious present and future, not to a defeated yesterday. I thank You. Amen.

TOWARD A CONTAGIOUS LIFE

Those who are wise will shine like the brightness of the heavens, and those who lead many to righteousness, like the stars for ever and ever. (Dan. 12:3)

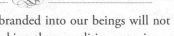

To have the qualities of Jesus branded into our beings will not be enough unless we become contagious, making these qualities outgoing, and placing them at the disposal of others. I love this saying: "No virtue is safe that is not enthusiastic; no heart is pure that is not passionate; no life is Christian that is not Christianizing." Here are seven steps toward contagion:

(1) In the inner structure of my being, I was made to be creative. If I am not spiritually creative, I fail to fulfill my destiny.

(2) To win others to a new life is the highest form of creative activity. I have a chance to be creative where it counts most. Spiritual creativity is denied to no one except those who deny it to themselves.

(3) Nothing is really mine until I share it with others. All expression deepens impression. Again, it is a law of the mind that whatever is not expressed dies. I want this life to be mine, for it is life's dearest treasure.

(4) I shall have the will to evangelize. So far the desire to evangelize has been in my mind and emotion; now it gets into my will. I have decided to share with others what has been shared with me.

(5) If I am afraid of being snubbed, I shall remind myself that I have a secret ally in every heart. There is something within the hearts of others that will take sides with me, for the human heart is made for this.

(6) If I fail, I will fail in doing what I should do. But perhaps the greatest failure is the failure to do anything.

(7) I may be unworthy, but God can use my very sins. Far from thinking of myself as being on a pedestal, I shall consider myself a humble pedestrian asking others to try the road I am trying.

O God, I bring You my noncreative life for Your touch. If my efforts falter, perhaps that will give You the greater chance to work. Whatever happens, I am committed to getting others committed to You. Amen.

HELPING OTHERS TO CHRIST (STEP 1)

Philip found Nathanael and told him, "We have found the one Moses wrote about in the Law, and about whom the prophets also wrote—Jesus of Nazareth, the son of Joseph."

"Nazareth! Can anything good come from there?" Nathanael asked.

"Come and see," said Philip. (John 1:45–46)

Perhaps you hesitate in attempting to win others to Christ because you are not sure how to proceed. I dislike exceedingly the idea of "selling religion"—it smacks of commercialism and conceives of our faith as a commodity.

Nevertheless, we can learn some things from those who sell commodities. I have watched the vendors who go through the trains. The ones who make a lot of sales usually do two things: First, they act as though their merchandise has real importance. But they must not overdo it; they restrain the importance. Second, they look straight at each passenger as if to give each one a personal invitation to buy. *Important* and *personal*—the two watchwords.

The sales manager of a national company gives four steps in presenting a commodity. Presenting the Christian way to people is similar: You answer four questions. First: *What is it?* Perhaps you will have to tell the person what faith is not, in order to clear away misconceptions. It is not a mere set of beliefs to be believed, an organization to be joined, a rite or ceremony to be undergone—it may and does involve these, but it is much more. It is a personal relationship with God, which involves a change (gradual or sudden) from the kingdom of self to the kingdom of God through the grace and power of Christ. The basis of life is shifted from self to God. His will becomes supreme. That will is interpreted to us in Christ. To be a Christian is to be a Christ-ian—to be committed to Christ in surrender and obedience.

More on this tomorrow.

O Christ, help me to help others see You. They see so many things built up around You that they do not see You. Help me to help someone bend the knee to You and You alone. For You are our very life. Amen.

HELPING OTHERS TO CHRIST (STEPS 2-3)

You have not received a spirit that makes you fearful slaves. Instead, you received God's Spirit when he adopted you as his own children. (Rom. 8:15†)

The second question in unfolding the Christian way to others is: *What will it do (for you)?* The answers are many: It will give you personal relations with a person—you will no longer be orphaned, estranged, out of gear with reality. You will find forgiveness and cleansing from all fears, resentment, guilt, inhibitions, and complexes. You will have the sense of inner unity—no longer at war with yourself. You will find the tyranny of self-centeredness broken; you will begin to think of others; you will begin to be a person who cares. You will find yourself part of a kingdom that is reality itself. You will have a cause—the kingdom—and that cause will be embodied in a person—Christ. Your faith will be at once personal and social. You will begin to say, "This is it!" Your life will be one long verification of your central hypothesis; it will be self-authenticating and self-verifying. Furthermore, it will give you power not merely to bear trouble, suffering, and frustration, but to use them and transmute them into character and usefulness.

The third vital question: *Who says so?* If just a few people here and there endorsed the Christian way, its worth would be doubted. But men, women, and young people in all ages, regions, and circumstances rise up and say, "I have tested it. Christ is a Savior not merely because I hope He will save me from hell and take me to heaven, but because He saves me here and now from gloom, despair, meaninglessness, purposelessness, sin, the tyranny of myself and my passions—He has made me free." This universal witness to a universal fact is one of the most solemn and reassuring things in life.

And if all this is so, then you may add, very quietly, "I too find that it works."

O Christ, help me to be Your witness. I hear in the media fervent appeals for what gadgets will do for me. Help me to witness all the more clearly and joyfully for You, O Eternal Reality. Amen.

HELPING OTHERS TO CHRIST (STEP 4)

[Jesus] said to the crowd, "If any of you wants to be my follower, you must turn from your selfish ways, take up your cross daily, and follow me." (Luke 9:23†)

----------------------------- ✎ -----------------------------

We come now to the last step of the four: *How can you get it?* Jesus gives the answer in the statement above.

He says *you must make up your mind*—"If any of you wants to be my follower…" Here is the great decision that decides all decisions. It is what they call in psychology "a major choice"—a choice you do not have to make over again each day; a choice into which the lesser choices of life fit, rather than a choice that fits into them. It is the choice that organizes everything around itself.

Next, *you give up yourself*—"you must turn from your selfish ways." The term literally is "fling away" or "utterly reject." It does not mean just doing without things here and there; it means a denial of self as central, as a primary factor. Self is subordinate and obedient to another will—the will of Christ. Self abdicates the throne, and Christ mounts it. You decide that He shall decide.

Next, *you take up your cross*. This doesn't mean merely to bear patiently the troubles that come upon you—it is deeper. It means you will deliberately, intentionally take upon yourself trouble, pain, sorrow, and sin, making them your own in order to free others from them.

Next, *keep up your cultivation*—"daily." There is a once-for-allness in this decision, and yet there is also daily discipline.

Finally, *gather up your loyalties into a single-minded devotion*—"follow me." You are not following this, that, or the other person—you are following Christ. People may let you down—He won't. Your faith is Christ-centric.

O Christ, the more I see in You, the more I see there is to be seen. I am on the great adventure of eternal discovery and eternal growth. My life's code is now a character, my law a divine life. I thank You. Amen.

HOW TO READ THE BIBLE (PART 1)

As for you, continue in what you have learned and have become convinced of, because you know those from whom you learned it, and how from infancy you have known the holy Scriptures, which are able to make you wise for salvation through faith in Christ Jesus. (2 Tim. 3:14–15)

One of the steps we mentioned yesterday was daily cultivation. When you are helping another person, get them to enroll in the school of the Word.

On board ship I saw two men begin the day in different ways. One, a businessman, came down early, picked up the newssheet, and turned at once to the stock-market report. His face would light up or fall with the market. Another man leaned over the rail each morning reading the Bible, and then looked out over the open sea in meditation. His face showed poise and strength. His happiness depended on eternal relationships, not temporal happenings.

In reading the Word each morning, take these steps:

(1) Relax. Only then are you receptive. Nothing can be inscribed on a tense mind. Let every muscle, every brain cell go limp. This attitude says along with the boy Samuel, "Speak, Lord, for your servant is listening" (1 Sam. 3:9–10). If you go stomping through a woods in a hurry, you will see little. But sit still, and the squirrels will come down the trees, the birds will draw near, and Nature will be alive in every twig and flower. The same is true with the Word.

(2) Recall. Ask these questions as you read: (a) Who is writing? (b) To whom? (c) For what purpose? (d) What is he saying? (e) How does this apply to me? (f) How shall I put it into practice? (g) When do I begin?

(3) Rehearse. If you find something that speaks to your condition, roll it over and over in the mind. It will become an atmosphere, then an attitude, then an act. When Jesus was pressed by temptation in the wilderness, He answered in the words of Scripture. These words had become a part of Him, and in the crisis they naturally passed from the stage of assimilation to act.

O Christ, I want the Word to be hidden in my heart so deeply that it becomes the hidden springs of action, determining my conduct and character. Amen.

HOW TO READ THE BIBLE (PART 2)

How can a young man keep his way pure? By living according to your word. I seek you with all my heart; do not let me stray from your commands. I have hidden your word in my heart that I might not sin against you. (Psalm 119:9–11)

More steps to take when reading the Word each morning:

(4) Retain. Do not merely rehearse a passage that gets your attention; deliberately plan to retain it. Commit it to memory. When a high school student in a Christian school assembly read the morning Scripture passage this way: "You will hate all nations for my name's sake," those who heard him did not seem surprised and shocked, for they didn't know the correct reading (see Matt. 24:9). That generation had not been trained in memorizing Scripture, and was mentally and morally the poorer as a result.

(5) Rejoice. Reading the Word is a tryst with God. Remember that all you have read is leading to His feet. The Bible is not a flat Bible from Genesis to Revelation—it is not a line like this: _____, but like this: /. It leads to Christ as the final goal and authority. He made His own word final, even in Scripture: "You have heard that it was said to the people long ago…but I tell you…" (Matt. 5:21–22). Revelation is progressive, culminating in Christ. He is the test and touchstone of all. Rejoice in Him.

(6) Realign. As you read this Word, keep realigning your life with this Life. In Korea, one girl did not come back for more Scripture instruction, and when asked why, she replied: "I haven't learned yet to practice fully what I've been taught." She felt she had to keep her practice abreast of the teaching. Quite right.

(7) Release. If you find something in the Word that gets hold of you, pass it on to somebody that very day. The repetition will help the retention, and it will also help lighten the path of the other person.

O Eternal Word, may my words be but echoes of You. Help me to be steeped in Your mind, fired by Your passion, and decisive with Your purposes. Amen.

REALISM IN THE BEATITUDES

Blessed are the poor in spirit, for theirs is the kingdom of heaven. (Matt. 5:3)

In a sense, Jesus began and ended in His whole ministry with His series of eight statements about "the happy ones," which we call the Beatitudes. They begin with the kingdom (Matt. 5:3) and end with the kingdom (v.10). As the kingdom was the framework in which all His teaching was set, the master-light in which everything was seen, so the kingdom is supreme here.

The Sermon on the Mount depicts the new order and the character of its citizens. No wonder the Harvard scholar Pitirim Sorokin, after reviewing the decay and breakdown of our social order, comes to the conclusion that any new order to replace the present one must be patterned after the Sermon on the Mount. This is the deliberate conclusion of a sociologist and not just a rhetorical gesture. The Sermon is turning out to be not idealism, but stark realism. The kingdom is reality—the only reality.

Jesus is saying here what He always insisted upon: "Seek first his kingdom and his righteousness, and all these things will be given to you as well" (Matt. 6:33). Get this straight, and everything else will come out straight.

But how do you get this supreme value straight—by holding it as a supreme idea? No, by submitting to it as a supreme loyalty. "Blessed are the *renounced in spirit* [literal translation], for theirs is the kingdom of heaven." The kingdom demands a renunciation on its very threshold, a renunciation at the deepest depths—in spirit. If we do not comply, nothing else will follow; if we do, then everything follows.

O God, I know whose bonds are upon my heart. I know what I must do. I must renounce at the center, in my very spirit. If the center is Yours, then all the circumference follows. I want to let the kingdom operate from the center of my being to the circumference of my relationships. Then I shall be a kingdom-controlled person. In Jesus' name, Amen.

RECEPTIVITY IN THE BEATITUDES

Blessed are those who mourn, for they will be comforted. Blessed are the meek, for they will inherit the earth. (Matt. 5:4–5)

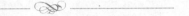

Jesus' recipe for happiness—"renounce"—reverses the ordinary recipe, which usually begins with "assert," "take," "realize." Which is correct?

Note that the first three beatitudes (Matt. 5) are all receptive instead of assertive. They esteem (1) the renounced in spirit—v. 3; (2) those who mourn over the mistakes, sins, and failures of themselves and others, as well as mourn for the coming kingdom—v. 4; (3) the meek, or the disciplined—v. 5. All three bespeak one thing: receptivity. These are all passive virtues.

Then follow three positive or active virtues: (1) the merciful—v. 7; (2) the pure in heart—v. 8; (3) the peacemakers—v. 9. Between these two sets, there is one beatitude that is both active and passive—v. 6: "Blessed are those who hunger and thirst for righteousness"—that is active—"for they will be filled"— passive. This verse is the pivot upon which the change is made from one kind of virtue to the other.

Now note that the kingdom way of life begins with receptivity. Is that right? Isn't that where all life has to begin? The seed in the ground receives moisture and nutrition from the earth and the air before it can begin to produce flower and fruit. An organism can expend only as much as it takes in, no more. If it doesn't begin with receptivity, it doesn't begin.

Scientists who don't sit down before the facts as a little child, who aren't prepared to give up every preconceived notion, who aren't willing to follow wherever nature will lead, will know nothing. They have to renounce, to mourn that they don't know, to be humble—or they get nowhere. The first immutable law of all life, material and spiritual, is receptivity. Life confronts us with the alternatives: receive or perish.

O God, I come to You renounced and receptive. Take my emptiness and make it full; take my foolishness and make it into Your wisdom; convert my paralysis into Your power. For I hunger and thirst for You. I really do. Amen.

ATTITUDE AND OUTCOME

(Now Moses was a very humble man, more humble than anyone else on the face of the earth.)... Then the LORD came down in a pillar of cloud; he stood at the entrance to the Tent and summoned Aaron and Miriam. When both of them stepped forward, he said, "...Why then were you not afraid to speak against my servant Moses?" (Num. 12:3, 5, 8)

If the first step in abundant living is receptivity, we may well ask what is received? The renounced in spirit receive the kingdom of heaven; the mourners receive comfort; the meek inherit the earth.

But note that the verse does not say the poor in spirit *belong to* the kingdom. It says the kingdom belongs to them—its powers are behind them; its resources are at their disposal; its very authority and power are at their command. They are universe-backed.

In the second beatitude about those who mourn, the outcome is specific— "they will be comforted" (Matt. 5:4). This word combines *com*—"together" and *fortis*—"brave," so the meaning is "brave together." There is a sense of human-divine togetherness; the mourners are adequate, not because of their strength, but because of their resources. You and Christ are afraid of nothing, because you can use everything.

In the third beatitude about the meek, the reward is again specific—"they will inherit the earth" (v. 5). The meek are not the weak—they are the trained, the disciplined, the receptive. They inherit not heaven only, but the earth. When the French people voted on the greatest Frenchman of all time, they passed by Napoleon and chose Louis Pasteur instead, whose scientific discoveries benefited so many. The meek inherited the world of affections and reverence. The earth belongs to the meek because it won't respond to the proud or the vaunting. It is made in its inner constitution to work in the Christian way.

O God, I see that the earth rots in the hands of those who try to take it by force, pride, and domination. It doesn't belong to them. It belongs to Your Son and to those who meekly follow Him. Help me to do so. Amen.

HUNGRY FOR GOODNESS

Blessed are those who hunger and thirst for goodness! They will be satisfied.
(Matt. 5:6 MOFFATT)

The group Jesus describes in this beatitude is reaching out for what? Money, fame, sex, power? No, goodness! And the result is that they are satisfied. Those who hunger and thirst for money, fame, sex, and power are forever unsatisfied—they are doomed to be always thirsty. The more they get, the more they want. Those who thirst for goodness yearn for what they are made for; hence they can be satisfied. If, on the other hand, the eye should thirst for darkness instead of light, the conscience for error instead of truth, the aesthetic nature for ugliness instead of beauty, the heart for hate instead of love—what would be the end? Dissatisfaction, frustration, conflict, and breakdown.

Goodness is our native air. We live to the extent that we live in goodness; we gasp and die if we try to live in evil. These are the alternating heartbeats of healthy, abundant living: outgoing for goodness—incoming with satisfaction; outgoing for goodness—incoming with satisfaction. A heart that beats with this rhythm lives forever.

But the heartbeat of the wrongly directed thirst is: outgoing for evil—incoming with dissatisfaction; outgoing for evil—incoming with dissatisfaction. This leads to heart failure—eternal heart failure.

Jesus said, "Everyone who drinks this water will be thirsty again" (John 4:13). Those who drink the waters of lust, money, power, fame, or thrills are doomed to remain thirsty. "But," continued Jesus, "whoever drinks the water I give him will never thirst" (v. 14). A central and fundamental satisfaction! A well of water within, springing up to everlasting life! This is a satisfaction that is popping with novelty and adventure.

O God, my Father, You are giving me two satisfactions—the satisfaction of fulfillment, and the satisfaction of growth. I am deeply satisfied with You, and yet I am forever reaching for more. I am so grateful. Amen.

DOING AND SEEING IN THE BEATITUDES

Blessed are the merciful, for they will be shown mercy. Blessed are the pure in heart, for they will see God. (Matt. 5:7–8)

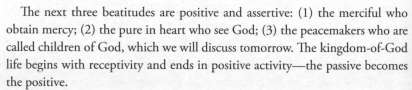

The next three beatitudes are positive and assertive: (1) the merciful who obtain mercy; (2) the pure in heart who see God; (3) the peacemakers who are called children of God, which we will discuss tomorrow. The kingdom-of-God life begins with receptivity and ends in positive activity—the passive becomes the positive.

The curious thing is that when Jesus turns from the passive, receptive side, the first thing He mentions is power wielded mercifully. He tells of masterful, dominating personalities who have people in their power, but who wield that power beneficently. Does receptivity bring power over others? Yes; a receptive person becomes a vigorous person. Divine resources make us humanly resourceful. But the vigor is constructive and redemptive; the power is controlled by love, the only safe power. Jesus had all power, but He used it not for Himself, not for the destruction of enemies, not to awe His hearers, but only for purposes of mercy.

The second outgoing quality is purity of heart that has a central insight—it sees God. Those who are receptive can not only do—they can see. There are two great types of personalities—those who desire to do, to achieve, to wield power, and those who desire to have insights, to know, to comprehend the relationships of things. The first are the people of action, the pioneers. The second are people of thought, the philosophers. Both types are produced out of receptivity, and both are needed. But the central insight is to see God at work in redemption, in science, in beauty, in the moral universe, overruling the affairs of humanity. The pure in heart are in the breathless adventure of seeing God everywhere.

O God, I want to be pure in heart, single-minded, so that my insights may be clear. I want to see You in the blade of grass, in the starry sky, in the rough-and-tumble of human events—and in my own heart. Then I am satisfied. Amen.

RECONCILIATION IN THE BEATITUDES

Blessed are the peacemakers: for they shall be called the children of God. (Matt. 5:9 KJV)

The undivided in heart see God. Where others see only dead matter, they see the Creator's delicacy of touch; where others see history as meaningless events, they see His Story. But they not only see; they also have the positive power to get other people to see and change and come to reconciliation on a higher level. Peacemakers find power to reconcile in three directions—between persons and God, between one person and another, and between the person and himself or herself. They have the power to help the person be at home with God, with fellow human beings, and internally.

If I were to pick out one verse that most nearly expresses the Christian gospel, it would be 2 Corinthians 5:18—"God…reconciled us to himself through Christ and gave us the ministry of reconciliation." God was in the positive business of an outgoing love that reconciled humans to Himself when they did not want to be reconciled. We now do what God does—He commits to us the same work of reconciling.

In two places Jesus calls us children of the Father, and for the same reason. One is this beatitude about peacemaking; the other comes late in the same chapter when he says: "Love your enemies! Pray for those who persecute you! In that way, you will be acting as true children of your Father in heaven" (vv. 44-45 †). You are most like God when you are bringing people together in reconciliation. When I was trying to find a basis for reconciliation between Japan and America, Admiral Nomura took my hand and said, "Thank you for what you are doing. Those who are trying to reconcile others are doing the work of heaven, for it is heaven's work to reconcile us." A non-Christian put his finger on the central Christian quality—reconciliation.

O God my Father, I want to be like You. Take out of me all antagonism, all divisions, all clashes, so that those I meet this day will instinctively feel that I breathe "Peace." In Jesus' name, Amen.

WHY PERSECUTION HAPPENS

Blessed are those who have been persecuted for the sake of goodness! The Realm of heaven is theirs. (Matt. 5:10 MOFFATT)

We come to the last of the "Blesseds." This one is the result of the other seven. Those people who are so receptive that they become positive and outgoing are a judgment to others—their lives become superior, and people do not like to be silently judged, so they kick back in persecution. Society demands conformity. If you fall beneath its standards, it will punish you; if you rise above its standards, it will persecute you. It demands an average, gray conformity.

But Christians are different—they are a departure upward; their heads are lifted above the multitude; hence, they get hit. "Woe to you," said Jesus, "when all men speak well of you" (Luke 6:26), for if they do, you are like them. Christians must therefore get used to the sight of their own blood.

But what is the result of being so positive that you are persecuted? "Theirs is the kingdom of heaven" (Matt 5:10). Note: They do not belong to the kingdom; the kingdom belongs to them. Its powers are with them, behind them, at their disposal.

The world reverses the formula—it begins with positive self-assertiveness but no receptivity. It soon uses up its resources and ends in receptivity by circumstances—it becomes a prey of environment, mastered by life, defeated, frustrated, empty. The kingdom life begins with humble receptivity and ends in mastery.

O God, I thank You that I have hold of the right end of life's handle, which is humble receptivity. Now I can wield the other end in positive achievement and output. I can never, never run out of resources, because I am simply the wire along which Your power runs. Keep me connected and insulated. Amen.

GRACE IN THE DUNGEON

"Then," the Eternal promises, "I will be god to all the families of Israel, and they shall be my people." For this is the Eternal's promise: "Those who survive the sword shall find grace in the dungeon." (Jer. 31:1–2 MOFFATT)

There are many who say: "I am caught in a web of circumstances that have tied me up completely. How can I have abundant living under these conditions?" In answer I refer you to the above passage. If you find grace at all, you must find it in the dungeon.

The people to whom this passage was addressed did find grace in their dungeon—they were purified in the Exile and became the instrument of God through that awful experience of national bondage. The dungeon became a door! You need not accept your circumstances as from God, but you can accept them as an opportunity for God to make you creative.

A young woman of twenty was confined to her bed for a year with a bad heart. She spent the first week in bitter rebellion. Then she came across my book *Christ and Human Suffering*, and it opened the possibility of not merely bearing suffering and frustration but also of using them. It was a revelation to her. The remaining fifty-one weeks of that year were the best of her life. She arose at the end awakened in soul and in mind. She determined to finish a college education and did so. She is one of the most promising and useful young people I know. Her frustration became fruitfulness.

Among the most beautiful of Paul s writings are these lines: "I, Paul, write this greeting in my own hand. Remember my chains. Grace be with you" (Col. 4:18). You would have expected him to say, "Remember my chains—God give me grace." But no, he puts it the other way: "Grace be with *you*." He had found grace in the dungeon enough and to spare; he could pass it on to others.

Gracious God and Father, help me not to whine or complain, but to find resources enough to pass on. For I know that Your grace is sufficient for me, not merely when life is free and open, but when life turns confining. Amen.

DUNGEONS MAKE OR BREAK US

I will know that you stand firm in one spirit…without being frightened in any way by those who oppose you. This is a sign to them that they will be destroyed, but that you will be saved—and that by God. For it has been granted to you on behalf of Christ not only to believe on him, but also to suffer for him. (Phil. 1:27–29)

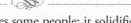

The dungeon experience crushes some people; it solidifies others. Conflicts may be of two kinds: the one where you come out on the lower, defeat side, and the other where you come out on the higher, victory side.

It was said of Jesus that He went into the wilderness "full of the Spirit" (Luke 4:1) and came out forty days later "in the power of the Spirit" (Luke 4:14). Fullness turned to power under the stress of temptation. The dungeon resulted in His being strengthened. The Evil One plays a losing game when he succeeds only in strengthening you through his temptations.

The account says, "Jesus said to him, 'Away from me, Satan! For it is written: "Worship the Lord your God, and serve him only."' Then the devil left him" (Matt. 4:10–11). The devil could not stand that word "only," because he knew that to tempt someone who holds a single-minded allegiance would only strengthen that person. Grace and more grace is found in the dungeon of temptation.

A gracious Christian woman said to her friend: "I know you dislike being ill. But I find the only thing to do is to get something out of every experience that comes to me. So make your illness give you something."

I find it hard to have to wait for people, but I've learned to make waiting useful by immediately turning to prayer. I find that praying keeps my temper from getting ruffled, and that I am not wasting my time. If you lie awake at night, don't fret—pray!

Gracious Father, let no moment of my life be empty and fruitless. If I don't know what to do, I will turn to prayer. I am grateful that I can always find grace in every dungeon. Amen.

FREEDOM THROUGH LIMITATIONS

[Paul]: *There was given me a thorn in my flesh, a messenger of Satan, to torment me. Three times I pleaded with the Lord to take it away from me. But he said to me, "My grace is sufficient for you, for my power is made perfect in weakness." Therefore I will boast all the more gladly about my weaknesses, so that Christ's power may rest on me.... For when I am weak, then I am strong. (2 Cor. 12:7–10)*

All our limitations, our dungeons, can be places where we find grace. I have always been grateful that I went to a small, obscure college, for it left me with the sense of being uneducated. I suppose that those who go to great institutions feel secure; to mention the name of their alma mater brands them as educated. I have felt no such security; so I have endeavored all my life to become an educated person. I gather from every moment, every occasion, and every conversation something to help me. The limitation has been a liberty.

The person who has discovered and revealed the wildflowers of Arkansas is shut-in, a woman crippled with arthritis. Although her hands are gnarled and twisted, she has painted exquisitely some 500 specimens. Harvard University wants to buy the collection, but there is currently a public movement to buy them for the state. Miss Whitfield cheerfully held up her twisted fingers and told how, by compensation, she was enabled to paint those delicate lines. Her cheer and her skill are beyond words.

I want to pay my tribute of gratitude to the single women of the world for whom life might have been a dungeon of loneliness had they not made it into something else. Around the world they have married themselves to human need; they have made every waif child their own; they have brightened families, while they themselves were familyless. They have found grace in the dungeon— and have given it. Bless them!

O Christ, You have shown me how to take hold of the briars of life and make those very stings into sensitiveness to others' hurt. I know that nothing can defeat me if I remain undefeated on the inside. I thank You. Amen.

MAKING IRRITATIONS INTO CHARACTER

My God, my God, why have you forsaken me? Why are you so far from saving me, so far from the words of my groaning? O my God, I cry out by day, but you do not answer, by night, and am not silent. Yet you are enthroned as the Holy One; you are the praise of Israel. In you our fathers put their trust; they trusted and you delivered them. (Psalm 22:1–4)

Two wealthy women with husbands in the lumber business went to live in the Northern woods. Both were from great cities. The one built a mansion in the woods, hired maids and butlers, imported her city friends for weekends, and tried to keep up the general social life of the city. She decayed—the dungeon got on the inside of her. The other woman lived in comparative simplicity, took an interest in her husband's employees, became one of them, and lifted their level. She is happy and is the salt of the situation.

There is no use fighting against the inevitable. Take hold of it and use it.

Granted, sometimes an evil seems to have no remedy. It is impossible to ignore—the iron of it enters the soul every day. What is to be done?

Take, for example, the dungeon of an unhappy marriage. Two things are possible. First, go over the whole matter anew, seeing if some of the reasons for the unhappiness are not in you. Be objective, even relentless with yourself. Don't defend yourself. If you find places where you are at fault, confess it to your spouse. Leave it to them to confess their own faults. Don't do it for them. Try honestly to find a way of agreement.

Second, if you cannot, then do what an oyster does when it gets an irritating grain of sand in its shell—it throws a pearl around the irritation. In the same way, you can build up the pearl of character around your daily grievance. You can find grace in the dungeon.

O God, my Father, I come to You with my dungeon life. You can either free me or give me grace here in this place. Daily we shall meet and work out life, in spite of. I thank You. Amen.

MAKING THE MOST OF CALAMITIES

We also rejoice in our sufferings, because we know that suffering produces perseverance; perseverance, character; and character, hope. And hope does not disappoint us, because God has poured out his love into our hearts by the Holy Spirit, whom he has given us. (Rom. 5:3–5)

Dungeons of various kinds often lead to grace. John Milton wrote *Paradise Lost* when blind. Clifford W. Beers was once in an insane asylum. Later he wrote *A Mind That Found Itself* and founded The National Commission for Mental Hygiene. The mentally upset owe much to a man who himself was mentally upset.

A man was set aside with a broken hip; while lying in bed, the wallpaper he had to face continuously gave him the idea of becoming a sketch artist, and he became a very successful one. He found grace in the dungeon.

A poet failed on the first night of a public reading and felt the next day that everybody was pointing the finger of scorn at him. He went home and wrote his greatest inspirational poem on the ability to endure when you fail. That poem fell into the hands of a man in the hospital who had lost both arms and feet, and it inspired him to become a public teacher. He became a very successful one.

Dr. Mary McCracken is totally crippled in her lower limbs by polio. The medical colleges of America refused to allow her to study medicine, saying she could never practice. She went to China, earned her medical degree at Peking Medical, ranked at the top of her class, came back to Philadelphia, the very city where she had been refused a medical education, and is practicing in an institution for crippled children—practicing in a wheelchair.

O God, these people have all found grace in a dungeon. Help me then to take limitations of any kind and make them into spurs toward life and achievement. May I do with my limitations what the river does with its banks—the more confining they are, the swifter the stream. May pain cause my life forces to flow faster. In Jesus' name, Amen.

GREATNESS BORN OUT OF TROUBLE

The LORD said, "I have indeed seen the misery of my people in Egypt. I have heard them crying out because of their slave drivers, and I am concerned about their suffering. So I have come down to rescue them from the hand of the Egyptians and to bring them up out of that land into a good and spacious land, a land flowing with milk and honey. (Ex. 3:7–8)

Great movements come out of dark periods. The notable historian Dr. Kenneth S. Latourette has traced some of them. In 1789 the French Revolution broke out and was followed by the Napoleonic wars, which lasted till 1815. In the span of those distressing years, the following events occurred:

—1792 (the year of the Reign of Terror in Paris): the Baptist Missionary Society was organized, growing out of the work of William Carey.

—1799 (when Napoleon was seeking to break Britain's communications with India): the Church Missionary Society was formed.

—1804 (about the time Napoleon was giving England the greatest threat of invasion she had faced in more than two centuries): the British and Foreign Bible Society was organized.

—1812 (while American ports were being blockaded by the British): *the first party of American missionaries sailed for India.*

When the world is at its worst, Christians are at their best. In Harold Church, Staunton, England, there is an inscription: "In the year 1653 when all things sacred were throughout the nation destroyed or profaned, this church was built to the glory of God by Sir Robert Shirley, whose singular praise it was to have done the best things in the worst times, and hoped for them in the most calamitous."

The Christian takes pains and makes them into pains of childbirth, bringing forth new movements.

O my Father, even in the hell of frustration and pain, You are inspiring and making Your children victorious. When the three Hebrews entered the furnace, it only burned off their fetters! Free me, even by fire. Amen.

FIVE STEPS OUT OF THE DUNGEON

The Lord replied [to Saul], "Now get up and stand on your feet. I have appeared to you to appoint you as a servant and as a witness of what you have seen of me and what I will show you. I will rescue you from your own people and from the Gentiles. I am sending you to them to open their eyes and turn them from darkness to light, and from the power of Satan to God." (Acts 26:16–18)

Our world as a whole is suffering in a dungeon of self-inflicted pain and self-chosen bondages. Can it find grace here?

Dr. Sorokin, the sociologist I have mentioned earlier, says that in order to make a transition, society must go through five stages. His sequence is interesting and startling, for it matches the very steps Christianity teaches:

(1) Crisis. As the old order goes to pieces, we are confronted with a choice of sinking with the old or choosing a new way. The Chinese have a word for *crisis* made of two characters: *danger* and *opportunity.*

(2) Ordeal. This is the consequence of having to change. Roots have to be torn up. The suffering may be acute.

(3) Catharsis—the cleansing from old ideas and old ways, especially the ones that led to this bankruptcy. Repentance, in Greek, is *metanoia*—literally, "change of mind," of outlook.

(4) Charisma, the Greek word for grace. We have to get God's grace—an empowerment to live in new ways.

(5) Resurrection. Life is reborn, individually and collectively. It had to get worse before it got better.

Perhaps you as an individual will have to pass through these five steps as well on your way to resurrection.

O God, You make us go through dungeons to open doors. But you love us too much to let us succeed on low planes. Precipitate the crisis, in order that we may go through the catharsis and end in resurrection. For we must be new—at any price. Amen.

THE CENTRAL AIM

The aim of the Christian discipline is the love that springs from a pure heart, from a good conscience, and from a sincere faith. (1 Tim. 1:5 MOFFATT)

In the remaining days of this year, we must gather up the strands we have been weaving. Perhaps the above verse sums it up.

"The Christian discipline" is a discipline, not merely a doctrine. Doctrine that does not discipline us is dead. Christianity is not merely something you believe, but something you believe enough to act upon. Your deed is your creed—the thing you believe enough to put into practice. You do not believe what you do not practice.

Undisciplined people waste their energies with themselves and their own tangles. The future of the world is in the hands of the disciplined—provided they are *disciplined to the highest*. If one is disciplined to less than that, then the discipline will exhaust itself. It isn't backed by the ultimate.

The Christian is disciplined to what? The preceding verse (1 Tim. 1:4) tells us—"the divine order which belongs to faith." That divine order is the kingdom of God. It was embodied in the divine person, Jesus Christ. We are, therefore, disciplined by a person who embodies an order, an embodiment that makes our discipline both personal and social—personal in that it is related to a person, and social in that it is related to a new order embodied in that person.

If we are disciplined to the embodied kingdom, we are bound to out-think, out-live, out-die, and out-experience every other way of life. We can give ourselves without question to the Christian discipline.

O God, help me now to be disciplined to this way with no reservations and no hesitations. May I fling every doubt, fear, and hesitation to the winds. Amen.

DISCIPLINED SPONTANEITY

Jesus answered, "Everyone who drinks this water will be thirsty again, but whoever drinks the water I give him will never thirst. Indeed, the water I give him will become in him a spring of water welling up to eternal life." (John 4:13–14)

If the Christian discipline is complete, reaching in to control and redeem our inmost thoughts and aspirations, then does it produce nothing but robots? Do we simply dance to the invisible strings of a master behind the scene?

No, a thousand times, no. The exact opposite is true. When we fulfill this will, we fulfill ourselves. Paul expressed this spontaneity in yesterday's text: "love that *springs*."

Here is what the world's totalitarians are aiming to achieve, and cannot. They cannot produce a love that springs up. Instead, their methods produce a hate that springs. They have to sit on a lid. God, on the other hand, takes off the lid. That is why it has often been said, "Love God, and do what you like." You are perfectly free, for you are free to do what you ought. Your desires and decisions fit in with the nature of reality—you are living with the grain of the universe, not against it.

Let this statement soak in with its full implications: "The highest in Christ is the deepest in nature." John's gospel asserts: "Grace and truth came through Jesus Christ" (1:17). Grace and truth are inseparable. When you are in grace, you are at the heart of reality. When you make the wise decision to be disciplined by the Christ kingdom, you harmonize with the fundamental truths written in you by that Christ. "Without him nothing was made that has been made" (John 1:3). The Christian discipline, therefore, produces the most truly spontaneous and natural person in the world—the real Christian. The law ends in a liberty—"love springs." The Christian is artesian.

God and Father, I surrender my lesser, uncontrolled loves of self in order to find a disciplined love of You. You are gathering up my discords into Your harmony, my jerky, bumpy ways of life into Your rhythm. I thank You. Amen.

FRUIT THAT EVAPORATES

[A lament against Babylon the Great]: *"They will say, 'The fruit you longed for is gone from you. All your riches and splendor have vanished, never to be recovered.'"* (Rev. 18:14)

If Christianity is the natural, common sense way to live, the opposite is also true: All evil has the doom of decay upon it. Just when the fruit is ripe, it vanishes. Just when evil promises most, it lets us down. Lust ends in disgust. Money, after you have toiled and labored for it, becomes a worry and anxiety.

Recently on the train, one soldier was telling another: "Do you know how you ended up your celebration last night? By spraying a woman opposite you with your vomit!" "Gosh," the other muttered in dismay, "and I promised my girlfriend I'd quit." Just when he thought he had reason to be happy, it was gone, and he humiliated himself.

There is another passage in Revelation that describes "the beast who once was, and now is not" (17:11). That is the biography of every "beast," demonic or human. There is no "will be." Evil has no future—it was and is not. Only of good can we say it "was and is and will be"—it has a past, a present, and a future. Evil, by its very nature, is self-destructive. It is an attempt to live against the nature of reality, and it ends only in self-destruction.

The New Testament therefore says in a number of places that sinners "perish"—they do so here and now; the life forces break down, disintegrate. Evil persons renders themselves unfit to survive. They will not obey the law of survival; so they perish. Romans 7:5 tells how "the sinful passions…were at work in our bodies, so that we bore fruit for death." Just when the fruit of evil is ripe, it rots. Such is a universal law.

Loving Ruler, You will not let us rest in self-destruction. Tender Lover of our souls, do not leave us alone. You are saving us by hard refusals. Do not soften those refusals, for they are Your preventive grace, holding us back from self-ruin. We thank You. Amen.

EVIL IS A PARASITE

These men are blemishes at your love feasts, eating with you without the slightest qualm—shepherds who feed only themselves. They are clouds without rain, blown along by the wind; autumn trees, without fruit and uprooted—twice dead. (Jude 1:12)

We must spend one more day on the self-destructiveness of evil, for many people have the idea that goodness is bondage, and evil is freedom. But we know that evil is freedom only to get into trouble with ourselves.

I was urging a politician to give up an illicit affair, for through it he was breaking up two homes—his own and the woman's—as well as generally snarling up his life. To ward off my appeal, he told of an English general who couldn't quite stomach the challenge of the Oxford Group with their four absolutes—absolute honesty, absolute purity, absolute unselfishness, and absolute love. The general had joked that he was going to organize another group whose principles would be the opposite: absolute dishonesty, impurity, selfishness, and hate.

The politician expected me to laugh. But instead, I replied: "Why not? Why don't you go in for evil and make it absolute? Why are you so tentative and hesitant? Why don't you sin with all the stops pulled out?"

"Oh," he replied, "we couldn't do that; it wouldn't work."

"Ah," I answered, "you have just given away your case. Evil has to have some good thrown around it to make it float. Pure evil would be self-destructive." You cannot build a society on absolute dishonesty, for no one would trust anybody; so with the other vices as well. Every dishonest person is a parasite upon the honesty of other people who hold the society together long enough for the person to practice dishonesty. Evil could not exist if there were no good surrounding it to keep it going.

O God, help me to rid myself of the evil parasites in my life. Let there be no decaying places in my life; make all points sound and under Your control. Amen.

DISCIPLINING THE WHOLE NATURE

May God himself, the God of peace, sanctify you through and through. May your whole spirit, soul and body be kept blameless at the coming of our Lord Jesus Christ. (1 Thess. 5:23)

The personality expresses itself in three phases: intellect, feeling, and will. So the Christian discipline produces a love that springs not just from a portion of our being, but from the total being. This is the echo of the words of Jesus, who said in Mark 12:30 that the highest commandment was to "love the Lord your God with all your heart" (the affectional nature), "and with all your soul" (the volitional nature), "and with all your mind" (the intellectual nature), "and with all your strength" (the physical nature). We are to do the highest thing in the world—which is to love—and to do it with every portion of our nature.

This is important—otherwise we can develop lopsided. To love God with the mind but not the heart or emotions produces the intellectualist in religion, lacking emotional drive and appeal. To love Him with the emotion but not the mind makes the sentimentalist in religion. To love Him with the soul or will but not the emotion makes the hard person of action who lacks lovableness.

The only really strong Christian is the one who lets love get hold of the total nature—mind, emotion, will, and body—so the whole being is caught up by a burning passion of love. This person is then like a glass lens that focuses the sun's rays, kindling love and devotion in others. Such a Christian is contagious. The disciplined make disciples.

O Lord, my consecration shall be the burning glass that gathers everything into one focus of love. Then and then alone can I kindle others. Let me find release from all contradictions, all cross-purposes, in order that I may burn for You. In Jesus' name, Amen.

THE MIND IS THE KEY

Be transformed by the renewing of your mind. Then you will be able to test and approve what God's will is—his good, pleasing and perfect will. (Rom. 12:2)

We have said that the whole person is to be disciplined—intellect, feeling, will, and body. The key apparently is the mind. According to the verse, this is how we reach transformation. Many would say that the nature transforms the mind, and there is a good deal of truth in that for we often think with our emotions, the mind hunting for reasons to justify attitudes. Nevertheless, the mind is the master transformer. "As [a man] thinks...so is he" (Prov. 23:7 NKJV).

The American Medical Association reports that football players raised their endurance 200 percent in three weeks by taking sugar tablets they believed contained gelatin, but which didn't. Other football players were given tablets that did contain the gelatin chemical, aminoacetic acid. They too improved 200 percent. "As [a man] thinks...so is he."

If you think you are beaten, you are. The mind renews the nature, and it can also resign the nature to defeat. But, with the Christian, all this is not simply a lifting of oneself by the bootstraps. Mind renewal, says the next portion of Romans 12:2, makes us "able to test and approve what God's will is." It is not a mind seeking to play tricks on itself, for that soon breaks down. You can kid yourself so far and no farther. Only when you are linked to reality can you make real progress. The Christian mind links itself to the will of God and taps into real resources for real living.

The mind thus stands between the will of God and nature; it is the key to linking the two. The mind throws the switch one way or the other. It links you to infinite resources, or entangles you in your own futile self.

O God, take all defeatism and fear from my mind. Lead me to affirmation, to achievement, to victory, to Your infinite resources. Give me a mind that minds its chief business—to find out the will of God. Bring me home. Amen.

DISCIPLINED BEYOND TIMIDITY

[Paul to Timothy]: *I remind you to fan into flame the gift of God, which is in you through the laying on of my hands. For God did not give us a spirit of timidity, but a spirit of power, of love and of self-discipline. (2 Tim. 1:6–7)*

Before we end this week's study of the Christian discipline, we must look at a similar passage as where we began seven days ago—and written to the same person, Timothy. The first (1 Timothy 1:5) began with discipline; now this one ends with it. The Christian way begins and ends in discipline.

The Christian discipline may be so hidden as to be almost unnoticeable. That is the point—to hide it away into habit, into the subconscious, so that the disciplined person appears to be spontaneous. A musician's creative spontaneity is actually coordinated discipline that has become second nature.

Paul puts his finger on the thing that dims people's spiritual life more than any other: timidity. If I had one gift to give myself and others, I would unhesitatingly give courage. We need rekindling of our divine gift. First of all, the courage to pay the price and take from God what He offers. That requires courage, for it shifts the whole basis of life from self-sufficiency to God-sufficiency. Then the next step: the courage to face up to the world and believe that this appropriated gift of God will meet every need—and to say so even when people are pathetically trying unworkable ways.

When I was traveling in China in 1937 through areas that were being bombed, this verse came to me again and again: "Whatever happens, be self-possessed, flinch from no suffering, do your work as an evangelist, and discharge all your duties as a minister" (2 Tim. 4:5 MOFFATT). Now here in America, I have to repeat it again and again.

O God, my Father, give me the steady courage of Jesus, who went on quietly, unruffled and unafraid, even though the end of the road meant disaster. I do not have to succeed. I have only to be true to the highest I know. Success and failure are in Your hands. Amen.

KEEP YOUR COMMISSION!

[Paul to Timothy]: *In the presence of God who is the Life of all, and of Christ Jesus who testified to the good confession before Pontius Pilate, I charge you to keep your commission free from stain. (1 Tim. 6:13–14 MOFFATT)*

This Scripture has spoken to me like a steady refrain down through many years. You and I hold a commission before God! It is a commission given to no one else—it is unique and different, for each of us is unique and different.

God is opening a fresh book through your character and life. If you do not respond, if you hold back and frustrate His purposes, that book will never be revealed. The world will be poorer—and so will you. The Laodicean church received a letter from Paul (see its mention in Col. 4:16), but it was lost and never shared with the wider church, as many of his other epistles were. Why? Perhaps because the Laodicean church was "neither cold nor hot" (Rev. 3:15). This lukewarm church did not have the insight or the loyalty to see the value of that letter. What might they have given to the world had they been spiritually keen and alert! They lost their commission!

I have just come from seeing a man who is going blind. As the shadows close in on him and the outer life fades, I suggested he would soon have to live "within." He sighed and said there was nothing there. He has not a thing on the inside but emptiness. He has lost his commission—and himself. He has missed both the purpose and the person. Had he grasped the purpose, now his inner person would be rich and full, adequate and essentially undisturbed as the outer fades out.

Keep your central treasure—your commission—so that if all else goes, you have the one thing that matters.

Gracious Father, I feel Your commission in my very bones. Help me to organize life around that one central fact, rather than organizing this purpose around some triviality. In Jesus' name, Amen.

FREE FROM STAIN

[Paul]: *I eagerly expect and hope that I will in no way be ashamed, but will have sufficient courage so that now as always Christ will be exalted in my body, whether by life or by death. For to me, to live is Christ and to die is gain. (Phil. 1:20–21)*

Yesterday's Scripture spoke about keeping our commission "free from stain." From stain of what? We shall begin at the periphery and work toward the center.

(1) Keep your commission free from the stain of unnecessary physical ailments. I say "unnecessary," for many of them can be avoided by proper living and right attitudes. In a mortal world the body breaks down sooner or later, but the soul is not necessarily subject to decay as the body is. Some people, however, pass on the sicknesses of mind and soul to their bodies.

An outstanding doctor of a great city said to me: "In my clinic we have decided that 75 percent of the people who come to us would be well if they changed their attitudes. They are throwing functional disturbances into their systems by wrong moral and spiritual attitudes." Here is one example: A letter from a highly cultured and intelligent woman came just this morning, relating that when her husband had begun to pay attention to another woman, she had broken out with eczema. Only when she surrendered the fear and worry to God did the eczema pass away.

Dr. W. C. Alvarez, the stomach specialist at the Mayo Clinic, says that 80 percent of the stomach difficulties that come to them are not organic, but functional. Wrong mental and spiritual attitudes throw functional disturbance into digestion. A woman said to me: "You're right; I lived with my son-in-law for five years. He developed a stomach ulcer and I developed arthritis. The tensions were responsible."

O God, I know this body of mine is made for faith and confidence, not for worry and anxiety and fear. Help me to help my body to be at its best for You. May I feed it with confidence and faith as well as with physical food. Amen.

FREE FROM WORRY AND FEAR

Do not be anxious about anything, but in everything, by prayer and petition, with thanksgiving, present your requests to God. And the peace of God, which transcends all understanding, will guard your hearts and your minds in Christ Jesus. (Phil. 4:6–7)

To have the best body God is capable of helping us to have, we must feed it with the best mental and spiritual food. Faith is food; worry and fear are poison.

(2) Keep your commission free from the stain of worry and fear. Worry is not merely weakness; it is wickedness. It is atheism. It says God has abdicated, and we have to hold the world together by our worrying. Actually, the opposite happens. Worriers wreck their world. Their bodies become more frail. Statisticians tell us that people who have annuities live an average of five or six years longer than those who do not. They are not killed off by worry about their finances.

A judge had to watch his diet carefully while trying cases in his court. But let him get out on the lake in a sailboat for several days, and he could digest anything! The worry upset his digestion.

Fears are usually homegrown. To impose fears on children is criminal. Learn to live by cheer, rather than by fear. Very few worries live long unless you give them careful nursing.

Newspaper columnist and syndicator George Matthew Adams tells about a man who set aside something called "the Worry Hour" for right after dinner. He planned to go to his library and settle down to worry in earnest. But he found he couldn't do it on schedule! The idea was absurd.

Another man had a better idea: a "Worry Tree" in his front yard, where he hung his worries before he came into the house. For the Christian, that "Worry Tree" is the cross. Hang your worries there.

O Christ, I do hang all my worries on Your cross. Compared to that cross, what have I ever suffered? Nothing can make me afraid. I thank You. Amen.

FREE FROM HATE AND RESENTMENT

Do not go about spreading slander among your people. Do not do anything that endangers your neighbor's life. I am the LORD. Do not hate your brother in your heart. Rebuke your neighbor frankly so you will not share in his guilt. Do not seek revenge or bear a grudge against one of your people, but love your neighbor as yourself. I am the LORD. (Lev. 19:16–18)

Continuing to move to the center of keeping our commission:

(3) Keep your commission free from the stain of hate and resentments. Throughout this war [World War II], we are now feeding our people mental and spiritual poison in the hate attitudes we are engendering. Hates are poisoning the air—and us, if we allow them.

When a newborn baby failed to gain in weight, Dr. Luther Emmett Holt, the famous pioneer of pediatrics, invariably left this prescription: "This baby is to be loved every three hours." He had found that babies are made for love, not for indifference, and when they do not have love, they do not thrive.

A refined and cultured woman reached out to shake my hand with her left hand, admitting, "I haven't been at war with others, but with myself—hence, this arthritis."

Then how can we get rid of hate and resentment? Frances Ridley Havergal, who wrote such beautiful hymns as "Like a River Glorious" and "Take My Life and Let It Be," was once so bad-tempered she used to lie on the floor and beat her head. How did she gain calm and poise? By doing what we all have to do, namely: bring the hate and resentment up and out; talk to the person concerned and ask forgiveness; then simply and humbly offer the hate and resentment to Christ, asking Him to bury them miles deep at the cross. You give the consent to have them taken out, and He will give the power. They will dissolve in His love.

The Christian faith shows itself completely sound when it insists on no harbored resentment. Psychology is saying the same.

O God, I am sick of hatred and the waste it makes. Let me be the friend of all. Amen.

FREE FROM HARSH ATTITUDES

Finally, all of you, live in harmony with one another; be sympathetic, love as brothers, be compassionate and humble. Do not repay evil with evil or insult with insult, but with blessing, because to this you were called so that you may inherit a blessing. For, "Whoever would love life and see good days must keep his tongue from evil and his lips from deceitful speech. He must turn from evil and do good; he must seek peace and pursue it." (1 Peter 3:8–11)

Another area in which to keep our commission:

(4) *Keep your commission free from the stain of harsh attitudes.* We must not only be free from hate, but also from harshness. Some people try to make others good by harsh attitudes. It doesn't succeed. As Jesus asked, "How can Satan drive out Satan?" (Mark 3:23). Can you, by acting like the devil, cast the devil out of people?

Paul says, "Treat one another with the same spirit as you experience in Christ Jesus" (Phil. 2:5 MOFFATT). There was a spirit about Him. He did and said many of the same things as others said and did, yet there was a difference. An aroma of graciousness made His deeds and words unique.

Paul ends one of his epistles this way: "This is how I write. The grace of our Lord Jesus Christ be with you all" (2 Thess. 3:17–18). When we write, do we say that? Or does our writing often leave a sting?

The spirit in which you do a thing gets noticed. Relief workers were once being thanked in Moscow by the Russian government for their assistance. The Quakers came last, and the emcee said: "Others may have fed more than these, but the Quakers wrapped every bottle of milk in a wrapper of good will." The gifts of the Quakers were different, and people never forgot, for the flavor lingered after the nourishment had gone.

Go out and do something today that nobody but a Christian would do. And be sure to do it in a Christian way.

O Christ, don't permit me to let the other person's conduct and attitude determine mine. Let me be unfailingly gentle and kind, no matter what I get in return. Amen.

FREE FROM PREJUDICE AND SELF-PITY

My dear brothers and sisters, how can you claim to have faith in our glorious Lord Jesus Christ if you favor some people over others? (James 2:1 †)

Godliness with contentment is great gain. For we brought nothing into the world, and we can take nothing out of it. (1 Tim. 6:6–7)

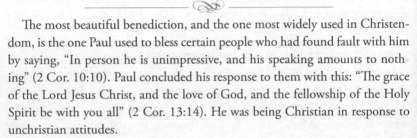

The most beautiful benediction, and the one most widely used in Christendom, is the one Paul used to bless certain people who had found fault with him by saying, "In person he is unimpressive, and his speaking amounts to nothing" (2 Cor. 10:10). Paul concluded his response to them with this: "The grace of the Lord Jesus Christ, and the love of God, and the fellowship of the Holy Spirit be with you all" (2 Cor. 13:14). He was being Christian in response to unchristian attitudes.

(5) Keep your commission free from the stain of prejudices. How we impoverish ourselves by these things! Color prejudice cuts us off from mental and spiritual enrichment through people of another color. God is the great artist, so He has made many colors. We are not artistic, so we insist on one color—white. We make a religion out of being white. Someone had a tulip bed in which there were all colors but one. So he bred a black tulip, which set off all the other colors. Prejudice against black would have impoverished that bed of tulips. That is what racial prejudice does to us.

(6) Keep your commission free from the stain of self-pity and complaint. We often speak of our sicknesses as "complaints." Indeed, sicknesses often come out of complaints. Feel sorry for yourself, and you will soon have a self worth feeling sorry for. Paul says: "I have learned to be content whatever the circumstances" (Phil. 4:11). He was often not content with the circumstances but in spite of them. His peace depended instead on his inner state of mind.

Gracious God, help me to live in a state that triumphs over all surroundings and conditions. For how can I feel sorry for myself when You are with me? With that fact secure, I can survive anything. I thank You. Amen.

FREE FROM EMPTINESS

I kneel before the Father, from whom his whole family in heaven and on earth derives its name. I pray that out of his glorious riches he may strengthen you with power through his Spirit in your inner being, so that Christ may dwell in your hearts through faith. (Eph. 3:14–17)

Finally, one more area in which to keep our commission:

(7) *Keep your commission free from the stain of emptiness.* This is the most frequent stain on the Christian soul. We are not bad—we are just not good enough. We lack the vital contagion. In Texas, where rain is desperately needed at times, someone asked a ranger about some clouds in the sky. He looked at them, shook his head, and replied, "They're just empties drifting by." How many of us are the moral and spiritual equivalent of just that! When people so desperately need the refreshing rain of abundant living, we are just empties drifting by.

In the passage quoted a week ago (1 Tim. 6:13–14), Paul says that you are to keep your commission free from stain in the light of two facts: First, "In the presence of God who is the Life of all"—in the presence of God's abundant fullness. Why be empty when you can attach yourself to His resources? The abundant life is not something we attain—it is something we *obtain*. If you try to attain without obtaining, all you produce is fussy doing.

A friend gave a lovely home to his sisters. Everything was ready for occupancy. The ranges were in, ready for cooking…but then it was discovered that the main line in the street had not yet been tapped. The whole apparatus was useless without obtaining the power. Life comes through attachment to power.

O God, I dare not be empty in a world of human need. For many look to me for help; may they not seek in vain. They come, like the man in Jesus' story, asking for bread at midnight. I must not be empty-handed. Give me bread. Amen.

FACING OUR PONTIUS PILATE

[Paul to Timothy]: *In the presence of God who is the Life of all, and of Christ Jesus who testified to the good confession before Pontius Pilate, I charge you to keep your commission free from stain. (1 Tim. 6:13–14 MOFFATT)*

Allow me to repeat the passage that began our study a week ago. It tells us to keep our commission in light of two things: (1) "In the presence of God who is the Life of all," which we considered yesterday; and (2) "In the presence...of Jesus Christ who testified to the good confession before Pontius Pilate." This full, abundant Life poured itself out in the face of opposition.

It is not enough to possess abundant life; that life must be expressed and lived out in the presence of some Pontius Pilate—something that stands to thwart this new life. If we meet it unflinchingly, this new life may well turn crimson on a cross. This business of being Christian in a world of this kind is no easy undertaking. We have to meet the equivalent of Pilate. And what would that mean?

To discover its meaning, let us ask not *who* crucified Christ, but *what?* Seven embodied sins combined to crucify the Son of God: (l) Self-interested moral cowardice, as seen in Pilate. (2) Vested class interests, as seen in the priests. (3) Envy—the priests. (4) Faithless friendships—Judas. (5) Ignorance—the multitude. (6) Indifference—the soldiers. (7) Race-prejudiced militarism—the Romans.

You will probably have to live out your abundant life in the face of one or more of these evils. The cross cannot be escaped. If you somehow avoid it, you also avoid its sequel—the resurrection. If you become a recessive personality, taking the line of least resistance, you will never be a resurrected personality. No cross, no creation.

God and Father, I see that I must stand up to life. Save me from all retreatism and lack of spiritual initiative. Help me to be calm and poised in the face of opposition. May none of this sour me. In Jesus' name, Amen.

OUT FROM THE PICTURE

The Word became flesh and made his dwelling among us. We have seen his glory, the glory of the One and Only, who came from the Father, full of grace and truth.... No one has ever seen God, but God the One and Only, who is at the Father's side, has made him known. (John 1:14, 18)

A little boy stood before a portrait of his absent father, then turned to his mother and wistfully said, "I wish he would step out of the picture." This little boy expressed the deepest yearning of the human heart. We who have gazed upon the picture of God in nature are grateful, but not satisfied. We want our Father to step out of the landscape and meet us as a person.

Someone may retort: "Why won't principles do? Why do we need a personal God?" Well, suppose you go to a child crying for its mother and say, "Don't cry, little one; I'm giving you the principle of motherhood." Would the tears dry and the face light up? Hardly. The child would brush aside your principle and keep crying. We all want not a principle nor a picture, but a person.

On Christmas the Father stepped out of the picture. The Word became flesh. Jesus is Immanuel—"God with us." He is the personal approach from the unseen. We almost gasp as He steps out of the frame. We didn't dare dream that God was like Christ. But He is. Just as I analyze the tiny sunbeam and discover in it the make-up of the gigantic sun, so I look at the character and life of Jesus, and I know what God's character is like. He is Christlike.

"You have an advantage," said Dr. Hu Shih, father of the Renaissance Movement in China, "in that all the ideas in Christianity have become embodied in a person." Yes, and the further point of our faith is this: The Christmas word must become flesh in me. I too must become the Word made flesh. I must be a miniature Christmas.

Gracious Father, help me this day to step out of the picture and let someone see the meaning of a Christian. May I be the Christmas message. Amen.

FACING CLASS INTERESTS

Then the high priest tore his clothes and said, "He has spoken blasphemy! Why do we need any more witnesses? Look, now you have heard the blasphemy. What do you think?"

"He is worthy of death," they answered. Then they spit in his face and struck him with their fists. Others slapped him. (Matt. 26:65–68)

We return to our commission to live out this new life in the face of opposition. We saw last week that you have to face your Pilate. While trying to get things done, say for the sake of a community, self-interested cowardice will block you. Public leaders, for private reasons, will look to see how your plans affect them—and will crucify those plans on the cross of self-interest.

What should you do? Meet your opponents with their own weapons—fight fire with fire? That is surely the way to get burnt. In a battle of beasts, the bigger beast wins. Instead, keep your Christian attitudes—they are your one real asset. There is always one thing open—you can suffer, and if necessary die, as Jesus did. Jesus conquered Pilate by not being like him. He broke Pilate by letting Pilate break his body, while He kept an unbroken spirit. Such a spirit will break anything that opposes it.

Furthermore, you will have to practice your commission in the face of vested class interests. You will have to meet your chief priests. Wrong attitudes can be embodied in a class as well as in an individual. People often think according to class interests instead of as persons. There is today a "class war," and the laborers did not create it—they simply proclaimed what they found. Sad to say, many of them then proceeded to embody the class interest they deplored in others.

What is left to you? You can suffer, and die if necessary, in order to have a classless society—the kingdom of God.

O Christ, give me power to face soured, selfish religion, and to die if necessary. Keep my soul from all class thinking. Help me to stand against it by word, deed, and attitude. Amen.

ENDURING FAITHLESS FRIENDSHIPS

Then one of the Twelve—the one called Judas Iscariot—went to the chief priests and asked, "What are you willing to give me if I hand him over to you?" So they counted out for him thirty silver coins. From then on Judas watched for an opportunity to hand him over. (Matt. 26:14–16)

The religious leaders, besides being wary about their class interests, were also envious and jealous of the growing power of Jesus. People were drawing away from them and crowding around Jesus. So green-eyed envy pushed up its head and slandered Him by twisting His meanings. Jesus was crucified on misquotations. Very often we will be too.

I heard about a religious leader who told a derogatory story about another religious leader. When the truth of it was questioned and the falsehood pointed out, the leader laughed it off by saying: "Well, anyway, it makes a very good story." It did, even if it left the reputation of another person lying wounded and bleeding. Envy twisted that story—and twisted itself into a snake.

Furthermore, you must sometimes endure faithless friendships—your Judas. Often those who dip their hand in the same dish will betray you. When money, position, or self-interest beckons, they fall away. It is not easy to keep from being embittered toward those who were once comrades in a cause and are now indifferent, or on the other side.

What can you do? Meet blister with blister? Two hot words never made a warm friendship. No, you are a Christian. "You must not rule your lives by theirs" (Lev. 18:3 MOFFATT). You can do what Jesus did. He died for the men who lied about Him. Their lies perished. He lived on.

O Christ, help me to do just that, or the equivalent of that, to those who betray me. And help me not to betray anyone else; help me to be true. Amen.

FACING DULL IGNORANCE

"Which of the two do you want me to release to you?" asked the governor.
"Barabbas," they answered.
"What shall I do, then, with Jesus who is called Christ?" Pilate asked.
They all answered, "Crucify him!"
"Why? What crime has he committed?" asked Pilate.
But they shouted all the louder, "Crucify him!" (Matt. 27:20–23)

Perhaps we will have to practice our commission in the face of another thing that crucified Jesus—ignorance in the multitude. For three years He had spoken as no man had spoken, pouring Himself out night and day to get the people to see. Yet in the end, the multitude chose a local, patriotic rebel and crucified a world redeemer.

When we meet ignorant opposition, what are we to do? Well, we can do what Jesus did. He prayed, "Father, forgive them, for they do not know what they are doing" (Luke 23:34). Then He died for them. We can do the same.

And someday the resurrection will come. I remember pleading in a conference in India for a move that would reconstruct the world church of Methodism. My proposal got tabled with a bang. Then, twenty years later, it was taken off the table and adopted almost to the letter. You can wait. "Whatever is born of God overcomes the world" (1 John 5:4 NKJV)—whatever is born of ignorance perishes. Be patient. Someday the stones thrown at you will be collected and stacked into a monument to your insight and foresight.

Grasp the truth in these words: "We also rejoice in our sufferings, because we know that suffering produces perseverance; perseverance, character; and character, hope" (Rom. 5:3–4). Hope is based on the solid reality of tested character. Verse 5 adds: "And hope does not disappoint us." With a hope based on that solid reality, we can wait.

O God, if we obtain nothing else out of the situation, we have the character left. We can commune with You here and now, no matter what is on the outside. This means we can put up with ignorant opposition. Amen.

FACING INDIFFERENCE

They crucified him, and parted his garments, casting lots…. And sitting down they watched him there. (Matt. 27:35–36 KJV)

This has to be the cruelest verse in literature. The soldiers "sat around" (NLT) in stolid indifference and watched Him go through His agonies.

It is easier to meet opposition than indifference. What do you do when people do not care? There is only one thing to do—keep on caring. Christians are people who care for people who do not care. Love does not change, no matter the changes in the other person.

Perhaps we have to do what one modern saint suggested: "Be so humble that you cannot be humiliated." I am told that in the Andes Mountains when the pack goats meet each other on a narrow ledge where it is impossible to pass, one will kneel and let the other walk over him—to the safety of both. Perhaps you will have to kneel and let people walk over you. Notice I said *kneel,* not knuckle. There is a difference: In kneeling you are bending low at the feet of Christ instead of knuckling at the behest of man. Kneeling is voluntary, and for His sake.

A bridge is something people walk on, but it leads from point A to point B. If you are to be a bridge between a person's indifference and their awakening, a bridge between groups and races, you will be walked on. Never mind; people may be getting somewhere when they walk on you.

A highly trained young doctor went to China as a medical missionary. While attending typhus cases, he was stricken by the disease and ravaged. When he heard there was a peasant woman who was about to die for lack of a cesarean operation, he asked to be carried to the operating room. Aides held him up, one on each side, as he saved the lives of the woman and her baby. But the shock was too much for him—in two days he was dead. He cared.

O Christ, You cared even when people sat watching You in open-mouthed indifference. Help me to care like that. When everything I love is trampled by indifferent feet, help me to go quietly on. I can wait for You. Amen.

FACING RACE-PREJUDICED POWER

Pilate then went back inside the palace, summoned Jesus and asked him, "Are you the king of the Jews?"

"Is that your own idea," Jesus asked, "or did others talk to you about me?"

"Am I a Jew?" Pilate replied. "It was your people and your chief priests who handed you over to me. What is it you have done?" (John 18:33–35)

We come now to the last of the seven things that crucified Jesus—and may crucify us. The Romans despised the Jews and made fun of their "king." They mocked a nation—in Him. So Jesus took the scorn, intended for the Jews, and bore it for the very Jews who were crying out for His crucifixion.

What are we to do in the face of racial prejudice that is linked with power? We can become embittered and sullen, or we can do what Jesus did—He suffered and died for the very ones who mocked Him. That possibility is always open.

Yesterday, I talked with a highly intelligent black cook—a graduate in chemistry from a great state university. He said, "I had high hopes as a student, but after trying in vain for two years to get a job as a chemist or a pharmacist, I gave up and became a cook." Prejudice had snuffed out those hopes.

Jesus died not only for the Jews but also for the Romans. Result? Out of a slave race came the world's greatest freedom. Rome and her military might perished, while Judea, in the person of the Christ, lives on today in the hearts of millions.

O Christ, You took all the racial insults into Your heart and emerged out of that sea of hate as the Son of Man, beyond race and insult. Help me to do the same. Help me to identify myself with the underprivileged and despised, accepting no privilege they cannot access. Break our sinful customs by the cross. Amen.

WELCOME, TOMORROW!

Everyone born of God overcomes the world. This is the victory that has overcome the world, even our faith. Who is it that overcomes the world? Only he who believes that Jesus is the Son of God. (1 John 5:4–5)

We have been talking this past week about the cross—but is that the last word? No! God's last word in human affairs is the victorious resurrection.

A great editor said: "On one side of my desk is a Bible, and on the other side is a typewriter. I try to make the two sides of this desk speak the same thing. For I know that if what I write in my editorials coincides with what is in that Book, it will live on; but if it is out of harmony with that Book, it will perish." That is our faith.

Someone asked the brilliant James B. Bashford why, when he could be an influential bishop in America, he chose to bury himself in China. He replied: "Because I believe in the resurrection." It has been said that "most people plot and plan themselves into mediocrity, while now and again somebody forgets himself into greatness." Bashford was one of these.

So was Dr. George Washington Carver, the saint and scientist, who did more for the agriculture of the South than anyone living or dead, white or black. He wanted to be an artist until a teacher said, "George, your people need agriculture more than art." He put his brushes away in a trunk and did not look at them for several years. He lost himself in people's need. And he unconsciously painted his image into the hearts of all of us.

I heard a minister tell of a small boy on a train who was suddenly and unexpectedly whisked into a long, dark tunnel. When the train emerged from the darkness, the sun was shining, and the boy exclaimed, "Mother, it's tomorrow!" Perhaps that is our final understanding for this year: Out of every interruption, every disturbance, every frustration, every sorrow, every dark tunnel, we can rescue a "tomorrow." If we do, we will find Abundant Living!

O Christ, we thank You that the best is yet to be. We salute the dawn with a cheer. For we have the "rising sun" (Luke 1:78) within us. Amen.